HUMOUR IN OLD ENGLISH LITERATURE

Humour in Old English Literature

Communities of Laughter in Early Medieval England

JONATHAN WILCOX

UNIVERSITY OF TORONTO PRESS
Toronto Buffalo London

© University of Toronto Press 2023
Toronto Buffalo London
utorontopress.com

ISBN 978-1-4875-4530-7 (cloth)   ISBN 978-1-4875-4570-3 (EPUB)
                                     ISBN 978-1-4875-4571-0 (PDF)

Library and Archives Canada Cataloguing in Publication

Title: Humour in Old English literature : communities of
laughter in early medieval England / Jonathan Wilcox.
Names: Wilcox, Jonathan, 1960– author.
Description: Includes bibliographical references and index.
Identifiers: Canadiana (print) 20230164722 | Canadiana (ebook) 20230164765 |
ISBN 9781487545307 (cloth) | ISBN 9781487545710 (PDF) |
ISBN 9781487545703 (EPUB)
Subjects: LCSH: English literature – Old English,
ca. 450–1100 – History and criticism. |
LCSH: English wit and humor – History and criticism. |
LCSH: Humor in literature. | LCSH: Comic, The, in literature.
Classification: LCC PR173 .W55 2023 | DDC 829/.0917 – dc23

Cover design: Val Cooke
Cover illustration: Album / British Library / Alamy Stock Photo

We wish to acknowledge the land on which the University of Toronto
Press operates. This land is the traditional territory of the Wendat, the
Anishnaabeg, the Haudenosaunee, the Métis, and the Mississaugas of the Credit
First Nation.

University of Toronto Press acknowledges the financial support of
the Government of Canada, the Canada Council for the Arts, and the
Ontario Arts Council, an agency of the Government
of Ontario, for its publishing activities.

Canada Council   Conseil des Arts
for the Arts   du Canada

ONTARIO ARTS COUNCIL
CONSEIL DES ARTS DE L'ONTARIO
an Ontario government agency
un organisme du gouvernement de l'Ontario

Funded by the   Financé par le
Government   gouvernement
of Canada   du Canada

Canada

Contents

Acknowledgments

The ideas in this book have preoccupied me for much of my career and benefitted immensely from discussion with the generous range of scholars and students interested in early medieval literature. Particular thanks go to Martha Bayless, Stacy S. Klein, John D. Niles, Gale Owen-Crocker, Hugh Magennis, Mercedes Salvador Bello, Simon Keynes, Megan Cavell, Jennifer Neville, Roy Liuzza, Richard Dance, Susan Irvine, Winfried Rudolf, and Elaine Treharne for discussions and insight and for invitations to present my work in progress. Thanks, too, to generations of students at the University of Iowa for stimulating my continuing enthusiasm for early medieval literature and to all my PhD students for the pleasure of sharing intellectual engagement with literature of the past.

I owe considerable thanks to the University of Iowa for providing institutional support throughout my career and particularly for the precious gift of research time through a Professional Developmental Assignment in 2017–18 when I began researching and writing this book in earnest. Warm thanks, too, to my colleagues in the Department of English for creating such a conducive place to teach, think, and write. Thanks, too, to the Fulbright Commission Iceland for giving me a change of scene and another place to try out some of these ideas during Fall 2019 while teaching at Háskóli Íslands. And thanks to the Office of the Vice President for Research, the College of Liberal Arts and Sciences, and the Department of English at the University of Iowa for subvention support towards the cost of publication.

A portion of the discussion of *Andreas* in chapter 5 was previously published as "Eating People is Wrong: Funny Style in *Andreas* and Its Analogues," in *Anglo-Saxon Styles*, ed. Catherine E. Karkov and George Hardin Brown (Albany: SUNY Press, 2003), 201–22. Other ideas have been worked out in different ways in numerous prior publications, as indicated in the footnotes, with appreciation for the editors and readers who work so hard to maintain the intellectual vitality of our field, and in many conference papers, with appreciation for all those organizers and audiences who stimulate and shape work as it progresses.

Particular thanks go to the three anonymous readers for the University of Toronto Press – this book is the better for your unheralded and generous labour of critique – and to the whole production team at UTP, with special appreciation to Suzanne Rancourt and Deb Kopka for guiding the production process so painlessly. And special thanks always to Denise K. Filios, my partner for discussion of all things medieval.

Abbreviations

ASE	*Anglo-Saxon England*
ASPR	Anglo-Saxon Poetic Records
BL	British Library
BT	Bosworth-Toller, *Dictionary*
CCCC	Cambridge, Corpus Christi College
CH I	Ælfric, *Catholic Homilies* I, ed. Clemoes
CH II	Ælfric, *Catholic Homilies* II, ed. Godden
DOE	*Dictionary of Old English*
DOML	Dumbarton Oaks Medieval Library
EETS	Early English Text Society
JEGP	*Journal of English and Germanic Philology*
MED	*Middle English Dictionary*
NM	*Neuphilologische Mitteilungen*
n.s.	new series
OED	*Oxford English Dictionary*
OEN	*Old English Newsletter*
o.s.	old series
PMLA	*Publications of the Modern Language Association*
PQ	*Philological Quarterly*
RES	*Review of English Studies*
s.s.	supplementary series

Exeter Book Riddle Numbers:
A Comparative Chart

This study, *The Riddle Ages* website, ASPR[1]	Muir[2]	Williamson, Orchard[3]
Riddle 1	1	1, lines 1–15
Riddle 2	2	1, lines 16–30
Riddle 3	3	1, lines 31–104
Riddle 4	4	2
Riddle 5	5	3
Riddle 6	6	4
Riddle 7	7	5
Riddle 8	8	6
Riddle 9	9	7
Riddle 10	10	8
Riddle 11	11	9
Riddle 12	12	10
Riddle 13	13	11
Riddle 14	14	12
Riddle 15	15	13
Riddle 16	16	14
Riddle 17	17	15
Riddle 18	18	16
Riddle 19	19	17
Riddle 20	20	18
Riddle 21	21	19
Riddle 22	22	20
Riddle 23	23	21
Riddle 24	24	22
Riddle 25	25	23

(Continued)

1 Megan Cavell, ed. and trans., *The Riddle Ages: Early Medieval Riddles, Translations, and Commentaries* (2013, redeveloped 2020: https://theriddleages.com/); George Philip Krapp and Elliott Van Kirk Dobbie, eds., *The Exeter Book*, ASPR (New York: Columbia University Press, 1936). This is the numbering used in much of the scholarship, often abbreviated K-D.

2 Bernard J. Muir, ed., *The Exeter Anthology of Old English Poetry*, 2 vols. (Exeter: University of Exeter Press, 1994; revised edition 2000).

3 Craig Williamson, ed., *The Old English Riddles of the 'Exeter Book'* (Chapel Hill: University of North Carolina Press, 1977); Andy Orchard, ed. and trans., *The Old English and Anglo-Latin Riddle Tradition*, DOML 69 (Cambridge, MA: Harvard University Press, 2021).

(Continued)

This study, *The Riddle* *Ages* website, ASPR	Muir	Williamson, Orchard
Riddle 26	26	24
Riddle 27	27	25
Riddle 28	28	26
Riddle 29	29	27
Riddle 30	30	28
Riddle 31	31	29
Riddle 32	32	30
Riddle 33	33	31
Riddle 34	34	32
Riddle 35	35	33
Riddle 36	36	34
Riddle 37	37	35
Riddle 38	38	36
Riddle 39	39	37
Riddle 40	40	38
Riddle 41	41	39
Riddle 42	42	40
Riddle 43	43	41
Riddle 44	44	42
Riddle 45	45	43
Riddle 46	46	44
Riddle 47	47	45
Riddle 48	48	46
Riddle 49	49	47
Riddle 50	50	48
Riddle 51	51	49
Riddle 52	52	50
Riddle 53	53	51
Riddle 54	54	52
Riddle 55	55	53
Riddle 56	56	54
Riddle 57	57	55
Riddle 58	58	56
Riddle 59	59	57
Riddle 60	60	58
Riddle 61	61	59
Riddle 62	62	60
Riddle 63	63	61
Riddle 64	64	62
Riddle 65	65	63
Riddle 66	66	64
Riddle 67	67	65

This study, *The Riddle Ages* website, ASPR	Muir	Williamson, Orchard
Riddle 68	68, lines 1–2	66, lines 1–2
Riddle 69	68, line 3	66, line 3
Riddle 70	69, 70	67, 68
Riddle 71	71	69
Riddle 72	72	70
Riddle 73	73	71
Riddle 74	74	72
Riddle 75	75, lines 1–2	73, lines 1–2
Riddle 76	75, line 3	73, line 3
Riddle 77	76	74
Riddle 78	77	75
Riddle 79	78	76, line 1
Riddle 80	79	76, lines 2–12
Riddle 81	80	77
Riddle 82	81	78
Riddle 83	82	79
Riddle 84	83	80
Riddle 85	84	81
Riddle 86	85	82
Riddle 87	86	83
Riddle 88	87	84
Riddle 89	88	85
Riddle 90	89	86
Riddle 91	90	87
Riddle 92	91	88
Riddle 93	92	89
Riddle 94	93	90
Riddle 95	94	91

HUMOUR IN OLD ENGLISH LITERATURE

Old English Literature and Humour

This book isn't meant to be funny. My intention is the serious business of explaining humour, which is a sure-fire way of killing the joke. I do, however, describe many moments within Old English literature that I think are funny and even more that might once have been thought so. By doing this, I sketch out a literary tradition different from the grim world of conflict and heroism and stoic resistance that is the usual sense of the period. In part, I do this by looking at works other than the poems of martial glory that usually receive attention, attending instead to riddles and runes, wisdom poetry and teaching dialogues, homilies and saints' lives. I also engage with traditionally valorized works, including *Beowulf*, from an unusual perspective to uncover their deployment of comic effects. Old English literature may not be bursting with eye-watering funniness, but there are enough humorous elements to merit their exploration and consideration of what insights they suggest.

Pursuing what is funny in a long-dead culture is, of course, challenging. Humour, it will be seen, depends upon incongruity, but it can be hard for readers in the twenty-first century to spot the congruities of a millennium ago, let alone when those expectations are being transgressed. Given the centrality of incongruity for creating the conditions for humour, much of this study is concerned with pursuing incongruities at the level of both content and style and then investigating further to consider how they are funny. Formal conventions sometimes provide a clue, although it is often hard to tell whether a violation results from inadvertance or an intent to be funny. Context provides a further clue. Individual instances often require considerable analysis to establish what is incongruous and how it is funny.

The task of analysis is made easier by the wealth of critical interpretation that has elucidated almost every aspect of Old English literature, and this study draws widely and appreciatively on previous scholarship. I am, however, pursuing a distinctive approach which has attracted relatively little prior scholarship. Contemporary critical thrusts show a particular interest in understanding issues of race and gender, or engaging with environmental and ecocritical concerns, while earlier studies often centred on philology, source study, and historical criticism, but few centred on questions of tone.[4] Concentrating on comic effects has, for the most part, been left out from these approaches, even though a focus on humour can contribute obliquely to many questions about both content and form. I hope the present study may encourage further readings of tone in Old English literature.

First, it will be useful to define the scope of the consideration here. Following that, I will survey modern theories of humour to pull out what is most fruitful for investigating the literature of early medieval England. I will consider descriptions of laughter, which proves a useful but not infallible index of humour, and introduce the most obviously funny genre in Old English, namely the riddles. I will conclude this introduction with three case studies of funny moments in the literature which can anticipate the appeal and challenges of what is to come in the body of the study.

Old English Literature

Old English literature is generally understood to comprise the corpus of surviving writing in English from the coming of the Germanic peoples in the mid-first millennium (Bede gives the date 449 CE) to the transition to a more French-influenced, less fully inflectional form of the language some significant time after the Norman Conquest of 1066 CE. In real-world terms, because of strategies of language policy and the writing and survival of manuscripts, most Old English writing survives from the reign of King Alfred (871–99 CE) onwards, with particular richness in the late tenth and eleventh century.[5] Virtually all the poetry in Old English that survives was written down within a few decades of the year 1000 CE, even

---

4 For an overview of critical approaches to Old English literature, see John D. Niles, *Old English Literature: A Guide to Criticism with Selected Readings* (Chichester: Wiley-Blackwell, 2016); Jacqueline A. Stodnick and Renée Trilling, eds., *A Handbook of Anglo-Saxon Studies* (Oxford: Blackwell, 2012). For more recent interests, see, for example, Dorothy Kim, ed., "Critical Race and the Middle Ages: A Special Cluster," *Literature Compass* 16, nos. 9–10 (2019).

5 Of the 421 manuscripts containing Old English known to N.R. Ker, *Catalogue of Manuscripts Containing Anglo-Saxon* (Oxford: Oxford University Press, 1957), only twenty-seven date from the middle of the tenth century or earlier; the other 394 all date from the second half of the tenth century or later (xv and 574–9).

though much of it was composed significantly earlier.[6] Old English prose translations developed from the time of King Alfred onwards, and there was an efflorescence of written vernacular prose in the late tenth and early eleventh century in the context of robust church activity known as the Benedictine Reform.[7] This was also a time of significant political upheavals, most evident in Viking raids during the reign of Æthelred (978–1013, 1014–16), Danish conquest under Cnut (reigned 1016–35), and Norman conquest by William (reigned 1066–87).[8] The development of recognizable institutions of the nation state and of the church coincided with the development of a book-based textual culture that would anticipate many facets of later English culture.[9]

I focus on literature written in Old English rather than the rich traditions of writing in Anglo-Latin and Old Norse that thrived in early medieval England, or the surrounding Celtic vernaculars. This is largely a pragmatic constraint to keep the study to a manageable scope, but it also allows me to illustrate the development of a particular vernacular literary tradition and to explore the overlooked comic moments in that tradition, with due acknowledgment of the rich overlap with related traditions.[10] Literature in English became less prominent with the ascendency of the Norman elite in the late eleventh century and the return of Latin for most church writings. When substantial English writings re-emerged in the high Middle Ages, there was a flowering of comic literature, particularly notable in the works of Geoffrey Chaucer, William Langland, and in late medieval drama, and these works have been the subject of much good discussion.[11] In this later period, comedy is often deployed for satire aimed at amending society,

---

6 R.D. Fulk and Christopher M. Cain, *A History of Old English Literature*, 2nd ed. (Oxford: Wiley-Blackwell, 2013) provides a useful survey, including probable dating.

7 In addition to Fulk and Cain, *History*, see Nicola Robertson, "The Benedictine Reform: Current and Future Scholarship," *Literature Compass* 3, no. 3 (2006): 282–99.

8 See, *inter alia*, Rory Naismith, *Early Medieval Britain, c. 500–1000* (Cambridge: Cambridge University Press, 2021); Elaine Treharne, *Living Through Conquest: The Politics of Early English, 1020–1220* (Oxford: Oxford University Press, 2012).

9 For an excellent contextualizing historical study, see Robin Fleming, *Britain After Rome: The Fall and Rise, 400–1070* (London: Penguin, 2010).

10 On humour in surrounding Latin traditions, see, in particular, Martha Bayless, *Parody in the Middle Ages: The Latin Tradition* (Ann Arbor: University of Michigan Press, 1996); Jan M. Ziolkowski, ed. and trans., *The Cambridge Songs (Carmina Cantabrigiensia)* (New York: Garland, 1994).

11 See, for example, Laura Kendrick, *Chaucerian Play: Comedy and Control in the Canterbury Tales* (Berkeley: University of California Press, 1988); David Wallace, ed., *The Cambridge History of Medieval English Literature* (Cambridge: Cambridge University Press, 1999).

contributing both to doctrine and to entertainment. While there are hints of such a tradition in early medieval literature, much of the humour looks quite different.

In accordance with a long tradition in Old English scholarship, literature is here understood in the broadest sense possible, essentially comprising anything that was written down and any oral performance that can be convincingly recreated from the surviving record. The process of survival radically skewed that record in ways that make difficulties for this project. In the vast majority of instances, scribes and book-makers of this period were monks or other ecclesiastics working in a regulated Christian culture.[12] Their domination of the chain of transmission explains why it is so difficult to know much about paganism or popular superstitions from the time, or about the daily life of common people, or about sex and romantic love, children and domestic affairs, or about frivolous entertainment where humour might abound. Some insight into all of these domains is still possible, but a modern reader has to work against the bias of a record that is heavily weighted towards edifying Christian learning and monastic culture, or towards the concerns of men of high status. Homilies and saints' lives in Old English provide some access to literature aimed at a broad audience, although, as will be seen, their potential for humour is limited by their strong moralizing imperative. The literature of learning will prove somewhat more conducive to deploying humour. The present study will read against the grain to construct as capacious a vision of early medieval English society as the surviving sources will allow.

Theories of Humour

The other term in need of clarification is humour. While there are occasional discussions of laughter from early medieval England, which will be duly noted, these prove only marginally helpful for discussing the creation or effects of humour. Modern scholarship, on the other hand, has provided rich investigations into the question of what constitutes humour and how it is created. I will draw on such modern humour theory to establish a framework for considering humour of the past.

Incongruity is fundamental. Different theorists use different terms and give different emphases, and yet all see some form of appropriate

---

12 See, *inter alia*, Richard Gameson, ed., *The Cambridge History of the Book in Britain;*
     Volume 1, c. 400–1100 (Cambridge: Cambridge University Press, 2012); Elaine
     Treharne, *Perceptions of Medieval Manuscripts: The Phenomenal Book* (Oxford: Oxford
     University Press, 2021).

doubleness at the heart of the perception of the comic.[13] Classical theorists of discourse had already elucidated this point. Aristotle comments how humour requires something contrary to one's previous expectations, while Cicero sees humour in either language or a thing itself deceiving expectation.[14] Modern theorists use a variety of expressions for the same fundamental observation, pointing to cognitive dissonance, or benign violation, or the yoking of opposites, or the clashing of conflicting scripts. In all such cases there is a duality, a transgression from what is expected, an effect neatly summarized by Schopenhauer as a perception that threatens a conception. This has been most fully theorized by cognitive psychologists: Hurley, Dennett, and Adams see the process as the sudden displacement of a strongly held but stealthily arrived at assumption in the mind.[15] For all serious theorists of humour, some doubleness of apprehension is at the heart of the process. For pinpointing humour, it is always useful to uncover the underlying incongruity.

While there is near-universal agreement on the need for such doubleness, incongruity alone is never sufficient to explain the creation of humour. Some incongruities are creepy, some plain odd, while only some trigger a humour response. What is needed is the right kind of incongruity that is somehow an appropriate inappropriateness.[16] Uncovering an incongruity and then showing that the inappropriateness is in some way comically appropriate is the work of this study.

All serious theories of humour, then, observe an underlying doubleness as a necessary prerequisite. The processing of that doubleness by the one appreciating the humour involves delight as one set of expectations gets replaced by another. That process can be summarized as incongruity resolution.[17] Different theorists, coming from varying disciplinary

---

13 See Noel Carroll, *Humour: A Very Short Introduction* (Oxford: Oxford University Press, 2014), for a handy brief introduction to humour theory, stressing the essential nature of incongruity; and Victor Raskin, ed., *The Primer of Humor Research* (Berlin: Mouton de Gruyter, 2008), for a useful collection of overviews. I use the terms funniness, humour, and the comic interchangeably for the sake of stylistic variation.

14 See Richard Janko, *Aristotle on Comedy: Towards a Reconstruction of Poetics II* (London: Duckworth, 1984); Edwin Rabbie, "Wit and Humor in Roman Rhetoric," in *A Companion to Roman Rhetoric*, eds. William Dominik and John Hall (Malden, MA: Blackwell, 2007), 207–17.

15 Matthew M. Hurley, Daniel C. Dennett, and Reginald B. Adams, Jr., *Inside Jokes: Using Humor to Reverse-Engineer the Mind* (Cambridge, MA: MIT Press, 2011).

16 See Elliott Oring, *Joking Asides: The Theory, Analysis, and Aesthetics of Humor* (Logan: Utah State University Press, 2016).

17 See John Morreall, *Comic Relief: A Comprehensive Philosophy of Humor* (Hoboken: Wiley, 2009).

approaches, give different emphases and contexts for understanding that mechanism. Raskin and Attardo provide a linguistic approach for unpacking jokes. Raskin has popularized the idea of clashing scripts as a way of describing the duality, which he characterizes as a Semantic-Script Theory of Humour (SSTH). This led to the grandly named General Theory of Verbal Humour (GTVH), involving the Logical Mechanisms of two opposed scripts.[18] Raskin has been working on computer recognition and generation of humour, while Attardo has attempted applying the same analysis to longer works, including humorous short stories.[19] The results, while expressed in language that none but computer coders and linguists could love, are valuable for pinpointing in a linguistic manner the very local mechanisms for generating humour in a textual environment, even as they lack a sensitivity to context or an ability to appraise subtlety in ways that would work well for literary criticism. What they do show is the productive power of incongruity at a linguistic level as a necessary but never sufficient cause of humour.

In order to be funny, the humorous incongruity must occur within the right paradox of identification and distance. McGowan suggests that there is no humour if we are disengaged, but also none if we are too close, so we need the right distance, either of emotional tenor or of time.[20] The incongruity must not be perceived as threatening or truly shocking. McGraw develops the helpful term "benign violation" to get at the way the incongruity must involve some break (of decorum or reason or level) and yet must not be so extreme as to be threatening.[21] The violation cannot be too benign, either, or it will come off as simply dull. Humour depends upon a kind of edginess to make it interesting even as it must avoid alienating an audience, since conscious disapproval will overcome any perception of humour. Boundary crossing is potentially fruitful, even as it is also particularly fraught, risking alienation.[22] Of course, the breaking point, either in the direction of dullness or of danger, varies for different members of

---

18 Salvatore Attardo and Victor Raskin, "Script Theory Revis(it)ed: Joke Similarity and Joke Representation Model," *HUMOR* 4, nos. 3–4 (1991): 293–347; Raskin, *Primer of Humor Research*.

19 Salvatore Attardo, *Humorous Texts* (Berlin: de Gruyter, 2001); Salvatore Attardo, "A Primer for the Linguistics of Humor," in *Primer of Humor Research*, 101–55.

20 Todd McGowan, *Only a Joke Can Save Us: A Theory of Comedy* (Evanston: Northwestern University Press, 2017).

21 Peter McGraw and Joel Warner, *The Humor Code: A Global Search for What Makes Things Funny* (New York: Simon and Schuster, 2014).

22 See Sharon Lockyer and Michael Pickering, eds., *Beyond the Joke: The Limits of Humour* (Basingstoke: Palgrave, 2005), on the risks and ethical issues involved.

an audience, hinting at some of the challenges facing those who create humour as well as those who would identify it from the past. The diversity of audience response needs to be considered in engaging the humour of the past just as with humour of the present. Even as the violation has to be perceived as benign for the audience to see it as humorous, the humour itself need not be particularly kind, potentially serving satirical or critical purposes, including mocking an out-group. Appreciating something as funny depends upon a community that shares certain knowledge, conventions, values, and expectations, and the process of laughing together can help cement that community.

There are other predictable constraints on the nature of incongruities that generate a humour response. The clashing perceptions in some way involve a shift from high to low, either in terms of register or decorum or some sense of tone. Again modern vocabulary for describing this phenomenon is more varied than the underlying concept. Bakhtin, in his account of the carnivalesque, describes an inversion of the higher order for the lower or of the head for the nether regions; Douglas comments on "a victorious tilting of uncontrol against control"; or, in the language of Herbert Spenser, consciousness is unawares transferred from great things to small.[23] Such a movement from high to low also explains humour's strong affinity with the taboo. Breaking decorum through exposing arenas usually left unstated provides an in-built incongruity that predictably moves from high to low. This is likely to generate a humour response from those audience members who view the transgression as benign, even as it will generate shock and disapproval from an audience for whom the taboo overrides the possibility of delight.

Timing is also crucial for making the incongruity humorous. For comedians, the pacing of delivery is well recognized as essential to the effect. In the incongruity-resolution model of humour, there is a need for the resolved sense to rapidly displace the false apprehension with a sudden flooding of understanding, and that sudden flooding is the trigger for laughter. The psychological explanation of Hurley *et al.* demonstrates at a theoretical level how the false apprehension is covertly built up and then confronted with an alternative understanding in a sudden displacement that would be disorienting were it not funny.

---

23 Mikhail Bakhtin, *Rabelais and His World*, transl. Hélène Iswolsky (Bloomington: Indiana University Press, 1984); Mary Douglas, *Implicit Meanings: Essays on Anthropology* (London: Routledge, 1977), chap. 7, "Jokes"; John Morreall, "Applications of Humor: Health, the Workplace, and Education," in *Primer of Humor Research*, 449–78.

More observational studies suggest the massive significance of framing. The humorist or humorous text signals the presence of humour (through voice or aspect or verbal markers), and the work of humour can then follow its own rules of not sense-making that will delight the audience that is receiving it.[24] The performance context can establish the humour, which, in turn, can cement social cohesion in the performance context. In a brilliant sociological study of Dutch joke tellers, Kuipers demonstrates how humour is about creating community and shows how fundamental class and gender are in the perception and response. In the communities that Kuipers explores, women are marked as humour appreciaters, men marked as humour producers.[25] Framing and the community aspect will be keenly pursued in the present study, even though fine-grained distinctions in audience responses of the past are notoriously hard to establish.

Irony presents an apparently contrary case, because in irony there are clashing scripts but the marker of humour is masked, enabling misunderstanding if the framing is not sufficient to tip off an audience to perceive the irony. This presents a particular challenge for humour of the long past, where it is hard to see the implicit markers, as can be seen in scholarly disagreements on the validity of reading irony in Old English literature.[26]

The conventions of humour are crucial for creating the right framing and cueing an audience to be appreciative, as seen for Dutch joke tellers (studied by Kuipers) or contemporary stand-up comedians (studied by McGraw and Warner). The verbal conventions of a joke work to establish appropriate receptivity in the audience hearing the joke. Canned laughter in television sitcoms was all about establishing the right context of receptivity in the audience. The crucial role of framing points to the need for considering performance contexts in thinking through the Old English examples.

Those essential elements – incongruity as benign violation, a tightness of timing, some movement from high to low, and an appropriate context – establish a useful basis for understanding humour of all kinds. In making more fine-grained distinctions, humour theorists are often seen as belonging to three distinct camps, which are worth briefly considering here. Incongruity theory is the most fundamental and has provided most of

---

24 See Michael Mulkay, *On Humour: Its Nature and Place in Modern Society* (Oxford: Polity, 1988) for an outstanding study.

25 Giselinde Kuipers, *Good Humor, Bad Taste: A Sociology of the Joke*, 2nd ed. (Berlin: de Gruyter, 2006, 2015).

26 See, for example, Elise Louviot, *Direct Speech in Beowulf and Other Old English Narrative Poems* (Cambridge: Bewer, 2016), in contrast with Tom Clark, *A Case for Irony in Beowulf, with Particular Reference to Its Epithets* (New York: Lang, 2003).

the theoretical work so far, but the other two approaches, superiority and release, also have utility. Superiority theory, derived from Aristotle and articulated by Hobbes and Bergson among others, suggests an appropriate domain for the incongruity, since the object is seen as in some way put down by the humour, with a sense of relief in the viewer that there do not go I.[27] In clarifying the approach, Hobbes articulates laughter as an expression of "sudden glory" at the realization of superiority, suggesting how perception of humour builds up the perceiver. Such humour is in some ways close to *Schadenfreude* since it is laughing at the revelation of folly, but the laughter can be mixed with sympathy and can be directed at one's previous self as well as at others. While the name makes this approach sound unpleasantly snobbish, the underlying theory is surprisingly productive for explaining how humour is a liberating and humanizing force. Bergson is particularly concerned with how such derisive laughter critiques the overly mechanistic. Superiority theory is fundamental to an understanding of satire: humour does social work through criticism, which appeals to the audience because of their disassociation from the object of the humour. Plato famously opposed such laughter, concerned that it was anti-social, yet most modern political comedy is of this type, suggesting the value of superiority theory for understanding comedy of social engagement.

Release theories of humour provide another way of thinking about the processes occurring during the resolution of the incongruity.[28] They suggest that the audience lives in a constant state of constraint, from which humour allows a temporary reprieve. Freud is the most famous exponent, suggesting that jokes (which for him are a limited subset of tendentious humour and are always about sex and violence) provide a momentary freeing from the repression of sexual and violent urges. Such release flags why the breaking of taboo can be such a fruitful arena for humour. A different version of release theory suggests that humour saves mental energy as the audience realizes that the set-up does not require serious problem solving. Play and the signals that define play prove to be a useful element in detecting humour.[29]

---

27 Henri Bergson, *Laughter: An Essay on the Meaning of the Comic*, transl. Cloudesely Brereton and Fred Rothwell (New York: Macmillan, 1911). See Barry Sanders, *Sudden Glory: Laughter as Subversive History* (Boston: Beacon, 1995) for an engaging account making use of superiority theory.

28 See Sigmund Freud, *Jokes and Their Relation to the Unconscious*, transl. James Strachey (London: Routledge, 1960); Elliott Oring, *Jokes and Their Relations* (Lexington: University of Kentucky Press, 1992).

29 See further Johan Huizinga, *Homo Ludens: A Study of the Play Element in Culture* (London: Routledge, 1949).

The mechanisms for the creation of humour might be summarized as follows, then: humour comes from an incongruity, a doubleness of script, clashing in some appropriate way. The appropriate inappropriateness often involves some surprising ambiguity of meaning or a shift in register or a departure from an expected form or a violation of level. The element of surprise speaks to an issue of timing in which the processing of the humorous stimulant needs to involve a rapid (or simultaneous) comprehending of the opposing scripts. The doubleness involves some turn downwards in register or decorum or moral seriousness, and hence humour is often taboo-breaking, which may add to its appeal. The whole process must grab an audience's attention and yet not repel that audience, which requires the right balance of empathy and alienation. The audience is often primed to be receptive to a perception of humour, and appreciating the humour can be a strongly social event. Some such understanding of the creation of humour will be of value throughout the study to come.

Laughter

Laughter is part of the sign language of the humorous mode, and some theorists take laughter as a convenient diagnostic for humour, but the relation proves tenuous in all cases and particularly vexed for understanding the past. While laughter has to appear spontaneous to be believed, observational studies show how it is social, interactional, and complicatedly controlled.[30] Laughter has some role as an ideal response to a humorous stimulus, but the correlation between laughter and humour is generally muted. Laughter is often a community-wide response and is so deeply social as to be contagious. Kuipers' study of joke-telling shows how laughter is valued as a community-building and community-affirming gesture. Laughter in the real world, though, more often derives from other causes than as a reaction to humour. Provine demonstrates that most laughter provides social cohesion in a conversational mode, where laughter is part of the conversational flow. Apparently, its exuberant use is curbed by a learned sense of decorum. In the United States, Provine shows that five-year-olds laugh 7.7 times per hour, whereas adults laugh on average once per hour.[31] Laughter can mark derision, suggest superiority, mask fear, register relief, express joy, or acknowledge a social compact in addition to its role as a response to humour.

---

30 See Robert R. Provine, *Laughter: A Scientific Investigation* (New York: Viking, 2000).
31 Kuipers, *Good Humor*; Provine, *Laughter*.

In Old English literature (as in the Bible), when laughter is mentioned, it is generally the laughter of scorn or derision that dominates, with occasional instances of relief or sociability.[32] This does not mean that early medieval audiences failed to laugh at the funny bits, but rather that quotidian laughter is rarely worth mentioning and therefore accounts of laughter are a poor index for uncovering moments of humour.[33] There are occasional accounts of the laughter of merriment, as when the captives in hell laugh in anticipating Christ's harrowing in the poem *The Prayer of St. John* (lines 19–21).[34] More common are examples of laughter of triumph, hostility, and scorn, as when the battle hero Byrhtnoth laughs in the poem *The Battle of Maldon* (lines 144–6) at the moment when he kills a Viking enemy in a last-ditch stand that is followed almost immediately by his own death.[35] This may be laughter of superiority, perhaps of relief, with an element of scorn, but it does not point to humour.

That lack of correlation should come as little surprise in an intellectual milieu dominated by the Bible, which generally takes a dim view of laughter. "Laughter I counted error: and to mirth I said: Why art thou vainly deceived?" says the voice of the preacher in Ecclesiastes 2:2.[36] The laughter of God in the Old Testament tends to be derisive: "I also will laugh

---

32 See Hugh Magennis, "Images of Laughter in Old English Poetry, with Particular Reference to the 'Hleahtor Wera' of *the Seafarer*," *English Studies* 73 (1992): 193–204; John D. Niles, "Byrhtnoth's Laughter and the Poetics of Gesture," in *Humour in Anglo-Saxon Literature*, ed. Jonathan Wilcox (Cambridge: Brewer, 2000), 11–32.

33 Unlike humour, mentions of laughter in early medieval English culture have been well studied: see Teresa Pàroli, "The Tears of the Heroes in Germanic Epic Poetry," in *Helden und Heldensage: Otto Geschwantler zum 60. Geburtstag*, eds. Hermann Reichert and Günter Zimmermann (Vienna: Fassbaender, 1990), 233–66; Magennis, "Images of Laughter"; T.A. Shippey, "'Grim Wordplay': Folly and Wisdom in Anglo-Saxon Humor," in *Humour in Anglo-Saxon Literature*, 33–48; Susanne Kries, "Laughter and Social Stability in Anglo-Saxon and Old Norse Literature," *A History of English Laughter: Laughter from Beowulf to Beckett and Beyond*, ed. Manfred Pfister (Amsterdam: Rodopi, 2002), 1–15; Daniel F. Pigg, "Laughter in *Beowulf*: Ambiguity, Ambivalence, and Group Identity Formation," in *Laughter in the Middle Ages and Early Modern Times: Epistemology of a Fundamental Human Behavior, Its Meaning, and Consequences*, ed. Albrecht Classen (Berlin: De Gruyter, 2010), 201–13.

34 The Exeter Book poem previously known as *The Descent into Hell* is so retitled in M.R. Rambaran-Olm, ed. and trans., *John the Baptist's Prayer, or The Descent into Hell from the Exeter Book: Text, Translation, and Critical Study* (Cambridge: Brewer, 2014).

35 See Niles, "Byrhtnoth's Laughter."

36 All Modern English renderings of the Bible will be from the Douay-Rheims translation of the Latin Vulgate, which was the dominant form of the text circulating in early medieval England. The King James Version sounds yet more pointed in this case: "I said of laughter, It is mad: and of mirth, What doeth it?"

in your destruction, and will mock when that shall come to you which you feared," according to Solomon in Proverbs 1:26.[37] What looks like the laughter of derision comes from both Abraham and Sara when the Lord promises them a son in their old age (Gen. 17:17, Gen. 18:10, Gen 18:12). The valence of laughter as joyful is hinted at when the resulting child is named "he laughs," Isaac (Gen. 21:6), but the dubious nature of laughter has been firmly established by then.[38]

If the Old Testament gives laughter a bad name by playing up derision over pleasure, the New Testament is equally suspicious of laughter within this world. As Christ says in his ministry to the poor: "Blessed are ye that hunger now: for you shall be filled. Blessed are ye that weep now: for you shall laugh.... Woe to you that are filled: for you shall hunger. Woe to you that now laugh: for you shall mourn and weep" (Luke 6:21–5). Present mirth may have present laughter, but what's to come is all too sure: merriment in this world is a sign of the heedlessness that presages torment in eternity, just as sorrow in this world will be turned around with eternal pleasure. The sense of these two verses requires an understanding of laughter as a symbol of pleasure – there is, after all, laughter in heaven – even as it is explicitly damning towards the creation of laughter in this world. Benedict of Aniane can say: "Since the Lord condemns those who laugh now, it is clear that there is never a time for laughter for the faithful soul."[39] This is an idea that will get explored further in chapter 6 on homiletic humour below. Otherwise laughter in the New Testament chimes with derision of the Old Testament, as when people laugh at Christ for his claim that he can bring anyone back from the dead (Matt. 9:24, Luke 8:53, Mark 5:40).

The Christian critique of laughter and of merriment in this world is picked up by some Christian commentators, such as John Chrysostom, who observes that Christ is known to weep, but never to laugh, "nay, nor smile but a little; no one at least of the evangelists hath mentioned this," and who famously posed the challenge "Christ is crucified and does thou laugh?"[40] The Benedictine Rule at first seems to prohibit laughter,

---

37 The Lord's laughter in the Psalms is similarly derisive: Psalms 2:4, 36:13 (KJV 37:13), 58:9 (KJV 58:8).

38 For a summary of patristic commentary on this scene, which tends to view Abraham's laughter as joyous and Sara's as the derision of doubt, see my "The First Laugh: Laughter in Genesis and the Old English Tradition," in *The Old English Hexateuch: Aspects and Approaches*, eds. Rebecca Barnhouse and Benjamin C. Withers (Kalamazoo, MI: Medieval Institute Publications, 2000), 239–69.

39 Quoted in Sanders, *Sudden Glory*, 130.

40 *Homilies on the Gospel of Saint Matthew*, homily 6; trans. Schaff 1888: 41. Chrysostom claims not to be entirely opposed to laughter: "And these things I say, not to suppress all laughter, but to take away dissipation of mind."

but then allows it in moderation. And while Bernard of Clairvaux in the 1120s famously opposed visual humour in the form of drolleries, churches, and religious manuscripts make many excursions into the comic.[41] The complexities of a Christian position that is broadly hostile to humour but makes some allowances are drawn out in chapter 6 below.

Old English audiences probably did laugh at what they perceived to be humorous, but such laughter is one of those quotidian and somatic responses that were not generally seen as worth recording. In a corpus skewed towards the ecclesiastical and those of high status due to the very nature of writing, everyday laughter does not make it to the record. The possibilities of positively valenced laughter are imagined, but often in a tellingly negative way. The Old English poem *Exodus* presents a fascinating example in a description of desolation on the death of the Egyptian first-born:

Wop wæs wide,   worulddreama lyt,
wæron hleahtorsmiðum   handa belocene.
(*Exodus*, lines 42–3)[42]

Lamentation was wide-spread, there were few worldly joys,
the hands of the laughter-smiths were clasped shut.

The poet is here emphasizing the scope of the desolation, and this is done by imagining a lack of laughter, a lack that is emphasized by a fancifully embodied sense of the construction of the laughter that is being denied. The locking shut (*belocene*) of the hands of the laughter-smiths suggests the absence of the worldly joy that came about when such entertainers could strike the harp and generate laughter as readily as a smith could craft the clasps and key for locking. "Laughter-smiths" is presumably a metaphor for comic entertainers, and such figures are apparently a recognizable part of society, even if they only get mentioned in the process of noting their absence.[43]

---

41 See Kendrick, *Chaucerian Play*; Sanders, *Sudden Glory*.
42 Peter J. Lucas, ed., *Exodus* (London: Methuen, 1977), 80. As Lucas shows, the context is both lamentation by the Egyptians on the destruction of the first-born and of the Israelites in exile. The poem is particularly rich in poetic compounds.
43 See, further, E.G. Stanley, "Wonder-Smiths and Others: *smið* Compounds in Old English Poetry, with an Excursus on *hleahtor*," *Neophilologus* 101 (2017): 277–304; and cf. the laughter-generating talents of Beowulf, which get noted only upon their extinguishing with his death, at *Beowulf*, lines 3020–1a, discussed in chapter 4 below.

Descriptions of laughter only occasionally help locate moments of humour, and so other means of analysis are needed. Rhetorical devices are often a useful clue. The specific devices by which humour is produced in Old English literature will be explicated in the analyses to come, but it may be useful to give a summary statement of some of the more predictable underlying methods here.[44] Understatement is one of the most common. Understatement is widespread in surviving early English literature, sometimes expressed in terms of a denial of the opposite, a rhetorical figure known as litotes (such as "not too bad" as an expression for being well). This is good for the creation of humour since it sets out an opposite idea which is then denied and so inevitably opens up incongruity, as will be seen in chapter 4. While understatement is particularly common in Old English, there is some fruitful use of overstatement to create humour, too, where the piling up of excess opens up an incongruity between the expression and the underlying sense, as will be seen in chapter 6. Both of these devices manifest irony since the surface statement is understood as differing from the underlying sense. This study will take something of a maximalist position in relation to detecting irony, which often underpins moments of humour.

The contradiction between social codes and the way people actually live can lead to a social incongruity manifest either in embarrassment or in satire, as will be seen in a surprisingly wide range of examples, including epic, hagiography, and romance, examined in chapters 4, 7, and 8. Play facilitates the perception of humour, and some playful genres are particularly inclined to be humorous. [45] This is seen most clearly in the case of riddles.

Funny Genres: Jokes and Riddles

In modern times, humour is most readily deployed in a crafted anecdote or brief story, delivered orally, and closing with an emphatic and surprising incongruity in a punch-line, a.k.a. a joke. The form has a long history, with references to joke-books in ancient Greece, one of which survives to

---

44 See, further, my "Understatement and Incongruity: Humour in the Literature of Anglo-Saxon England," in *Humour in the Arts: New Perspectives*, eds. Vivienne Westbrook and Shun-liang Chao (New York: Routledge, 2019), 59–77.

45 See, further, Martha Bayless, "Merriment, Entertainment, and Community in Anglo-Saxon Culture," in *The Daily Lives of the Anglo-Saxons*, eds. Carole Biggam, Carole Hough, and Daria Izdebska (Tempe, AZ: ACMRS, 2017), 239–56 on the centrality of play and community to generating merriment.

the present.[46] Jokes are a perfect case study for most humour theorists, in part because of their brevity, in part because their sole purpose seems to be the creation of humour, and in part because they are so amenable to the techniques of social science research.

Indeed, one strand of the social science study of humour has been to uncover the world's funniest joke:

> Two hunters are out in the woods when one of them collapses. He doesn't seem to be breathing and his eyes are glazed. The other guy whips out his phone and calls emergency services. He gasps, "My friend is dead! What can I do?" The operator says, "Calm down. I can help. First, let's make sure he's dead." There is a silence, then a gunshot. Back on the phone, the guy says, "Okay, now what?"[47]

This joke was selected through international polling on the internet, as explained by McGraw and Warner. There is a risk that the methodology encouraged what might be the joke least likely to set up barriers of offence, perhaps making this the least unfunny joke. The incongruities are glaring, hingeing on the conflicting scripts within which the operator's reassuring third sentence can be interpreted, with the ambiguity rapidly pinpointed by the other guy's action. The outcome may have a little extra force from flirting with taboo, since killing a friend is presumably that, and yet nobody gets hurt, since it is only a joke, making it a benign violation, even as the joke pokes fun at the literal-mindedness of the second hunter, who is the object of mild satire, releasing a superiority humour response. The framing of the story clearly announces that this is a joke and so encourages a humour response. The context of the retelling clarifies that laughter is an expected response. The switch from high to low may come in the move between something deadly serious and the casual flippancy of the joking structure.

There is no recognized tradition of jokes as such surviving from early medieval England and few from the later Middle Ages until the joke-book compendiums of the early modern period. Comic sermon exempla may present a medieval equivalent, as discussed in chapter 6 below. Rather than jokes, the form most recognized as humorous from early medieval England is the riddle. Riddles are central to this study. Riddles dwell on paradoxes, which often involve comic incongruity, and feature many secondary techniques of humour. They imply an interactive performance,

---

46 See Barry Baldwin, trans., *The Philogelos, or Laughter-Lover* (Amsterdam: Gieben, 1983).
47 "World's Funniest Joke," from McGraw and Warner, *The Humor Code*, 114.

with an audience that chooses to be engaged and not alienated by the ambiguities and dualities of the form. The audience is primed to laughter by the context and probably contributes to the hilarity by competing to provide the best answer. Riddles in Old English will provide the backbone of this study. They fit within a tradition of Anglo-Latin riddling and much good recent work has been devoted to tracing links with that tradition.[48] This book will take a different tack, examining them in the context of other literature in Old English, including, unusually, such hortatory vernacular oral pieces as homilies and saints' lives.

Chapter Outline

Following this introductory account of theories of humour, chapter 1 introduces the most recognizably funny surviving Old English works, namely the riddles. I provide a detailed interpretation of a single example, Riddle 51 (generally solved as a quill and three fingers), working slowly over the clues to establish how the various stages of riddle solving each generates comic effect. Many of the features investigated are common to other riddles, such as the false picture that gets built up at the same time as the true one, and the comic interplay between the two. I also look closely at Riddle 44 (generally solved as a key) as an example of a riddle of *double entendre*, showing how the consistent doubling in such riddles particularly parades incongruity, while the shift in levels of decorum makes it easy to establish that the incongruity is funny. The humour of the comic duality would be particularly activated by the liveliness of a riddle-solving community, where tension is generated by the risk of an audience member shouting out the unspeakable solution.

Riddles are not the only genre of short pieces that play with ambiguities that call for interpretation from a challenged audience. The thought-games of riddle solving are encouraged, too, in interpreting statements of

---

48 See Andy Orchard, "Enigma Variations: The Anglo-Saxon Riddle-Tradition," in *Latin Learning and English Lore: Studies in Anglo-Saxon Literature for Michael Lapidge*, eds. Katherine O'Brien O'Keeffe and Andy Orchard, 2 vols. (Toronto: University of Toronto Press, 2005), I, 284–304; Andy Orchard, ed. and trans., *The Old English and Anglo-Latin Riddle Tradition*, DOML 69 (Cambridge, MA: Harvard University Press, 2021); Andy Orchard, *A Commentary on the Old English and Anglo-Latin Riddle Tradition* (Cambridge, MA: Harvard University Press, 2021). See also, Dieter Bitterli, *Say What I am Called: The Old English Riddles of the Exeter Book and the Anglo-Latin Riddle Tradition* (Toronto: University of Toronto Press, 2009); Megan Cavell, ed. and trans., *The Riddle Ages: Early Medieval Riddles, Translations, and Commentaries* (2013, redeveloped 2020: https://theriddleages.com/).

proverbial wisdom, explored here in a less familiar example, the so-called *Durham Proverbs*. These often prove to be funny, deploying many devices similar to the riddles. After considering the humour at some length, I ground an initial understanding of potential audiences for these works by turning to the implications of the manuscripts in which they survive, particularly the Exeter Book. This builds up the surprising picture of a monastic or similar setting as one attested venue for the enjoyment of the humour.

Riddles in general seem to be more suited for listening than reading, and yet some of the tricks of the Exeter Book riddles complicate that picture. In chapter 2, I consider one of those tricks, namely the use of runes within the riddles. These provide a rich source of humour by making incongruity manifest through language play. Often the runic letter needs to be articulated as the word that names the letter, even as the sense depends on understanding the word as the letter itself, although, on one occasion, regular words that are also the names of runic letters need to be understood as the runic letter and not as the concept that the word usually names. The doubleness of understanding needed to crack such puzzles depends on a highly literate sense. Breaking that initial code usually gets only part-way to a riddle's solution since what is revealed is often an anagram, which requires further literate puzzling to solve, with further potential for humour. As a consequence, poems that seem to describe objects prove to be describing language, even as that language then points back to an object. I show that such jumping between levels and systems of signification is itself often a source of humour as an audience processes a sometimes dizzying sequence of violations which, nevertheless, add up to a rational solution if viewed with enough care. Self-consciousness about language proves to be a recurring point of humour.

Nor are riddles the only works that exploit the dual signification of runic letters. Those runes are reified in the poetic riddle-contest of *Solomon and Saturn I*, where the very shape of the runic letter-forms within the Pater Noster prayer are seen to skewer the devil in a scene presented with exuberant excess. Once again, there is a dizzying play of levels as letters which sound out the power of the prayer prove to have power in and of themselves. In addition, *The Rune Poem* repeats the trick of each rune serving as both letter and the concept of the word that articulates that letter. In this case, further humour arises from the pithy form of the wisdom contained in each stanza of the poem, provoking proverb-reading techniques analogous to those deployed on *The Durham Proverbs*. Interpretation of such lettered humour probably went on, among other places, in a schoolroom context, which would also have appreciated the riddles and the proverbial wisdom, and I close out chapter 2 by exploring an exuberant version of that environment by drawing on the imaginative pedagogical dialogue of Ælfric Bata.

Humour can arise from incongruities of form as well as content, and in chapter 3 I consider the interesting example presented by a plenitude of acoustic poetic effect in passages of extended rhyme in Old English verse. Because rhyme is not a structural component for Old English meter and is quite rare, those instances where it does occur are loudly noticeable. I consider how the piling on of rhyme in Riddle 28 and in *The Rhyming Poem* creates a comic effect. In both these cases, familiar conventions combine with the formal oddity to generate the humour. This is an effect that would be appreciated by poetry connoisseurs of all kinds, and I close out the chapter with recoverable examples of audiences of poetry appreciation at strikingly different social levels, namely within the court of King Alfred and among the farm workers on the estate of Abbess Hild's monastery at Whitby.

A more rhetorical formal characteristic is a more common source of humour: the use of understatement. This sets up incongruity because information is doled out in too cautious or partial a manner. Old English literature appears to relish a particular form of such understatement, namely litotes, where an assertion is stated by means of denying its opposite ("I'm not too bad" standing for "I am well"). When tweaked appropriately this is often wryly funny. The use of such understatement proves to be endemic in heroic literature, where it often works to build up the insouciance of a hero in the face of threat, as I show in chapter 4. Such insouciance plays into the construction of a heroic ethos, seen widely in surviving Old Norse sagas and poetry. That provides one framework for reading *Beowulf*, seeing it as a work conducive to the community of warriors in the mead-hall lovingly sketched within the poem. But I suggest that the humour in *Beowulf* can be fruitfully interpreted in other ways, too. While comic insouciance may be a heroic ideal, the poet presents King Hrothgar as constantly teetering on the edge of comic embarrassment for all his attempts at insouciance. In the second half of the chapter I read the presentation of Hrothgar's court in terms more usually applied to reading a romance like *Apollonius of Tyre*. Attending to the implied etiquette and close reading the narrator's presentation of the king and his actions, I suggest that Hrothgar is constantly in danger of being outfaced by Beowulf and the poet is happy to parade his discomfiture in a comic way. Humour derives from displaying the risk of embarrassment at breaking decorum within the kingdom of Denmark in a manner that would appeal to audiences inclined to laugh at the elite warriors in the mead-hall.

Laughing at heroic conventions is explored further in chapter 5. Sometimes humour derives from the clash of competing generic expectations, and this is particularly apparent in poems that exploit heroic conventions to relate a Christian story. *Judith* has long been recognized as deploying some of the conventional elements of battle poetry in a surprising way to advance a plot in which a non-martial woman overthrows a hyper-masculine warlord. I pursue how reversals of expectation are played out at many levels here to create comedy. In a similar manner, *Andreas* mixes elements of battle poetry with conventions of didactic hagiographical literature to comic effect. The overlapping of language also used in *Beowulf* raises the possibility that *Andreas* is parodying a specific surviving poem, although I suggest instead that the work is parodying a tradition more broadly. The trickiness involved in both of these poems invites comparison with a comic trickster presented elsewhere in the *Beowulf* and *Judith* manuscript, namely Alexander from *The Letter of Alexander the Great to Aristotle*. Such tricks of genre would invite laughter from many poetry connoisseurs, and in this chapter I explore its reception by an intellectual courtly audience such as the learned power-house of women known to be gathered around Queen Edith.

Chapter 6 moves to a body of literature rarely considered in the same breath as humour, namely Old English homilies and related preaching texts. The reputation for dourness in this preaching corpus is largely justified, I concede, looking at biblical hostility to mirthful laughter and the sober instincts of Ælfric. Nevertheless, some homilists make use of comic exempla to spice up their moral message, and I show how the Old English translation of Gregory the Great's *Dialogues* presents material particularly suited to this purpose. I analyse two homilies which do make use of humour, both now anonymous, namely Napier 46 and Vercelli 9. These homilies create humour by using some of the techniques seen to be productive elsewhere in this study, such as understatement, breaking taboo, and most fully through over-statement and exaggeration. Such exaggeration is also used to comic effect in a clerical satire, *The Seasons for Fasting*, which delights in skewering the bad conduct of priests until, alas, the poem breaks off incomplete. While the audience for much of the humour in this chapter is the broad Christian community gathered for services in church, this clerical satire usefully conjures up a contrasting possibility, namely the ale house, which is a productive locus for imagining the reception of comic literature of all kinds.

If the pickings are somewhat slim for homiletic humour, they are altogether more generous for hagiographic humour, as I show in chapter 7. On the one hand, humour here comes in the form of a kind of decorous and restrained comedy that might help keep an audience's attention during an extended narrative without ever threatening to disrupt the pre-ordained coordinates of a saint's life – the kind of humour that Ælfric would approve of and occasionally himself practises. On the other hand, there are examples of a more unrestrained humour of human interest, particularly apparent in three anonymous prose hagiographies, each inclining towards a kind of hagiographic romance, where embarrassment and irony, upset and inversion, all get richly deployed. The humour here might shock a controlling church authority like Ælfric but was presumably seen by some religious authorities as effective for conveying a story and useful for keeping an audience's attention. This is humour designed to draw in a broad range of early medieval Christian society. I suggest that a pious secular household, such as that of Ælfric's patron, the Ealdorman Æthelweard, would provide the broad-ranging audience appropriate for these works if they were read out before the extended family along with their servants and workers gathered in a single place.

Finally, from hagiographic romance, I turn in chapter 8 to the one generally recognized example of romance surviving in Old English – *Apollonius of Tyre* – to show how this story of human interest is often recounted with a considerable comic flourish. I focus on the humour that becomes apparent from attending to the tone and ironies as the king's daughter, Arcestrate, goes about covertly wooing Apollonius, side-stepping expectations of gender by operating through indirection. This creates multiple comic incongruities as well as significant scope for embarrassment, which turn out to boost an audience's sympathy for the human predicament of the characters. This late Old English example most anticipates the conventions and possibilities of Middle English romance. Its inclusion here serves well as a reminder of the legitimacy of reading other Old English works in the style of romance, even as it appropriately closes out the study by pointing to conventions that will be more apparent in subsequent literature.

The value of studying humour through the corpus of early medieval literature is explored in the conclusion, where I suggest that the sequence of works treated here sketch out a possible alternative literary tradition to the more standard one of dour heroic achievement. Humour serves to emphasize the wonder of the world and the flawed and partial human perceptions of it in a way analogous to a good riddle. Different audiences would appreciate different elements of the humour, as grounded in the discussions at the end of each of the chapters. While much of the humour comes from reinforcing a Christian ideology, I suggest that a surprising amount creates satire aimed at the manly men of the heroic tradition. Humour turns the world upside-down, and attending to it in early medieval English literature provides an antidote to the excessively male-centred, elite, martial values that the period is most famous for, even as it also serves an enduring function by being entertaining.

Three Brief Case Studies

As a taste of such entertainment after so much groundwork, it may be nice to anticipate a few funny moments. The three examples below anticipate three different aspects of the discussion to come. Bibliographical references and fuller contextual discussions are provided in chapters 4, 7, and 1, respectively.

Killer Understatement: A Water-Monster Slower on His Fins

A small and incidental detail from *Beowulf* demonstrates that poem's pleasure in understatement and the potential this has for creating humour. As Hrothgar and the Danes and Beowulf and the Geats follow the bloody tracks of the dying Grendel, they come to a body of water in what is presented as a strikingly uncanny landscape. As they first arrive, one of the Geats shoots a creature within the water, one of the *nicras* ("water-monsters," 1427b), and the poet reports:

> he on holme wæs
> sundes þe sænra   ðe hyne swylt fornam.
> (*Beowulf* 1435b–6)[49]

> it was the slower of swimming
> in the water because death took it off.

This is a strikingly inefficient way of describing a kill, with a dilatory effect created by the narrator giving details about swimming speed before giving the key information that the beast has been carried off by death. Upon processing that latter piece of information, the earlier statement gets reanalysed as an incongruous understatement. The beast is not just the slower of swimming, it is now the slower at everything, and not just a little bit slower, but so much slower that it has stopped (and the warriors duly reach for it with boar-spears to bring it to the headland for gazing upon). The scene has built up the uncanniness of the context, which the unnamed Geat is both working to control and contributing to by killing the beast. The phrasing here suggests a glimmer of humour within that construction of the uncanny. The information about the killing had been anticipated

---

49 *Beowulf* is cited from from R.D. Fulk, Robert E. Bjork, and John D. Niles, eds., *Klaeber's Beowulf: Fourth Edition* (Toronto: University of Toronto Press, 2008). Translations from Old English are my own unless otherwise noted.

earlier in the sentence with a report that the hard battle-arrow stood in the water-beast's vitals and deprived it of life and *yðgewinnes* (1434a, "of striving in the wave"). Motion is apparently crucial to the water monster's being and definitional of its life. The loss of that movement bodes ill for the beasts of the mere, anticipating a triumph of human order. In addition, the extreme understatement of equating death with a slowing down in the water creates a momentary puzzle, a brief delay, and a switch from a high register of horror to a lower one of pedantic zoological explanation. The narrator sees the value of a moment of humour for establishing a frisson of fear.

The doubleness here, then, comes from learning one message from the explicit sense of the words (water monster slowed down) and then processing it and arriving at a different sense (water monster dead). It is an incongruity where one set of expectations (account of water monster natural history) has been replaced with another (account of water monster demise). This shift is sudden, as one statement gets reanalysed in terms of the other. In a bigger context, the use of such understatement and inversion encourages a sense of the omnipresent underlying potential for reversal. Something is rotten in the state of Denmark, and it behooves an audience to be attentive and not to take the movements of water monsters, or of anyone else, for granted. The implications of this kind of humour for the poem will get worked out in chapter 4 below, while the potential humour of the dilatory effect will prove to be deployed too in some of the funny homilies discussed in chapter 6.

The Insouciance of the Sizzling Saint: Laurence on the Grid-Iron

A person being tortured should want the pain to stop. That is a stealthy but firmly held expectation that often gets flipped in the story of martyrs. Instead of expressing the anguish of a body impaled, martyrs generally show disdain towards their tormentor as they transcend the mere bodily to express an unbowed spirit. Since the incongruity is already expected, baked into the genre, its straight manifestation may not be perceived as funny, but if the difference between expectation and narrated event is particularly acute, then the extremity of the gulf may activate the potential for humour. That is what happens when St. Laurence calls to his tormenter from the grid-iron on which he is being burned to turn the other side and then eat. The clashing scripts are between torture, a body suffering pain as it is burned alive, and the discourse of cooking. What makes it so striking is that the meat itself is giving the instructions. For a moment this is like the geese rising up from the spit in the *Land of Cockayne* declaring their juicy doneness, except that it is a human being on the stake. The saint's utterance is incongruous at so many levels. At a normal level, he should not be speaking and his spirit should be bowed; at the exceptional level of a martyred saint, his spirit should be defiant, but he should be pointing towards piety rather than jesting about roastedness. Laurence articulates saintly insouciance by crafting an apparent joke.

There is an element of moving from high to low in both substance and tone here as pain and death is turned into cheeky verbal defiance. There is suddenness as an audience processes the implications of what the saint is saying: not just that I am unbowed but also that I am calling myself a piece of meat and suggesting you, the torturer, do what is implied by that. And the audience is primed to expect funny business of some sort, as this is the climactic moment in the narrative of a saint's life, a martyrdom that will hurt the body but liberate the soul and see the birth of an exemplary figure into the community of saints. Ultimately this is a moment of delight rather than dolour that can, at the level of narrative, be perceived as a benign violation rather than a threatening one. The humour both provides a memorable detail and a moment of relief for the audience, reminding us of the ultimate point of spirit superseding flesh that is always encoded in these encounters. The insouciance displayed here will be seen to mark much of the heroic literature discussed in chapter 4, and the incongruity in hagiography will be developed further in chapter 7.

Inverted Probabilities: A Witch in Unusual Locomotion

Ne swa þeah treowde þeah þu teala eode, cwæþ se þe geseah hægtessan æfter heafde geongan.
(Durham Proverbs, no. 11)

I would not trust you anyway, even though you walked properly, said the one who saw the witch pass by on her head.[50]

Incongruities abound here. The context is one of a series of aphorisms or proverbs, so an audience expects some brief statement that will turn to metaphoric wisdom. It is an inversion of sorts for such an utterance to begin with a negation, since this risks not presenting rather than presenting

---

50 Text from Olof Arngart, ed. and trans., "The Durham Proverbs," *Speculum* 56, no. 2 (1981): 288–300; translation my own but drawing heavily on Richard Marsden, ed., *The Cambridge Old English Reader* (Cambridge: Cambridge University Press, 2004), 305.

something. The inverted statement is itself enigmatic ("I wouldn't trust you nevertheless even if you went so" is what it seems to be saying on a first read through). That initial utterance is reanalysed on account of the qualification describing the one who is doing the seeing. That qualification provides an abundance, or even an excess, of information. The viewer saw a sight that was anything but commonplace: a *hægtessan*, a witch. These probably did not walk the fields of early medieval England in any regular way. There has already been a jolt of the unexpected in the discovery that the one who walked in some exceptional way was a witch, but there is a full carnivalesque inversion as the witch apparently traveled *æfter heafde*, "after the head" (i.e. upside-down?). This is clearly some sort of turning against expectations presenting the topsy-turvy world of the wrong side up.

The complexity of the image encourages a double take in the manner of a riddle. On re-reading or re-hearing, the incongruity of the image becomes dominant. This is apparently something quite bizarre: a witch passing by travelling on her head. A further re-reading for the wisdom dispensed makes surprisingly little of this fundamental oddity: the onlooker's lack of trust had already been in place and is not shifted by such bizarrerie. Apparently the onlooker can spot a witch for her essentialist characteristics, regardless of her means of locomotion. By extension, the aphorism seems to suggest that essential identity is readable, which is curiously at odds with other proverbs along the lines that clothes make the person. Indeed, the spectacular and exuberantly comic visual image of this proverb may serve to undercut the apparent wisdom. Persons passing by on their head are in such attention-grabbing form that the onlooker is surely foolish to discount the memorable image.

The bizarre, surrealistic surface here presents an immediate incongruity that risks resolving into further incongruities in a manner similar to a riddle. This proverb is rich in humour of the absurd, and interpreting it proves less than straightforward. The humour of the inverted witch keeps listeners on their toes and nicely illustrates the potential pleasure – and humour – of puzzles. While this is the only witch to enter this study, there will be plenty of incongruous inversions. Engaging with the pleasurable puzzle of riddles and of proverbs will be the work of the first chapter.

Chapter One

Risible Riddles and Witty Wisdom: The Appeal of Playful Puzzles

The Exeter Book Riddles are generally considered funny, unusually so among surviving Old English literature, and this makes them a good starting point for the present study. Solving riddles, especially riddles of artful concealment, is intuitively a funny business. The riddle-solving process overlaps with the humour-perceiving process described in the introduction. Riddles revel in ambiguities and surprise, proceeding through an incongruity-resolution mechanism. They often flirt with taboo, overcoming inhibitions in ways congruent with release theories of humour. Resolving the incongruities brings a sense of superiority at out-smarting the riddle challenger and other would-be solvers as well as at overcoming the challenge. The audience for riddles chooses to enter a world of play where the challenges are seen as entertaining and not as threatening. Riddles are often engaged as a community activity, where an audience is primed for laughter, which is amplified by the rivalry and one-upping that goes on as individuals in the communal audience vie with each other to solve the challenge. Riddles, then, are understandably seen as funny.[1]

Incongruity is built into the riddle genre through the oblique form of the presentation and through the distance between an initial understanding, often building on false clues, and the reanalysis of all the details once the riddle is solved.[2] The incongruities need to be held in mind with an

---

1 On the overlapping mechanisms of riddles and humour, see my "Humour and the Exeter Book Riddles: Incongruity in Riddle 31," in *Riddles at Work in the Anglo-Saxon Tradition: Words, Ideas, Interactions*, eds. Megan Cavell and Jennifer Neville (Manchester: Manchester University Press, 2020), 128–45.
2 On riddles in general, see W.J. Pepicello and Thomas A. Green, *The Language of Riddles: New Perspectives* (Columbus: Ohio State University Press, 1984); Annikki Kaivola-Bregenhøj, *Riddles: Perspectives on the Use, Function, and Change in a Folklore Genre* (Helsinki: Finnish Literature Society, 2001).

unusual degree of simultaneity since an audience both absorbs what it is being told and reanalyses the details to construct alternative possible solutions. Once a likely solution is settled upon, humour derives from the distance between the once-imagined possibilities of the riddle's false propositions and the newly discovered solution. This is a process that happens in miniature at every step of the unfolding riddle puzzle as well as in a sustained way across the riddle as a whole.

The Old English riddles so richly exemplify different techniques of humour that I will begin each of the subsequent chapters with analysis of a pertinent example. Here I will introduce the corpus and uncover some of the tricks of language that make the Old English riddles funny before grounding the discussion with a fuller account of two characteristic examples, one straighforwardly wondrous, one bawdily so, in Riddles 51 and 44.[3] After introducing this most-famously funny Old English genre, I will turn to a less familiar example in the wisdom of proverbs. A sequence known as *The Durham Proverbs* proves to exploit some of the same tricks of puzzlement and incongruity as the riddles and so creates humour in a similar way. I will conclude by exploring an early medieval audience that appreciated the humour of both of these works.

Old English Riddles

The vast majority of riddles in Old English survive in a single manuscript, namely the Exeter Book (Exeter Cathedral Library, MS 3501, fols. 8–130), a compendium of Old English poetry, mostly religious, written in a script of the second half of the tenth century.[4] The riddles occur in three clusters towards the end of the collection. The book has suffered damage, leading to the loss of a few riddles from the end and partial loss within some texts. In addition, the boundary between works is sometimes uncertain,

---

3 Pinpointing specific Exeter Book riddles is vexed, as they have been subject to multiple numbering schemes. I use that of George Philip Krapp and Elliott Van Kirk Dobbie, eds., *The Exeter Book*, ASPR (New York: Columbia University Press, 1936), since this numbering enjoys wide circulation, including in Cavell, *The Riddle Ages*. A chart correlating the numbering in different recent editions is provided in the prefatory matter above.

4 The complete collection is ed. Bernard J. Muir, *The Exeter Anthology of Old English Poetry*, 2 vols. (Exeter: University of Exeter Press, 1994; revised ed., 2000), and quotations are drawn from this edition. The place of origin is contested, as discussed at the end of this chapter. On the organization of the collection, see Patrick W. Conner, *Anglo-Saxon Exeter: A Tenth-Century Cultural History* (Woodbridge: Boydell, 1993); John D. Niles, *God's Exiles and English Verse: On the Exeter Anthology of Old English Poetry* (Exeter: University of Exeter Press, 2019).

including at the opening of the sequence, where some editors see three riddles while others see a single first riddle. This makes it hard to say how many riddles the collection once contained. Compounding the challenge, there is also controversy over which poems in the collection constitute riddles since none is titled in the manuscript. "The Husband's Message," for example, is generally now classed as an elegy, even as some see it as a riddle.[5] It seems likely that the compiler aimed for a collection of one hundred riddles, which would match the Anglo-Latin riddle collections by Aldhelm, the combined collection of Tatwine and Eusebius, and the earlier collection by the North African/Late Roman poet Symphosius, but the surviving text only comes somewhat close to that number.[6] The once-standard edition of Krapp and Dobbie, whose numbering is used in this study, identifies ninety-five separate riddles, some of which are fragmentary and one of which is repeated. The valuable edition of Williamson identifies ninety-one, in which it is followed by Orchard, while Muir's complete edition of the Exeter Book identifies ninety-four.[7] The sequence has been presented in an impressive array of editions with valuable commentary, and there are many appealing translations into Modern English.[8] I will adopt the numbering of Krapp and Dobbie, while citing the text from Muir, and providing my own translations, drawing on the published scholarship.

The subject within a riddle is often characterized as a *wiht* ("a creature"),[9] a noun with an appealingly capacious sense, animate or inanimate, animal or human. Sometimes the riddle deploys prosopopeia and presents its description in the first person, while on other occasions the *wiht* is described in the third person, but with the voice of the riddler still very close to the subject

---

5 See S. Beth Newman Ooi, "Crossed Lines: Reading a Riddle Between Exeter Book Riddle 60 and 'The Husband's Message'," *Philological Quarterly* 100 (2021): 1–22.

6 On the continuity of the riddling tradition from Anglo-Latin to Old English, see the studies cited in the introduction, note 49, above.

7 Krapp and Dobbie, *Exeter Book*; Craig Williamson, ed., *The Old English Riddles of the 'Exeter Book'* (Chapel Hill: University of North Carolina Press, 1977); Orchard, *OE and Anglo-Latin Riddle Tradition*; Muir, *Exeter Anthology*. See the prefatory matter above for a table comparing the different riddle numbers.

8 For editions, see the preceding note. Notable translations include Craig Williamson, trans., *A Feast of Creatures: Anglo-Saxon Riddle-Songs Translated with Introduction, Notes and Commentary* (Philadelphia: University of Pennsylvania Press, 1982); Kevin Crossley-Holland, trans., *The Anglo-Saxon World: An Anthology* (Oxford: Oxford University Press, 2009); Greg Delanty and Michael Matto, eds., *The Word Exchange: Anglo-Saxon Poems in Translation* (New York: Norton, 2011); Cavell, *The Riddle Ages*.

9 *Wiht* is defined by BT s.v., definition I: "a wight, creature, being, created thing."

described.[10] Many of the texts close with the formulaic challenge "Saga hwæt ic hatte" (say what I am called) or "saga hwæt hio hatte" (say what it is called), or a variant, setting up a performance context in which the audience is pitted against the riddle challenger. Many incorporate a certain mocking defiance of the would-be interpreters, encouraging a contest of talking back by audience members who can display their wit. Even though there are no solutions in the manuscript, there is a scholarly consensus on the likely solution for most of the riddles, although a few remain unsolved.[11]

The subjects thus given voice include many from the natural world, such as a *wiht* whose garment is silent on land and on water yet sounds out when carrying it through the air (in the swan of Riddle 7); tools of agrarian life, such as a creature with many teeth and a useful snout that proceeds downwards as it usefully plunders (in the rake of Riddle 34); objects of the heroic world, such as a battle-worn creature who takes many blows but is healed by no doctor (in the shield of Riddle 5); tools from the world of study, such as a creature fallen from his martial seat and deprived of his twin now that he serves at a desk (in the ink-horn of Riddle 88); and objects from the Christian world, such as the tongue-less *wiht* that nevertheless speaks of salvation (in the inscribed patten or chalice of Riddle 48). Occasionally the concept is larger, as in the cosmological storm riddle that opens the collection (Riddles 1–3), or the riddle solved as creation which is drawn from the Latin example by Aldhelm (Riddle 40).

The different riddles within the Exeter Book were probably created by more than one author and gathered from more than one place.[12] The first forty constitute a somewhat ordered collection, beginning with the cosmic storm and ending with creation, but after that the sequence becomes increasingly miscellaneous, with many in the second half addressing an object already covered in the first half, a few apparent fragments, and a stray example in Latin (Riddle 90).[13] One instance (Riddle 30) occurs

10 See Peter Orton, "The Exeter Book *Riddles*: Authorship and Transmission," *Anglo-Saxon England* 44 (2015): 131–62, who classifies the collection by such techniques.

11 For the solutions, see in particular Donald K. Fry, "Exeter Book Riddle Solutions," *Old English Newsletter* 15, no. 1 (1981): 22–33; John D. Niles, *Old English Enigmatic Poems and the Play of the Texts* (Turnhout: Brepols, 2006), chap. 4, "Answering the Riddles in their Own Tongue"; Cavell, *The Riddle Ages*.

12 See Orton, "Exeter Book *Riddles*"; Mercedes Salvador-Bello, *Isidorean Perceptions of Order: The Exeter Book Riddles and Medieval Latin Enigmata* (Morgantown: West Virginia University Press, 2015).

13 See Salvador-Bello, *Isidorean Perceptions*, who provides the best account for the logic of their arrangement. On the Latin riddle, see Mercedes Salvador-Bello, "Exeter Book Riddle 90 Under a New Light: A School Drill in Hisperic Robes," *Neophilologus* 102 (2018): 107–23.

twice within the collection, with small but telling differences between the two texts.[14] A riddle describing the paradoxical form of a garment not weaved from cloth but from metal, a mail-coat (Riddle 35), survives in another copy, preserving the evidence for a long transmission history, and this is likely to also be the case for many others, even though alternative versions have not survived.[15] These riddles, then, were probably in wide circulation, getting performed in untold contexts that are no longer recoverable, and the surviving collection provides only a small fragment of what once circulated. It is, though, an impressive fragment, featuring riddles that work with considerable artistry to describe diverse subject matter through diverse poetic practices and tricks of obfuscation, often with considerable wit.

Funny Naming

While the method used to craft the puzzle differs in different riddles, underlying all of them is a pleasure in language. The very call to "say what I am called" gives prominence to a name, unstated in the text, and yet necessary as a resolution. This establishes a kind of in-built punning, since the unstated name designates both some external object in the world beyond the text yet also constitutes a word that the riddle-poet can flag with various linguistic tricks. Some critics ponder whether the answer may not be a word but rather the object itself, although, paradoxically, this would make the play of language more noticeable, as the riddle-poems convey the inadequacy of a name to convey all the facets of the object described. As Beechy puts it: "riddles are obsessed with the relationship between form and meaning, and thus involve a tension among the poetic function (form; message referring to message), the referential function (meaning; message referring to the world outside the message), and the metalingual function (the code, the set of symbols through which communication can occur)."[16] The multiple thrusts

---

14 See R.M. Liuzza, "The Texts of the Old English *Riddle 30*," *The Journal of English and Germanic Philology* 87 (1988): 1–15; A.N. Doane, "Spacing, Placing, and Effacing: Scribal Textuality and Exeter Riddle 30 a/b," in *New Approaches to Editing Old English Verse*, eds. Sarah Larratt Keefer and Katherine O'Brien O'Keeffe (Cambridge: Cambridge University Press, 1998), 45–65.

15 See my "Transmission of Literature and Learning: Anglo-Saxon Scribal Culture," in *A Companion to Anglo-Saxon Literature*, eds. Phillip Pulsiano and Elaine M. Treharne (Oxford: Blackwell, 2001), 50–70.

16 Tiffany Beechy, *The Poetics of Old English* (Ashgate, 2010; repr. New York, Routledge, 2016), 93; cf. Seth Lerer, *Literacy and Power in Anglo-Saxon Literature* (Lincoln: University of Nebraska Press, 1991).

of the riddle technique imbue even the quotidian with wonder. As Daley explains: "The riddle itself models a form of responsiveness *as* wondrous: it narrates a way of seeing something that may itself be ordinary but, when transposed in the riddle-form, is *wrætlic*, providing a new order for the mind to perceive, read and imitate. The poetic language of the riddles becomes the means for enchanting different forms of creation, for imbuing things with a wonder proper to them, and for reorienting the mind with a proper disposition and responsiveness to the surrounding world."[17] Through their playful process, riddles bring out a pleasure in both the adequacy and inadequacy of language.

Sometimes the play with language is fairly straightforward, such as the redeployment of letters in an anagram. The bow of Riddle 23, for example, gives its name in reverse in the first line, with a bald statement that it is doing so, albeit now with a spelling error that complicates the solution: "Agof is min noma eft onhwyrfed" ("Agof [for Agob, i.e. *bow* inverted] is my name, turned back again," line 1). This opens a riddle that proceeds to present many of the paradoxes and misdirections that establish comic incongruities. The subject-object is personified and presented with a voice, a breast, limbs, and the ability to spit. It possesses volition and control and manifests an independent streak common in such riddle objects, here expressed through the ability to refuse to obey its master, which is something it does when unbound, "nymþe searosæled" ("unless skillfully tied," 16). This is setting up a shadow description of the riddle subject as a human. Humour comes from the incongruity between a thinking, attitudinous human subject and an inanimate object made of wood and string that turns out to be the true solution. The opening anagram suggests that an audience will delight in working out the riddle clues even once the answer is apparent. Indeed, it suggests that the riddler specifically wanted the audience to key in quickly to the right solution to appreciate and enjoy the full range of paradoxes and incongruities that are then described. There is a pleasure in playing with linguistic form, recognizing and righting a name that is *onhwyrfed* ("turned about") at the start of the process, even as such naming facilitates appreciating riddling humour deployed through

---

17 Patricia Dailey, "Riddles, Wonder, and Responsiveness in Anglo-Saxon Literature," in *The Cambridge History of Early Medieval English Literature*, ed. Clare A. Lees (Cambridge: Cambridge University Press, 2013), 451–72 at 469. On wonder in the riddles, see also Peter Ramey, "The Riddle of Beauty: The Aesthetics of *Wrætlic* in Old English Verse," *Modern Philology* 114 (2017): 457–81; Peter Ramey, "Crafting Strangeness: Wonder Terminology in the Exeter Book Riddles and the Anglo-Latin Enigmata," *Review of English Studies* 69 (2018): 201–15.

the rest of the text.[18] Anagrams play a significant role in a number of riddles, establishing an incongruity of language.

Another aspect of such language play is apparent in the code-switching of alphabets through the use of runic letters alongside the more customary roman script of early English vernacular minuscule. Runic letters break up the flow of the reading experience at many levels. They visibly stand out in the manuscript, and a reader has to decide whether to treat each form as a letter or articulate the name of the rune. That name disrupts the flow of sense, as it can stand either for the referent generally named by this word or for the rune-letter itself. Such alternatives create both humorous incongruity and secondary puzzles that always call attention to language. Runes are used sparingly in the Exeter Book riddles and their system of signifying differs in different instances, as will be explored in chapter 2.

Even when they are not playing with letter forms, many of the riddles display a self-consciousness about writing or the play of language. A significant number re-animate the magic of the writing process by describing elements of the scriptorium.[19] One such example, Riddle 51, will be considered further in this chapter. Such consciousness is wittily encoded in a riddle presenting the paradoxical work of a bookworm, Riddle 47, as discussed at the opening of chapter 2 below. It is seen, too, in a riddle that presents the transcendent wonder of the creation of a book in Riddle 26 (Bible or Gospel-book), discussed at the opening to chapter 7. Riddles wittily play with language and language's embodiment in writing and enjoy displaying that play.

The techniques of such play are often akin to the techniques of Old English poetry, in which innovative compounding of nouns creates kennings, coinages that metaphorically describe an object through a pithy

18 Megan Cavell, *Weaving Words and Binding Bodies: The Poetics of Human Experience in Old English Literature* (Toronto: University of Toronto Press, 2016), 179–84 explicates the humorously paradoxical binding/unbinding of the object. There is a further level of linguistic play if the form of the opening initial letter *a* in the Exeter Book is distorted to provide an additional visual clue, as suggested by Winfried Rudolf, "Riddling and Reading—Iconicity and Logographs in Exeter Book Riddles 23 and 45," *Anglia* 130, no. 4 (2012): 499–525.

19 See Laurence K. Shook, "Riddles Relating to the Anglo-Saxon Scriptorium," in *Essays in Honour of Anton Charles Pegis*, ed. J.R. O'Donnell (Toronto: PIMS, 1974), 215–36; Robert DiNapoli, "In the Kingdom of the Blind, the One-Eyed Man Is a Seller of Garlic: Depth-Perception and the Poet's Perspective in the Exeter Book Riddles," *English Studies* 81 (2000): 422–55; Dieter Bitterli, *Say What I am Called: The Old English Riddles of the Exeter Book and the Anglo-Latin Riddle Tradition* (Toronto: University of Toronto Press, 2009), chap. 7.

condensation or a compressed riddle.[20] Conversely, the solution of a riddle sometimes revivifies the image underlying a compound word of everyday use through a kind of etymological play. The creature that captures the attention of many people with a modulating voice in Riddle 8, for example, is probably hinted at in the characterization as *eald æfensceop* ("traditional/ old evening-poet," line 5a), which puns on the name *nihtegale*, "nightin-gale" (etymologically "night-singer") that is the likely solution.[21] Naming may be yet more playful in the salacious clues to Riddle 45, when a lord's daughter grasps and covers I-know-not-what bone-less thing rising in the corner, in a *double entendre* description of dough rising. The woman's activity may play on the etymology of the word for a high-status woman, *hlæfdige*, "lady" (etymologically "loaf-kneader").[22] Riddles that play on the more or less dormant underlying sense of a common name suggest the punning pleasure of bringing that name to life, exploiting an incongruity of language that elicits humour.

Humorous play with language, then, is a fundamental element of the pleasure of Old English riddles. In addition to the pleasure of naming that comes from arriving at a riddle's solution, it is also evident in the false leads and puzzling clues of a riddle's development. The humour of this development is particularly obvious in the *double entendre* riddles, where the duality of a respectable and a bawdy solution guarantees a consistently appropriate incongruity, super-charged with the added frisson of flirting with the violation of taboo, as I will illustrate in an analysis of Riddle 44. But humour inheres in the very form of the riddle, and so it will be useful to start by looking at the mechanisms that create humour in a non-bawdy example, namely the scriptorium example of Riddle 51.

Tracking Humour in Riddle 51

Riddles necessarily operate through clashing scripts as they present clues that can be read in multiple ways. In an initial reading (or listening), no possible meaning or grammatical construction or image pattern can be

---

20 See Peter S. Baker, *Introduction to Old English*, 3rd ed. (Chichester: Wiley-Blackwell, 2012), chap. 14, for an introductory account of the poetic technique; Ann Harleman Stewart, "Kenning and Riddle in Old English," *Papers on Language and Literature* 15 (1979): 115–36 for the overlapping methods of kennings and riddles; Hannah Burrows, "Riddles and Kennings," *European Journal of Scandinavian Studies* 51, no. 1 (2021): 46–68, for the case in Old Norse.

21 See Bitterli, *Say What I am Called*, 46–56.

22 See Rudolf, "Riddling and Reading," who uncovers further puns in establishing multiple layers of interpretation.

dismissed, since it may provide the crucial clue to an answer. Throughout the riddle, an audience guesses at a likely solution and tries to re-interpret meaning, grammar, and image patterns to support that solution. During the process, any chosen solution is only a heuristic and may prove unsustainable, so the riddle form encourages an audience to keep in mind sustained ambiguities that are almost always incongruous and often comically so. Riddle 51 demonstrates this well.

Ic seah wrætlice   wuhte feower
samed siþian;   swearte wæran lastas,
swaþu swiþe blacu.   Swift wæs on fore
fuglum framra;   fleag on lyfte
deaf under yþe.   Dreag unstille   5
winnende wiga   se him wægas tæcneþ
ofer fæted gold   feower eallum.
(Riddle 51)[23]

I saw four wondrous creatures
travel together; their tracks were dark,
very black traces. It was swift on the journey,
bolder than birds; it flew in the air,
dived under the wave. The striving warrior
laboured untiringly who shows them the ways
over plated gold for all four of them.

Riddle 51 describes the sight of a group of *wihte* (here spelled *wuhte*). Such *wihte* are often explicitly *wrætlic* in the riddles, as in the collocation here (where *wrætlice*, "wondrous," is probably the accusative plural feminine form of the adjective qualifying the *wuhte*, although it could also be an adverb, "wondrously," describing their movement). *Wonder* is an emotion the riddle form encourages, and this characterization is something of a tease in terms of clues, since any object, from the quotidian rake to the complexly crafted loom, or from a simple swan to all of creation, is wondrous when viewed through a riddle's indeterminacy. The noun phrase, then, sets up here, as in many of the riddles, a kind of place-holder with a hint of agonistic defiance in relation to the audience: the objects or

---

23 Riddles of the Exeter Book are quoted from Muir, ed., *Exeter Anthology* (although with the numbering from ASPR). Translations are my own, drawing on the editions and translations cited in notes 7 and 8 above, while aiming to reflect the Old English quite closely.

creatures being described are wondrous for an audience that is capable of perceiving that wonder.

To arrive at a solution, the audience needs more specific clues, and the emphasis on leaving a dark track looks like it might be a useful one. The presence of tracks, *lastas* and *swaþu*, seems to clarify that the *wihte* are animals or humans, since these would leave tracks, although this is also the mark left by the plough of Riddle 21 or metaphorically by the creature (probably a book) of Riddle 95, so non-animate objects might leave tracks, too. The doubled description of the dark tracks in the formulation at line 2b and again at 3a deploys the characteristic poetic technique of variation, which generally hints at multiple facets of something of importance. A riddle's difficulty of meaning encourages a hyper-sensitivity to poetic technique which can itself be funny, and so the variation is likely to provide a meaningful clue. The emphasis here seems to be on the darkness of the tracks, which are not just *swearte*, "black," but also, in a half line rich in poetic technique – chimingly half-rhyming, half-assonating – "swaþu swiþe blacu" ("very dark traces," line 3a). While *swiþe*, "very," is an extremely common intensifying adverb in general, it is quite rare in the riddles, which have a premium on specificity of language that this intensifier usually lacks. The alliteration of *swiþe* here intrudes into the stress pattern, with the adverb either trumping the more significant adjective to carry the second stress of the a-verse, or risking too much prominence as it enters into the alliterative pattern while only carrying secondary stress. An attentive audience picks up information both from the semantic load of the words and also from the hints of the poetic form. Apparently, the darkness of the tracks is an emphatic clue – unless it is a blind – and a well-attuned audience, tracking the description as attentively as possible, might be particularly conscious of a usually run-of-the-mill intensifying adverb, or fearful that they are over-emphasizing a simple uninteresting filler. The riddle challenge encourages a potential *mise en abyme* of interpreting interpretation, with a potential for humour in the category slippage which could ultimately prevent any certainty about any meaning.

Syntax provides clues as well as semantics and poetic technique. A paradoxical four-in-one status gets emphasized by the verb forms here. The four creatures left multiple tracks captured through a plural verb agreement in lines 2b–3a (*wæran*), but from line 3b onwards these four creatures are described in verbs that are grammatically singular (*wæs*, *fleag*, *deaf*), suggesting the four have come together as a *wiht* that has a single identity. Again, an attuned audience would be picking up a probable clue to the solution, or worrying that they might be tracking irrelevant trivia, creating tension to be released with a resolution and a sense of comic incongruity.

This four-in-one team is swift on its journey, bolder or more eager than birds ("fuglum framra"), and operates in multiple elements, presumably on the earth, where they/it left those tracks, but also explicitly in the air and under water (*fleag on lyfte/deaf under yþe*, "flew in the air,[24] dived under the wave," lines 4b–5a). That the riddle subject is *framra* than birds illustrates an ambiguity that comes from semantic range. The adjective, here in the comparative, can mean "stronger," "bolder," "braver," or "more eager," and any of these senses could be relevant and a clue to the answer. The multiplicity is challenging and potentially triggers a humour response.

Subsequent clauses in the riddle provide a series of statements that seem fairly unambiguous in metre, syntax, or sense, but illustrate the further level of ambiguity in that they could be more or less metaphorical. The slipperiness between metaphor and literal sense is an important part of the game in all riddles. The statement of flying in air suggests that the creatures are birds, except that other objects also move through air in a way that might metaphorically be considered flying, and the earlier assertion that the creature(s) is/are bolder than birds logically suggests that it/they are not (a) bird(s) – if such regular logic applies in a riddle – and the likelihood that the object under investigation in a riddle should not be explicitly named in the clues given by the riddle seems to eliminate birds – unless the solution is some particular kind of bird or there is some trickery around birdiness. The possibly birdy/possibly not birdy subject-object(s) dived under the wave. Seabirds come to mind, but the same objections apply. Other creatures dive, of course, or the verb could be a metaphor for something like diving that is not diving. Indeed, the wave is a standard poeticism for the sea, home to literal waves, although the metaphor could be more broad-ranging and so the word that appears to mean "sea" may or may not mean sea. Presumably any motion into any liquid could be metaphorically a diving under the wave – unless the implication of wetness is a blind and the metaphor is pulling in some different more remote direction yet.

The words of the riddle-poem are now providing both likely and unlikely possibilities of sense and overtones, with incongruity in the slippage. The process of interpretation involves attempting to keep open all the possibilities, and there is inevitable incongruity resulting from too many meanings. There is a risk that a frustrated audience will find the incongruities annoying rather than amusing as sense breaks down, but the

---

24 *Fleag on* from MS *fleotgan*, which appears to mean something like "floaty [on] air," but the emendation is adopted by most modern editors, including Muir, and the basic clue would remain in place with either reading.

expectations of the genre have established a promise of game playing with a possible solution at the end of it, rather than ultimate frustration.

With Riddle 51, the riddle-solving audience is now holding in mind a four-in-one team that leaves a particularly dark track that is swift and that seems to fly through something that seems like air and seems to dive into something that seems like the sea. The riddle concludes with a final sentence that seems to point in a different direction: a striving warrior laboured ceaselessly, *Dreag unstille*, or acted in a not-still manner, he who shows or makes known (*tæcneþ*) the ways over the ornamented or plated gold for the four in all. Now the avian team seems to be under the guidance of a single warrior, who is labouring at a task, and there is another clue about the element in which they are operating, namely over ornamented/plated gold. The task that the labouring warrior guides them in is the tokening of the ways, which are presumably the places where they are leaving the tracks that are strikingly dark and black.

Certain clues have now become emphatic, namely the four-in-one, the dark tracks, the movement across different mediums, and the striving warrior controlling the team. The avian clues hint that the answer somehow is like a bird but is not a bird. The success of the clues here is apparent in that this is one of the few Exeter Book riddles which almost all modern critics answer in the same way. The moving team of four are a quill pen and three fingers (or two fingers and a thumb), dipping into an inkwell and then writing on parchment, governed and controlled by a scribe, who is here imagined as a striving warrior. Apparently, the scribe is writing a high-status book, if the surface is literally decorated with gold leaf, or a valued text, if the gold is a metaphor for the edification to be gathered from the writing. The scribe is characterized both through the labour, that is the act of writing, and the martial status of one who struggles agonistically through learning. The solution of a quill pen and its guiding fingers, then, accounts for the totality of the clues provided by the riddle, as any good solution must.[25] It is confirmed by numerous analogues, where other scriptorium riddles work with some of the same conceits as here, often marvelling at writing as a leaving of a dark track on a light surface.[26]

What makes this puzzle and its resolution funny? As I have tried to suggest, there is a constant incongruity generated by the multiple possibilities of language and poetic effect in the presentation of a riddle.

---

25 On the conditions for solving a riddle, see John D. Niles, "Exeter Book Riddle 74 and the Play of the Text," *Anglo-Saxon England* 27 (1998): 169–207 (repr. in Niles, *Enigmatic Poems*, chap. 1).

26 On the Latin use of these motifs, see especially, Bitterli, *Say What I am Called*, part 3.

The inevitability of that incongruity makes all riddles potentially funny, unless the audience is pushed to reject a comic response, either through frustration at the break-down in meaning (particularly likely for a riddle that is too hard to solve) or from a recoil at the senses becoming apparent (particularly a risk for riddles that break taboo). Another source of humour lies in the appropriate inappropriateness of the relationship between the solution and the false leads established by the misdirecting clues, a pattern called by Murphy the focus of a riddle, and perhaps more clarifyingly labelled the false focus.[27] The account of flying establishes a false focus on birds here, and the false focus is particularly appealing in its relation to the ultimate solution. A writing implement is like a bird both through metaphor and metonymy, because both fly through the air, and because a quill is made from a bird feather. That collocation is still more marked in Old English, where the solution is a kind of pun since the word *feþer* means both "feather" (or, in the plural, "wing") and "quill, pen."[28] The most common raw material for quills was probably goose feathers, which gives added force to the aquatic avian clue.

With a solution in mind, the *framra* clue of line 4a both applies and obfuscates in multiple ways. The quill's closeness to the scribe-warrior makes it bolder than the bird-kind from which it came, since birds generally avoid proximity to humans. It is more eager than birds, since it follows the directives of its controlling warrior with particularly high precision. Also, it is metaphorically bold as it enters into the war against ignorance implied by the metaphor of the scribe as a warrior. The trace of the pen on the parchment is a track, since the pen leaves marks that allow the one pursuing the wisdom it lays down to follow those tracks, just as an animal can be pursued through its tracks, but the tracks of the quill are exceptionally black in view of the colour of the ink. There may be a further punning clue here in the overlap of the term *blac* to convey both dark colour and the word for ink.[29] There is further paradox in the track, which is initially the conceptual line contained within the scribe's mind as the way of representing the sound and sense of words that become a track for others to follow through the miracle of writing, an idea pursued further in chapter 4 below. The incongruities of pen as bird, writing as track, and parchment as

27 Patrick J. Murphy, *Unriddling the Exeter Book Riddles* (University Park, PA: Penn State University Press, 2011), 18: "an underlying metaphor that lends coherence to the text's strategy of obfuscation."

28 DOE, s.v. *feþer*, senses 1, 2, and 3.

29 This is a suggestion of Murphy, *Unriddling*, 85.

ground, all have particular appropriateness so that false focus and solution are in satisfying tension.

The status of the scribe sets up more humour here. The controller of the four-in-one team is a labouring figure, striving (*winnende*) and not at all still (*unstille*). This sets up the process of writing as a significant labour, which seems inappropriate in view of the minute bodily motions involved, even as it is particularly appropriate for the never-easy control called for by the writing task, as a commonplace that recurs in scribal colophons makes clear: "Tres digiti scribunt totum corpusque laborat" ("Three fingers write and the whole body labors").[30] The build-up of the scribe implied by the metaphor of *winnende wiga* ("the striving warrior," 6a) is more playful still, as it sets up the one who has written this text as in some way a heroic and martial figure, amplifying the agonistic play of the riddle. If the one writing it is a striving warrior are we, the riddle audience, competing warriors? Is the battle of wits getting imaged as a regular battle?

But there is more humorous paradox in view of the likely status of the scribe. In early medieval England, the technology of writing was a preserve of monastic communities, and a scribe is most likely to be a monk. In another recurring image, the monk is often seen as a warrior for Christ as his prayers fight the devil.[31] This may be commonplace, but it appropriates for the clerical orders the high status usually preserved for the order who fight. There is, then, a certain ironically self-referential comedy in the one providing the text elevating the status of one who provides the text. Within this riddle, presented in the "I saw" format, the I-observer who witnessed wonders turns out to be the very wonder that the striving warrior is creating for the I-observer to witness. The self-praise in a scribe writing out such a flattering portrait of the high status and ceaseless labour of the scribe sets up incongruity at the level of decorum in light of the expectation for a monk to be humble.[32]

The mechanisms of obfuscation here generate a comic response in ways that will recur across many riddles, even as the specific details of this riddle generate specific moments of comedy. Laughter by the end may reflect the humour of superiority theory, as unpacking all of these ironies shows mastery over the challenge and also makes the riddle-interpreters superior to the monk-scribe who has set himself up as superior to the thane-warrior. An attentive audience gets to harness apparently incompatible clues to

---

30 Cited in Bitterli, *Say What I am Called*, 148.
31 Noted from Cassiodorus, for example, in Niles, *God's Exiles*.
32 A similar paradox is seen in the portrait of the scribe Eadwig; see Richard Gameson, "The Colophon of the Eadwig Gospels," *Anglo-Saxon England* 31 (2002): 201–22.

arrive at a solution that is in some sort of happy relationship to all the false solutions momentarily suggested.

The hint of breaking decorum with the scribal boast here is common in scriptorium riddles, but the power of impropriety is even easier to see in riddles that conjure up thoughts of sex. This proves to be quite common among the Exeter Book riddles, as the next example will demonstrate.

A Key to Comic Doublings: Riddle 44

Humour is particularly clear in a subset of riddles in which a consistent strand of doubleness is hard-baked, namely those that hinge upon sexual *double entendre*. Riddle 44 can serve as a good example.

> Wrætlic hongað　bi weres þeo,
> frean under sceate.　Foran is þyrel.
> Bið stiþ ond heard,　stede hafað godne;
> þonne se esne　his agen hrægl
> ofer cneo hefeð,　wile þæt cuþe hol
> mid his hangellan　heafde gretan
> þæt he efenlang ær　oft gefylde.
> (Riddle 44)

> A wondrous object hangs by a man's thigh,
> under a lord's garment. It is pierced in front.
> It is stiff and hard, has a good place;
> when the man raises his own garment
> above his knee, he wants to greet
> with his hanging head the familiar hole
> that, equally long, he often filled before.

A wondrous object (*wrætlic* again, here used as a substantive adjective) establishes some degree of obfuscation in this description, but surely just about any audience will quickly resolve the clues as pointing to a male sex organ. That solution appears to account for the totality of the clues: the place (by a man's thigh and under his garment), the aspect (hanging), the characterization (pierced in front, with a hanging head, and stiff and hard in certain attitudes), the activity (filling a hole, and that a familiar one of matching dimensions which he has often filled before). *Efenlang* in line 7a[33] carries some ambiguity,

---

33 The MS has *efe lang*, which is probably a spelling variant or a spelling error, and most editors emend to *efenlang*.

since it might apply to the object (nominative singular masculine, agreeing with *he*), suggesting that the mystery object was sometimes before equally proportioned to the hole, or to the place that the object is entering (accusative singular neuter, agreeing with *þæt cuþe hol*), suggesting that the object enters a familiar hole that is the same length as itself. The very ambiguity plays to the sexual solution, adding a certain pleasurable paradox about fit to an otherwise rather obvious sexual description.

For this riddle to work, though, it must also be apparent to an audience that the obvious answer is unspeakable. The taboo on calling out "penis" or its equivalent (perhaps *se sceamigendlica*; see chap. 5) is implied by the very straightforwardness of the fit between the clues and this solution. A riddle should not be that easy to solve, and such an easily fitting answer which is socially unacceptable is clearly a trap. Once the anatomical solution is put aside, the clues need to be reanalysed, creating the dualities of humorous incongruity. In this case, the clue about place, hanging by a man's thigh and under his garment, could apply to anything attached to a belt. The object needs to be stiff and hard, as would anything crafted from metal, and pierced in front. The special characteristic of this object has to do with its filling reiteratively a hole in some way particularly suited to it. That clue might suggest a sword or dagger fitting into its sheath, but the placement under rather than over a garment, and the piercing at the front, makes more likely a key. This has the added benefit of the special significance of the keyhole, which is a hole specially crafted for just the dimensions of this particular stiff and hard piece of metal, a wonder brought to life by the riddle.

Once again, part of the humour comes from the relationship between the false focus (the penis) and the solution (the key). In addition to the slight similarities of appearance, the overlap is also more fundamental: a key bestows control for the one who holds it, and, in a gender-hierarchized society, a phallus implies the same sort of control. A key gives access to treasure, and the bodily analogue probably implies an attitude towards women's sexuality as a treasure to be guarded and opened up.[34] The patriarchal implications are strong but masked by the devices that create the humour. The move from the bawdy body to innocent household activity provides a shift in register that encourages the laughter of release, augmented by the realization of escaping from what would otherwise be

---

34 See Edith Whitehurst Williams, "What's So New About the Sexual Revolution? Some Comments on Anglo-Saxon Attitudes Toward Sexuality in Women Based on Four Exeter Book Riddles," *Texas Quarterly* 18 (1975): 46–55.

taboo. This is a riddle that would surely have an audience of many different types laughing.

Riddle 44, then, provides another example of humour from the appropriate inappropriateness of the relation between the false solution and the true. If the structural humour is somewhat straightforward, the social impact of the humour is more complicated. Even as the itemization of anatomical detail looks like a phallic boast, it is possible to read the riddle as bestowing a critique on the one bearing the implement that is uncovered. He is a *wer* in line 1b, a male human being, in a gender clue that is crucial for the anatomical solution. This man has a high status in line 2a as a *frea*, a lord. This makes sense for the respectable solution, as a key suggests wealth to be kept locked up.[35] In line 4a, though, the man is an *esne*, usually connoting a man of low status, in particular a servant.[36] The contradictory status terms set up a comic disparity. Is this a comment on the man who is proud of his key, believing it provides him status as a *frea*, while in fact he has to wield it just like any *esne*? At the respectable level, that would satirize a belief that valuables provide status. At the anatomical level, the satire is yet more powerful. A man who is proud of his phallic implement believes that it gives him status as a *frea*, even as he is an *esne*, serving this very part of his anatomy and following where it leads. The object may not be quite so *wrætlic* as he believes. The hint of satire at the strutting masculinity of the one who praises his implement runs through many a riddle in the collection. It is perhaps worth noticing the similarity of the covert humorous mockery of the strutting quill-wielder in Riddle 51 and of the strutting key-wielder in Riddle 44. Social attitudes may be as open to humour in the Old English riddles as the wonders of the observed world, and men who think they are in command may be the appropriate butt of the joke, using the humour of satire to undercut some of the privileges assumed in a patriarchal society.

The humour may serve to cut the sexual assertiveness down to size, but a different set of associations could establish an altogether more pious reading, with potential humour in the gap between piety and bawdry. The word *frea* is always a potential pun in Old English since it describes both a secular powerholder and the ultimate divine authority, the Lord.[37] The

---

35 Keys are occasional finds in women's graves, while key-like girdle hangers are associated only with women but seem to be distinctively early and Anglian; see Gale R. Owen-Crocker, *Dress in Anglo-Saxon England*, revised and enlarged edition (Cambridge: Boydell, 2004), 66–7.

36 See DOE, s.v. *esne*.

37 See DOE, s.v. *frea*, sense A "human lord or ruler"; sense B "divine lord or ruler."

latter plays into an image cluster of Christ as the key-holder, unlocking the doors of heaven for Christians who are good in this world. A fulcrum for this interpretation is the erotic play with lock and key in the Song of Songs 5:4–6, a sexualized account of lovers that was often interpreted as a metaphor for Christ's relation to the human soul, keying into the content of the preceding Exeter Book text, Riddle 43, which is generally solved as describing soul and body.[38] The result is an edifying interpretation, but the explicit sexual imagery – both of the riddle and of the Song of Songs – carries enough surface shock to generate a frisson of comic incongruity in the distance between bawdiness and doctrine, a distance exploited in the eleventh-century comic Latin of the Cambridge Songs.[39]

The anatomical sense is impossible to avoid in this and other *double entendre* riddles, and the breaking of taboo gives the edginess that helps establish them as funny. Humour derived from the release of repression would be amplified in many performance contexts by the risk of an audience member breaking taboo and shouting out the obvious answer or bantering on the sexual sense. The evidence of the surviving manuscript suggests that these riddles were also appreciated in a more decorous context, as will be explored at the end of this chapter. First, it will be seen that strikingly similar mechanisms are at work creating humour in a different series of short, self-contained puzzle-texts, namely *The Durham Proverbs*.

Witty Wisdom in *The Durham Proverbs*

The Durham Proverbs were written out in the middle of the eleventh century, probably at Canterbury, into originally blank leaves between a hymnal and a collection of canticles in MS Durham, Cathedral Library, B. III. 32, fols. 43v–45v.[40] The collection comprises forty-six pithy statements in both Old English and Latin. It is hard to establish which language came first, and the modern editor thinks they may have been a classroom exercise in translation from Old English into Latin.[41] This suggests a

---

38 See Mercedes Salvador-Bello, "The Key to the Body: Unlocking Riddles 42–46," in *Naked Before God: Uncovering the Body in Anglo-Saxon England*, eds. Benjamin C. Withers and Jonathan Wilcox (Morgantown: West Virginia University Press, 2003), 60–96, esp. 76–82.

39 Ziolkowski, ed. and trans., *Cambridge Songs*, lyric 49.

40 Arngart, ed., "Durham Proverbs."

41 Ibid. Some of the proverbs seem to have enjoyed prior circulation in both languages, as shown by Thijs Porck, "Treasures in a Sooty Bag? A Note on Durham Proverb 7," *Notes Queries* 62, no. 2 (2015): 203–6. Their humour has been discussed by Shippey, "Grim Wordplay."

schoolroom context that will be explored more fully at the end of the next
chapter. First, though, it will be useful to see how proverbs can create
humour through some of the same mechanisms as riddles. One example,
No. 11, has been cited above, where the humour derives from the comic
inversion of expectations stretching to a kind of grotesquerie, along with a
structure hinged on inversion. Similar comic turns are common throughout the collection.

The structure of the proverbs often leads to humour through a form of
comic timing. That is evident in the second item in the collection:

> Freond deah feor ge neah. byð neah nyttra.
> (Durham Proverb 2)

> Friends avail far or near; they are more useful near-by.
> (Latin: Amicus tam prope quam longe bonus est.)

The first half of the Old English here is a gnomic statement that friends
are of value no matter where they are, a proverb which partakes of a gen-
erosity of spirit and suggests the underlying wisdom that friendship transcends mere practical limitations. That upbeat observation stands alone
in the Latin but gets comically inverted through the second half of the
Old English, where the word *neah* ("near") becomes a fulcrum, picked
up to undercut the spirit of idealism expressed so far. The qualification
suggests a more cynically pragmatic world where friends are more useful
if they are nearer, presumably because they are able to provide practical assistance while in proximity. The rapid turn from high idealism to
low practicality establishes comic incongruity. The underlying wisdom is
probably drawn from Proverbs 27:10 ("Thy own friend, and thy father's
friend forsake not: and go not into thy brother's house in the day of thy
affliction. Better is a neighbour that is near, than a brother afar off"),
but given a pithiness of form and suddenness of inversion that creates
humour. The Old English version, but not the Latin, works through the
tight timing of surprise to convey its paradoxical wisdom with a jolt of
humour.

Humorous acknowledgment of limitations to idealism becomes evident
in other proverbs in the collection, too, such as Durham Proverb 18:

> Ða ne sacað þe ætsamne ne beoð.
> (Durham Proverb 18)

> Those don't quarrel who are not together.
> (Latin: [S]ol[i] illi non contendunt qui in unum non conueniunt.)

Here the wisdom implied has a similarly pragmatic logic. Quarrelling is a problem, and the ideal solution is tolerance and charity to all. After the Old English proverb presents a main verb in the negative, the expected resolution is some version of an idealistic statement (e.g. those don't quarrel who love one another). In place of that, the proverb offers a solution that is extremely practical – people who are not in proximity are not in a position to quarrel with one another – so practical and obvious, indeed, as to be a surprising inversion of the expectations of proverbial wisdom, and thereby incongruously comic.

A similar structure is seen in another example that plays further with paradox:

> Hwilum æfter medo. menn mæst geþyrsteð.
> (Durham Proverb 8)
>
> Sometimes after mead, people most thirst.
> (Latin: Post medum maxime sitit.)

In this case, the initial phrase could be expected to continue with many different possibilities (e.g. sometimes after mead, people do foolish things), but not with the consequence that is here specified of the drink not quenching thirst and instead creating a superlative further thirst. The failures of alcohol to ultimately satisfy despite its pleasures is a paradox beloved of the Old English riddlers (see Exeter Book riddles 11, 18, 27, and 28, discussed below). The practical wisdom in this Durham Proverb is comic in its paradox, but there may be yet more to it. Additional humour comes from the dissonance between a literal sense based on the alcoholic beverage – an addictive substance that upsets the recipients' judgment so that the desire for a drink is fuelled by the very act of drinking – and the more metaphorical wisdom that the proverb hints at – the fulfilment of a desire is rarely the satisfaction that brings that desire to an end. The movement between literal and metaphorical creates comic incongruity. The gulf between localized pragmatic sense and broadly transcendental wisdom creates a frisson of humour by playing so radically with levels of interpretation.

Humour comes from the distance between imagery and underlying wisdom in another example:

> Gyfena gehwilc underbæc besihþ.
> (Durham Proverb 28)
>
> Every gift looks back.
> (Latin: Omnia dona retrorsum respiciunt.)

The sentiment here is that every gift generates the expectation of reciprocity, an idea expressed more explicitly in the Old Norse wisdom poem, *Hávamál*, line 165, "Ey sér til gildis giǫf" ("A gift always looks for a return").[42] By making the gifts themselves the subject of a verb of gazing, emphasized by the rather convoluted direction of the gaze implied by *underbæc*, the Durham Proverb plays up the personification of the non-animate, creating a comic incongruity in the same manner as the riddles deploying prosopopeia. The proverb presents the gift as a twisted body looking backwards and behind, which creates a concrete image that a listener needs to transcend to pick up the implied wisdom. The oscillation between concrete and abstract, convoluted and dignified, vehicle and message, creates comic incongruity, here carried on the back of an imagined contorted body.

Sometimes the wisdom of the proverb is not clear, even as the humour is. Durham Proverb 6 uses the attributes of animals, partly anthropomorphizing them, partly playing off their expected animal natures, to deliver a message that is surely funny even if the fundamental sense is debatable:

God ger byþ þonne se hund þam hrefne gyfeð.
(Durham Proverb 6)

It is a good year when the dog gives to the raven.
(Latin: Bonus annus quando canis coruo exibet.)

The idea of a dog giving to anyone raises a smile at the incongruity of such personification of a canine beast and is matched by the incongruity of a raven acting in a manner appropriate to receive such largesse. There are multiple ways of reading a context that would make sense of this comic image. Presumably there is an expectation of underlying competition between dog and raven for food, and the proverb imagines the pleasure of a time that would lack such a contest. If the dog is a domestic creature, then the foodstuffs may be human scraps, which dogs would usually guard from carrion birds but which are imagined as so plentiful that there would be sufficient for dogs to give away to their traditional rivals; in other words, it would be a good year when even dogs, who only get leftovers, would themselves have leftovers – a vision of broad-ranging well-being imagined through a minor beast fable. On the other hand, the

---

42 The analogue is cited by Arngart, ed., "Durham Proverbs," 298.

underlying image would connote differently if the creatures are imagined as the traditional beasts of battle (usually a wolf and an eagle, but wild dog and raven would fit), since then the imagined excess would be from carrion left on the battlefield, suggesting a particularly prolific slaughter. The humour would now have a distinctly aggressive edge: it would be a good year for the victor if the conquering army produced so much slaughter that carrion creatures were not in competition, but a terrible one for the vanquished. But an opposite reading is also possible. It would be a good year for humans with a peace-loving desire when the beasts of battle needed to cooperate on account of a lack of carrion provided through slaughter, i.e. the traditional competitors would need to work together if there were no wars and universal peace had broken out. Bestial comity would imply even greater well-being among humans.

All of these senses, it seems to me, are reasonable possibilities for the proverb, and all are premised on the basic incongruity of viewing human values through a focus on beasts. The distance between the proverb's concrete instantiation and its implied wisdom creates the space for humour, potentially making the mind both merry and wise. Deciding which is the right sense here calls for the kind of collaborative/competitive participation required of the audience of the riddles, too, in a setting that would be particularly alive to comic cues. In this particular proverb, the multiplicity of meanings sets up another level of humour, since a single image allows such a plenitude of possibilities to be raked over and argued for, some the direct opposite of others.

If anthropomorphized animals can trigger comic incongruity, so, too, can human absurdity, as in the following:

Ne mæg man muþ fulne melewes habban &eac fyr blawan.
(Durham Proverb 43)

A person may not have a mouth full of meal and also blow the fire.
(Latin: Non potest os ambo plenum ferrine et ignem sufflare.)

Again, the proverb presents incongruities as it unfolds, with the final clause giving unexpected development to the opening. Presumably the wisdom here is the desirability of not doing two things at once.[43] The image that conveys that truism presents the physical humour of a person ingesting food who simultaneously blows out onto the fire. The inelegance of bodily

---

43 As Shippey, "Grim Wordplay," suggests in his analysis.

mal-functions is a staple of slapstick humour.[44] Perhaps the image is the funnier for the incendiary implications: presumably the grain dispensed from the mouth would serve as kindling to the fire, threatening the imagined blower with injury as well as embarrassment. Wisdom comes from an imaginatively comic image.

Occasionally it is the sound of the words more than the underlying image that generates the humour, as in:

Betere byþ oft feðre þonne oferfeðre.
(Durham Proverb 37)

It is better to be often loaded than overloaded.
(Latin: Meliora plura quam grauia honera fiunt.)

The pleasure of the verbal echo from *oft feðre* to *oferfeðre* suggests the pleasure of acoustic puns. The humour from repeated sounds is analysed in chapter 2 below. In the context of proverbs, such self-conscious verbal play emphasizes the underlying trope that language can capture the values of the world, and yet language can also assert its own set of values. The verbal dexterity substitutes for fanciful imagery, since the message is literally true even as the idea is generalizable beyond the carrying of loads (i.e. better to work slowly but steadily than take on too much at once, whatever the task). The rhyming, alliterating, and assonating balance of this pair was apparently particularly appreciated in the early Middle Ages, since this proverb also survives in a small proverb cluster in MS BL Royal 2 B. v, fol. 6r, with this part of the phrasing intact ("Selre byð oft feðre þænne oferfeðre").[45]

The pleasure of rhyme and repeated sounds is evident in another of the proverbs that survives not in the Durham Proverbs but in BL Royal 2 B. v, fol. 6r, and also in BL Cotton Faustina A. x, fol. 100r:

Hat acolað, hwit asolað,
leof alaðaþ, leoht aðystrað.
(Dobbie, "Latin-English Proverbs," lines 3–4)[46]

---

44 Bergson, *Laughter*, analyses laughter as a response to the inelasticity demonstrated by such bodily missteps.

45 Printed Elliott van Kirk Dobbie, ed., *The Anglo-Saxon Minor Poems*, ASPR 6 (New York: Columbia, 1942), cxi, n. 4, in the context of discussing the two metrical proverbs in this cluster of four.

46 Dobbie, *Minor Poems*, 109.

Heat cools, white soils,
a dear one palls, light falls.

This appears to be verse, unlike the prose of the Durham Proverbs, even though the boundary between prose and verse is a porous one that these pithy utterances often flow through.[47] In this case the form is particularly heightened: audible in each line is the tight structure of alliterating noun (or adjective standing as a noun) followed by verbs that alliterate, grammatically rhyme, and also either rhyme or assonate on their stressed syllable, while the prefix repeated in four verbs across two lines adds to the sound play.[48] The resulting acoustic effects are a significant part of the pleasure of the proverb in a manner similar to *The Rhyming Poem*, discussed below. Indeed, the first line echoes a line of *The Rhyming Poem* (line 67), and here, as there, the heightened form creates a striking effect on the ear that is potentially funny itself, even as the wisdom the proverb announces centres on the passing of earthly happiness. A proverb appealing to the sense of sound can make the mind merry even in contemplation of transience, a paradox that will also be seen in *The Rhyming Poem*.

One final cluster of proverbs illustrates particularly well the comic potential of the form. A small subset of the Durham Proverbs use the qualification of an utterance by an imagined speaker in the manner of Durham Proverb 11 cited in the introduction. That mechanism, known as a Wellerism since the trick was popularized by Dickens through the character of Sam Weller in *The Pickwick Papers*, has the potential to make comic or suggestive any utterance, as with the joke tagline, "as the actress said to the bishop," which sexualizes an otherwise innocent assertion. As Shippey explains, "an innocuous or uninteresting statement is transformed by inventing a fantastic, ridiculous, or obscene context in which it is said to be said."[49] The trick turns out to be recurringly productive of humour in each Durham Proverb that uses it.

---

47 See Angus McIntosh, "Wulfstan's Prose," *Proceedings of the British Academy* 35 (1949): 109–42; Thomas A. Bredehoft, "Ælfric and Late Old English Verse," *Anglo-Saxon England* 33 (2004): 77–107. This example is analysed by Emily V. Thornbury, "Light Verse in Anglo-Saxon England," in *The Shapes of Early English Poetry: Style, Form, History*, eds. Irina Dumitrescu and Eric Weiskott (Kalamazoo: Medieval Institute Publications, 2019), 85–106, at 88–9, showing how the proverb is playing with normal language to prioritize form.

48 The Latin has fewer acoustical effects but is marked by dissyllabic rhyme, with the third clause differing slightly in effect: "Ardor frigesscit, nitor squalescit, / amor abolescit, lux obtenebrescit."

49 Shippey, "Grim Wordplay," 41.

Durham Proverb 44 demonstrates how such a turn adds humour and paradox to a strikingly straightforward statement:

Wide ne biþ wel, cwæþ se þe gehyrde on helle hriman.
(Durham Proverb 44)

Things are not well all over, said one who heard crying out in hell.[50]
(Latin: [...] ait qui a[udiu]it [clamorem in] infern[o].)[51]

The initial statement here is a rather vague but probably unexceptional generalization, "wide ne biþ wel" ("things don't go well all over the place"), which has the hint of aphoristic wisdom in its compression and in the balance of the alliteration between the two adverbs. This rather anodyne message about the discomfort of everyday life is suddenly made much sharper through the surprising qualification of a speaker who has overheard the final judgment of the damned. This involves such an extreme contrast between the quotidian and the transcendent and such a shift in implied register that it creates a striking incongruity. The wisdom implied is that one should not complain about one's suffering, and the exaggeration makes for a memorable way of suggesting that people should keep their sense of their woes in proportion. The qualification nuances the message, but once again in a way that calls for group discussion to interpret. Hell is as bad as it gets in a Christian cosmography, so if the two clauses are sequential, the explicit put down that the one who is hearing the screaming in hell knows all about such grief from everyday experience (*wide*) risks trivializing the ultimate torment. While that may sound like a blasphemous understatement of the woes of hell, if angels are understood to laugh at the sinners in hell, the joke here may be very much on the side of the angels. On the other hand, if the qualifying phrase is understood as a past perfect tense, such that the imagined speaker is now about to apply wisdom acquired elsewhere, namely from a sojourn within ear-shot of hell, there is a startling shift in register and significance between wisdom acquired from contemplation of the ultimate last things and the current source of woe. There is then a degree of overkill for the underlying message that present sorrow is not all that bad. In either reading, incongruity is generated both by the

---

50 Ibid. translates more idiomatically: "There is trouble all over, said he who heard the screaming in hell."
51 "The first part of the Latin sentence is missing. What is left of it is corrupt, and has been conjecturally restored in the text," Arngart, ed., "Durham Proverbs," 300.

uncanniness of the context and by the mechanism of surprising qualification which forces a reconsideration of the opening statement.

Humour is similarly created by the surprising qualification in the following proverb:

> Age þe se þe æfter cige cwæþ se þe geseah hungor of tune faran.
> (Durham Proverb 45)

> He can have you who calls after you, said the one who saw hunger depart from the habitation.
> (Latin: [T]e habe[a]t qui te uocet [ai]t qui famem uidit abeuntem.)

This time the humour is reinforced through the personification, with *hungor* apparently imagined as a character who can travel away from a human habitation (with overtones of the kind of personification allegory seen in *Piers Plowman*). The opening utterance is another obvious truism ("age þe se þe æfter cige," "that one can have you who calls after you"), which is given a proverbial ring from the chiastic balance of verbs and repeated pronouns. The qualification makes the unexceptional statement suddenly undesirable through an arrestingly specific addition: it would be folly to desire the personification of hunger. At its most metaphorical, the wisdom now seems to arise from an imagined test case in which something that would seem always to be true is no longer true, or rather true but self-evidently not desirable. Again, the uncanniness of the image and the incongruity between halves of the proverb create possibilities for proverbial wisdom through humour.

A somewhat similar mechanism is seen in an earlier example:

> Ne saga sagan cwæð se geseah hwer fulne healena seoþan.
> (Durham Proverb 15)

> Don't tell tales, said the one who saw the foul pot of puss seething.[52]
> (Latin: [N]ec caro carnem emendat dixit qui caccabum plenum ponderosum coxit.)

---

52 There are many possibilities for the sense here. If *hwer*, which above is seen as the masculine noun "pot, cauldron," is read as a spelling of the common adverb *hwær*, then "Don't tell stories, said the one who saw where the foulness of puss was seething" might be likely. Arngart, ed., "Durham Proverbs," 296–7, suggests a sense of "as they brew, so let them drink" assuming two opening nouns and building on a possible sense

The mechanism here is similar to that in Proverb 45, since the straight-forward initial utterance (if it be the straightforward "don't tell tales") is qualified by the fanciful following scenario, which establishes an unlikely test case. The underlying image here seems to match that of the Cook's portrait in *The Canterbury Tales*, with an unsavoury bodily excrescence juxtaposed all too closely to food preparation (if that is the implication of *seoþan*). Even if the wound merely superates (another possible sense of *seoþan*), the fact that this pot is *fulne* gives a fair clue that this might be an occasion on which it would be wise to tell tales, either to warn the person with the wound or to warn others whose food preparation is looking distinctly unhygienic. The reversal created by the juxtaposition, as well as the enigmatic bizarrerie of the imagined situation, create humour through the distance between proverbial wisdom and unseemly embodied scenario.

A final example uses the characteristic structural trick in relation to another fanciful image, once again with multiple possibilities for interpreting the underlying wisdom:

> Nu hit ys on swines dome cwæþ se ceorl sæt on eoferes hricge.
> (Durham Proverb 10)

> Now it is at the pig's discretion said the man sat on the boar's back.
> (Latin: Nunc in iudicio porci dixit maritus sedens in apro.)

This time it is not a regular utterance that is inverted, but instead an utterance that is already striking. Comic inversion is immediately apparent here, even in the opening statement, as the *dom* (which is such a weighty concept in Old English, be it underlyingly "glory" or "judgment") is attributed to an animal rather than a human, all the more striking as this is an animal low down on the hierarchy of imagined nobility (*swin*, "a domestic pig"). There is additional humour in the qualification which also contains an inversion as the human (*ceorl*, "a man," with possible overtones in Old English of a humble freeman, a peasant, or possibly, following the sense of the Latin, a husband) is sitting not on an animal that constitutes a conventional steed (such as the horse explored in Durham Proverb 41) but on a creature that, presumably on account of both size

---

of the Latin version. Even though it varies from the Latin, seeing *saga* and *sagan* as the related imperative verb and noun seems a more likely reading of the Old English, and this is accepted by Marsden, *Old English Reader*, 306, who offers the translation "Tell no tales, said he who saw the pot full of hydroceles boil." He comments: "This is the most obscure of the proverbs, no doubt owing to transmission error."

and disposition, is generally considered inappropriate for human carriage (*eofor*, "a wild boar"). The placement of human on boar-back sounds like one of the drolleries characteristic of manuscript marginal illustrations of just a slightly later date, a grotesque inversion of normal standards.

If *swin* and *eofer* here denote the same beast, the *ceorl* is showing bad judgment, giving too much discretion over to a mere animal. Both the humour and the underlying wisdom tilt in a slightly different direction if the *swin* and *eofer* are not the same creature. While giving one's *dom* over to a beast may always be unwise, the *ceorl* may have made a rational but mistaken judgment to trust himself to a creature that he believes to be tamed and domesticated by man's control (*swin*), and he will be in for an unpleasant shock when he realizes that he is instead relying on the wild, untamed version of the related porcine beast, a wild boar (*eofor*). In either case, the *ceorl* has given up the power of control inappropriately, with more or less disastrous results to follow, and the moral becomes one of exercising caution in one's judgment (perhaps parallel to the need for perceptive observation sacrificed in the case of the witch in Durham Proverb 11).

Such is the somewhat literal reading of this eye-catching proverb. In the Latin version, *maritus* connotes a married man, a "husband," and this is a possible sense for the Old English *ceorl*. In such a case, the animal imagery is probably hinting at an anti-feminist medieval gibe at marriage, with the *ceorl* ceding power to his wife, which is here seen either as straightforwardly grotesque (if there is just one creature with synonymous names), or as a particularly bad judgment as the man assumes that the wild one has been domesticated (in the case of a meaningful difference between *swin* and *eofor*). The implied mockery of the hen-pecked husband suggests an aggressive mosogynist comedy aimed at controlling a man who fails to control a woman seen later as a traditional subject in misericords and in the presentation of Noah and his wife in medieval drama. That type of humour is not usually visible in surviving Old English literature but is certainly a possibility here. As with the riddles, the range of possibilities deriving from this striking and improbable image might best get unpacked through audience discussion. A mixed-sex audience might break down along gender lines in engaging with the implications of the marital status (as is scripted into some of the misogynist gibes in later medieval drama).

These proverbs certainly open up a potential for wisdom, and many of them achieve it through the frisson of humour, which makes them memorable, even as the humorous incongruity oftentimes complicates arriving at a straightforward understanding. Retaining and revising multiple mental images parallels the root cause of incongruity in the riddles. The wisdom often achieves its effect through humour.

Performance Contexts: Communities
of Laughter at the Exeter Book

The mead hall provides one obvious setting for listening and rowdily respond-ing to both the riddles and proverbs discussed here. The paradigmatic descrip-tion comes in the extended intermission between monster fights in *Beowulf*, when characters within the poem, and those listening to it, settle down for an extended story about Danish action visiting Frisians in Finnsburh. The noisi-ness of this audience is described by the poet and, at the end of the tale, the audience responds with laughter, as explored more fully in chapter 4 below. This scene imagines the pleasure in humour in an audience comprising a dis-tinctly small subset of society: masculine (apart from Queen Wealhtheow and her daughter), elite, martial, and secular. The high-status manly men gathered in the mead hall in *Beowulf* would provide an appropriately lively audience for engaging with riddles in general, and especially those with sexual over-tones, but both riddles and proverbs would also play well elsewhere, such as in an environment of learning, and this will be explored further in the next chapter. Other scenes of performance suggest a probable audience of much broader social range, including the gathering of workers that incorporated the shy cattle-herder on the estate at Whitby, or the ale house tipplers imagined in *The Seasons for Fasting*, or the audience of a salacious female entertainer described in *The Life of Mary of Egypt*, as will be seen in subsequent chap-ters.[53] In other words, gatherings of women or of men, of high status or of low, might all find mirth in contending to solve the Exeter Book riddles or striving to parse the sense of the Durham Proverbs, whether listening in the field or in the workshop, on the street or in the household.

But such works did not appeal only to secular society, as is suggested by the manuscripts in which they survive, and these manuscripts allow the reconstruction of another audience for such entertainment. The Exeter Book (Exeter Cathedral Library, MS 3501, fols. 8–130), which contains the Old English riddles among a compendium of Old English religious poetry written in the second half of the tenth century, is worth consid-ering for the audience it implies.[54] Any book copied at that time would

---

53 The other copy of Riddle 35, written in MS Leiden, Rijksuniversiteit, Vossianus Lat. 40 106, fol. 25v, preserves evidence of early Northumbrian provenance, grounding possible recital of the Old English riddles at Whitby in the time of Cædmon; see, most fully, A.H. Smith, ed., *Three Northumbrian Poems: Cædmon's Hymn, Bede's Death Song, and The Leiden Riddle* (London: Methuen, 1933).

54 The script of the single scribe is dated by Ker, *Catalogue*, 153 to the second half of the tenth century, by Muir, ed., *Exeter Anthology*, to ca. 965–75; while others mostly accept a date range of 970–90.

have been written by a scribe in a monastic or ecclesiastical scriptorium, writing much as the *winnende wiga* of Riddle 51.[55] While the specific place of origin of the Exeter Book is uncertain, a strong case has been made for Christ Church, Canterbury, or for Glastonbury Abbey.[56] Later, the book was given to Exeter Cathedral by Bishop Leofric, who moved the episcopal see from Crediton to Exeter in 1050 and who describes his gifts to the cathedral community in a donation list from 1069–72, including "i. mycel englisc boc be gehwilcum þingum on leoðwisan geworht" ("one large book in English about various things composed in verse").[57] The book the riddles are included in, then, circulated in clearly ecclesiastical contexts.

The poems within the Exeter Book are all untitled, but the names given by modern editors give a good sense of their subject matter. The collection begins with *Christ I (The Advent Lyrics)*, *Christ II (The Ascension)*, and *Christ III (Christ in Judgement)* and continues with hagiographical poems about Guthlac and Juliana and many shorter poems, including the so-called Old English elegies and a number of poems of religious wisdom.[58] Interspersed among these are the three blocks of riddles. The Exeter Book, then, places the riddles in a context of pious and contemplative vernacular poetry, which suggests a pious and contemplative audience for the riddles, too. One possible use would be to provide listening material in a religious community, either in a monastery (like Glastonbury) or in a cathedral community (like Christ Church, Canterbury, of the possible origin, or Exeter of its later provenance). Monastic communities pursued a life described in *The Rule of St. Benedict* or its tenth-century English adaptation, the *Regularis Concordia*, which proscribe private devotional reading, with a suggestion that a monk receive a new book every year at

---

55 See, e.g., Gameson, *History of the Book*.

56 See especially Richard Gameson, "The Origin of the Exeter Book of Old English Poetry," *Anglo-Saxon England* 25 (1996): 135–85, who demonstrates the unlikelihood of Exeter, as suggested by Conner, *Anglo-Saxon Exeter*.

57 See Michael Lapidge, "Surviving Booklists from Anglo-Saxon England," in *Learning and Literature in Anglo-Saxon England; Studies Presented to Peter Clemoes*, eds. Michael Lapidge and Helmut Gneuss (Cambridge: Cambridge University Press, 1985), 33–89, at 64–9.

58 See Muir, ed., *Exeter Anthology*, as well as Christopher A. Jones, ed. and trans., *Old English Shorter Poems, Volume 1: Religious and Didactic*, DOML 15 (Cambridge, MA: Harvard University Press, 2012); Mary Clayton, ed. and trans., *Old English Poems of Christ and His Saints*, DOML (Cambridge, MA: Harvard University Press, 2013); Robert E. Bjork, ed. and trans., *The Old English Poems of Cynewulf*, DOML 23 (Cambridge, MA: Harvard University Press, 2013). Niles, *God's Exiles*, gives a fuller account of the various genres and rationale for the collection.

Lent.[59] The range of contents of the Exeter Book would serve well for such devotional reading, even if a book in Latin would be more likely in a reformed monastery. An individual monastic reader would gain wisdom, and pleasure, not just from the pious scriptural poems but also from the wondrous puzzles of the riddles. Another possible use would be as edifying reading aloud over meals. Here the riddles present a challenge on account of their implicitly interactive quality more than for any indecorousness, since shouting out a proposed answer would seem to violate expectations of quiet, even as moderate laughter was licit.[60] The cathedral communities probably followed a monastic routine less stringent than in reformed monasteries, peopled by a more capacious clerical community, potentially including married priests and their families.[61] This would be a good audience for entertaining and yet edifying reading material. Construing riddles would entertain such a community and also lead them to contemplate the plenty of God's creation.

Christ Church, Canterbury, one possibility for the writing of the Exeter Book, is also the likely place of origin of MS Durham, Cathedral Library, B. III. 32, into which the Durham Proverbs were placed in the middle of the eleventh century. The proverbs could well serve as edifying yet entertaining reading for a cathedral community. In addition, this is where Ælfric Bata was training young monks and developing the practice dialogues described in the next chapter. Such monks in formation might benefit from a training in the range of vernacular poetic styles that the Exeter Book riddles demonstrate, and the lively schoolroom context that Ælfric Bata creates is a perfect setting for the comic cut and thrust of witty speculation and called out answers. Canterbury is also a likely training ground for higher ecclesiasts, who might appreciate a broad induction in vernacular literature that includes the riddles and the wisdom to be drawn from the Durham Proverbs, as suggested in chapter 8 below. In addition to secular

---

59 Bruce L. Venarde, ed. and trans., *The Rule of Saint Benedict*, DOML (Cambridge, MA: Harvard University Press, 2011), chs. 8, 48; Thomas Symons, ed., *Regularis Concordia: The Monastic Agreement* (London: Nelson, 1953), chs. 19, 25, 29, 40, 54, 55, 56. See M.B. Parkes, "*Rædan, Areccan, Smeagan*: How the Anglo-Saxons Read," *Anglo-Saxon England* 26 (1997): 1–22; Nicholas Howe, "The Cultural Construction of Reading in Anglo-Saxon England," in *Old English Literature: Critical Essays*, ed. R.M. Liuzza (New Haven: Yale University Press, 2002), 1–22.

60 Niles, *God's Exiles*, makes the point that the riddles would fit in a monastic and edifying reading context. On rules about laughing, see chapter 6 below.

61 See John Blair, *The Church in Anglo-Saxon Society* (Oxford: Oxford University Press, 2005), esp. 360–7; Julia Barrow, *The Clergy in the Medieval World: Secular Clerics, Their Families and Careers in North-Western Europe, c. 800–c. 1200* (Cambridge: Cambridge University Press, 2015).

audiences, then, it is easy to see many a responsive ecclesiastical audience for the humour of the Old English riddles and the Durham Proverbs.

These are works that could have been enjoyed by a wide range of early medieval English society, from the learned audiences implied by the manuscripts to the broad-ranging audiences described in subsequent chapters. In any of these contexts, laughter begets more laughter, and riddles and proverbs both display the world anew and cement the social relations of those who puzzle and laugh together. The appeal of riddles is suggested by the presence of riddling elements in much Old English literature.[62] Riddles and proverbs have mass appeal, which could include the learned and pious as well as the unlearned and profane. One subset of the riddles imply a specifically lettered audience, and the humour that comes from such work will be considered in the next chapter.

---

62 As well demonstrated by Rafał Borysławski, *The Old English Riddles and the Riddlic Elements in Old English Poetry* (Frankfurt am Main: Peter Lang, 2004).

Chapter Two

Laughing at Letters:
Runic Riddles and Riddling Runes

A famous Old English riddle presents the paradox of a literal bookworm, that is a moth in its larval state, which eats up text but is not one whit the wiser (Riddle 47). This is not the best riddle at obscuring its solution – a work that begins "Moððe word fræt" ("a moth ate words," 1a) and is generally solved as a word-eating moth might be thought to fail in a riddle's duty of obfuscation – and yet the underlying paradox of a parasite consuming language without understanding is so appealing it is a favourite for illustrating issues of textuality and has elicited a wealth of perceptive readings.[1] This is a riddle that makes manifest the paradox of the word made flesh. Oral performance gets transformed into marks on parchment to be decoded by those in the know, who get to chew on the wisdom thereby revealed.[2] The book moth fails to understand the wisdom, or to get the joke, but a wise audience does both.

In this chapter, I will consider humour that arises from making language manifest. There is always something incongruous in calling attention

---

1 See, for example, Ann Harleman Stewart, "Old English Riddle 47 as Stylistic Parody," *Papers on Language and Literature* 11 (1975): 227–45; Fred C. Robinson, "The Artful Ambiguities in the Old English 'Book-Moth' Riddle," in *Anglo-Saxon Poetry: Essays in Appreciation*, eds. Lewis E. Nicholson and Dolores W. Frese (Notre Dame, IN: University of Notre Dame Press, 1975), 355–62; Lerer, *Literacy and Power*, chap. 3; Peter Ramey, "Writing Speaks: Oral Poetics and Writing Technology in the Exeter Book Riddles," *Philological Quarterly* 92, no. 3 (2013): 335–56; Jordan Zweck, "Silence in the Exeter Book Riddles," *Exemplaria* 28, no. 4 (2016): 319–36; Martin Foys, "The Undoing of Exeter Book Riddle 47: 'Bookmoth'," in *Transitional States: Change, Tradition, and Memory in Medieval Literature and Culture*, eds. Graham D. Caie and Michael D.C. Drout (Tempe, AZ: ACMRS, 2018); Benjamin A. Saltzman, *Bonds of Secrecy: Law, Spirituality, and the Literature of Concealment in Early Medieval England* (Philadelphia: University of Pennsylvania Press, 2019), chap. 8.

2 On images for meditative reading, see Parkes, "*Rædan*"; Howe, "Cultural Construction."

to the physicality of letters rather than allowing them to invisibly do
their magic of visually sounding out language, and the book moth riddle
generates humour by parading this slippage. Another way of creating a
similar jolt in perspective comes from switching the code of the letters
used, and this happens when the flow of cursive early English minuscule that is the norm for Old English manuscripts gets interrupted by
the deployment of runic letters, with their distinctive angular look and
different system of interpretation. A cluster of riddles use this trick to
comic effect, while a whole poem based on the technique, *The Old English Rune Poem*, often generates humour through the code-switching.
Another poem, *Solomon and Saturn I*, constitutes almost an apotheosis
of alphabetical embodiment as runic letters spell out the Lord's Prayer
and, in the process, battle the devil. The extremity here may well carry
comic overtones, even if it is deployed for a serious purpose. All such
humour calls for considerable interpretive skills from an audience that
would need to be knowledgeable in two alphabets and think in terms of
letters. This chapter will end by considering a work aimed at training
such an audience, the Colloquies of Ælfric Bata, which imaginatively
pictures a classroom deploying mirth and thereby presents one possible
venue for savouring such linguistically humorous wisdom in addition to
the puzzles and proverbs of chapter 1.

Riotously Runic: Riddles 24, 42, 19, 64, and 75/76

I will begin by considering riddles that make the instantiation of language
visible in a particularly prominent way through logographic code-switching.
The riddles that do so always generate a jolt of humour from the trick,
which gets deployed in strikingly different ways in different instances.
Runes habitually perform a coded riddling, since each rune stands both for
the sound of a letter and for the name that the rune bears. For example, the
E-rune, ᛗ, is named *ēþel*, a word that usually carries the sense "homeland,"
and so the runic letter within a manuscript can either straightforwardly
provide the sound of an *e*, or can stand for the regular semantic load of
the word *ēþel*, with a regular sense of "homeland," or a specialist sense
of the runic letter itself.[3] The *Beowulf* scribe, among others, occasionally uses this rune to stand as an abbreviation for the word "homeland,"
and the use of the runic form may carry with it overtones of an earlier or

---

3 See DOE, s.v. *ēþel*. For additional explication, see Victoria Symons, *Runes and Roman
   Letters in Anglo-Saxon Manuscripts* (Berlin: de Gruyter, 2016); Dieter Bitterli, *Say What
   I am Called: The Old English Riddles of the Exeter Book and the Anglo-Latin Riddle
   Tradition* (Toronto: University of Toronto Press, 2009), chap 7.

non-Christian writing system, probably without any frisson of comedy.[4] The riddles, on the other hand, fully activate the potential for incongruity to create linguistic humour.

Two bird riddles from the Exeter Book, Riddles 24 and 42, nicely illustrate contrasting strategies for creating comic play through runes. Riddle 24 provides a good example to start.

Ic eom wunderlicu wiht,   wræsne mine stefne –
hwilum beorce swa hund,   hwilum blæte swa gat,
hwilum græde swa gos,   hwilum gielle swa hafoc;
hwilum ic onhyrge   þone haswan earn,
guðfugles hleoþor,   hwilum glidan reorde   5
muþe gemæne,   hwilum mæwes song,
þær ic glado sitte.   .ᛉ. mec nemnað,
swylce .ᚠ. ond .ᚱ.   ᚠ. fullesteð,
.ᚻ. ond .ᛁ.   Nu ic haten eom
swa þa siex stafas   sweotule becnaþ.   10
(Riddle 24)[5]

I am a wonderful creature, I vary my voice,
sometimes I bark like a dog, sometimes I bleat like a goat,
sometimes I honk like a goose, sometimes I yell like a hawk,
sometimes I imitate the grey eagle,
the voice of the bird of battle, sometimes I open my mouth
with the voice of the kite, sometimes the song of the seagull,
where I sit cheerful. G names me,
likewise Æ and R, O helps,
H and I. Now I am named
as these six letters clearly signify.

---

4 See, for example, Adam Miyashiro, "Homeland Insecurity: Biopolitics and Sovereign Violence in *Beowulf*," *postmedieval: a journal of medieval cultural studies* 11 (2020): 384–95. The enthusiastic embrace of magical potential of runes in R.W.V. Elliott, *Runes: An Introduction* (Manchester: Manchester University Press, 1959) is opposed by an anti-fanciful approach of R.I. Page, *An Introduction to English Runes* (London: Methuen, 1973). See Robert DiNapoli, "Odd Characters: Runes in Old English Poetry," in *Verbal Encounters: Anglo-Saxon and Old Norse Studies for Roberta Frank*, eds. A. Harbus and R. Poole (Toronto: University of Toronto Press, 2005), 145–62 for an appealingly balanced view.

5 Bernard J. Muir, *The Exeter Anthology of Old English Poetry*, 2 vols. (Exeter: University of Exeter Press, 1994; revised ed., 2000), substitutes bold upper-case roman letters for the runes of the manuscript here and throughout. The runes are restored in this study, with reference to the editions of Krapp and Dobbie and Williamson. Muir retains the manuscript punctuation at these points, which can be valuable.

The plenitude of sounds in the first sentence here keys into the humorous presentation of a creature adept in mimicry. While clauses introduced by *hwilum* ("sometimes") often provide useful clues in the riddles by demonstrating different aspects of the creature under consideration, the version here is excessive: seven such clauses itemizing the sound world of eight different creatures is the kind of disproportionate expansion that generates humour through its very excess, especially as the list incorporates six different verbs of sounding, themselves each ear-catching, with the alliterating and grammatically rhyming pairs *beorce* and *blæte* and *græde* and *gielle*, rounded out with the more distinctive *onhyrge* and *muþe gemæne*. The breadth of reference adds to the incongruity in view of the wide range of animal sounds, from dog to goat to birds. This is a list of disparate distinctive noises which have little in common beyond being unmelodious to a human listener. The recurrence of bird sounds – there are five different avian species named – keys into the likely domain for a solution. The speaker is a mimic of many creaturely sounds, with a specialty in different bird cries. The creature is apparently upbeat in disposition in view of the adjective in line 7a (*glado*, "happy"), where the feminine grammatical form suggests a female subject.

Like the bookworm riddle, this is a riddle that plays with the crossover between oral and literate understanding. The answer is clinched in the runic passage, where the use of letters is explicitly noted, turning from sound to text. The incorporation of runic forms makes those letter stand out visually but masks the different effect that would come in hearing the riddle read out. Here the performer has puzzling options. The metre and alliteration work straightforwardly if the runes are read out as standard rune names:

> þær ic glado sitte.   *Giefu* mec nemnað,
> swylce *æsc* ond *rad*   *os* fullesteð,
> *hægl* ond *is*.   Nu ic haten eom
> swa þa siex stafas   sweotule becnaþ.

This is how the riddle must have been recited, but the result would be baffling in meaning for the first-time listener before the clue provided by the final sentence:

> where I sit cheerful. *Gift* names me,
> likewise *ash-tree* and *riding*, *god/mouth* helps,
> *hail* and *ice*. Now I am named
> as these six letters clearly signify.

Even in the challenging environment of a riddle, this sounds drunkenly incomprehensible unless a listener catches the full implications of the verb "nemnað." In this case, though, the sense of incongruous incomprehensibility would last only until the reference to "þa siex stafas" ("the six staves *or* letters") which "sweotule becnaþ" ("clearly signify"). This would confirm an auditor in the need to think back over the otherwise nonsensical utterance, listening for letter names. That clue activates the full sense of the verb *nemnað* of line 7b, encouraging a listener to attend to a naming process. A visual reader of the poem does not face the same challenge, since the runes are so visibly marked as distinctive letters, standing out in their angularity from the surrounding insular minuscule script. A reader's challenge is to maintain the flow of the poetic form by mentally or verbally articulating the rune signs as the names that they convey and yet comprehending them as letter names rather than the concept the words usually convey.

These six runic letters spell out G Æ R O H I, an itemization which continues the play of gibberish since there is no such Old English word. Instead, as with the bow of Riddle 23 described in chapter 1, the audience needs to rearrange those six letters to find the name of a creature that mimics others, especially birds, with a somewhat rasping or screeching sound, while giving off an air of happiness. Working out an anagram to arrive at a solution once again emphasizes the naming process: *nemnað* of line 7b again carries emphatic force, and the riddle does not need to articulate a command to "name what I am called," since naming is the only possibility in arranging letters. The anagram *higoræ* (an alternative spelling of *higera*) is the Old English word for a female jay or magpie (*pica*) and so provides a convincing solution.[6] The riddle then neatly resolves into a description of a bird with a reputation for mimicry and clowning, but only after parading tricks of literacy.

The interpretive operations required by the runes are complex, starting with the need to identify that they are there (in an oral performance), or to register how to articulate them (in a reading). Once identified as letters, the runes need rearranging for the anagram. At both of those stages, there is the temporary presence of nonsense. This itself creates a comic incongruity in a world where texts should make sense. The paradox of the process of interpretation is emphasized by the loud and onomatopoeic aural effects of the first half of the poem, which play up the screeching behaviour of a living bird that happens to carry this name rather than the nature of

---

6 DOE s.v. *higera*, *higere*. See also Peter Kitson, "Old English Bird-Names (1)," *English Studies* 78 (1997): 481–505 at 496.

the word that names that creature. The incongruity of letter names that are also standard elements of the lexicon briefly adds to the humour in a riddle that has already established its comic credentials. All parts of this riddle thereby parade the arbitrary nature of language within an engaging and non-threatening environment of play that ensures the incongruities are seen as comic.

The puzzle is probably easiest to solve for a collective audience trying out different riddle-solving strategies, which would create an environment primed for finding things funny. Such an audience would presumably be hooked by the rhetoric of the variations in the first half of the poem, either revelling in the onomatopoeic power of animal-sounding verbs or perhaps interacting with the premise of the riddle by continuing the sequence of possible similes of animals and their sounding verbs. Once faced with or hearing the runes, the laughter of an audience might first come from frustration at tripping over the puzzle, followed by satisfaction at resolving the clashing scripts and recognizing the wonder of the incongruities. The rearrangement of letters for the anagram requires the audience to step back from the deictic presentation of the clues to a contemplation of text at a different level, a movement between levels, or metalepsis, that often creates a comic shock. At the end of all this, an audience is likely to laugh from a sense of superiority at finally cracking the code and solving the riddle.

But straightforward substitution of the name for the runic letter does not work to interpret all the riddles of runic trickery.[7] Riddle 42, for example, uses a different kind of fowl play in presenting an avian runic anagram.

Ic seah wyhte   wrætlice twa
undearnunga   ute plegan
hæmedlaces;   hwitloc anfeng
wlanc under wædum,   gif þæs weorces speow,
fæmne fyllo.   Ic on flette mæg   5
þurh runstafas   rincum secgan,
þam þe bec witan,   bega ætsomne
naman þara wihta.   Þær sceal Nyd wesan

---

7 See Niles, *Enigmatic Poems*, chap. 6, on the need for different strategies in different poems; Bitterli, *Say What I am Called*, chap. 7 for a good reading of the runic tricks in the riddles.

twega oþer   ond se torhta Æsc
an an linan,   Acas twegen,   10
Hægelas swa some.   Swa ic þæs hordgates
cægan cræfte   þa clamme onleac
þe þa rædellan   wið rynemenn
hygefæste heold   heortan bewrigene
orþoncbendum?   Nu is undyrne   15
werum æt wine   hu þa wihte mid us,
heanmode twa,   hatne sindon.
(Riddle 42)

I saw two wondrous creatures
indulge in amorous play outside
without concealment; the fair-haired female,
proud beneath her garments, received her fill,
if that work went well. Through runic letters
I can tell to warriors in the hall,
to those who know books, the names of both
of those creatures together. There must be N
two times and that bright Æ
once in the line, two As
and as many Hs. So have I unlocked
with the key of skill the fetters of the treasury-door
which held the riddle firm in mind
against men skilled in mysteries, its heart concealed
by bonds of cunning? Now it is manifest
for men at wine how those creatures,
the low-minded pair, are called among us.

Once again, there are multiple elements that will encourage laughter in the audience. The opening presents the surprise of sexual activity outside and displayed without concealment (*undearnunga ute*), a breaching of decorum and taboo that establishes an initial frisson of humour. The solution of the riddle is then presented *þurh runstafas* ("by means of runic letters," line 6a), which sounds like it will be a straightforward display of runic letters, but in practice works in the opposite manner to Riddle 24. This time the Exeter Book manuscript does not contain any actual runic letter forms, but rather the rune names are spelled out as words which are in no way visually marked. Modern editors choose to capitalize the relevant words, but the manuscript gives no formatting clue. The rune names work satisfyingly to fit the alliteration and metre and do not call attention to themselves as anything other than the sense of the word articulated – except that such a reading fails to make any sense:

There must be *necessity*
two times and that bright *ash-tree*
once in the line, two *oaks*
and as many *hails*.

The passage comes out sounding like an arboreal excess after an incomprehensible doubling of an abstract concept and some odd bad weather. Once again, this would encourage laughter at the incongruity of nonsense where sense was expected. For the passage to make sense, key nouns must be construed as letters. There are multiple clues that flag this as a trick and help an audience break the code to a more rational solution. The riddle makes clear that the answer is available to those who are book-learned (7a), who need to be *rynemenn* ("people skilled in mysteries" or "rune[-knowledge-able] people" 13a), and the riddle twice states that runic letters provide the naming of the two riddle subjects (7b–8a, 15b–17). A rune-savvy audience should be alert for rune names and so able to hear the key nouns as naming runic letters, namely two Ns, one Æ, two As, and the same number of Hs, rather than their more common but nonsensical regular referents. Once again, there is further obfuscation in that these letters then need reordering to arrive at the anagrammatical *hana* and *hæn*, "cock and hen,"[8] which are the creatures portrayed in unconcealed conjugal relations.

Here, then, the imagined presence of runic letters involves a switch of levels that breaks the expectations of the frame with a kind of bluff and double-bluff as the names of runic letters need to be found and operated with, even though there are no runes in sight. Modern critics stress the important cultural work such frame-breaking serves. Lerer points to the heightened attention the riddle directs towards writing itself and its celebration of organizing the mundane world through literary artistry.[9] Salvador sees a pun between the *wihta*, the beasts who lack reason, and those who *witan* with the wisdom of exegetes, matching a dichotomy between body and soul, and so reads the riddle as demonstrating that "literacy leads to salvation."[10] Bitterli stresses the wine-hall setting and concludes, "the oral poet in the hall becomes a nostalgic double for the Old English writer at his desk. Riddle 42, therefore, reflects the cultural changes that marked

---

8 DOE, s.v. *hana* and *henn*.
9 Lerer, *Literacy and Power*, chap. 3.
10 Salvador-Bello, "Key to the Body," 66.

early England, as it negotiated the transition from orality to literacy and the shift from one linguistic system to another: from the obsolete practice of runic communication that harked back to the pagan past to the roman alphabet and its use in a Christian scribal culture."[11] Such cultural work is clearly important, but the incongruities are also glaringly funny.

Comic potential has been built up from the opening, and resolution of the runic trick makes earlier responses comically incorrect. Unconcealed sex out of doors is eye-catching but indecorous, as is stressed by the formulation that this pair "plegan | hæmedlaces" ("indulge in sex-play" or "play the marriage game," 2b–3a), in which the compound noun is a uniquely surviving formulation, a *hapax legomenon*, perhaps coined for this occasion.[12] The shockingness of that open sexual exposure comes from the audience's salacious assumption that we are watching human coitus, an assumption that is encouraged by the riddler's blinds at the opening, where the recipient of the fecundity of fillingness (5a) is blonde-haired (*hwitloc*, 3b),[13] haughty (*wlanc*, 4a),[14] a wearer of garments (*under wædum*, 4a), and a virgin or woman (*fæmne*, 5a).[15] At first, this all seems a straightforward description of human activity, surprising only for its openness. It is only on breaking the code and arriving at the solution that the alternative meaning of each of these terms becomes apparent: a barnyard fowl can also be white in its coverings (*hwitloc*, 3b), haughty in appearance (*wlanc*, 4a), and covered in feathers (*under wædum*, 4a), while *fæmne* (5a) can signify a female chicken as well as a female human. If an audience was initially shocked at the flaunting of sexual activity, that shock presumably evaporates to be replaced with laughter as the audience keys into a vision of productive and commonplace barnyard fecundity in place of human exhibitionism. Sex in the barnyard by the poultry is not salacious so much as domestic economy, necessary for the production of eggs, putting paid to the titillation of the openness (1–3a), and perhaps giving point to the *weorc* of 4b. The parading of human sexual activity which then needs to be reanalysed as poultry doing their barnyard thing creates doubleness with the right distance between high and low to generate humour. Such chicken-brained sexual workers are presumably literally *heanmode* ("low minded," 17a),

---

11 Bitterli, *Say What I am Called*, 131.

12 On the challenges and potential of engaging Old English sexual language, see Julie Coleman, "Old English Sexual Euphemism," *Neuphilologische Mitteilungen* 93, no. 1 (1992): 93–8; Julie Coleman, *Love, Sex, and Marriage: A Historical Thesaurus* (Amsterdam: Rodopi, 1999).

13 Also a unique formation in this form, although *hwitloccedu* survives in Riddle 80.

14 The term often carries sexual connotations; see Coleman, "Sexual Euphemism."

15 The term usually means a virgin but can also refer to a woman; see DOE, s.v. *fæmne*.

unlike the high intellectual acumen called for from the riddle's solvers. Cracking the runic code creates another level of doubleness, leading again to laughter of relief and superiority by those who succeed in doing so.

But those very solvers get mocked more thoroughly than the livestock depicted. Indeed, if the first half of the riddle is comic for the blind of a barnyard coupling unexpectedly substituting for human sexual activity, the second half is funny for the way it pokes fun at the riddle-solving audience. The riddle taunts an audience imagined as *rincum* ("warriors," "men," 6b) *on flette* ("on the floor" that stands for the hall, 5b), and *werum æt wine* ("men at wine," 16a). Such an audience sounds like a secular martial masculine group, rowdy warriors in the hall, as seen, for example, in *Beowulf*. Is the riddler taunting such an imagined audience because they are not those "þe bec witan" ("who know their books," 7a), nor *rynemenn* ("men skilled in mysteries," 13b), and who therefore, for all their strength and conviviality, may not hold the key to break through these bonds of cunning (lines 12a and 15a)? Indeed, is the taunt that this secular masculine audience may be happy to stay at the unexamined level of thinking about human sex in the open, *undearnunga* (2a), thereby missing what is *undyrne* (15b) if they only knew their *futhorc*? The agonistic aspect of riddles is here emphasized and may encourage a kind of class critique in which warriors of learning get to laugh in superiority at warriors of the hall in the manner already seen in the pen and fingers riddle (Riddle 51) above. There is a certain preening self-confidence in referring to the riddle as locked behind the fetters of the treasury-door, its heart concealed by bonds of cunning (lines 11b–15a). Those who do not hold the key of learning risk being laughed at by this riddle.

The presence of runes in a riddle, then, creates an ambiguity that is a good source of humour, but the comedy is brought out, too, by other elements of these tricky poems. In Riddle 24, humour is emphasized by the display of the mimicking persona, to be solved by the puzzle of the anagram; in Riddle 42, the humour is emphasized by the apparent lack of decorum, by the mocking tone, and by the puzzle of runes that need to be understood even when not present. In two further riddles, Riddles 19 and 64, the runic puzzle is significantly harder, probably adding to the humour of the pieces by requiring further energy from the solvers, even if the puzzles are not embedded in such a funny context.

Ic [on siþe] seah   .ᚻ ᚱ ᚠ
ᚻ. hygewloncne,   heafodbeorhtne,
swiftne ofer sælwong   swiþe þrægan.

Hæfde him on hrycge   hildeþryþe
.ᛀ ᚠ ᛗ. nægledne rad   5
.ᚠ ᛂ ᛗ ᚹ. Widlast ferede
rynestrong on rade   rofne .ᛚ ᚠ
ᚠ ᚠ ᚻ. For wæs þy beorhtre,
swylcra siþfæt.   Saga hwæt ic hatte.
(Riddle 19)

I saw a proud bright-headed SRO
H on the track,
a very swift one run over the plain.
It had on its back a battle-strong NOM.
AGEW rode the nailed one.
The wide track, strong-flowing,
carried in riding a brave CO
FOAH. The trip was the brighter,
the journey of such ones. Say what I am called.

The riddle text makes no mention of the runes, but they need to be read as
their names to make the verse work, whereupon the verse lines have necessary alliteration and credible scansion:

Ic on siþe seah   sigel, rād, ōs,
hægl hygewloncne,   heafodbeorhtne,
swiftne ofer sælwong   swiþe þrægan.
Hæfde him on hrycge   hildeþryþe
nȳd, ōs, mon   nægledne rad   5
āc, gifu, eoh, wynn.   Widlast ferede
rynestrong on rade   rofne cēn, āc,
feoh, ōs, āc, hægl   For wæs þy beorhtre,
swylcra siþfæt.   Saga hwæt ic hatte.

Once again, though, if such a recitation were to suggest the sense of the
words the rune names generally convey, the text would be sorely lacking
in sense:

I saw a proud bright-headed *sun, riding, god/mouth*
hail on the track,
a very swift one run over the plain.
It had on its back a battle-strong *necessity, god/mouth, man.*
Oak-tree, gift, horse, joy rode the nailed one.

The wide track, strong-flowing,
carried in riding a brave *torch, oak*
treasure, god/mouth, oak, hail. The trip was the brighter,
the journey of such ones. Say what I am called.

This would constitute nominal craziness with way too many nouns even
for the noun-rich, variation-common form of Old English poetry, and no
apparent sense.

In this case, the visual arrangement of the runes in clusters provides an
added clue. The runes need to be understood solely as letters, and those
clusters of letters then have to be read backwards, whereupon the riddle
begins to make sense, as translated above.[16] Solving the riddle clusters does
not in itself solve the riddle here, even though some earlier commentators stopped at the clunkily literalistic solution, "A man upon horseback
with a hawk on his fist."[17] Instead, most critics see the runic terms as a
sequence of metaphors that establish a mini-riddle, elegantly decoded by
Williamson, who associates the solution with the Old English kennings
merehengest, "sea-horse," or *sæmearh*, "sea-steed," or *yðhengest* "wave-
horse," which are recurring poeticisms for "ship."[18] The hawk is a metaphor for the ship's sail, and the plain or path or ways that are ridden over
are obscured descriptions of the sea. A further refinement has been proposed by Griffith, who suggests that the riddle clusters in their inverted
arrangement encode a further clue by spelling out an acronym *snac*, the
name for a swift sailing vessel or small warship.[19] That possibility adds a
further frame-breaking twist that again makes the mechanisms of language
incongruously visible.

The elements of humour described for the previous runic riddles
are all present here, with some further twists. The metalepsis of riddle
clues that turn out to be alphabetical spellings has already been posited as a cause of humour. Here a solution begins with that process

---

16 The third cluster presents an editorial choice, since the reading "wega" could work as
    the genitive plural "of the ways" ("he rode the wide track of the ways"), or it could
    be an alternative spelling of "wiga," "man or warrior," which would then provide an
    expressed subject for the clause. Either reading is possible, and the alternatives do not
    change the interpretive strategy required or the ultimate solution.

17 Frederick Tupper, Jr., ed., *The Riddles of the Exeter Book* (Boston: Ginn, 1910; reprint
    Darmstadt: Wissenschaftliche Buchgesellschaft, 1968), 108, building on Trautman's
    decoding of the runic clusters.

18 Williamson, *Old English Riddles*, 186–8, notes to his Riddle 17.

19 Mark Griffith, "Riddle 19 of the Exeter Book: *snac*, an Old English Acronym," *Notes
    Queries* 237 (1992): 15–16.

but then careens back to the more regular style of riddle solving once those letters have been arrived at and rearranged. The resulting elements become clues for arriving at the ship solution, and then the level changes again if Griffith is right about seeing an acronym to name the type of ship. Breaking the frame is always comic in the self-consciousness created by the shift in level; doing so three or four times approaches the dizzying. This will have a humorous effect so long as an audience is not simply alienated by the complexity. I suggest (in chapter 5 below) that there may be yet another breaking of the frame, albeit a much simpler one, if the riddle text of the Exeter Book is taken literally, since the final question does not ask about the object described but about the one positing the puzzle, the riddler. In such a reading, the incongruity of working on the difficult clues without needing to adds a further cause for laughter, provided an audience does not block any appreciation of comedy on account of frustration.

Riddle 64 works runes in a trick that is almost as complex.

Ic seah .ᚹ. ond .ᛁ.   ofer wong faran,
beran .ᛒ. ᛗ.;   bæm wæs on siþþe
hæbbendes hyht   .ᚺ. ond .ᚠ.
swylce þryþa dæl,   .ᚦ. ond .ᛗ.
Gefeah .ᚠ. ond .ᚠ.   fleah ofer .ᛏ
ᚻ. ond .ᛈ.   sylfes þæs folces.
(Riddle 64)

I saw W and I journeying over the plain,
carrying B E; H and O
was the owner's joy for both on that journey
likewise a portion of power, Þ and E.
F and Æ rejoiced, flew over EA
S and P of that people themselves.

Again the riddle has good alliterative verse lines and adequate metre if the rune names are read out:

Ic seah *wynn* ond *īs*   ofer *wong* faran,
beran beorc, eoh;   bæm wæs on siþþe
hæbbendes hyht   *hægl* ond *ōs*
swylce þryþa dæl,   *þorn* ond *eoh*.
Gefeah *feoh* ond *æsc*   *fleah* ofer *ēar*   5
sigel ond *peorð*   *sylfes* þæs folces.

And again the resulting reading would not be very satisfactory in terms of sense:

> I saw *joy* and *ice* journeying over the plain,
> carrying *birch*, *horse*; *hail* and *oak-tree*
> were the owner's joy for both on that journey
> likewise a portion of power, *thorn* and *horse*.
> *Treasure* and *ash-tree* rejoiced, flew over *earth/grave*
> *sun* and *game?* of that people themselves.

Instead, what is needed here, most commentators agree, is taking the runes for their letter sounds and taking pairs as a single unit and then building from such initialism to the appropriate word. Such a system is the more likely in view of the resulting similarities with Riddle 19, even though it presents some challenges towards the end. Williamson spells out the following words from the runic letters: *WIcg*, "horse," *BEorn*, "man, warrior," *HAfoc*, "hawk," *ÞEgn*, "thane, man, servant, retainer," *FÆlca*, "falcon," and *EASPor*, "water-track."[20] Once again, the ship is a metaphorical horse, occupied by a man, with a sail like a hawk or falcon. Williamson suggests this is part of the power (line 4a), as the ship has both oars and sails, and that *hæbbendes* of line 3a should be derived from *hebban* (rather than the more obvious *habban*), thereby portraying the sail as the "lifter's joy." While Williamson sees the last three runes constituting a single cluster, which he reads as the unrecorded *ea-spor*, "water-track" (i.e. the wake of the ship), Bitterli would see these as two separate groups, namely runic EA alone standing for *eard*, "earth," and *SPor*, "track."[21] A likely translation, then, is:

> I saw a horse journeying over the plain,
> carrying a man; the hawk
> was the owner's [or raiser's] joy for both on that journey
> likewise a portion of power. The man/servant
> rejoiced; the falcon flew over the water-
> track of that people themselves.

The difficulties here suggest how runes within a riddle can present an overabundance of incongruities. As so often in riddles, the challenges of interpretation play best to a group dynamic and beg the offering of competing

---

20 Williamson, *Old English Riddles*, 325–7, notes to his Riddle 62.
21 Bitterli, *Say What I am Called*, 90.

solutions, which would provide the agonistic and witty context in which every incongruity is seen as funny.

One last riddle incorporating runes has the potential to be significantly funnier, even as it presents yet a different challenging puzzle. Two lines from the Exeter Book appear to constitute two short riddles, edited by Krapp and Dobbie as Riddles 75 and 76, the first ending with a sequence of four runes:

> Ic swiftne geseah   on swaþe feran
> .ᛗ ᛏ ᛚ ᚻ.
> Ic ane geseah   idese sittan.
> (Riddles 75 and 76)[22]

> I saw a swift one travelling on the track
> DNLH.
> I saw a woman sitting alone.

The runes here appear to operate differently from the other examples, since they are not integrated into the poetic text and reading out the names would fail to scan or alliterate. Commentators assume that instead they provide a coded answer to Riddle 75, perhaps incorporated into the text from the margin in a similar manner to an intrusive coded clue incorporated into Riddle 36. As presented, the runes fail to spell any recognizable Old English word, either read forwards or backwards, but they do if the third rune is emended from an L, ᛚ, to a U, ᚢ, which has a somewhat similar form, whereupon the runes read backwards spell out *hund*, "dog." The swiftness of the creature described in line 1 might favour such a solution, but the riddle text is so short that this has not achieved universal acceptance.[23] Mackie assumed a different coding system and so supplied omitted vowels, reading the letters backwards to arrive at *HæLeND*, "Saviour."[24] That either a dog or Christ are credible for a solution suggests the

---

22 While this is Riddles 75 and 76 in the ASPR numbering used here, Muir, ed., *Exeter Anthology*, treats this as one text, his Riddle 75 and consequently numbers Riddles 77–95 as Riddles 76–94. The different numbers are presented in the table in the prefatory matter of this study.

23 First proposed by Benjamin Thorpe, ed. and trans., *Codex Exoniensis* (London, 1842), 487. Bitterli, *Say What I am Called*, 106–9 reinforces this solution by pointing to the convention of seeing dogs as swift.

24 W.S. Mackie, ed. and trans., *The Exeter Book, Part II: Poems IX–XXXII*, EETS o.s. 194 (London: Oxford University Press, 1934), 77.

unreasonably large range of possibilities for something simply described as swift on the track.

The line following the four runes was long read as a separate riddle, equally challenging for its brevity, featuring a feminine persona sitting alone, until Williamson suggested combining the two as a single riddle. He supplies a different vowel to the runic sequence read backwards to arrive at a solution that provides comic surprise: *HLaND*, "piss."[25] As Williamson explains: "The swift piss of man is seen to travel on the road or track. The piss of woman by implication is hidden." He further observes, "The distinction between modes of pissing is often the source of jokes and stories.... This is the musing distinction made, I think, by the Old English riddler – men piss on the path while women may only be seen squatting alone."[26] Such a solution has been enthusiastically embraced by some commentators but rejected by others.[27]

A different reading of the runes was proposed by Dewa, who suggested that the third rune deploys a substitution code, whereby the L-rune, which stands in formation midway between a U-rune and an I-rune, might indicate both, suggesting the solution to the two surrounding riddles as both *hund* "dog" and *hind* "hind, female deer," the hunter and the hunted.[28] This suggestion is refined by Niles, who sees the relevant L-rune as a visual pun that has been lost in transmission: "The symbol that is now to be read at this point has resulted from a scribe's misunderstanding of the riddler's intention, which was to present the reader with an ambiguously drawn ᚢ, ᚱ, or ᛁ (the runic equivalents of the roman letters **U**, **L**, and **I**, respectively)."[29] He thereby solves the riddle as *hund ond hind*, "hound and hind," or "dog and doe," with the hound a hunting dog running along the track and the hind frozen in its attempt to hide.

The jostling solutions to Riddle 75/76, all of which seem to me quite credible, enact the process whereby a community of scholars competes and cooperates to arrive at the best solution. Runic script embedded in insular minuscule flags a challenge that calls for code-breaking. Because there is no single system, decoding runes in the riddles requires uncertain work by the audience of would-be solvers. Such work is apparently visual and so implies learned book-literate readers, even as Riddles 24 and 42 both thematize an aurally received text. The process of decoding would be rife with

---

25 Williamson, *Old English Riddles*, 352–6, notes to his Riddle 73.

26 Williamson, *Old English Riddles*, 355.

27 It is endorsed by Muir, *Exeter Anthology*, 716; Delanty and Matto, *Word Exchange*, but rejected by Niles, *Enigmatic Poems*, chap. 3.

28 Roberta J. Dewa, "The Runic Riddles of the Exeter Book: Language Games and Anglo-Saxon Scholarship," *Nottingham Medieval Studies* 39 (1995): 26–36 at 35.

29 Niles, *Enigmatic Poems*, 98.

the potential for humour, as a crowd initially shouted "dog," even as Mackie risked sounding square with his answer of "Our Saviour," whereas Williamson would elicit a giggle at his cheek as he shouted out "piss" (where the colloquial register contributes to his cheekiness, whereas a shout of "urine," which is the DOE's definition of *hland*, would generate a smile at the learned discourse level for such a basic function), while Niles would amplify Dewa's first shout of "hound and hind," and Wilcox would cry out half-heartedly that it might be the "hand" of the scribe.[30] Sometimes humour accrues from the ingenuity of the riddle, as in the description of the mimicking bird of Riddle 24 and the heavily coded ships of 19 and 64, sometimes the humour accrues from the ingenuity of the solutions, as in these suggestions about Riddle 75/76, while some solutions have the added frisson of breaking taboo, as in Riddle 42.

The disconcerting proximity to nonsense probably boosts the humour of all the riddle examples, but not all runic substitutions are funny. Similar techniques of reading are called for in the epilogues to four religious poems signed by Cyn(e)wulf, who famously embeds his name through the incorporation of runic letters.[31] Each of these sequences requires the runic letters to be read out as the noun that names the letter in order to maintain the metre, even as those same words are understood as letters, which can be rearranged into the name Cynewulf (or Cynwulf). The passages centre on such serious issues as death and judgment, which are not obviously conducive to the incongruities being received as comic, and Cynewulf seems to tamp down rather than play up any possibility of seeing humour here. While encouraging an agonistic spirit in the audience – some of these examples continue to generate critical controversy over how they should be read[32] – these passages

---

30 I suggest this solution in "The Riddle of the Page: Material Enticement to the Old English Riddles of the Exeter Book," in *Manuscript Materiality in the Classroom and Beyond*, eds. Ellen K. Rentz and Michelle M. Sauer, a special issue of *SMART: Studies in Medieval and Renaissance Teaching* 25, no. 2 (Fall 2018): 75–87.

31 On Cynewulf, see Daniel J. Calder, *Cynewulf* (Boston: Twayne, 1981); Earl R. Anderson, *Cynewulf: Structure, Style, and Theme in His Poetry* (London: Associated University Presses, 1983); but note the cautions against thinking in terms of a modern sense of authorship from Jacqueline A. Stodnick, "Cynewulf as Author: Medieval Reality or Modern Myth?" *Bulletin of the John Rylands University Library of Manchester* 79 (1997): 25–39; Jason R. Puskar, "Hwa Þas Fitte Fegde? Questioning Cynewulf's Claim of Authorship," *English Studies* 92 (2011): 1–19.

32 See Page, *Introduction*, 206, rejecting Elliott, *Runes*; Niles, *Enigmatic Poems*, chap. 8; Jill Hamilton Clements, "Reading, Writing, and Resurrection: Cynewulf's Runes as a Figure of the Body," *Anglo-Saxon England* 43 (2014): 133–54; Emily V. Thornbury, *Becoming A Poet in Anglo-Saxon England* (Cambridge: Cambridge University Press, 2014), 120–35; Symons, *Runes and Roman Letters*, chap. 3.

function to raise consciousness of interpretation for the purpose of edification rather than for comic play.[33] A different poem, though, uses runic substitutions for edifying effect that also allows the play of humour.

Killer Runes: *Solomon and Saturn I*

Solomon and Saturn I provides an instantiation of runes in service of a serious
purpose, but with a deployment that also comes across as funny. This poem
presents an exchange in Old English verse between two rival figures of wisdom centring on the nature and properties of the Pater Noster prayer.[34] It lays
out the power of the prayer by describing the power of the very letters that
constitute it, which fight against the devil. These letters stab and wound their
metaphysical opponent in a strikingly physical way, which jarringly switches
levels of interpretation as the letters move from sounding phonemes that
constitute language into physical objects, visible on the page, and capable of
leaping from it into a fighting posture. The idea contributes to a serious theological purpose, suggesting the power of language to effect moral outcomes
and of prayer to defeat evil, but the extremity of the movement between
epistemological levels is so incongruous as to generate laughter.

This extreme instantiation of the power of letters comes into play as
Solomon tells Saturn of the ability of the prayer to cause harm to the devil
and make him flee:

> gif ðu him ærest on ufan   ierne gebrengest
> prologa prima   ðam is .ᚳ. P. nama;
> hafað guðmæcga   gierde lange,
> gyldene gade,   ond a ðone grimman feond
> swiðmod sweopað;   ond him on swaðe fylgeð
> .ᚠ. A . ofermægene   ond hine eac ofslihð.
> .ᛏ. T . hine teswað   ond hine on ða tungan sticað,
> wræsteð him ðæt woddor   ond him ða wongan brieceð.
> (*Solomon and Saturn I*, from CCCC 422, lines 88–97)[35]

> if you first bring the angry one on him from above,
> prologa prima, the name for that one is P;

---

33 See Tom Birkett, "Runes and *Revelatio*: Cynewulf's Signatures Reconsidered," *Review
    of English Studies* 65 (2014): 771–89.

34 On the tradition, see Carolyne Larrington, *A Store of Common Sense: Gnomic Theme
    and Style in Old Icelandic and Old English Wisdom Poetry* (Oxford: Oxford University
    Press, 1993); Brittany Erin Schorn, *Speaker and Authority in Old Norse Wisdom Poetry*
    (Berlin: de Gruyter, 2017).

that warrior, a brave one, has a long rod,
a golden goad, and ever swipes
at the grim fiend; and on his track follows
A with a mighty power and also strikes him.
T injures him and stabs him in the tongue,
twists his throat and breaks his cheeks.

The assailants here are the opening letters of the "Our Father" prayer in Latin. All prayer would be considered potentially efficacious against the forces of evil in a Christian world view, and this prayer carries particular heft as words spoken by Christ to guide his followers in a text that is prominent from recurrent liturgical use.[36] Nevertheless, rarely is the power of the prayer so atomized as to be presented as the martial ability of each individual letter to physically engage with the forces of evil. The poem presents these letters in their order within the words of the prayer (with the proviso that each letter is only spelled out once). The encounter each letter has with the devil is strikingly embodied, with R shaking him by the hair, N and O scourging him, and S knocking his teeth out. Q and V scourge him again; I, L, and C battle him; and F and M send fiery arrows.

Such imagination of the extreme power of letters picks up on the recurring Christian concern with the logos fully displayed in the opening of the Gospel of John. Wade suggests it resonates with an Augustinian sense of language "to focus attention on the materiality of language and to discourage views of language as metaphor" with the poet differentiating "between arbitrary, human language (the spoken Pater Noster) and divine, ideal language (the living letters)."[37] Such an apotropoeic understanding of letters resonates with the power of language seen in the Old English charms.[38] O'Brien O'Keeffe points out how S, G, and T silence the devil by stabbing his tongue and points to one level of

---

35 Daniel Anlezark, ed. and trans., *The Old English Dialogues of Solomon and Saturn* (Cambridge: Brewer, 2009), who also provides extensive commentary.

36 See Stephanie Clark, *Compelling God: Theories of Prayer in Anglo-Saxon England* (Toronto: University of Toronto Press, 2018).

37 Erik Wade, "Language, Letters, and Augustinian Origins in the Old English Poetic *Solomon and Saturn I*," *The Journal of English and Germanic Philology* 117, no. 2 (2018): 160–84 at 161.

38 See Thomas D. Hill, "Tormenting the Devil with Boiling Drops: An Apotropaic Motif in the Old English 'Solomon and Saturn I' and Old Norse-Icelandic Literature," *The Journal of English and Germanic Philology* 92, no. 2 (1993): 157–66; James Paz, "Magic That Works: Performing *Scientia* in the Old English Metrical Charms and Poetic Dialogues of Solomon and Saturn," *Journal of Medieval and Early Modern Studies* 45, no. 2 (2015): 219–43.

duality: "The silencing of the devil is thus accomplished by the speaking of the Pater Noster. And herein lies the crux of the double understanding of writing, letters and speech in the poem. Speaking the words of the prayer (a notion implicit in an oral mentality) invokes its power, which the poem conceptualizes as being situated in its letters (a notion suggesting a literate mentality)."[39] Such a picture is highly memorable, and Dumitrescu incisively plays up the mnemonic and disciplinary value of the dialogue within a pedagogical context.[40] The military exploits enter into the tradition of the violent encounters between sins and vices in the *Psychomachia* tradition[41]; the symbolic reading of the order and even shape of the letters enters into a learned tradition of alphabetic significance and esoteric alphabets.[42] In addition, I am suggesting that the frame-breaking is funny.

At one level, incongruities come from the letters ceasing to serve as phonetic representation and instead playing up their physical form, in the manner seen in the runic play of the riddles, but there is more. The examples of the letters fighting are so physical and so warrior-like as to be surprising in relation to mere letters, no matter how embodied they are. The incongruity is played up by the poet since both their martial skills and their letter-ness are repeatedly stressed. The poem survives (in fragmentary state) in two manuscripts, and in one of these, CCCC 422, the scribe provides both roman and runic letter form for each letter, visually playing up the presence of the letters through the two alternative instantiations. The poet plays up the very shape of the letter forms: C is characterized as "geap stæf" (124b) "rounded, curved, or bent letter", while G is "se geapa" (134a, the rounded one), both comments which apply more clearly to the insular roman form of the letter than the runic. Wade gives a helpful account of the life given to these letters:

> When one utters the Pater Noster, one does not actually fight the devil oneself. Instead, one calls upon these living letters, who then rush into battle. The

39 Katherine O'Brien O'Keeffe, *Visible Song: Transitional Literacy in Old English Verse* (Cambridge: Cambridge University Press, 1990), 50–9.

40 Irina Dumitrescu, *The Experience of Education in Anglo-Saxon Literature* (Cambridge: Cambridge University Press, 2018), chap. 2.

41 See John P. Hermann, "The Pater Noster Battle Sequence in *Solomon and Saturn* and the *Pyschomachia* of Prudentius," *Neuphilologische Mitteilungen* 77, no. 2 (1976): 206–10.

42 See E.J. Christie, "By Means of a Secret Alphabet: Dangerous Letters and the Semantics of *Gebregdstafas* (*Solomon and Saturn I*, line 2b)," *Modern Philology* 109, no. 2 (2011): 145–70.

letters have their own personalities, and each letter engages in different kinds of actions against the devils, from setting fire to one devil's hair to breaking another's teeth. The enumeration of these battles emphasizes the letters' individuality. Although there is a reciprocal function of prayer in *Solomon and Saturn I* (I say a prayer, and, in exchange, God sends letters to fight for me), the power of the prayer is not found in the words uttered by the speaker but in the living letters themselves, which are ultimately created by God.[43]

That serious theological purpose is made memorable in the poem through the dramatic version of the letter skewering flesh, which is funny in its incongruity.

Such comedy of metalepsis, that is, breaking the frame through switching levels, is a recurring trick of modern humour, and there are hints that it is also funny here, since the poet articulates the possibility of the contest making the mind merry. In the opening of the dialogue, Saturn asks how the canticle is to be practised in the mind:

> ðam ðe his gast wile
> meltan wið morðre,   mergan of sorge,
> asceadan of scyldigum?
> (*Solomon and Saturn I*, MS CCCC 422, lines 54b–56a)

for him who wants to steel the mind against trespass, make merry from sorrow, sunder from sins.

"Mergan of sorge" in line 55b is open to alternative understandings. It may be a continuation of the metallurgical imagery started with *meltan* at line 55a and best translated as "purify from sorrow," as Anlezark suggests, but I think a more obvious interpretation is "make merry from sorrow," with a verb building on the common adjective *myrige/mirige*, "pleasant, delightful, sweet" (BT), cognate with "merry." Runic letters often serve to make the mind merry in Old English, especially when boldly battling embodied badness.

Such can be seen, too, in the related further poetic dialogue *Solomon and Saturn II*. Here the two figures of wisdom trade conceptual riddles.[44] They reflect on the nature of learning in ways that thematize the process

---

43 Wade, "Language, Letters, and Augustinian Origins," 171.
44 On the tradition, see further Elaine Tuttle Hansen, *The Solomon Complex* (Toronto: University of Toronto Press, 1988); Fulk and Cain, *History*, chap. 10; T.A. Shippey, ed. and trans., *Poems of Wisdom and Learning in Old English* (Cambridge: Brewer, 1976).

of interpretation. Solomon responds to Saturn's question about the dumb creature which is very wise and has seven tongues, each tongue with twenty tips, each tip with the wisdom of an angel (a version of the inexpressibility topos, always open to comedy through its excess, which will be investigated further in chapter 5 below):

> Bec sindon breme,   bodiað geneahhe
> weotodne willan   ðam ðe wiht hygeð,
> gestrangað hie ond gestaðeliað   staðolfæstne geðoht,
> amyrgað modsefan   manna gehwylces
> of ðreamedlan   ðisses lifes.
> (*Solomon and Saturn II*, lines 60–4)

> Books are glorious, they often declare
> the appointed will to the one who thinks about it at all,
> they strengthen and make firm the steadfast thought,
> make the mind of each person merry
> from the mental oppressions of this life.

The response flags the entertainment possible from such wisdom: books are glorious and edifying, and they specifically "amyrgað modsefan" ("cheer/delight/make merry the mind," 63a). This instance of *amyrgan* is a unique survival in Old English but again builds on the common adjective *myrige/mirige*, "pleasant, delightful, sweet."[45] Here the image is clearly of a lightening of the mind since it opposes "ðreamedlan" ("mental oppressions").[46] Edification is an unsurprising outcome for an instructional dialogue, and the claim that it makes the mind merry points to an appreciation for the humour to be had from book-learning.

The idea is borne out by the striking climax of this riddle-dialogue, which sees Saturn defeated but elated:

> Hwæðre wæs on sælum   se ðe of siðe cwom
> feorran gefered.   Næfre ær his ferhð ahlog.
> (*Solomon and Saturn II*, lines 335–6)[47]

---

45 DOE s.v. *amyrgan*, "to cheer, delight."
46 This is Anlezark's gloss for another challenging term, building on T.J. Gardner, "*Þreaniedla* and *þreamedla*: Notes on Two Old English Abstracta in '-lan'," *Neuphilologische Mitteilungen* 70 (1969): 255–61.
47 Edited by Anlezark as "Solomon and Saturn Poetic Fragment," lines 8–9. *Solomon and Saturn II* is fragmentary in the surviving MS, CCCC 422, and an earlier fragment is assumed by most editors to be its displaced conclusion: see Shippey, *Poems of Wisdom*, 89.

Nevertheless he was happy, he who had come on that journey, travelled from afar; he had never before laughed from his heart.

There are textual complications here, but it seems that Saturn's reaction to losing this riddle contest is to experience real pleasure expressed through laughter.[48] Wisdom and the exchange of riddles is evidently seen as cathartic and perhaps as downright funny.

Funny Runic Wisdom: *The Rune Poem*

One poem combines the metaleptic duality of runic letters with the presentation of wisdom in riddling style, namely the runic abecedarium known as *The Old English Rune Poem*. This work presents pithy wisdom in paradoxes that each start out through punning on the name of a runic letter.[49] Every stanza is a puzzle that can generate delight, using many of the techniques of the Exeter Book riddles, such as anthropomorphism and a sense of an object's utility to humans, simultaneous disclosure and concealment, verbal polysemy, periphrasis, kennings, and metaphor, along with word play of various kinds.[50] Sometimes, although not always, this deployment generates humour.

The enigmatic quality of *The Rune Poem* is nicely captured in the stanza on *lagu*, the L-rune, the name of which means "the sea, water":[51]

"Lagu" byþ leodum   langsum geþuht,
gif hi sculun neþun   on nacan tealtum,

---

48 For a reading of Saturn's laughter as relief, see Tiffany Beechy, "Wisdom and the Poetics of Laughter in the Old English Dialogues of Solomon and Saturn," *The Journal of English and Germanic Philology* 116 (2017): 131–55.

49 After the damage to MS BL Cotton Otho B. x in the 1731 fire in the Cottonian Library, the poem survives only in Hickes's 1705 edition. Maureen Halsall, ed. and trans., *The Old English "Rune Poem": A Critical Edition* (Toronto: University of Toronto Press, 1981), provides a full edition, translation, and commentary; and the poem is also edited and translated in Shippey, *Poems of Wisdom*; Robert E. Bjork, ed. and trans., *Old English Shorter Poems; Volume II: Wisdom and Lyric*, DOML 32 (Cambridge, MA: Harvard University Press, 2014). My translations draw on those of Shippey and Halsall in particular.

50 The list is taken from Paul Sorrell, "Oaks, Ships, and the Old English *Rune Poem*," *Anglo-Saxon England* 19 (1990): 103–16.

51 Text from Halsall, *Rune Poem*, but with the rune name in quotation marks. Hickes's transcript, on which all editions are based, gives rune, equivalent roman letter, and rune name, but an earlier version probably gave only the rune whose name was to be spoken and then explicated in the same way as in most of the runic riddles discussed so far. Halsall gives the rune followed by its name in brackets.

and hi sæyþa swyþe bregaþ,
and se brimhengest bridles ne gymeð.
(*The Rune Poem*, lines 63–6)

The sea/water seems interminable to people,
if they must venture on an unsteady boat,
and the sea-waves terrify them greatly,
and the sea-stallion does not pay heed to its bridle.

The perception of the object of the stanza, *lagu*, acquires a menacing aspect through the qualification of the last three lines. This is not a comic turn, but rather an effect of wonder, awe, and fear in those who have experienced the out-of-control instability of a disturbed sea. In conveying that fear, the poet deploys an incongruity that probably generates momentary humour by activating the kenning of the sea-horse, *brimhengest*, here seen with attributes appropriate to its equestrian form (*bridles ne gymeð*, "does not pay heed to its bridle"), but clearly established by the context as a ship. Both the initial double sense of *lagu* and the play with the *brimhengest* may briefly register as comic, although the incongruities don't have the up-down effect or the right context for sustaining any humour.

Other examples use similar techniques for a more sustained humorous effect. The challenges of controlling a steed get a comic treatment in an earlier stanza presenting the runic letter R:

"Rad" byþ on recyde rinca gehwylcum
sefte, and swiþhwæt ðam ðe sitteþ onufan
meare mægenheardum ofer milpaþas.
(*The Rune Poem*, lines 13–15)

Riding, for every warrior in the hall, is
easy, but very vigorous for the one who sits above
a powerful horse on the paths marked by mile-posts.

Here the surprising turn in the second line creates the incongruity, and the shift in tone works in a way that establishes the humour. The idea of riding as *sefte*, "soft, easy, pleasant," is established for each of the warriors (*rinca gehwylcum*), a designation of the riders which builds up the expectations for their martial valour, but it is soft only because they are "on recyde" (in the hall), which, while it is a martial environment, is not one suitable for active horsemanship. Presumably the going is so easy as the warriors are recounting their travels while sitting around in comfort rather than actually doing the riding on the road.[52] External reality asserts itself with the alliterating *swiþhwæt*, "very vigorous," which is the sensation for the one who is actually in the saddle. The difficulties of the activity are hinted at in the positioning of the rider's perspective (*onufan*, sitting "upon from above"), in the quality of the horse (*mægenheard*, "strength-hardened"), and in the nature of the land traversed (*milpaþas*, "ways marked by mile-markers"). All this suggests hard riding, and the reversal implied by the initial qualification comically undercuts the boldness of those who ride only in talk. The fulcrum lies in the innocent copula in line 14a (*and*), here serving as an adversative connection. Satire at those who speak in comfort rather than act is one element of the humour here. The underlying wisdom moves from the abstract of boasting to the practical down-to-earth nature of real labour, denying expectations in a movement from ideal to distinctly pragmatic in a manner seen in some of the *Durham Proverbs*. The Old English *Rune Poem* is matched by one in Old Norse, and the analogous stanza there also involves a shift of perspective from high to low, in that case by describing the joy of the rider and then the labour of the horse, which generates a comic jolt.[53] The comic jolt of the Old English is more satirical in view of the implied critique of heroic boasting and the metaphoric jab at those who are full of talk rather than action.

One other stanza of *The Rune Poem* also jokes about the riders of horses. The E-rune, "Eh," is named through another word for horse (lines 55–8), in this case characterized as a joy to noblemen, who converse, prosperous on the steed. The last line provides a sly additional detail:

and biþ unstyllum   æfre frofur.
(line 58)

and it is always a comfort for the restless.

---

52 BT plays up this reading by seeing *rad*, s.v., as a pun on furniture of a house and the fittings of a horse. The general sense of "riding, going on horseback" seems more likely here, as Halsall, *Rune Poem*, 112, observes.

53 "'Reið' er sitjandi sæla / ok snúðig ferð / ok jórs erfiði" ("Riding is joy of the rider / and speedy journey / and labouring of the horse"), ed. and trans. Halsall, *Rune Poem*, 184, appendix B.

Given its movements, a horse would be a comfort to those who don't want
to be still. The obviousness of the statement is reinforced by the form of
the adjectival noun *unstyllum* "for the unstill ones," suggesting here some
humour from litotes, with the comic incongruity coming from understatement by means of a reversal of a negative attribute.

Punning duality creates comic effects in some of the other rune stanzas.
The description of *æsc*, the runic letter for a front a-vowel, Æ, spoken as
a word that means "ash," plays more clearly with riddling conventions:

> "Æsc" biþ oferheah,   eldum dyre,
> stiþ on staþule;   stede rihte hylt,
> ðeah him feohtan on   firas monige.
> (*Rune Poem*, lines 82–4)
>
> Ash is very tall, precious to mankind,
> strong on its foundation; it holds its place rightly,
> even if many men fight against/attack it/them.

Here the tallness and the value to people and the firmness on a foundation
all fit with the arboreal nature of the ash tree. All those attributes, though,
might apply to one of the most famous products of the ash tree in Old
English poetry, namely the ash spear, which is also often designated simply
æsc.[54] Holding its place rightly is an obvious attribute of a tree (provided
it doesn't fall down) but a more notable attribute for a spear, which often
operates in coordination with others when under attack by many men, at
which point its extreme size, its value, its firmness on its foundation, and
above all its keeping its right place, are all crucial to the fighting tactic of
a shield-wall. The ash spear (*æsc*) is collocated with the shield for both
Byrhtnoth and Byrhtwold as the implements that these warriors shake as
they begin their speeches of defiance in *The Battle of Maldon* (lines 42–3
and 309–10). The stanza, then, reasonably conjures both the ash tree and a
spear made from ash.[55] Whichever was the poet's intent, the play between
the two solutions embeds some fundamental incongruity in the ambigu-
ous referents for a single word, and the simultaneous embrace of readings
that carry conflicting metaphoric implications creates the opportunity for

---

54 DOE, s.v. *æsc*, sense 3.
55 Niles, *Enigmatic Poems*, 281–3, reads the stanza as punning on both the tree and
    another metonymy designated by *æsc*, namely "a light, swift ship, especially a Viking
    ship" (DOE, sv *æsc*, sense 2).

humour in the manner of the resonance between false and true solution in the riddles.

A neighbouring stanza designating another tree also has some comic play:

"Ac" byþ on eorþan   elda bearnum
flæsces fodor;   fereþ gelome
ofer ganotes bæþ;   – garsecg fandaþ
hwæþer ac hæbbe   æþele treowe.
(*Rune Poem*, lines 77–80)

Oak provides for the sons of men on earth
fodder for meat; it often travels
over the gannet's bath; -- the ocean tests
whether the oak has noble faith/may hold as a noble tree.

The poem appears to present multiple aspects of the oak in the manner of the riddles, namely as fodder for pigs and also as the material for constructing a ship. This ship image is more heroic than the perilous vessel seen in the *lagu* stanza. The point is most emphatic at the end, which seems to revolve on a pun on *treowe*. The primary sense is the startling one of the ocean testing whether the oak may have a noble faith, suggesting a ship that is not going to sink on the sea, and working grammatically with feminine *treow*, "truth, faith, troth" (BT s.v. *treow*, fem.), but the context is such as to inevitably conjure up the idea of masculine *treow*, "tree, wood" (BT s.v. *treow*, masc.). This is a noble tree if it satisfies the test at sea, just as it is a useful tree on land ("on eorþan," 77a) for its feeding of those creatures who become meat for humans.[56] Holding the dualities of the pun and of the description in mind activates comic incongruity in the manner of the riddles.

A further arboreal example creates humour in a different way.

"Ðorn" byþ ðearle scearp,   ðegna gehwylcum
anfengys yfyl,   ungemetun reþe
manna gehwylcun   ðe him mid resteð.
(*Rune Poem*, lines 7–9)

---

56 J.R. Hall, "Perspective and Wordplay in the Old English *Rune Poem*," *Neophilologus* 61 (1973): 453–61, at 456–7 unpacks the pun, providing analogues for the usage here and showing the way the grammar works. See also Sorrell, "Oaks."

Thorn is extremely sharp, for any warrior
painful in the grasp, immeasurably fierce
for any person who rests among them/it.

The humour here comes about from a doubly unexpected anticlimax. The ubiquity of the evil described is emphasized with two out of six half-lines stressing how the danger applies widely ("for each of thanes," 7b; "for each of human beings," 9a). The object's danger comes about because it is very sharp (with the emphatic adverb in 7a, *ðearle*). With such a build-up, the audience is surely expecting something wondrous or paradoxical (just like the paradox of the oak that travels over the ocean or the ash that sustains against human attack). Instead, though, this object is sharp in the most obvious way, as a spiky protuberance on vegetable matter, namely a thorn. It is undeniably sharp, but there is surely some folly in the thanes (particularly given their status) who get felled by such an obvious feature of nature. The vegetable matter is imagined as having malign agency to the extent that it is *reþe* (fierce), and emphatically so since it is "ungemetun reþe" ("immeasurably fierce" 8b). In its favour, though, the object appears to exercise this malign agency only in restricted circumstances, namely against those who attempt to make their bed among it (9b), which seems a self-evidently foolish choice for any thane or any person. Hall points out that the fierceness described here seems more appropriate to the preceding stanza, describing a wild ox (*ur*, the aurochs, of lines 4–6), which had been described in terms of its horns.[57] The contrast from large to small and the bathos of the description of vegetable matter in mock-heroic terms shape up this stanza as funny. It conveys some good proverbial wisdom – sharp things hurt when they skewer – but of such a literally appropriate kind that there is comic distance between the expected abstract message and the literal picture presented. Within that picture, the danger is so much brought on by the folly of the one that suffers that the poet appears to be satirizing the noble folk afflicted by thorns. The object is so small and so natural that the attribution of so much malign agency, or even so much attention, seems like a comic incongruity.[58]

All of the stanzas in *The Rune Poem* bounce from letter name to the regular object designated by that letter name, creating a recurring incongruity that might raise a smile, even as the effect gets somewhat dulled through

---

57 Hall, "Perspective," 454.
58 Niles, *Enigmatic Poems*, 263–4, sees a pun on thorn and "hawthorn-hedge."

its frequent repetition. This stanza may just bring that incongruity back to sharpness in playing with the very shape of the letter imagined. The letter thorn, Þ, is generally written in manuscripts with a rounded bow, but the runic form has a pointed one, using the straight lines characteristic of the script. If such were the case in the presentation here, the letter itself would match the description of the imagined thorn in its sharpness, and the physical character of the lettering would correspond with its verbal power in a disorientingly literal manner, as seen above in *Solomon and Saturn I*. Enforced self-consciousness about the physical nature of letters is recurringly funny and often, as here, played for further comic effect.

The puzzles of *The Old English Rune Poem*, then, create paradoxes and incongruities that match the humour of some of the riddles, while the recurring conceit of a symbol that is both a letter and a word matches the trick of the runes in the riddles and elsewhere. The hint of satire at the martial class in the *Rad* stanza or in the *Thorn* stanza picks up a hint also seen in the riddles. These are supremely lettered games which call for an audience schooled in letters who might take satisfaction in laughing at (and out-doing) warriors in the hall.

Laughter in Class and the Colloquies of Ælfric Bata

The process of riddle and rune interpretation surely brings out a competitive spirit in the audience who would engage interactively with the material, and the mead hall is far from the only place to imagine a lively community responding to such puzzles. As has been seen, Riddle 42 imagines two distinct audiences: one group are the *werum æt wine* ("men at wine-drinking," 16a), apparently the aristocratic secular audience in the hall, who are taunted for their failure to solve the riddle. In contrast are those people "þe bec witan" ("who know books," 7a), the *rynemenn* ("people skilled in mysteries/runes," 13b), who have the key to unlock the sense held in bonds of cunning, very much like the imagined *winnende wiga* ("striving warrior") scribe of Riddle 51 discussed in chapter 1. In a joke that would be particularly appreciated by the community of the literate, the *rynemenn* establish their learning as superior to the martial skills of the more obviously favoured elite of society, those manly and martial men drinking wine in the hall. Those *rynemen* would have required academic training, which, in early England, implies education in a monastic or ecclesiastical setting. A final work will illustrate the possibilities for humour in such an educational setting.

Ælfric Bata, writing in Canterbury in a similar milieu to that where the Durham Proverbs were preserved, identifies himself as a student of Ælfric the homilist (discussed in chapter 6 below), and wrote two colloquies which provide trial conversations for training students in Latin.[59] These are imaginative dialogues which enable a student to practise speaking Latin and build up vocabulary and grammar usage in imagined dramatic scenarios. As Porter explains, Ælfric Bata has assimilated the random scenes of his source "into a coherent dramatic representation of human characters in monastic settings" and, like any good language pedagogue, works to keep his students' attention by making these conversations entertaining.[60]

Ælfric Bata makes explicit claim to the use of humour. He closes out the first series of his colloquies with serious concern for the souls of his students, but before that he provides a discussion of his method:

> As you've learned in this speech, my boys, and as you read in many places, joking is often mixed with wise words and sayings [iocus cum paientiae loquelis et uerbis inmixtus est et sepe coniunctus].

He goes on to explain:

> For that reason I've written and arranged these speeches in my own way for you young men, knowing that boys speaking to one another in their way more often say words that are playful [ludicra uerba] than honourable or wise, because their age always draws them to foolish speech, frequent joking, and naughty chattering [ad inrationabilem sermonem et ad frequens iocum et ad garrulitatem indecentem]. And if they're allowed, they'd rather play and joke foolishly [ludere et iocare … inspienter] with their pals and peers, and in this they take great pleasure.[61]

Ælfric Bata envisages a classroom community of laughers delighting in joking and playful speech. Classroom work on solving the Old English riddles or on understanding the wisdom of *The Durham Proverbs* or *The Old English Rune Poem* would provide an environment for such joking, chatter, and play.

---

59 Ælfric Bata was probably the teacher at Christ Church, Canterbury, or St. Augustine's, Canterbury: see Scott Gwara, ed., and David W. Porter, trans. and intro., *Anglo-Saxon Conversations: The Colloquies of Ælfric Bata* (Cambridge: Boydell, 1997); Christopher A. Jones, "The Irregular Life in Ælfric Bata's *Colloquies*," *Leeds Studies in English* 37 (2006): 241–60.

60 David W. Porter, "Anglo-Saxon Colloquies: Ælfric, Ælfric Bata and *De raris fabuilis retractata*," *Neophilologus* 81 (1997): 467–80 at 471. See also Dumitrescu, *Experience of Education*, chap. 3.

61 Gwara and Porter, *Anglo-Saxon Conversations*, 170–1, Colloquy 29 "The Master Instructs the Boys," translated by Porter.

Ælfric Bata teaches what he preaches. Colloquy 8 of the first series, for example, begins with a student-monk, presumably the young oblate learning Latin, imagined as serving his elders at table but then being invited to join in the feast. At first the vocabulary is rich in politeness, but then the senior voice becomes improbably persistent in importuning excess. The student tries multiple answers of polite deferral ("Really, I'm not hungry, father, or thirsty either. But anyway I'm willing to drink once or twice or three or four more times before we leave," Gwara and Porter, 97). By Colloquy 9, the practice scenario drops such moral decorum, first with an imagined trip to the toilet, with the oblate serving a senior monk's needs (Gwara and Porter, 99–101), palpably and obviously contrary to the monastic rule, and then through another student voicing the pleasure of excessive drinking:

> All right, if I can have some drinking horns, sir.
>   We have to get some for you. Server, go get a great horn full of the best beer, and give it to him right away so he can hold a horn for drinking in his hand. (Gwara and Porter, 101)

I assume this is already occupying the world of wish fulfilment, comically inverting the discipline of monastic life, with or without an obscene pun. Even if oblates drank beer, surely it is a fantasy to imagine the master ordering for the student a horn full of the best beer (even if that might be a handy locution should the oblate ever be involved in entertainment outside the cloister). The excess becomes clearer as the student gets to riff on the form *cornu*, a fourth declension neuter noun with, exceptionally, identical forms in nominative, accusative, and ablative,[62] the sense of which will soon be seared into even the most reticent memory:

> I want to drink from the horn. I ought to have the horn, to hold the horn. I'm called horn! Horn is my name! I want to live with the horn, to lie with the horn and sleep, to sail ride, walk, work and play with the horn. All my kith and kin had horns and drank. And I want to die with the horn! (Gwara and Porter, 103)

The dialogue goes on, imagining alternatives and playing with linguistic forms, but all in a context that is memorable in its counter-disciplinary lack of abstemiousness and decorum. By the end of this speech, the cellarer's

---

62 See Gwara and Porter, *Anglo-Saxon Conversations*, 40–1.

disapproval at such excess is imagined ("but this lightheartedness is making our cellarer unhappy, I think," Gwara and Porter, 103), even as this voice of sobriety is here fantastically counter-imagined ("No, brother, believe me ... it doesn't make me at all unhappy," Gwara and Porter, 103). And the drinking scene goes on with greater excesses still (Gwara and Porter, 105–7), concluding in a tipsy compline, whose competence as liturgical performance might well be questioned.[63]

Even if monastic constraints on eating and drinking may have been partly relaxed for young oblates, who are the students learning colloquial Latin, they were surely never as relaxed as this! The *Land of Cockayne*-like imagination here serves up vocabulary and grammar practice in Latin with a scenario so inappropriate to the monastic regime as to be comically incongruous and therefore highly memorable. It looks like this was a winning pedagogical strategy as student drunkenness is a frequent point of passing reference throughout the colloquies. Surely this constituted a standing joke, capitalizing on laughter and play in the classroom to cement memory.

If excesses of eating and drinking constitute one clear case of counter-monastic discipline, talking back to the master (who elsewhere is imagined as a stern disciplinarian and the wielder of a literal rod and whip for beating and scourging the children-scholars) is surely even more so. This is imagined to excess in Colloquy 25, which begins with the master abusing the student, at first with an air of verisimilitude ("You've come late; you're always coming late to your reading or your work, because you're always slow and lazy, slothful, idle, and bad," Gwara and Porter, 137), giving practice in a range of synonyms for sloth. The dialogue then offers a fuller range of vocabulary, turning with increasing unlikelihood to the exuberantly scatological:

> You idiot! You goat shit! Sheep shit! Horse shit! You cow dung! You pig turd! You human turd! You dog shit! Fox shit! Cat turd! Chicken shit! You ass turd! You fox cub of all fox cubs! You fox tail! You fox beard! You skin of a fox cub! You idiot and halfwit! You buffoon! (Gwara and Porter, 139)

which does not sound much better in the original Latin:

> Tu sochors! Tu scibalum hedi! Tu scibalum ouis! Tu scibalum equi! Tu fimus bouis! Tu stercus porci! Tu hominus stercus! Tu asini scibalum! Tu uulpicule

---

63 See Gwara and Porter, 107, notes 80 and 81.

omnium uulpiculorum! Tu uulpis cauda! Tu uulpis barba! Tu nebris uulpiculi! Tu uechors et semichors! Tu scurra! (Gwara and Porter, 138)

In the biggest surprise of them all, this provokes a matching response in the voice of the student:

> I would like you to be totally beshat and bepissed for all these words of yours. Have shit in your beard! May you always have shit in your beard, and shit and turds in your mouth, three and two times and eight and one, and I none at all ever! Now your words reveal the truth, that you are a buffoon and a fool and a silly blabbermouth. (Gwara and Porter, 139)

This fantasy of answering back gets but mild rebuke from the teacher, who starts steering the dialogue towards ultimate good, as both boy and master then start exchanging aphorisms from Proverbs in the kind of practice that might also have laid the groundwork for discussing and translating the Durham Proverbs.

This exchange gives students access to a vocabulary and syntax of insult and to an impressively extensive scatology. It seems unlikely that such an insult-exchange with a superior would constitute imaginable real life in the classroom – as Jones points out, the various monastic rules are all about creating a disciplined subject.[64] Still, as Foucault would so cogently come to articulate, that kind of discipline leaves as its residue an obsession with precisely those things that are suppressed, and parading them allows for significant if shocking relief.[65] This is a particularly clear example of humour from crossing taboo, with the implied release of constraint allowing for the release of laughter in any audience not reacting with outrage or shock.

Jones suggests that the dialogues satirize the strictness of reformed monastic ideology.[66] While that is surely one good use, it is also possible that they provide a release valve from the discipline of that strict ideology, acquiring added frisson from that context. Dumitrescu emphasizes the fictional nature of the whole scenario and how the shock, including of the sternly disciplinarian master, contributes to the effect.[67] In all these ways,

---

64 Jones, "Irregular Life."
65 Michel Foucault, *Discpline and Punish: The Birth of the Prison*, trans. Alan Sheridan (New York: Pantheon, 1977).
66 Jones, "Irregular Life."
67 Dumitrescu, *Experience of Education*, chap. 3.

the dialogues attest to a brilliant pedagogy.[68] The repeated parading of the unspeakable so violates taboo, so inverts decorum, and so revels in excess as to also generate considerable humour.

Such a classroom of laughter would be one appropriate site for engagement with the humorous proverbs of *The Durham Proverbs* and with ingenious riddles of all kinds. As a multilingual and book-centred community, it would also be an ideal audience for the linguistic and alphabetical puzzles pursued in this chapter. The riotous students pictured in the colloquies would relish the competition of the runic puzzles and delight at the comedy to be had from letters, all the more so for the sudden relaxation from otherwise stern discipline. This would be a place for community laughter delighting in the reversal of expectation. Perceiving the incongruities could serve an ultimately theological purpose of understanding the wonder of the created universe. Delight in such material could also be viewed in terms of superiority theory, building up a community that acquires power by knowing its letters rather than through force of arms. Ælfric Bata's schoolroom presents a surprising but ideal venue for engaging with humorous literature of all kinds and a particularly good fit for funny riddles, witty wisdom, and ludicrous letters.

---

68 See, further, Gwara and Porter, *Anglo-Saxon Conversations*, 56; Harold C. Zimmerman, "Drinking Feasts and Insult Battles: Bringing Anglo-Saxon Pedagogy into the Contemporary Classroom," *Pedagogy* 13, no. 2 (Spring 2013): 229–44.

Chapter Three

Metrical Mirth:
Sonorous Sounds and
Rambunctious Rhymes

While letters on parchment and letter codes can create comic incongruity, the same is also true of sounds and sound-play.

> Haha and hehe getacniað hlehter on leden and on englisc, forðan ðe hi beoð hlichende geclypode. (Ælfric's *Grammar*)[1]

> "Ha ha" and "he he" signify laughter in Latin and in English, because they are called out laughing.

So observes Ælfric in his *Grammar*, indicating the sound of laughter which is, itself, funny. Reduplicating sounds in a language not given to reduplication break expectations of phonology, and mere repetition can be funny in an appropriate domain, as Chaucer famously exploits for a climactic moment in his later comedy.[2] The trick of the runes investigated in the last chapter is inherently a visual effect, requiring a learned and literate audience that either reads the manuscript page or imagines the letters when rune names are read out. Other humour in Old English poetry, though, depends on the sounds of language and so could be relished by any listening audience without needing to draw on the specific skill of writing.

Sound is always significant for poetry, of course. Heightened sound effects contribute to the humour in the verbs describing the voice of the *higoræ* in Riddle 24, for example, as described above. Riddle 7 provides another avian example, as it describes a creature whose garment is silent on the earth or on the water but sings out when it raises the subject aloft, a paradox of silence and sound which is captured in a series of acoustically

---

1 Julius Zupitza, ed., *Ælfrics Grammatik und Glossar* (Berlin: Wiedmann, 1880), 279.
2 "'Tehee!' quod she, and clapte the wyndow to," *The Miller's Tale*, line 3740, ed. Larry D. Benson, *The Riverside Chaucer*, 3rd ed. (Boston: Houghton Mifflin, 1987), 75.

chiming but semantically contrasting verbs, where *swigað* (is silent, line 1) contrasts with *swogað*, *swinsiað*, *singað* (lines 7–8, the creature's garments "swish," "sound out," "sing"). Onomatopoeic play hints at the wingbeats of the mute swan described by the riddle in an ear-catching way that would generate a smile in an attentive audience.[3]

One recurring indicator of humorous sound effects in Old English poetry is the presence of rhyme. Rhyme is strongly marked precisely because it is not a metrically required element. Old English verse predictably proceeds in two-stress units paired through the regular use of alliteration.[4] The alliteration is structural and through its chiming, alongside the concision of the half-lines, signals poem-ness in an effect more easily appreciated in listening than in looking, since manuscript page layout generally provides no visual clues of metrical form.[5] Vocabulary, too, marks poetic form, since Old English poets deploy a distinct poetic diction. Performance context, distinctive language use, and chiming alliteration, then, would all call attention to the presence of poetic form, but not rhyme, which comes into play only in some of the late verse contained in the *Anglo-Saxon Chronicle*.[6] Sustained use of rhyme across multiple lines is extremely rare in classic Old English verse and occurs to a significant extent in just three instances: Riddle 28, *The Rhyming Poem*, and towards the conclusion of Cynewulf's *Elene*.[7] I will argue that the first two cases both establish an incongruity of form that is humorous in its effect.

---

3 I explore the acoustic effect of Riddle 7 (swan) in the context of the paradoxes of the poem in "'Tell Me What I Am': The Old English Riddles," in *Readings in Medieval Texts: Interpreting Old and Middle English Literature*, eds. David F. Johnson and Elaine Treharne (Oxford: Oxford University Press, 2005), 46–59.

4 For handy introductions to the metre of Old English verse, see Donald G. Scragg, "The Nature of Old English Verse," in *The Cambridge Companion to Old English Literature*, 2nd ed., eds. Malcolm Godden and Michael Lapidge (Cambridge: Cambridge University Press, 2013), 50–65; Haruko Momma, "Old English Poetic Form: Genre, Style, Prosody," in *The Cambridge History*, 278–308; Baker, *Introduction*, chap. 13.

5 See, *inter alia*, O'Brien O'Keeffe, *Visible Song*; Daniel Donoghue, *How the Anglo-Saxons Read Their Poems* (Philadelphia: University of Pennsylvania Press, 2018).

6 E.G. Stanley, "Rhymes in English Medieval Verse: From Old English to Middle English," in *Medieval English Studies Presented to George Kane*, eds. Edward Donald Kennedy, Ronald Waldron, and Joseph S. Wittig (Woodbridge: Brewer, 1988), 19–54, provides a convenient catalog and discussion; and cf. Michael McKie, "The Origins and Early Development of Rhyme in English Verse," *Modern Language Review* 92 (1997): 817–31.

7 Cynewulf also uses rhyme for a climactic description of heaven at *Christ II*, lines 591–6, but this is less sustained and probably relates to a tradition of aurally heightened description in the homiletic tradition, while *The Ruin* has a less extended use of rhyme.

Augustan wits knew that too self-conscious or elaborate a display of poetic effects generates humour, as Alexander Pope famously outlines performatively in his *Essay on Criticism*:

'Tis not enough no harshness gives offense,
The sound must seem an echo to the sense:
Soft is the strain when Zephyr gently blows,
And the smooth stream in smoother number flows;
But when loud surges lash the sounding shore,
The hoarse, rough verse should like the torrent roar:
When Ajax strives some rock's vast weight to throw,
The line too labors, and the words move slow.

The same kind of self-conscious play is on display in those instances where rhyme becomes super-abundant in Old English verse.

Riddling with Rhyming Form: Riddle 28

Riddle 28 takes such acoustic effects of verse to an extreme.

Biþ foldan dæl   fægre gegierwed
mid þȳ heardestan   ond mid þȳ scearpestan
ond mid þȳ grymmestan   gumena gestrēona,
corfen, sworfen,   cyrred, þyrred,
bunden, wunden,   blǣced, wǣced,   5
frætwed, geatwed,   feorran lǣded
tō durum dryhta.   Drēam bið in innan
cwicra wihta: clengeð, lengeð,
þǣr þǣr ǣr lifgende   longe hwīle
wilna brūceð   ond nō wið spriceð,   10
ond þonne æfter dēaþe   dēman onginneð,
meldan mislīce.   Micel is tō hycganne
wīsfæstum menn,   hwæt sēo wiht sȳ.
(Riddle 28)[8]

A portion of the earth is beautifully adorned
with the hardest, and with the sharpest,
and with the fiercest of treasures of men,

---

8 In this case I have added indications of vowel length to facilitate subsequent discussion.

cut, rubbed, plied, dried,
bound, wound, bleached, leached,
adorned, reformed, led from afar
to the doors of men. Joy of living creatures
is on the inside: there where those living before for a long time
enjoy desires and do not at all speak against it,
it clings, lingers,
and then after death it begins to judge,
to declare variously. It is much
for wise people to think what that creature may be.

This whole poem is a bravura performance of sound. The opening resonates with especially powerful audible effects. Beyond the requisite alliteration, the first line contains assonance between stressed syllables in *dǣl*
and *fǣgre* and ear-catching secondary alliteration in the palatal *g* sounds
within the b-verse. The sound effects become louder in the next line and
a half (lines 2–3a), where the thrice-repeated preposition and demonstra-
tive, the thrice-repeated superlative ending and grammatical rhyme, and
the assonance between stressed syllables within line 2 all chime loudly
in the ear. The specialness of such sound effects seems to trump regular
requirements of Old English metrical form: all recent editors point out
that line 2 is lacking in alliteration and yet hardly needs emending when
so many secondary effects serve to stitch together the two half-lines.[9] The
next lines launch rhymes of a particularly striking kind:

corfen, sworfen,   cyrred, þyrred,
bunden, wunden,   blǣced, wǣced,
frætwed, geatwed,   feorran lǣded.
(lines 4–6)

cut, rubbed, plied, dried,
bound, wound, bleached, leached,
adorned, reformed, led from afar.

The sound effects here are breathtaking. Ten past participles in succession
lead to five half-lines with the fastest rhyming effect possible, namely a
rhyming stressed syllable followed by a rhyming unstressed syllable, with

---

9 As remarked by Williamson, *Old English Riddles*, 224 (note to his riddle 26.2); Bernard J.
  Muir, *The Exeter Anthology of Old English Poetry*, 2 vols. (Exeter: University of Exeter
  Press, 1994; revised ed., 2000), 630 (note to riddle 28, line 2).

no intervening syllables to dilute the effect.[10] The rhyming sound is magnified in the a-verses, as the rhyme incorporates a consonant cluster rather
than a simple consonant following each stressed vowel. The effect eases
in the sixth half-line, but even here an eleventh past participle, *lǣded* in
line 6b, associates with the pair in line 5b through assonance and joins the
grammatical rhyme of unstressed endings running through lines 5b and 6.
If even occasional rhyme is chimingly noticeable in Old English verse, this
tsunami of echoing sounds is downright mesmerizing. It would likely create a smile of appreciation at the bravura nature of the aural pyrotechnics
in a kind of humour generated by the metrical form.

Notable sound effects continue throughout the riddle, if slightly less
heated than in that opening charge. The collocation *in innan* at 7b is ear-
catching in the rapid repetition of a syllable, while *cwicra wihta* at 8a plays
with further assonance and grammatical rhyme, leading to the emphatically chiming bisyllabic true rhyme (and playful part identity) of doubled
verbs *clengeð, lengeð* at 8b. The musicality continues with grammatical
rhyme in lines 10–11, emphasizing the sequence of three parallel verbs.
In all likelihood, the very chiming of the rhyming sounded funny, as this
excessive aural patterning occurs on top of the regular rhythm and structural alliteration of verse.

Such striking sound effects would surely be treated by a riddle-solving
audience as a clue to the riddle's solution, as more muted ones were in the
avian Riddles 24 and 7. Riddle 28 is, however, one of the few complete
Exeter Book riddles where modern critics do not agree on a likely solution. In view of that, I will work over the clues to present the case for a
number of convincing but competing solutions and thereby suggest some
of the pleasure – and potential for humour – in trying to solve a high-
octane riddle.

The ear-catching sounds of the opening come in a description of the
process of creation, which, as well as being noisy, sounds distinctly painful for the material involved. Pain suffered by an object in manufacture
is a recurring trope of the riddles, often evoking sympathy for inanimate
things. In Riddle 26, the book that is crafted from parchment begins by
articulating the skin's loss of life at the hands of an enemy. In Riddle 83,
gold voices its brooding resentment at its wrenching treatment by humans,
for which it exacts suitable revenge. Here in Riddle 28, the pyrotechni-
cal pile-up of past participles is painful in content, but the sound turns it
into a celebration of a reiterative and rhythmically mesmerizing process of
manufacture. The unusual and dazzling poetic effects presumably signal

---

10 I assume a probable true rhyme for *frætwed, geatwed* masked by the spelling.

an unusual and dazzling object which goes through a torturous process of manufacture that gets loudly celebrated, presumably on account of the happy outcome that comes about through the pain. The very unsubtleness of the noisy process adds to the taunting power of the riddle, as is apparent in a more conventional way at the end, where the riddler spells out the thought required of people fast in wisdom (*wīsfæstum menn* 13a) to say what this *wiht* may be.

Such wisdom has proved hard for modern critics, who have offered many conflicting suggestions. Two of the most appealing see the riddle subject as a book made of parchment[11] or an alcoholic drink made from some cereal crop.[12] For the former, the bravura passage describes the violent dousing, washing, stretching, scraping, smoothing, and sanding preparation of the animal skin needed to turn it into parchment. Bitterli nicely matches verb to process: "first the animal skin is 'cut' (*corfen*, 4) 'rubbed' clean (*sworfen*, 4), and soaked and 'turned' (*cyrred*, 4) in the lime bath before it is 'dried' (*þyrred*, 4) and 'bound' (*bunden*, 5) onto a wooden frame so that it can be stretched and 'wound' (*wunden*, 5); next the parchment sheet is 'bleached' (*blæced*, 5) and 'softened' (*wæced*, 5) with pumice stone, 'adorned' (*frætwed*, 6) with ink by the scribe, and finally 'equipped' (*geatwed*, 6) with a binding."[13] In the opening, either the beast (most likely a sheep or cow) is hyperbolically built up as the hardest, sharpest, and fiercest, or these attributes describe the blade used to flay the beautifully adorned one to provide the skin that then is subject to the loud process of manufacture.[14] The whole celebration of a torturous flaying which paradoxically leads to edification resonates with the torture of a saint's body with its paradoxically joyous result, as Bitterli also suggests.[15] The joy that the parchment brings is the

---

11 Parchment was proposed by Waltraud Ziegler, "Ein neuer Lösungsversuch für das altenglische Rätsel Nr. 28," *Arbeiten aus Anglistik und Amerikanistik* 7 (1982): 185–90; endorsed by Hans Pinsker and Waltraud Ziegler, eds. and trans., *Die altenglischen Rätsel des Exeterbuchs* (Heidelberg: Winter, 1985), 212–14, notes to their Riddle 26; and built on by Dieter Bitterli, *Say What I am Called: The Old English Riddles of the Exeter Book and the Anglo-Latin Riddle Tradition* (Toronto: University of Toronto Press, 2009), 178–88, who favours the refinement of an edifying book made from parchment.

12 Tupper, *Riddles*, suggests "ale," and Krapp and Dobbie, *Exeter Book*, accept "beer/ale." Niles, *Enigmatic Poems*, 114–17, refines this to ale and its source, barley.

13 Bitterli, *Say What I am Called*, 184. See the discussion of the energetic process of parchment making in Jonathan Wilcox, ed., *Scraped, Stroked, and Bound: Materially Engaged Readings of Medieval Manuscripts* (Turnhout: Brepols, 2013), and references there.

14 The knife is part of the focus for working the parchment in the analogous edifying book Riddle 26 at lines 5–6.

15 Bitterli, *Say What I am Called*, 178–82, 185–6.

edification contained inside the resulting book, which presumably contains Christian wisdom (like the Gospel-book or Bible of Riddle 26), and which speaks out from the now-dead creature, a paradox of speech and silence, life and death, also explored in Eusebius's riddle on parchment, among other Latin analogues.[16] This dead object made from a living beast offers to living readers eternal life for those who heed the message before their death.

In this reading, the reference to the doors of men (line 7a), punningly picked up by the following *in innan* (line 7b), is a reminder of the door to salvation that the opening of the book can offer. In the ending, the wise riddle solvers are called on to understand what is at stake: the Christian wisdom that the book offers, metaphorically suggesting the eternal life of Christian salvation. For all the violence of construction, the outcome is a happy one, matching a similar paradox in the case of the saint, whose suffering turns to good effect in a kind of Christian comedy. In such a reading, the logic of the bravura rhymes has to do with signalling the wonder of God's creation, celebrating the power of artisans whose activity can have such beneficent effect. The humour of the rhymes and the acoustic effects are an expression of the Christian joy at creation and a celebration of the incongruous paradoxes that allow for life after death.

If, though, the solution is an alcoholic beverage, then the whole poem is far more ironic. The sounds of the bravura passage would now celebrate the threshing and fermentation of the barley to create the alcoholic drink, presumably beer or ale. The opening becomes a somewhat playful metaphorical description of barley growing in the field, with its spiky grain ends making it appear the hardest, the sharpest, the fiercest. The verbs of the bravura production passage are explicated by Niles, who favours the solution *bere ond ealu*, "barley and ale": "The barley is then cut and malted, and reference is made to the process by which it is harvested, then dried, threshed, and turned, then soaked and allowed to germinate before being fermented in the malting house."[17] Tupper matches the description to the John Barleycorn ballad, where "the barley is 'cut by the knee,' 'tied fast,' 'cudgeled full sore,' 'hung up,' 'turned o'er and o'er,' 'heaved in a pit of water,' 'tossed to and fro,' 'wasted o'er a scorching flame,' 'crushed between two stones.'"[18] The joy the riddle subject offers is very much a transitory joy within this world; it clings and lingers in the deceptive perception of those imbibing, or in the unhappy outcome of those who feel the booze's after-effect.

---

16 Eusebius, Enigma 32; see Ziegler, "Ein neuer Lösungsversuch"; Bitterli, *Say What I am Called*, 182–4.

17 Niles, *Enigmatic Poems*, 115.

18 Tupper, *Riddles*, 137.

The death and judgment that the drink offers are presumably meta-phorical, playing with the paradox of a joy which rapidly turns to woe, although Niles sees the bibulous suffering in a judgment scene. The mock-ing tone of the closing taunt suggests that the *wisfæst* ought to know that drink offers a false promise, yet the affliction of those who have been liv-ing for a long time who do not speak against it suggests that age is not a guarantor of wisdom in this respect. The witty critique of the dangers of alcohol matches the neighbouring Riddle 27 with its description of mead. The bravura rhymes of the opening signal the elaborate work and skill that, in this case, is deployed for questionable effect, and the heady sound effects may be replicating the disorienting effect of the subject: dazzling the audience into an altered state through rhyme is somewhat akin to the dazzling effect the alcohol will offer. That effect is comic in the moment, if ultimately questionable. Laughter is directed here at those who unwisely revere drink and also derives from the cleverness of its revelation.

Both these readings account for the bravura rhymes of the opening as an elaborate process of creation and then account for the two key paradoxes of the second half: the contrast between the living and dead (lines 8a, 9a, 11a), and the contrast between not speaking and then judging and speaking after death (lines 10b–12a). Be it book or booze, the riddle catches attention through comic rhyming at the process of production, and thereafter offers either ultimate salvation or a deadly hangover. Given how neatly these two solutions fit the clues on offer, and how each echoes a nearby riddle solu-tion (Riddle 26 is the Bible or Gospel-book, Riddle 27 is mead, and both have overlapping language and concepts), it seems likely that both answers would be offered by a contemporary riddle-solving audience, despite the extremity of the contrast between the two. Whichever interpretation is thought of as the true one, relegating the other to the blind, the extreme difference between the possibilities is appealingly incongruous for read-ings of the same text, and the clashing answers likely expanded the humor-ous effect as different riddle solvers shouted out either Bible or beer.

Unless, of course, the solution is something else entirely. The musicality of the poetic effects might encourage the idea of a musical instrument as the solution. Trautman suggests "harp," Shook suggests "tortoise-lyre" (pointing to Symphosius's Riddle 20), and Williamson suggests "yew-horn," pointing to the wooden horn discovered in the River Erne.[19] A musical instrument works well for the paradox of not speaking alive and

---

19 Moritz Trautmann, "Die Auflösungen der altenglischen Rätsel," *Beiblatt zur Anglia* 5 (1894): 46–51; Laurence K. Shook, "Old-English Riddle 28 — *Testudo* (Tortoise-Lyre)," *Mediaeval Studies* 20 (1958): 93–7; Williamson, *Old English Riddles*, 218–26, notes to his Riddle 26.

metaphorically speaking when dead and crafted. The joy of the music might be an appropriate accompaniment to laughter of merriment. While such solutions have particular appeal for picking up on the sounds, there are difficulties with some of the details. The opening lines do not seem particularly motivated for any of the musical instrument solutions and Williamson, for example, has to insist that the horn is made from the hardest wood, namely yew, the leaves of which are the bitterest and grimmest for being poisonous, which seems oddly tangential.

The possible solution pattern-welded sword, on the other hand, would have very different overtones. Göbel and Göbel match the verbs to the process of manufacturing such hardest, sharpest, and grimmest blades:

> The various kinds of iron were cut to form rods (*corfen*), smoothed (*sworfen*), and partly thinned out into wires which were then twisted (*cyrred*). During his work the smith alternately cooled the metal and then heated it in the forge (dried it: *pyrred*). The various pieces of iron were then bound and wound (*bunden, wunden*) and beaten out again…. The finished blade was then polished (*blæced*) and showed a high degree of elasticity due to the complicated process of production…. Such a springy iron blade is called *wæced* (resilient) in the riddle. The swords were adorned with the pattern-welded design of Damascus steel as well as with the artful shape of their hilts (*frætwed, geatwed*).[20]

In this reading, the sounds of the passage mimic the sound of the blacksmith at work, while the following paradox of speech in death has to do with the words of the proud owner in contrast with the disapprobation of one killed by the riddle subject.

Once again, these two solutions, musical instrument or pattern-welded sword, involve working through the verbs of the process of creation with considerable aplomb, even as both are open to possible objections. Once again, the dichotomy between life-enhancing musical instrument and life-depriving instrument of warfare suggests the possibilities of humorous play through contrasting answers. In all these solutions, modern critics' ingenuity most likely replicates the ingenuity of an early medieval audience. All four solutions explored here have in common the idea of a highly wrought, highly valued object. The sound effects of the rhymes describing its formation play up wonder at the constructedness of the object and are themselves so highly wrought as to invite a smile at their

---

20 Heidi Göbel and Rüdiger Göbel, "The Solution of an Old English Riddle," *Studia Neophilologica* 50 (1978): 185–91, at 190–1.

ingenuity. The broad array of credible solutions shows how this riddle would have been particularly ripe for the febrile atmosphere of riddle solving proposed in any of the communities imagined in this book. In such a set-up, any answer could be greeted by laughter and an attempt at further one-upping.

The very fact that this acoustic plenitude of rhyme occurs within a riddle makes it more likely the exceptional form would contribute to mirth and would be received with laughter. That this is not inevitably so for bravura rhymes is seen in the case of Cynewulf, who, at the end of his poem about St. Helena's finding of the true cross, crafts a purple passage of extended rhyme (*Elene*, lines 1236–51a) describing the power of poetic technique. This comes before a particularly challenging version of his runic signature describing the coming of age and affliction, all in the context of contemplating death and judgment.[21] The rhyming self-referentiality of the contemplation of poetic creation might elicit a smile of acknowledgment by an audience who hears the powerful sound effects and realizes their thematic appropriateness, and the following runic passage might encourage riddle solving as it destabilizes sense, but the context is entirely serious.[22] The incongruities in this case encourage heightened attention in an audience led to eschatological Christian contemplation, but Cynewulf demonstrates that chiming rhyme can be exploited for wholly serious purposes.

One further example of overabundant rhyme provides a more interesting test case in terms of humour. What if a poem that pursues the pattern of happiness followed by grief followed by hints of salvation that is common in the Old English elegies proceeded with a superabundance of rhyme? Such is the case for a poem that bears its most striking attribute in its editorial title, *The Rhyming Poem*. Building on the argument for comic form presented in this chapter, I will suggest that the result was a cause for laughter even in a genre committed to revealing sorrow.

---

21 On the rhetorical heightening, see Cavell, *Weaving Words*, 234–8, 243–4; Samantha Zacher, "Cynewulf at the Interface of Literacy and Orality: The Evidence of the Puns in *Elene*," *Oral Tradition* 17, no. 2 (2002): 346–88. On unlocking the runes, see Niles, *Enigmatic Poems*; Birkett, "Runes and *Revelatio*."

22 See Éamonn Ó Carragáin, "Cynewulf's Epilogue to *Elene* and the Tastes of the Vercelli Compiler: A Paradigm of Meditative Reading," in *Lexis and Texts in Early English: Studies Presented to Jane Roberts*, eds. Christian J. Kay and Louise M. Sylvester (Amsterdam: Rodopi, 2001), 187–201; Thornbury, *Becoming a Poet*, 128–34; Saltzman, *Bonds of Secrecy*, 194–7.

Rhymes to Die By: Funny Form in *The Rhyming Poem*

While the bravura rhymes of Riddle 28 are striking for their acoustical impact, the eighty-seven-line poem in the Exeter Book called by modern editors *The Rhyming Poem* outdoes them by a considerable margin. Rhyme runs throughout in a *tour de force* of form. The language play is so prominent and the form so surprising and so controlling that I will argue that these effects create humour even though this is not the conventional interpretation of the poem and even though the subject matter seems on the surface to be rather sombre, describing loss and death.[23]

The Rhyming Poem tells a story of a joyful past which has given way through sorrow and loss to a miserable present, with thoughts of impending death alleviated by thoughts of Christian salvation.[24] As one of its editors explains: "The poem contrasts the speaker's former happy and prosperous state with his present bitterness, and links his decline to the corruption of the world generally."[25] This movement is broadly similar to that in other, more famous, Old English elegies, such as *The Wanderer* and *The Seafarer*, with which the poem is clustered in the Exeter Book, suggesting that the Old English compiler of that collection saw it in such light.[26] It is generally seen by modern commentators as a weak example of the elegiac genre. The cycle of happiness to misery is worked out in relation to a persona, apparently a king, who is less clearly individuated than in other elegies. Many modern critics suspect that rhyme in this case has got in the way of reason, an assessment well summarized by Klinck: "the exigencies of the form compelled the author to use many rare words, perhaps nonce-words, making the poem obscure, and occasionally, when the problem is compounded by textual corruption, almost impenetrable."[27] An earlier generation of critics were more scathing. Conybeare, its first editor, pointed to the "absurd intricacy of the metre" and observed how the poet

23 Useful editions include O.D. Macrae-Gibson, ed. and trans., *The Old English Riming Poem* (Cambridge: Brewer, 1983); Anne L. Klinck, ed., *The Old English Elegies: A Critical Edition and Genre Study* (Montreal: McGill-Queen's University Press, 1992); Muir, ed., *Exeter Anthology*, 262–5, 570–80; Bjork, *Shorter Poems*, 90–7, with facing page translation.

24 See O.D. Macrae-Gibson, "The Literary Structure of 'The Riming Poem'," *Neuphilologische Mitteilungen* 74 (1973): 62–84; Karl P. Wentersdorf, "The Old English *Rhyming Poem*: A Ruler's Lament," *Studies in Philology* 82 (1985): 265–94; and the editions cited in the note above.

25 Klinck, *Old English Elegies*, 40–1.

26 Muir, *Exeter Anthology*; Niles, *God's Exiles*.

27 Klinck, *Old English Elegies*, 40; see also Anne Klinck, "*The Riming Poem*: Design and Interpretation," *Neuphilologische Mitteilungen* 89 (1988): 266–79.

was "obliged to sacrifice sense to sound, to a more than ordinary extent"; Mackie, in his edition of the Exeter Book, labels it "incoherent babbling"; Pearsall called it "a lunatic exercise," in which "sense, like everything else, is sacrificed to rhyme."[28] Clearly some modern readers consider form that is excessively prominent as simply incompetent.

But what form it is! The poem follows the usual metrical rules of Old English verse, with two stressed half-lines joined by alliteration, and recurringly uses the most stringent version with double alliteration in the a-verse, so that three of the four stressed syllables in each line consistently alliterate. This already tight form is augmented with the additional acoustic effect of rhyme, which is tightly controlled throughout the whole poem. The end of each a-verse rhymes with the end of the b-verse, so that every full verse line not only alliterates three times but also rhymes internally. In many instances, the same rhyme carries across multiple lines, and many times further acoustic effects add to the strong sense of baroque constructedness.

The opening lines demonstrate some of these patterns:

Me lifes onlah   se þis leoht onwrah,
ond þæt torhte geteoh,   tillice onwrah.
Glæd wæs ic gliwum,   glenged hiwum,
blissa bleoum,   blostma hiwum.
(*The Rhyming Poem*, lines 1–4)

He who revealed this light gave me life
and brought forth that brightness, graciously revealed it.
Joyously was I glad, in hues was I clad
in colors of delights, in the blossoms' hues.[29]

The spellings in line 2 and 4 obscure what were probably true rhyming sounds, although the specific forms have occasioned much debate among critics, and many competing emendations have been offered. With that caveat, it is easy to see the consistent alliteration (marked with underlining) and rhyme (marked in bold):

Me lifes onlah   se þis leoht onwrah,
ond þæt torhte geteoh,   tillice onwrah.

---

28 The opinions are assembled and cited by Macrae-Gibson, *OE Riming Poem*, 11–12.
29 The poem is quoted from Muir, ed., *Exeter Anthology*. Because of the manifold challenges in establishing the sense, I here cite the published translation of Bjork, *Shorter Poems*, 91–7.

Glæd wæs ic gliwum,   glenged hiwum,
blissa bleoum,   bloɜtnɪa hiwum.

The rhyme is all the more prominent for twice continuing across two lines for a sequence of four rhymes, while the alliteration is emphasized by the consonant clusters in lines 3 and 4. Incidental effects include the repetition of the prefix syllable *on-* in the first two lines, the grammatical parallelism in many of the half-lines, and the repeated words at the end of each of the line pairs.[30] To translate such a passage meaningfully would require replicating the sound of the language play as much as conveying the semantic value of the words, and such a translation has been crafted by James W. Earl:

My life He lent   who life insent,
Founded the firmament   with fair intent.
Delight-endued   in dresses hued
I was bloom-imbued,   blossoming-hued.[31]

This opening establishes a tight, acoustically notable verse form. This is not just maintained throughout the whole poem, but actually enriched and complicated further. Examples will usefully illustrate some of the remarkable effects.

The poetic persona describes past happiness:

Scrifen scrad glad   þurh gescad in brad,
wæs on lagustreame lad,   þær me leoþu ne biglad.
Hæfde ic heanne had,   ne wæs me in healle gad,   15
þæt þær rof weord rad.   Oft þær rinc gebad,
þæt he in sele sæge   sincgewæge,
þegnum geþyhte.   Þenden wæs ic in mægen,
horsce mec heredon,   hilde generedon,
fægre feredon,   feondon biweredon.   20
Swa mec hyhtgiefu heold,   hygedryht befeold,

---

30 Although the latter is sometimes emended away as scribal error: see, for example, Christopher Abram, "The Errors in *The Rhyming Poem*," *Review of English Studies* 58 (2007): 1–9. The part of speech, and hence the grammatical structure (and sense) is also open to debate, with different editors treating *geteoh* in line 2a as a verb or a noun (with or without emendation).

31 James W. Earl, "Hisperic Style in the Old English 'Rhyming Poem'," *PMLA* 102 (1987): 187–96, corresponding with lines 1–4. This will be provided as a second translation throughout this discussion.

staþolæhtum steold,   stepegongum weold
swylce eorþe ol,   ahte ic ealdorstol,
galdorwordum gol.   Gomen sibbe ne ofoll,
ac wæs gefest gear,   gellende sner,   25
wuniendo wær   wilbec bescær.
Scealcas wæron scearpe,   scyl wæs hearpe,
hlude hlynede,   hleoþor dynede,
sweglrad swinsade,   swiþe ne minsade.
(*The Rhyming Poem*, lines 13–29)

The appointed ship sailed through the passage onto the broad course,
was on the ocean path where the vessel did not fail me.
I had high rank; for me, nothing was lacking in the hall
where the proud troop moved about. A warrior often waited there
in the hall so that he might see the weight of treasure,
useful to retainers. While I was strong,
the brave praised me, protected me in battle,
fairly upheld me, defended me from enemies.
Thus the hope-gift held me, the household retainers
surrounded me, I held the high seat, ruled their goings
as the earth gave nourishment, I possessed the high throne,
sang the words of charms. The joy of peace did not decrease,
but the war was constant in gifts, resounding harp string,
continuing pledge, cut off the river of affliction.
Men were sharp; clear was harp,
loudly it sounded, the sound resounded,
the music melodious, diminished not for us.

Outskipped the slip,   outstripped the rip,
The grey sea's grip   guiding my trip,
In high hallship   had I worship.
Loving lordship   and loyal hoardship
Would not withhold   the weighted gold
From the battle-bold.   Then bore I glory.
Proud men me praised,   proudly upraised,
Defended in frays,   my foes amazed.
So with hopegift halled,   to highseat called,
Thought-troop enthralled   I was throne-installed.
The harvest and the herd   I held in my word,
Kingship I cultured,   kinship ennurtured.
That giftyear gladhand   I granted bookland,
Pledges were planned   that promised to stand.

Strings were sounded,   singing abounded,
The harp was handed   to him who commanded
The stronghold splendid.   Song never ended.

The sentiment here is rather conventional. The persona works through the markers of happy kingship, including distributing treasure and receiving loyalty in amity marked by the sounds of happy song and the harp. The sound effects, on the other hand, are anything but conventional. This excerpt begins with quadruple rhyme in line 13. Rhyme and double alliteration continue with massive prominence throughout, with the same rhyming syllable running across the first four lines here for eight consecutive rhymes, except that the augmentation in line 13 makes for ten rhymes in four lines. The trisyllabic examples at lines 19–20 and 28–9 call particular attention to the rhyme. Rhythmical forms are also repeated and play across many lines. In most Old English poetry, the rhythmical type varies between half lines, but in this poem sixty of the eighty-seven lines comprise half-lines of the same metrical type, with many of the remainder very close.[32] Secondary sound effects abound, with additional assonance and secondary alliteration adding to the prevailing chime of the rhyme. Repeated rhyming sounds will continue to be prominent throughout the poem with nineteen consecutive grammatical rhymes running across lines 28–37. Rhyme here is used in "amazing overwhelming abundance."[33] This is a *tour de force* of sound that will elicit a smile from a poetry-conscious audience at the sheer audacity of the sound.

Almost exactly midway through the poem, at line 43, the persona turns from a happy imagined past to a troubled present. The sound effects continue in full force, as in the following:

Werig winneð,   widsið onginneð,
sar ne sinniþ,   sorgum cinnið,
blæd his blinnið,   blisse linnið,
listum linneð,   lustum ne tinneð.
(*The Rhyming Poem*, lines 51–4)

The weary one labors, the wide journey begins,
pain does not abate, gapes with sorrows,
his renown ceases, he desists from joy,
he parts from skills, goes not at will.

---

32 See Macrae-Gibson, *OE Riming Poem*, 6.
33 Earl, "Hisperic Style," 187.

Too late he learns   what his life earns,
In sorrow discerns   his sorrow's returns.
He sadly sojourns,   ceaselessly yearns,
And still he spurns   his soul's concerns.

Here the sentiment risks being banal, but the rhymes are spectacular, with the single bi-syllabic rhyme continuing across eight half-lines, perhaps the more prominent for the long central consonant, with the slight variation in grammatical rhyme, each rhyming word a verb in a consistent variation of word (or short phrase) followed by verb. This is arrestingly tight audible form.

Sound effects ramp up yet further as the description of woe continues:

Wercyn gewiteð,   wælgar sliteð,
flahmah fliteþ,   flan mon hwiteð,
borgsorg biteð,   bald ald þwiteþ,
wræcfæc wriþað,   wraþ að smiteþ
singryn sidað,   searofearo glideþ,
gromtorn græfeþ,   græft hafað,
(*The Rhyming Poem*, lines 61–6)

The joyous kin departs, the slaughter-spear tears,
the hostilely determined one fights, wickedness polishes the arrow,
sorrow that comes from borrowing gnaws, the bold cuts off the old,
a time of exile fetters, wrath fouls the oath,
continual grief spreads wide, cunning glides,
fears anger mines deep, the grave imprisons

Sin's kindred sighs,   spear fearsome flies,
Knife life denies,   at night light dies,
Fate's hate defies,   fine lines unties,
The breath of death betrays   the bold old one's days,
Sorrow's arrow slays,   the snare near lays,
Rage engages lies,   rip ship destroys.

In a scheme that is already hair-raisingly challenging, the poet has inserted an additional rhyme within each half-line by rhyming the two elements of a compound word, as in *flahmah*, or two neighbouring syllables, as in *bald ald*. The effect is achieved by exploiting the potential for a prominent secondary stress in a half-line of Sievers's type D and E, even if the precise metrical pattern is hard to pin down.[31] Some of the identities of sound are approximate, although these might reflect tighter forms loosened in the course of scribal transmission. In any event, looseness would not spoil the effect since the clanging chiming forms are so audibly established that they would be continued in the mind's ear even when approximate. It is easy to see why Pearsall labelled this a lunatic exercise, although Earl's spectacular translation nicely hints at the appeal of the lunacy. Many of the compound words here are *hapax legomena*: the poet is probably coining new words to fit the pattern. This is in addition to the regular rhyme between half-lines, which itself is retained with a single rhyme across ten half-lines. The effect of such sound-patterning is an extremity of baroque-sounding pyrotechnics.

In a characteristic move of the elegies, the poet finally turns from contemplation of misery to thoughts of the death of the body:

Þonne lichoma ligeð,   lima wyrm friteþ,
ac him wenne gewigeð   ond þa wist geþygeð,
oþþæt beoþ þa ban   an,
ond æt nyhstan nan   nefne se neda tan
balawun her gehloten.   Ne biþ se hlisa adroren.
(*The Rhyming Poem*, lines 75–9)[35]

Then the body will lie, the worm will gnaw the limbs,
and it will experience joy and take the feast,
until all alone there will be naught but bone,
and at the last none except the inescapable lot
appointed for men. That fame will not fall away.

Soulless he sleeps   while the serpent eats,
The worm who wastes,   wallows and feasts
Till be there bone,   alone.
And now is none   but necessity's own,
Evilly allotted.   Honour is not departed.

The formal effects continue. There is a surely deliberate break-down with that oh-so-felicitous incompleteness in line 77, "oþþæt beoþ þa ban an."

---

34 Macrae-Gibson, *OE Riming Poem*, 7, suggests a modified version of Sievers A2 and D types.
35 Muir, ed., *Exeter Anthology*, fills out line 77b to "gebrosnad on an."

Thornbury demonstrates that metrical trouble begins at line 75 and that the first half-line of line 77 would already feel light since it lacks the requisite double alliteration. As she aptly puts it, by line 77b "the worms have eaten the verse."[36]

The poet closes out with exhortation to contemplate the joys of heaven:

þær moncyn mot   for meotude rot
soðne god geseon,   ond aa in sibbe gefean.
(*The Rhyming Poem*, lines 86–7)

where mankind, glad before the measurer, will be allowed
to see the true God and always rejoice in peace.

Where mankind might   in the Maker's sight
Find God's favour   forever and ever.

And so the poem comes rhymingly to its end with a brief homiletic conclusion.

The whole poem, then, enacts the thought-world and many of the images familiar from the Old English elegies, augmented by some traditions of homiletic poetry, but does all this in a form that is unparalleled in Old English and that screamingly calls attention to itself. That form is so controlling, and the language so difficult, that it is fiendishly difficult to translate.[37] It must have been even more difficult to create, and that, of course, is the point. Earl celebrates the characteristics that hostile critics regret, pointing to the playfully erudite poetic obscurantism of the style and suggesting that it is not a problem if the verse form leads to distortion, since "distortion is the point here. By imposing such stringent formal demands on himself, the poet willingly gives himself over to linguistic play…. It is not desperation but wit."[38]

Earl himself revels in the puns and difficulties as well as in the baroque form. He explains line 13 with its quadruple rhyme, quoted above, as "not so much a puzzle to solve as a host of ambiguities to relish." His explanation is worth citing at length:

Gescad means "distinction" or "separation" as well as "reason." The immediate context here, established by *lagustreame* ("sea-stream") in the next

---

36 Thornbury, "Light Verse," 93–4.
37 See James W. Earl, "A Translation of 'The Rhyming Poem'," *Old English Newsletter* 19, no. 1 (Fall 1985): 31–3, in addition to Earl, "Hisperic Style."
38 Earl, "Hisperic Style," 191.

line, has to do with the sea; the larger context is the growth of a child into adulthood, for which this momentary reference to a sea voyage would seem to be metaphorical. In this larger context of growing up, *gescad* could comfortably mean "reason"; but in the immediate context it could also refer to the narrow channel that leads into the open sea.… Now what of the peculiar word *scrad*? If we keep in mind both the metaphorical meaning of the sea imagery – the growth of a child – and the vegetation and clothing images that dominate the first twelve lines of the poem, *scrad* has a broad range of interesting connotations here.… The poet has given us a hapax legomenon that may well be a nonsense syllable associated with several clusters of appropriate meanings.… In the end, we have no satisfactory "trot" for such a line. On one level it means "the appointed shrouds glided through the channel into the broad sea"; on another, "the chosen slip of a boy moved through reason into the wide open world of adult-hood"; and there are many other glosses as well.[39]

Such complexities are also opportunities for interpretation, best relished by the kind of puzzle-solving community posited for the riddles and the proverbial and runic challenges already considered in this study

One further interpretation by Earl will help confirm the point. For line 34,

Treow telgade   tir welgade

he points to the clear pun on *treow* as both "truth, loyalty" in parallel with *tir*, and the other sense of the word as "tree," which is picked up by the uniquely surviving following verb, itself "certainly derived from *telga*, which means a "branch" or "root," and so is probably a coinage meaning "to put forth shoots."" Earl suggests how this pun has expanding ramifications: "The following line, 'blæd blissade,' partakes in the pun too; for *blæd* means not only 'prosperity' but also 'leaf' or 'blade' (as in a blade of grass) and 'flower' or 'fruit'.… Given these puns, is it going too far to point out that 'tir welgade' 'glory enriched' might contain a hidden *welig*, a willow? and that the following stave 'gold gearwade' 'gold was prepared' might contain a hidden *gearwe*, a yarrow?"[40] Such a flourish of puns gives a good sense of how an appreciative audience would likely be discussing possibilities and talking through playful linguistic complexity with laughter.

---

39 Earl, 193–4.
40 Earl, 193.

The complexities of such form can be condemned or delighted in, and recent critics have been more appreciative than those of the past. Davis points to the riddling effect of the poem, relating the enigmatic first-person and juxtaposed states of existence to Riddle 26 (the Bible or Gospel-book), where a creature is transformed into an edifying function. For Davis, the point of *The Rhyming Poem* is essentially celebratory in a self-conscious and yet serious way that ties in to the linguistic self-consciousness explored in the previous chapter: "Far from looking backward and confirming lament, the poem offers its own writing as the reverse of a life to death process, as testimony to the potential honour of a life and thus the possibility of salvation."[41] She sees the frustrations of the poem's surface form as part of the effect: "Its constant rhyme and quick, regular metre speed the poem forward, yet this movement is resisted by the poem's arresting wordplay and contorted syntax, generating tension between the rushing movement of transient time and the suspense of that movement." I am suggesting that such tension frustrates expectations in a way that allows for the creation of humour.

In another perceptive recent treatment, Thornbury explores the poem as an example of formal light verse, that is verse "in which meter has been reified" and language is obliged to conform to form. Thornbury points to the coinages and rare usages in *The Rhyming Poem* to show how the stringent form "prompts poet and audience to view words as malleable." She shows how the poet bends language to fit the metre, concluding, "Form does not obscure the *Rhyming Poem*'s meaning: form *produces* its meaning."[42] I am suggesting that such triumph of form over content is itself an incongruity that is funny.

There are analogues for this kind of elaborate linguistic play in surrounding poetic traditions. A likely inspiration for the form is the playful obscurantism of the hermeneutic (or hisperic) style of much Anglo-Latin poetry of the period: fiendishly difficult word-play, obscure linguistic borrowings, and unreasonable-seeming constraints are all features of this learned Latin style.[43] This does not in itself generate humour, particularly once this becomes an expected convention, but the potential is there. Another parallel occurs in Old Norse. Egill Skallagrímson's *Hǫfuðlausn*, "Head-Ransom," is the poem he composes (according to *Egils saga*) on

---

41 Kathleen Davis, "Old English Lyrics: A Poetics of Experience," in *The Cambridge History*, 332–56, quotations from 341 and 340.
42 Thornbury, "Light Verse," 88, 90, 95.
43 Earl, "Hisperic Style"; see also Michael Lapidge, "The Hermeneutic Style in Tenth-Century Anglo-Latin Literature," *Anglo-Saxon England* 4 (1975): 67–111; Rosalind Love, "Insular Latin Literature to 900," in *The Cambridge History*, 120–57.

inadvertently falling into the hands of his archenemy, Eirik Bloodaxe, at York. He needs something exceptionally showy to impress a leader who has sworn to kill him and has many reasons to do so. The resulting poem in praise of Eirik takes Old Norse Eddic poetic form, which is already strikingly tight, and ups the stakes by adding additional consistent rules of rhyme and assonance. The result is a poem so aurally striking that even his archenemy is wowed by it, although many have assumed Eirik's response of "that was well recited" is a comic jab, suggesting that the dedicatee failed to understand a praise poem that in content is mostly a sequence of commonplaces mixed with self-praise strung together with impressive sound.[44] Egil's recital takes place in the middle of the tenth century, which is approximately the date most commentators assume for *The Rhyming Poem*. Since these two outliers from their tradition create their sound effects in analogous ways, some critics have assumed that one borrows form from the other (with both directions posited), even as the current consensus is that both take inspiration from the rhymed Latin hymnal tradition and possibly hermeneutic Latin style.[45] For my purposes, Egil's example is of particular interest for the hint that deployment of the form could be part of an elaborate joke.

Building on Thornbury's insight, I am arguing that, as with other examples of light verse, the extreme control of the metrical pattern itself makes for humour. The exuberance of form in *The Rhyming Poem* is so outré, and so much at variance from expectation, that form alone would make this poem seem funny in the sense of humorous as well as in the sense of peculiar. The incongruity here is of language too audibly fitting to an imposed and unlikely metrical constraint. It is probably relevant that the genre of elegy to which the poem belongs is so strongly marked as to be well established for a modern audience and presumably for a medieval one, too. *The Rhyming Poem* fulfills the tropes of the genre with relatively familiar, perhaps even bland, details. That makes understanding the content relatively undemanding, leaving the audience free to gasp at the sound and find it funny. It may seem improbable that an audience would laugh at an account of earthly discomfort and impending death, but this will prove a surprisingly common focus for humour in heroic or hagiographic literature (see chapters 4 and 7 below). As in saints' lives, the movement of the elegiac genre is an ultimately happy one as present sorrow leads to a focus

---

44 See John Hines, "Egill's *Hǫfuðlausn* in Time and Place," *Saga-Book* 24 (1995): 83–104; Matthew Townend, "Pre-Cnut Praise-Poetry in Viking Age England," *Review of English Studies* 51 (2000): 349–70.

45 See, especially, Klinck, *"Riming Poem"*; Klinck, *Old English Elegies*.

on ultimate salvation. The playfully erudite poetic obscurantism and the exuberant excess of acoustic form encourage the audience to an appropriate reaction of laughing in the face of death.

In Modern English verse, the potential for humour is dulled by the long tradition of rhyme as a controlling metrical feature, but sufficient excess can re-establish comedy from form alone. The comic potential of excessive rhyme can be nicely illustrated from a playful example by a Romantic poet. "The Cataract of Lodore" by Robert Southey (1774–1843) is worth quoting at some length to establish the cumulative effect of a plenitude of rhyme:

"How does the water
Come down at Lodore?"
…
From its sources which well
In the tarn on the fell;
From its fountains
In the mountains,
Its rills and its gills;
Through moss and through brake,
It runs and it creeps
For a while, till it sleeps
In its own little lake.
…
Collecting, projecting,
Receding and speeding,
And shocking and rocking,
And darting and parting,
And threading and spreading,
And whizzing and hissing,
And dripping and skipping,
And hitting and splitting,
And shining and twining,
And rattling and battling,
And shaking and quaking,
And pouring and roaring,
And waving and raving,
And tossing and crossing,
And flowing and going,
And running and stunning,
And foaming and roaming,
And dinning and spinning,
And dropping and hopping,

And working and jerking,
And guggling and struggling,
And heaving and cleaving,
And moaning and groaning;
And glittering and frittering,
And gathering and feathering,
And whitening and brightening,
And quivering and shivering,
And hurrying and skurrying,
And thundering and floundering;
Dividing and gliding and sliding,
And falling and brawling and sprawling,
And driving and riving and striving,
And sprinkling and twinkling and wrinkling,
And sounding and bounding and rounding,
And bubbling and troubling and doubling,
And grumbling and rumbling and tumbling,
And clattering and battering and shattering;
Retreating and beating and meeting and sheeting,
Delaying and straying and playing and spraying,
Advancing and prancing and glancing and dancing,
Recoiling, turmoiling and toiling and boiling,
And gleaming and streaming and steaming and beaming,
And rushing and flushing and brushing and gushing,
And flapping and rapping and clapping and slapping,
And curling and whirling and purling and twirling,
And thumping and plumping and bumping and jumping,
And dashing and flashing and splashing and clashing;
And so never ending, but always descending,
Sounds and motions for ever and ever are blending
All at once and all o'er, with a mighty uproar, -
And this way the water comes down at Lodore.
(Robert Southey [1774–1843] from "The Cataract of Lodore,"
Poetry Foundation website)

This dizzying example is a particularly appealing analogy, as it uses some of the very same structural effects as the Old English *Rhyming Poem* in elevating sound over content, with ever-more elaborate self-imposed structural constraints. It is not that a waterfall is a particularly funny subject, but rather the sheer exuberance of the poem's form is funny, and the conventional subject matter contributes by leaving the audience free to appreciate the sounds. Incongruity springs from a formal excess that breaks with any possible sense of measure in language and pushes towards displaying rhyme and synonymy to an almost impossible extreme. The incongruity is in language that obeys the rules of form over those of meaning and efficiency. Settling on the sense of such *esprit de formes* is less important than revelling in the sound and laughing at how language can do more than merely make sense. That is the effect of *The Rhyming Poem*, too.

A Laughing Community of Poetry Connoisseurs

The extended rhyme of this chapter is a *tour de force* of form that would be particularly appreciated by an audience well attuned to Old English verse conventions. Such audiences were probably very common. Whereas writing and runic knowledge were the domain of scholars and ecclesiasts, listening to and appreciating poetry would have been massively widespread, with poetry appreciators in all classes of society. Such experience only gets recorded, though, in exceptional circumstances. I will end this chapter with a grounding in two appreciators of poetry who were so exceptional that their experience was preserved: King Alfred in his youth, and the humble cowherd Cædmon. The two constitute a valuably contrasting pair in their differing positions in society, and so their receptivity to vernacular poetry can stand in for many others.

A nuanced sense of King Alfred's appreciation for poetry is preserved in the famous biography written by Asser. Asser recounts how, as a youth, and before he could read, Alfred:

> was a careful listener, by day and night, to English poems, most frequently hearing them recited by others, and he readily retained them in his memory....
>
> One day, therefore, when his mother was showing him and his brothers a book of English poetry which she held in her hand, she said: "I shall give this book to whichever one of you can learn it the fastest." Spurred on by these words, or rather by divine inspiration, and attracted by the beauty of the initial letter in the book, Alfred spoke as follows in reply to his mother, forestalling his brothers (ahead in years, though not in ability).... [He clarifies the challenge and the reward.] He immediately took the book from her hand, went to his teacher and learnt it. When it was learnt, he took it back to his mother and recited it.
>
> (Asser's *Life of King Alfred*, chaps. 22–3)[46]

---

46 William Henry Stevenson, ed., *Asser's Life of King Alfred*, with an intro. by Dorothy Whitelock (Oxford: Oxford University Press, 1959), 20; translation from Simon Keynes and Michael Lapidge, trans., *Alfred the Great: Asser's Life of King Alfred and Other Contemporary Sources* (Harmondsworth: Penguin, 1983), 75.

The anecdote has many implications. A pre-literate Alfred is attracted by the written book, apparently drawn to it by the visual beauty of the illuminated initial. He commits an act characteristic of an oral culture – memorizing a notable amount of text after hearing it – motivated by a very literate prize – the book itself. As son of the king, Alfred has privileged access to a teacher, as well as to such a prize, and Asser is concerned, in his semi-hagiographic style, to establish Alfred's inspired way with learning that will next see him learn the divine offices of the monastic hours and then certain psalms and many prayers (chap. 24), thereby establishing the king's holy credentials. Asser is anticipating Alfred's love of learning that will lead him to gather the group of learned advisors with whom he will translate into English those works that are most necessary for all people to know.[47]

For all that, there is little reason to doubt the credibility of Alfred's enthusiasm for English verse. The story hints at the multiple communities within which he might have listened to poetry and discussed it without needing to read, explicitly with his teacher, potentially with his brothers (who are the competitors that he outsmarts in this story), and certainly with his mother. In addition to this family context, Asser suggests that hearing poetry has been a recurring part of his life in view of the placing comment that he was habituated to listening to poems "by day and night … most frequently hearing them recited by others" ("die noctuque solers auditor, relatu aliorum saepissime audiens"). Alfred was a member of multiple communities of listeners long before he adopted the more learned community of scholar-helper-readers. The latter group constitutes another example of *rynemenn*, a learned community that would have enjoyed learned riddles and the code-switching challenges of the runes and the interpretation of proverbs seen in the previous chapters. Alfred's earlier community of listeners are not marked as literate, even as he and they enjoyed the poetry, and presumably attended to the poetic technique as they listened. These enthusiasts would likely laugh in appreciation at the formal exuberance of Riddle 28 and *The Rhyming Poem*.

Such laughing communities of poetry appreciators need not be confined to the elite. At the other end of the social spectrum lie the agricultural workers of Hild's double monastery at Whitby who assembled as a group when a cause of mirth was declared. The well-known story of their poetry appreciation is told by Bede in his *Ecclesiastical History of the English People* in order to show the miracle of the first Christian poet.[48] The build-up

---

47 Asser, chaps. 76–88; Alfred's Preface to the Old English translation of Gregory's *Cura Pastoralis*, available in Keynes and Lapidge, *Alfred*, 124–7, and widely elsewhere.

48 Book IV, chap. 24; Bertrand Colgrave and R.A.B. Mynors, eds. and trans., *Bede's Ecclesiastical History of the English People* (Oxford: Oxford University Press, 1993).

to the miracle nicely suggests a more quotidian context of poetic recital. As described in the Old English translation, because he had not learned any poetry, Cædmon showed his customary and repeated shyness when he saw the harp approach:

> in gebeorscipe, þonne þær wæs blisse intinga gedemed, þæt heo ealle sceoldon þurh endebyrdnesse be hearpan singan.[49]

> in beer-drinking, when there was deemed to be a cause of joy, that they should all sing in turn alongside the harp.

This is a domestic and secular scene, albeit on a monastic estate, as is clear from Bede's insistence that Cædmon had not yet taken orders and in his subsequent retreat to the cow-shed. When commanded by a divine figure in a dream, he proves capable of telling the story of creation in verse, which might suggest to a rationalizing audience that he had listened to enough performances of poetry to internalize the metrical patterns. The other participants at the *gebeorscipe* provide evidence that such poetic performances were unremarkable at such a communal gathering. Excepting Cædmon, each participant was confident enough to take their turn reciting, suggesting they had either memorized some poems (potentially including Old English riddles) or they had internalized command of Old English poetic technique enough to sing something new. Their gathering *in gebeorscipe* (in beer-drinking) suggests that the mead-hall image for communitarian listening and banter need not be limited to the masculine martial elite. The agricultural workers at Whitby are an audience that would surely laugh at the agonistic challenge of the riddles and smile at the incongruity of the metrical *tours de force* in Riddle 28 or *The Rhyming Poem*.

Asser attributes to Alfred an exceptional literary skill, and Bede sees Cædmon provided with a miraculous ability in his subsequent creation of religious verse, but the qualities of listening to and appreciating poetry presumably went unrecorded for countless others. Riddle 28 and *The Rhyming Poem* are deeply exceptional in their form, but laughing at their deviation from the norm is likely to have been a pleasure for any of the many experienced listeners to poetry in early medieval England.

---

49 The story is widely anthologized; here cited from Baker, *Introduction*, 211.

Chapter Four

Heroic Humour:
Comic Insouciance and
Embarrassments of Etiquette

This chapter will consider the humour that runs through some of the most famous literature from early medieval England, the heroic literature of combat and honour. Like so much else, this world, too, is touched on in Old English riddles, some of which feature the martial world of valour and violence, glory and gory, that is the norm of heroic literature. The riddles contribute to that world in such a slant way as to be comic and, in the process, often hint at a critique of values that are normally celebrated in heroic poetry. This is particularly apparent in some riddles that portray weapons of war as if they were humans, as when a foot-soldier can regret that he need not expect the comfort of doctoring despite his skilful resistance (in the shield of Riddle 5) or a soldier who will not obey anyone when unbound, even as he is skilful at his deadly craft when bound (in the bow of Riddle 23).[1] Casual violence and implied pain is turned to comedy because the speaking and complaining subject proves to be no more than an inanimate implement. There is humour in the insouciance expressed in the face of danger, which is an element that runs through much heroic literature. The incongruity carries a satiric edge, too, since the speaking object which becomes a subject through the trick of prosopopeia gives lightly masked voice to the human who deploys the riddling implement, creating momentary sympathy for those at the lower end of heroic hierarchies.[2]

---

1 On these riddles as a group, see Edward B. Irving, Jr., "Heroic Experience in the Old English Riddles," in *Old English Shorter Poems: Basic Readings*, ed. Katherine O'Brien O'Keeffe (New York: Garland, 1994), 199–212; E.G. Stanley, "Heroic Aspects of the Exeter Book Riddles," in *Prosody and Poetics in the Early Middle Ages: Essays in Honor of C. B. Hieatt*, ed. M.J. Toswell (Toronto: University of Toronto Press, 1995), 197–218.
2 For more, see my "Objects that Object, Subjects that Subvert: Agency in Exeter Book Riddle 5," *Humanities* 11, no. 2 (2022): 33.

The social critique advanced by such humour will be the concern of the second half of this chapter.

One riddle makes the point particularly well. Riddle 20, while regrettably incomplete due to the loss of a leaf from the Exeter Book, is generally solved as sword. In this case, a speaking and sentient subject that has opinions and feelings and sounds like a well-rewarded, particularly loyal hall-retainer turns out to be a mere implement of warfare. The paradox of an object that speaks has a built-in incongruity that is always likely to evoke amusement in an audience. This speaker is particularly insouciant about killing and causing harm, both at his lord's behest and also "æt his freonde" ("near, at, *or* by means of his friend," 16a), suggesting a certain danger for friend as well as foe in such comic boasting. There is also a surprising amount of comedy of manners as the speaker regrets not having children unless he is disloyal to his lord (perhaps because a sword will only get melted down and recycled if it fails in battle, but suggesting a human follower who gives up family to be a hall-thane), and the subject-object regrets being chided by the woman he angers (with hints of a phallic boast) just before the poem breaks off incomplete. Riddle 20 presents humour with an edge, as the speaking and boasting sword/retainer demonstrates and satirizes the human cost of the system of martial glory, and this edge will be seen in some of the material in this chapter.

The Insouciance of Heroes

Insouciance in the face of threat is a common trope of heroic literature and the display is often appropriately inappropriate enough to generate humour through the incongruity between adversity and response. Such an attitude serves to build up the character of the hero. A minor example in a short fragmentary text will establish the point. While the corpus of heroic literature in Old English is thin and, for the most part, sombre, one of the few surviving pieces starts with a joke, at least in its present fragmentary state. *The Finnsburh Fragment* begins:

> Hleoþrode ða,   heaþogeong cyning:
> "Ne ðis ne dagað eastan,   ne her draca ne fleogeð,
> ne her ðisse healle   hornas ne byrnað,
> ac her forþ berað;   fugelas singað,
> gylleð græghama,   guðwudu hlynneð,
> scyld scefte oncwyð.   Nu scyneð þes mona
> waðol under wolcnum;   nu arisað weadæda
> ðe ðisne folces nið   fremman willað.
> Ac onwacnigeað nu,   wigend mine,

habbað eowre linda,   hicgeaþ on ellen,
winnað on orde,   wesað on mode!"
(*Finnsburh Fragment*, lines 2–12)[3]

The battle-young king then made a speech:
"This is not day dawning from the east, nor is a dragon flying here,
nor here are the gables of this hall burning,
but here we will bear forward; birds will be singing,
the grey-coated one will howl, the battle-wood will resound,
shield will respond to shaft. Now this moon shines
wandering under the clouds; now woeful deeds will arise
which will carry out this people's enmity.
But wake up now, my warriors,
take your linden-shields, think about valour,
fight at the front, be in high spirits!"

The situation portrayed here can be inferred from the rest of the fragment and from allusions to the same story within *Beowulf* (lines 1063–159).[4] Faced with a night-attack, Hnæf, the young leader of a party of Danes visiting Frisia, comments on what is not happening. He then observes that the beasts of battle and the implements of war will soon be making their sounds in view of the hostility he is able to see by the shimmering light of the moon. Finally, the business of the speech kicks in at lines 10–12 as Hnæf commands his warriors to wake up and reach for their shields and for their courage.

That command seems like a rational reaction for a battle leader in potentially hostile territory facing a nighttime attack. The opening of the speech, though, is altogether less efficient – startlingly so in view of the presumable need for rapid action. Rather than getting to business, Hnæf engages with three possible sources of a glimmer of light in order to deny them: day is not dawning in the east, a dragon is not passing by sending forth fire, and the roof of the hall is not burning. This is an extreme form of litotes, describing what is happening by denying what is not happening. There is a significant disproportion between the need for a rapid response and the leisure of the enumeration established by the broad range of the list, which is almost infinitely extensible (e.g. nor are the surrounding bushes on fire, nor is a smith working on forging metal, nor has a volcano erupted, etc.).

---

3 Cited from Fulk et al., *Klaeber's Beowulf*, 283. The text survives only in the 1705 edition by Hickes and has required numerous emendations by different editors. In addition to the lacunae at beginning and end, there is probably something missing before line 5.
4 See Fulk et al., *Klaeber's Beowulf*, 273–9, and commentary on lines 1063–159.

This is striking incongruity of pacing likely to generate a smile in an audience as it catches on to the trick.

Such startling inefficiency does not make Hnæf look like a bad battle leader. On the contrary, the dilatory nature of the call to action builds him up precisely because it allows him to show insouciance in the face of danger. The humour of such an inappropriately slow response to battle turns out to be a recurring feature of this kind of narrative.[5] Such a leisurely periphrasis allows a battle leader to show that he has accurately appraised the situation and understands the threat, to convey that threat to his men and to the audience, and yet to do so without sounding threatened. A leader who gets to joke under pressure demonstrates the kind of carefreeness beloved of heroic narrative and this particular trick allows him both to convey the pressure and the insouciance with a certain lightness of touch.

A different version of this comic insouciance is particularly apparent among heroes in Old Norse sagas, who often deploy a kind of sardonic humour to display fearlessness in the face of death through last words that are notable for not engaging in the emotions the occasion would seem to warrant.[6] The last words of Atli in *Grettir's Saga* provide a paradigmatic example, as he comments, "Broad spears are now in fashion," as he receives his death-wound from the thrust of one.[7] In the attack on Gunnar in *Njal's Saga*, Thorgrim climbs onto the roof to discover whether the hero is at home, is stabbed through the thatch, and makes it back to Gizur, leader of the attackers:

> Gizur looked up at him and asked, "Is Gunnar at home?"
> "That's for you to find out," replied Thorgrim, but I know that his halberd certainly is."
> And with that he fell dead.[8]

---

5 See Patrick Sims Williams, "'Is It Fog or Smoke or Warriors Fighting? Irish and Welsh Parallels to the *Finnsburg* Fragment," *Bulletin of the Board of Celtic Studies* 27 (1978): 505–14. *Klaeber's Beowulf*, 286, calls it a commonplace.

6 Such humour in Old Norse literature of Viking activity is nicely analysed by Tom Shippey, *Laughing Shall I Die: Lives and Deaths of the Great Vikings* (London: Reaktion, 2018). See, also, my "Famous Last Words: Ælfric's Saints Facing Death," *Essays in Medieval Studies* 10 (1993): 1–13.

7 Guðni Jónsson, ed., *Grettis saga Ásmundarsonar* (Reykjavik: Íslenzka Fornrit, 1936), chap. 45 (p. 146): "Þau tíðkast nú in breiðu spjótin"; translation from Jesse Byock, trans., *Grettir's Saga* (Oxford: Oxford University Press, 2009), chap. 45 (p. 122). For further examples, see Shippey, *Laughing Shall I Die*.

8 Magnus Magnusson and Hermann Palsson, trans., *Njal's Saga* (London: Penguin, 1960), chap. 77 (p. 169).

The punctilious precision of Thorgrim's answer signals through a joke his sang-froid and lack of self-pity at a moment when he might be expected to show either self-concern or, in the convention of last words, transcendental wisdom. The cool treatment of a climactic moment in such an anticlimactic way is an appropriate inappropriateness to craft sardonic humour.

Old English heroic literature may not deploy precisely this comic trick, but Hnæf in the *Finnsburh Fragment* is not the only leader to establish his cool with the use of sardonic verbal humour. The Old English heroic poem in celebration of the tenth-century English defeat in Essex, *The Battle of Maldon*, centres on a moment of stasis as the opposing forces face off across the River Pante (the Blackwater estuary). Because of the tidal river, the two sides are unable to attack each other but they are able to parlay. The exchange between an unnamed Viking messenger and the English leader, Byrhtnoth, is rich in aggressive humour by both parties. The Viking messenger offers to hold off from battle if Byrhtnoth will buy off the Viking forces in language that is laced with insult:

"Me sendon to þe   sæmen snelle,
heton ðe secgan   þæt þu most sendan raðe
beagas wið gebeorge;   and eow betere is
þæt ge þisne garræs   mid gafole forgyldon,
þonne we swa hearde   hilde dælon.
Ne þurfe we us spillan,   gif ge spedaþ to þam;
we willað wið þam golde   grið fæstnian.
Gyf þu þæt gerædest   þe her ricost eart,
þæt þu þine leoda   lysan wille,
syllan sæmannum   on hyra sylfra dom
feoh wið freode   and niman frið æt us,
we willaþ mid þam sceattum   us to scype gangan,
on flot feran,   and eow friþes healdan."
(*Battle of Maldon*, lines 29–41)[9]

"Bold seamen sent me to you,
commanded me to tell you that you may quickly send
rings in return for protection; and it will be better for you all
that you buy off this spear-rush with tribute
than that we share battle so hardily.
We don't have to kill each other, if you are prosperous enough;

---

9 D.G. Scragg, ed., *The Battle of Maldon* (Manchester: Manchester University Press, 1981), 58.

we want to secure peace in return for that gold.
If you agree to that, you who are richest here,
that you want to redeem your people,
give to the seamen in their own judgment
wealth in return for peace, and take a truce from us,
we will take ourselves to our ships with those treasures,
depart onto the sea, and keep a truce with you."

The speech is dripping with defiance, often expressed through a comic mode.[10] The messenger's offer – *beagas wið gebeorge*, "rings in return for protection" – is not an honourable option for an English battle leader to pick up, even if it was increasingly the policy of King Æthelred in the wake of this battle defeat.[11] The messenger wittily inserts a wedge between the leader and his troops as he moves between singular you, *þu/þe*, and plural you, *ge/eow*. In line 30, he is asking Byrhtnoth, singular, to send the treasure (or, more insultingly, saying that he *most*, "might/would be allowed to"[12] send treasure), even as stopping the impending battle would be better for you plural (lines 31b–33). At line 36, he turns to the leader as the individual who must make the agreement, picking him out through a loaded periphrasis: "þu ... þe her ricost eart" ("you ... who are here the most powerful," would normally be the sense of the Old English *ricost*, but it is tempting to see here an early instance of what will become the subsequent sense of the word, "you ... who are here the richest"), with the hint that any settlement money will come out of the hide of the leader, not the assembled and listening troops. The underlying offer, "niman frið æt us" ("to take a truce from us"), is rhetorically formed to be unpalatable in view of the prepositional clause. The messenger is aiming to unpick English unit cohesion while going through the motions of a parlay that wittily asserts Viking superiority.

To which provocation, Byrhtnoth does what any good leader needs to do: he out-rhetorics his opponent's rhetoric with a display of verbal wit that shows he understands what is at stake and is still capable of both insouciance and defiance (*Battle of Maldon*, lines 45–61). Byrhtnoth replies not

---

10 Many commentators have observed the rhetorical power here, such as Fred C. Robinson, "Some Aspects of the *Maldon* Poet's Artistry," *The Journal of English and Germanic Philology* 75 (1976): 25–40; Shippey, "Grim Wordplay."

11 See, *inter alia*, Simon Keynes, "The Historical Context of the Battle of Maldon," in *The Battle of Maldon, AD 991*, ed. Donald Scragg (Oxford: Blackwell, 1991), 81–113.

12 See Scragg, *Maldon*, 69, note to line 30.

as an individual but for the people as a whole: "Gehyrst þu, sælida, hwæt
þis folc segeð?" ("Do you hear, seafarer, what this people say?" 45). He
mimics the Viking messenger's play with second-person pronoun number, first addressing himself specifically to the messenger (you singular,
line 45) but thereafter associating him with the full Viking force that will
not avail (*eow*, you plural, line 46 on). He picks up the Viking's insulting
word *gafol* ("tribute") and returns it (at lines 46 and 61), improving on it
with a specific term for the tax of war-gear paid to a lord on the death of
a retainer, *heregeatu* (the heriot, at line 48), but with the clear implication
that the weapons will be presented with point and edge first, that is, as
implements deployed in battle, rather than as a gift to avoid battle.[13] This
is witty one-upping.

Byrhtnoth establishes a clear tone of sarcasm in his reply:

> To heanlic me þinceð
> þæt ge mid urum sceattum   to scype gangon
> unbefohtene,   nu ge þus feor hider
> on urne eard   in becomon.
> (*Battle of Maldon*, lines 55b–58)

> It seems too miserable to me
> that you take yourselves back to your ships with our treasures
> unfought, now that you have come thus far
> hither into our land.

Again, he is echoing the wording of the Viking messenger, with mock-
concern for the group's far travelling. The sarcasm of his speech is
stressed through the delay of the post-positioned, climactic *unbefohtene*
at line 57a. Witty verbal sparring anticipates the impending play of battle (*grim guðplega*, "grim battle-play" 61a), which the poem proceeds to
narrate. In the subsequent battle, when Byrhtnoth is cut down, his fall
comes immediately after his laughter, which expresses a spirit of defiance and sardonic scorn rather than reflecting a response to humour,[14]
but the verbal artistry he displays earlier shows how wry humour is
valued in heroic literature, building up the agonistic spirit of successful
warrior-leaders.

---

13 See Nicholas P. Brooks, "Arms, Status and Warfare in Late-Saxon England," in *Ethelred
the Unready*, ed. David Hill (Oxford: BAR, 1978), 81–103.
14 See, in particular, Niles, "Byrhtnoth's Laughter."

Comic Insouciance in *Beowulf*

Such humour of insouciance is occasionally seen in *Beowulf*. Perhaps the clearest example revolves around Beowulf's orders for the disposing of his body were he to fail in his fight with Grendel. When Beowulf anticipates this fight in speaking to Hrothgar, he lays out the ease of bodily disposal with a joking tone:

> Na þu minne þearft
> hafalan hydan,   ac he me habban wile
> dreore fahne,   gif mec deað nimeð:
> byreð blodig wæl,   byrgean þenceð,
> eteð angenga   unmurnlice,
> mearcað morhopu –   no ðu ymb mines ne þearft
> lices feorme   leng sorgian.
> (*Beowulf*, lines 445–51)[15]

You will not need
to hide my head, but he will have me
salted with gore, if death takes me;
he will bear off the bloody corpse, he will intend to taste it,
the solitary-walker will eat me unmourningly,
stain the moor-retreats – you will not need to sorrow longer
for the feeding of my body.

The incongruity here first derives from an adversary who eats those whom he kills. This is clearly contrary to the usual etiquette of early medieval (and most) battle poetry, but does have the incidental benefit of solving the need to tend to the corpse. The language deployed by Beowulf plays up the paradox with a pun: the monster intends to *byrgean* (448b) a body that he has made bloody, which here carries the sense of "taste" rather than the equally possible and more appropriate in context sense of "bury."[16] The table manners of the human-consuming adversary add to the humour. Beowulf imagines a bloody end for himself, which would provide good sauce for Grendel's palate, if also making his domestic arrangements rather messy (*mearcað morhopu*, "stain

---

15 All citations are from Fulk et al., *Klaeber's Beowulf*. Translations are attentive to the commentary and glossary of this edition.

16 DOE has two distinct entries for the verb at the centre of the pun: *byrgan* 1 "to bury (someone)"; *byrgan* 2 "to taste, partake of (food or drink)."

the moor-retreats"). The unsentimental imagination of the disposal of his own body establishes Beowulf's insouciance with comic incongruity, even as a key adverb applied to Grendel, who will eat *unmurnlice* ("unmourningly," 449b), reminds an audience of the appropriate decorum upon death (*murnlice*), denied by the not-at-all-*murnlice* monstrousness of Grendel.[17] A similar effect is achieved through Beowulf's subsequent request that in such a circumstance his non-comestible battle-garment be sent back to Hygelac (lines 452–5a), which hints at Beowulf's emotional investment in his own loss and reminds the audience of his affection for his king, but does so without sentimentality.[18] There is a secondary joke at lines 450b–51, as Beowulf explains that Hrothgar will no longer need to be concerned with feeding his guest either, since he will have become food for the monster.[19] The improbability of balancing such concern for his host's larder with the death of himself creates the incongruity that flags the utterance as a comic one. In the whole passage, Beowulf is playing on a doubleness of script by taking a topic treated with serious attention throughout the poem – funerary rites and the respectful disposal of the dead are a recurring preoccupation of this poet[20] – and making light of it to show his unconcern at his own death. This is classic sardonic humour of heroic literature.

Another source of humour lies in the understatement that characterizes Beowulf's engagement with his opponents in the up-beat first half of the poem, during his encounters with Grendel and Grendel's mother, where it serves as a kind of aggressive goading. In a double understatement at a climactic moment of Beowulf's battle with Grendel, the narrator observes of Beowulf:

Nolde eorla hleo   ænige þinga
þone cwealmcuman   cwicne forlætan,
ne his lifdagas   leoda ængum
nytte tealde.
(*Beowulf*, lines 791–4a)

---

17 *Klaeber's Beowulf*, cxi, refers to the tone of "decorously ironic understatement" created through *un*- prefix words.
18 In keeping with the observation of Shippey, *Laughing Shall I Die*, who establishes that, in Viking culture, the heroic ideal is to outwardly give no sign of concern at explicit danger even as some emotion shows through in uncontrolled expression.
19 George Clark, "The Hero and the Theme," in *A Beowulf Handbook*, eds. Robert E. Bjork and John D. Niles (Lincoln: University of Nebraska Press, 1997), chap. 14, 271–90, at 278.
20 See Gale R. Owen-Crocker, *The Four Funerals in Beowulf and the Structure of the Poem* (Manchester: Manchester University Press, 2000).

The protector of men would not by any means
allow the slaughterous visitor to leave living,
nor did he reckon the days of his life
of use to anyone.

Beowulf's first intention here is ironic since Grendel will, indeed, leave living and remain alive (the range of *forlætan* here allows for a possible sense
of leave as in depart or leave as in continue to exist, both of which will happen in the short term). That irony, though, is not a humorous one. It is in
the additional explanation that humour arises. Given the perspective of the
opening statement, it is not a surprise that Beowulf would not reckon the
days of Grendel's life of use to anyone. This is a form of litotes, expressing
a sentiment by denial of its opposite. Indeed, it is such an inverted way of
expressing a desire for an adversary's death as to be comically incongruous.
Through such phrasing, the narrator implies that Beowulf thinks even during the fight scene with the wit of agonistic heroic humour.

The same joke through understatement is deployed after the flight of
Grendel, where it is focalized through the onlookers who have followed
the bloody tracks of the monster to the mere:

> No his lifgedal
> sarlic þuhte   secga ænegum
> þara þe tirleases   trode sceawode.
> (*Beowulf*, lines 841b–43)

The loss of his life
did not seem sad to any of those men
who gazed upon the track of the glory-less one.

Whatever modern sympathies he may elicit, Grendel has been portrayed
within the poem as a disruptive and antisocial force towards the Danes and
one who is most emphatically lacking in *tir*, "glory." That his loss of life
did not seem *sarlic* ("sad," "grievous") to the Danes is so much an expression of the obvious as to be comically incongruous. Again the rhetorical
form of the understatement by means of a negative uses litotes to stress the
disjunction, which is emphatically at odds with the presumed jubilation
of the crowd.[21] At this moment there is a lightness of tone in the relief of
the Danes, expressed here through a triumphalist joke, even if, once again,

---

21 On the use of litotes throughout Old English literature, see Frederick Bracher,
   "Understatement in Old English Poetry," *PMLA* 52 (1937): 915–34; Roberta Frank,

there is a certain irony in letting down their guard, since the narrative will soon undercut their sense of well-being through the subsequent visit of Grendel's mother. The understatement involves a mini-reversal which marks the present happy moment with humour before a subsequent turn of *edwenden*, "reversal."[22]

These two examples are imagined from the viewpoint of the hero and of the onlookers, but the narrator gets in on the act, too, deploying some of the same agonistic humour, sometimes through litotes, sometimes through delay. When Grendel bursts into Heorot, the narrator describes his flame-like eyes as a prominent feature displaying "leoht unfæger" ("un-beautiful light," 727b). Given the general ghastliness of the scene, the light is presumably not even a little bit *fæger*, and the expression through such an inappropriate negative creates momentary humour, even though Grendel's subsequent laughter (730b) is not a reflection of anything funny, but rather aggressive exultation by one who has an expectation of a satisfying slaughter. When Beowulf's sword is described as *unslaw* ("not-blunt," 2564a), it is a humorously understated way of conveying that the weapon is sharp indeed, albeit, ironically, not fit for the task at hand of engaging the dragon.[23]

A more straightforward example of the narrator deploying humour comes in a moment of narrative aplomb around the revelation of the outcome of Beowulf's fight with Grendel. The narrator comments on the sign of his victory with meaningful delay:

> Þæt wæs tacen sweotol
> syþðan hildedeor   hond alegde,
> earm ond eaxle   – þær wæs eal geador
> Grendles grape –   under geapne hrof.
> (*Beowulf*, lines 833b–36)

> That was a clear sign
> after the battle-bold one laid the hand,
> arm and shoulder – there was altogether
> all of Grendel's grip – under the spacious roof.

"*Beowulf* and the Intimacy of Large Parties," in *Dating Beowulf: Studies in Intimacy*, eds. Daniel C. Remein and Erica Weaver (Manchester: Manchester University Press, 2020), 54–72.

22 On the recurring pattern of *edwenden*, reversal, within the poem, see especially T.A. Shippey, *Beowulf* (London: Arnold, 1978).

23 The example is cited as carrying "a touch of humour" by *Klaeber's Beowulf*, cxi.

The revelation comes in measured order as the audience of the poem learn here how much damage has been done to Grendel. At first the clear sign would appear to be Grendel's hand, but the poet proceeds to itemize the additional pieces of anatomy, namely arm and shoulder, before giving a summary statement that this is the complete grip. Delay in giving the full manifestation of the sign allows for greater emphasis through a kind of aggressive humour, here suggesting the present harmlessness of the once formidable Grendel.

This kind of sardonic humour of laconic understatement or delay is evident throughout the poem. As touched on in the introduction above, a water beast is *sundes þe sænra* ("the slower of swimming," 1436a) because death had taken it. Presumably the beast is more than just the slower of swimming – rather it is completely slow in all aspects now that death has taken it – but the leisure and false precision of the comparative construction comically emphasizes the death, while amplifying the uncanny nature of the body of water occupied by Grendel's Mother. Sometimes the same effect comes about because of the narrator's choice to withhold a key negator or qualifier, so that an audience at first assumes a positive and then realizes it has been mischievously misled. As Beowulf relies on the shield especially crafted to withstand the dragon's fire, the order of the Old English description is crucial:

> Scyld wel gebearg
> life ond lice   læssan hwile
> mærum þeodne   þonne his myne sohte.
> (*Beowulf*, lines 2570b–72)

> The shield protected well
> his life and his body for less time
> for the glorious lord than his intention sought.

The primary joke here is played by starting with an utterance using *wel* so that it seems as if the shield is serving its purpose well, only to have this reversed through the qualifying clause that switches "well" to "less well," or, rather, well for less duration than well would normally be expected to connote. Further leisure and redundancy is evident in the statement of point of view: that his *myne*, "intention, thought," would seek/desire that the shield work to protect him does not really need spelling out since it is inherent in the idea of a shield. That the poet spends the time is a reminder of the expectation that is being failed with a laconic leisureliness that establishes through its very inappropriateness the urgency of the current situation.

This is a trick that the poet soon repeats with a matching litotes centred on the sword, which

> bat unswiðor
> þonne his ðiodcyning   þearfe hæfde.
> (*Beowulf*, lines 2578b–79)

> bit less strongly
> than the lordly king had need of it.

The failing sword surely did bite *unswiðor* ("less strongly") than intended, given Beowulf's clear intention to use the sword to kill the dragon. The litotes creates emphasis and makes clear that the implied point of view is Beowulf's. While the dire circumstance of losing life in the fight with the dragon is hardly a laughing matter, the phrasing implies a kind of stoic acceptance of the deadly failure of technology to deliver safety, thereby playing off and contributing to the comic insouciance of the doomed hero.

Heroic insouciance and agonistic verbal wit, stressed through understatement and a certain dilatory effect, are appropriate elements that help build up a hero. Moments of sardonic humour celebrate the heroic ethos of the poem and contribute to the broadly upbeat tone of the first part of *Beowulf*, where even if successes are ringed about with ironies and *edwenden* will come all too quickly, there is a hopefulness in the youthful exploits of Beowulf. Another strand of humour in this section of the poem may be more surprising. For all the heroic action, the first part of *Beowulf* contextualizes the story through a rich consciousness of high-status hall etiquette. Drawing out that etiquette, the poet shows how characters manoeuvre around the ever-present threat of embarrassment and occasionally fail to fend it off. The poet's presentation of such concerns creates a kind of comedy of manners that often serves to undercut a straightforward sense of heroic values. Uncovering this layer of humour involves being sensitive to poetic hints and what is implied but not said as well as to the ironies of the expressions that are used. Since attending to such hints is not the most common way of reading the poem, I will explore this aspect at some length to demonstrate the alternative comedy of *Beowulf*.[24]

---

24 A recent translation that effectively hints at much of the comedy discussed here is Maria Dahvana Headley, *Beowulf: A New Translation* (New York: Farrar, Straus, and Giroux, 2020).

Court Comedy in *Beowulf*

Even as it centres on the rich action of slayings by monsters and slayings of monsters, *Beowulf* is very much concerned with the human world of etiquette and good deportment in heroic society. This is particularly apparent in the first two-thirds of the poem and especially in its early stages, as the hero must first enter the kingdom of Denmark to arrive at the challenge and then must work to keep his entry from outfacing his host. Such a world provides abundant opportunity for a comedy of manners and a type of humour that may undercut some the apparent heroic values. Rather than insouciance in the ever-present face of death, the comedy of manners plays up the need to save face by means of verbal control with the risk of mockery for any unaddressed failures.

Such stakes are set up quite clearly in the opening part of the poem. Expectations for appropriate speech practices are first established through the challenge by the guard at the coast as the Geats make their initial approach to Denmark, as has been often noticed.[25] Here the stress on decorum and appropriate speech is evident as the group of Geats work their way closer to the centre of the Danish court at Heorot. The rather verbose coastguard makes the point:

> Æghwæþres sceal
> scearp scyldwiga   gescad witan,
> worda ond worca,   se þe wel þenceð.
> (287b–89)

> A sharp shield-warrior
> must know the difference between the two,
> words and deeds, he who thinks well.

While *Beowulf* seems to be a poem about deeds, it is every bit as concerned with words, as the emphasis on speeches in either direct or implied discourse attest.[26] This is still more apparent when Beowulf and his fellow travellers get into Heorot.

---

25 See, for example, Andy Orchard, *A Critical Companion to Beowulf* (Cambridge: Brewer, 2003), 203–12.

26 Some 1,300 of 3,192 lines are direct speech: see *Klaeber's Beowulf*, lxxxvi–lxxxviii. On speeches in the poem, see Peter Baker, "Beowulf as Orator," *Journal of English Linguistics* 21 (1988): 3–23; T.A. Shippey, "Principles of Conversation in Beowulfian Speech," in *Techniques of Description: Spoken and Written Discourse; A Festschrift for*

As he learns of Beowulf's visit, King Hrothgar is quick to parade his knowledge of the young hero and to hint at the appropriateness of the young man's visit in view of the favours he, Hrothgar, had done for the father (lines 372–6, 457–72). In return, Beowulf is careful not to outface his host as he proposes to take on Grendel with self-confidence matched by verbal tact:

> Me wearð Grendles þing
> on minre eþeltyrf   undyrne cuð.
> (409b–10)

> The business of Grendel
> was made known to me in my homeland.

"Grendles þing" is semantically rich – Grendel's affair or possibly a formal meeting with Grendel or even the judicial case of Grendel.[27] Beowulf uses the same term later in his speech to describe his planned encounter with Grendel, "ana gehegan/ðing wið þyrse" ("hold a meeting *or* settle the dispute alone with the giant," 425b–26a).[28] The latter instance looks like verbal play that imagines a proposed fight as some kind of legal exchange, while the former instance may be jokingly understated for the broken benches and denuded nighttimes that Grendel has created for Heorot. The understatement is played up as Beowulf observes that the matter has become the opposite of secret (*un-dyrne*), a litotes that is mildly comic in its tactful inappropriate slightness for describing the well-known affair (as discussed above).

Things get more fraught in talk around the dilemma of the Danes who have not been eaten by Grendel, since their survival depends on a degree of circumspection that is the opposite of heroic bravado. This was spelled out by the somewhat neutral voice of the narrator at lines 138–43:

> Þa wæs eaðfynde   þe him elles hwær
> gerumlicor   ræste sohte,

Malcolm Coulthard, eds. John M. Sinclair, Michael Hoey, and Gwyneth Fox (London: Routledge, 1993), 109–26; Robert Bjork, "Speech as Gift in *Beowulf*," *Speculum* 69 (1994): 993–1020; Orchard, *Critical Companion*, chap. 7; Elise Louviot, *Direct Speech in Beowulf and Other Old English Narrative Poems* (Cambridge: Bewer, 2016).

27 On the range of sense, see *Klaeber's Beowulf*, 141 note to line 409b.
28 The translation offered by *Klaeber's Beowulf*, 141, note to line 425b f., with the suggestion that the phrase is here applied ironically to battle.

bed æfter burum,   ða him gebeacnod wæs
gesægd soðlice   sweotolan tacne
healðegnes hete;   heold hyne syðþan
fyr ond fæstor   se þæm feonde ætwand.
(138–43)

Then it was easy to discover one who sought for himself
rest at a greater distance elsewhere,
a bed among the women's quarters, when the hatred of the hall-thane
was manifest and truly told through a clear sign;
he held himself afterwards further away and more secure,
he who escaped from that enemy.

Even this narratorial statement risks a certain mocking tone. The comparative adverb, "gerumlicor" ("more roomily," 139a) is as ignominious as it is awkward since the destination is a bed "æfter burum," that is, among the bowers of the women's quarters.[29] That the movement is one of escape is emphasized by the verb at 143b (ætwand, "escaped") and also by the zeugma of the two further comparative adverbs, "fyr and fæstor" ("further away and more secure," 143a), where the linking shows just what is the motivation for the action these warriors are taking when faced with a *feond*. Since these are the warriors who usually lie down for the night on the benches of the hall, any *bed* may be inappropriately soft, let alone one among the *buras*. That "bed æfter burum" is not the appropriate sleeping quarters for the male warriors tracked in this sentence is further emphasized by the poet's ironic choice of term for the one opposing them: *healðegnes hete* ("the hatred of the hall-thane," 142a) gives Grendel the appropriately inappropriate rank of hall-thane, presumably because he is usurping by night the function that ought to be maintained by the regular martial attendants of the hall. The term will have re-established its more appropriate valence when Grendel finds the *healðegnas* gathered around Beowulf at 719b, although these are the Geatish warriors, who have displaced the ones who should be in this particular hall, namely the Danish thanes. Since the compound word *healðegn* is unique to these two instances, it may have been coined

---

29 DOE, s.v. būr1, gives the definition "private room, chamber, or dwelling place for use of royalty, nobility, or well-born ladies." *Klaeber's Beowulf*, note to 138–40a, points to the implication that the *buras* are outlying buildings which served as living and sleeping quarters for persons of rank. The usage here strongly associates them with feminine quarters, as in the subsequent passage discussed below, and analogous with the infamous *bur* in the Chronicle account of Cynewulf and Cyneheard.

by the poet, emphasizing the artfulness of the implied irony.[30] Even the "clear token" (*sweotolan tacne*, 141b) has loaded overtones, since this will be the phrase used to describe Grendel's grip that serves later as a far more glorious token of Beowulf's victory (833b), but here serves as an understatement for the devastation and death that this night-visiting hall-thane brings. The language of this passage suggests that the poem's narrator is quietly mocking the cowardice of the Danish warriors, whose predicament has become both embarrassing and a little comic, but without spelling out any condemnation.

Beowulf gets to articulate that ignominy, but with appropriate displacement, when he rounds on Unferth, who, as many commentators have observed, serves precisely the function of being a goad to test out Beowulf within the court and subsequently a scapegoat for the cowardice of the Danish retainers who have not stood up to Grendel.[31] Unferth is marked out as a particularly appropriate object for such scorn in view of the narrator's unusual turn to interiority when he makes explicit Unferth's envy of Beowulf and his desire to be bested by none (lines 501b–5). After his verbal sparring with Beowulf, the collectivity of Danes laugh at Unferth in response to Beowulf's lengthy speech of rejoinder (611–12a), expressing collective joy and relief in their belief in the heroic potential of their visitor, even as the laughter reduces Unferth to silence. The poet returns to Unferth's discomfiture as the Danes get to gaze upon the sign of Beowulf's victory, where Unferth's silence is explicitly noted (980–1). Laughter here appears to be an expression of relief rather than a reflex to humour, but comes with an element of comic derision.

The character protected by this scapegoating of Unferth is his boss, Hrothgar, King of the Danes, whose joy at Beowulf's speech is stated explicitly (607–10), suggesting that he takes a significant lead in the subsequent laughter (611–12a). Hrothgar's position is a tricky one and the vocabulary used to describe him constantly risks slipping into meaningful irony.[32] As the alpha male, he should command the hall which so clearly stands as a synecdoche for his kingdom, but which he will now need to

---

30 The editors of *Klaeber's Beowulf*, 125 suggest the compound "is apparently coined for the occasion" in their note to line 142.

31 On the verbal sparring with Unferth as flyting, see Carol J. Clover, "The Germanic Context of the Unferþ Episode," *Speculum* 55 (1980): 444–68; Ward Parks, *Verbal Dueling in Heroic Narrative: The Homeric and Old English Traditions* (Princeton, NJ: Princeton University Press, 1990); Peter S. Baker, *Honour, Exchange and Violence in Beowulf* (Cambridge: Brewer, 2013), chap. 3.

32 For an extended reading of epithets as ironic, see Tom Clark, *A Case for Irony in Beowulf, with Particular Reference to Its Epithets* (New York: Lang, 2003).

give up to a visiting hero. Irony at such ineffectualness lurks in the narrator's account of Hrothgar's approval of Beowulf's speech:

Þa wæs on salum   sinces brytta
gamolfeax ond guðrof;   geoce gelyfde
brego Beorht-Dena;   gehyrde on Beowulfe
folces hyrde   fæstrædne geþoht.
(607–10)

Then the dispenser of treasure, grey-haired and battle brave,
was happy; the lord of the Bright-Danes
counted on help; the guardian of the people
heard in Beowulf steadfast thought.

Hrothgar is *on salum* ("happy," 607a)[33] because he can believe in the proffered assistance, having heard in Beowulf *fæstrædne geþoht* ("thought firm of purpose," "steadfast thought," 610b). So far, so good, but this implies a contrast, hinting that Hrothgar has become habituated to hearing thought that is not *fæst-ræd*. Would that be from his own retainers, particularly from Unferth, whose help against the monster, by contrast, he has not been able to believe in? If that is the case, the rather conventional characterization as *sinces brytta* ("distributor of treasure," 607b) and *folces hyrde* ("guardian of the people," 610a) risk carrying more irony since the circulation of treasure these terms encode has failed to achieve the loyal monster-slaying supporters it ought, while Hrothgar would not seem presently to live up to a description as guardian of a people. The dilemma is amplified in the other epithets here. *Gamolfeax* ("grey-haired," 608a) captures the seniority of the aging king, perhaps emphasizing his domain as wisdom rather than action,[34] but the collocating *guðrof* ("battle-brave," 608a) risks being jarringly inappropriate about the one who, in the business of Grendel, is not going into battle (would that make him *guð-unrof*?). No explicit criticism is made of the good king, but the poet's choice of language here might give an attentive listener pause. Laughter is explicitly directed at Unferth, but the alert listener might notice the risk that the aging king could be an equally appropriate object of such laughter.

---

33 The spelling varies between *on sālum* here and *on sǣlum* (643, 1170, 1322), with a possible play on the similar-sounding word with a short vowel, *on sælum* "in the halls," which is the meaningful locus ringing through these passages.

34 The classic study is R.E. Kaske, "*Sapientia et Fortitudo* as the Controlling Theme of *Beowulf*," *Studies in Philology* 55 (1958): 423–56, who laid out the competing options.

The awkwardness of Hrothgar's position becomes yet more apparent as the day wears on, and he needs to leave the hall to avoid the danger of Grendel. How to get him out without losing face, as he would if he were seen as running away in fear? The narrator again presents the king in language that an attentive audience could see as mocking, even as the king himself attempts to re-establish control through his own verbal dexterity, expressed indirectly, I believe, by his own crafting of a joke. After describing Wealhtheow's success in establishing the decorum of hospitality by circulating the cup (612b–41), the poet returns to the scene of happiness in the hall, but then establishes an abrupt break:

> Þa wæs eft swa ær   inne on healle
> þryðword sprecen,   ðeod on sælum,
> sigefolca sweg,   oþ þæt semninga
> sunu Healfdenes   secean wolde
> æfenreste.
> (642–46a)

> Then again as before noble words were spoken
> in the hall, the troop of warriors was happy,
> there was the happy sound of the victorious people, until suddenly
> the son of Halfdane wanted to seek
> his evening rest.

The mood of the troop *on sælum* (643b) matches that of their lord, who earlier was *on salum* (607a), and so the hall once again resounds with the happy communal sounds of a group that recognizes a likely saviour in the visiting hero. As before, there are discordances in the language here that are surely deliberate: the choice of compound noun for the group (*sigefolc*, "victorious people," 644a) strongly risks a hint of irony, since they have not been victorious in relation to Grendel so far. The compound noun for the buzz of language, *þryðword* ("strong or brave or noble words," 643a, a unique formation and so perhaps the poet's coinage) contributes to the same uneasy sense, since speech which is *þryð* has not yet been matched with action which is so. The happy sounds last *oþ þæt* (a conjunction that often brings an unhappy reversal in the narrative of this poem) *semninga* ("suddenly," 644b, an adverb that rarely bodes well and that here carries the alliteration of the line) the lord of the hall wanted to seek out, or intended to visit (*secean wolde*), evening rest, or bed for the night (*æfenreste*, 646a). Every leader must get his rest (presumably), but choosing to spell out this biological necessity risks giving it undue prominence, and the weight of the adverb piles on the emphasis. The appropriate incongruity of the language hints with gentle humour that something is not well in the state of Denmark.

If an attentive audience is already attuned to spotting something a little ignominious in Hrothgar's actions, the next passage brings out the point and shows the poet more clearly laughing at the leader of the Danes:

> wiste þæm ahlæcan
> to þæm heahsele   hilde geþinged,
> siððan hie sunnan leoht   geseon meahton
> oþ ðe nipende   niht ofer ealle,
> scaduhelma gesceapu   scriðan cwoman
> wan under wolcnum.
> (646b–51a)

> he knew battle was intended
> by the formidable one in that high hall,
> since they could see the light of the sun
> until night came darkening over all,
> the shapes of darkness came gliding
> dark under the clouds.

The subject of the verb of knowing in the first clause is presumably Hrothgar, the son of Halfdane, the last subject mentioned (at line 641), even though the knowledge he carries is quickly shifted to an unspecified plural *hie* (648a), presumably all the Danish retainers, all equally attuned to the foreboding movement of the sun. There is some potential mockery at their lack of resilience, both in the timing of the perception and in the expansion of the description. Grendel presents a threat to the hall at night, but if the Danes have perceived the danger since they could first see the light of the sun (i.e. dawn), there is no part of the day when Grendel's domination has not been wracking their psyches.[35] The Danes have become unduly attentive to the movement of the light. They perceive that threat comes with the movement of darkness over the earth, and the nature of that movement is here conveyed through a verb of motion, *scriðan* ("to glide, move, wander, stride," 650b) that was used before of Grendel's locomotion (163b) and is just about to be strikingly so used again (at line 703a). Indeed, the one doing the gliding in the present

---

35 Some editors save the Danes' psyche by emending line 648b to "geseon ne meahton," an emendation forcefully rejected by *Klaeber's Beowulf*, 156, note to 646b ff. Fulk et al. point to the possibility that the *ahlæca* here may refer to Grendel or Beowulf, but most critics assume this is a reference to Grendel.

passage is not entirely clear. Is this simply dusk, the regular transition from light to darkness? It is here spelled out as the *scaduhelma gesceapu* ("the shapes of darkness," or, more literally, "the forms of the coverings *or* helmets of shadow," 645a), where the compound word is unique, again perhaps the poet's coinage, probably playing off the emphasis on not-entirely-efficacious helmets throughout the poem. If it is, the poet seems to be ventriloquizing an unhealthy Danish perspective that is investing the coming of darkness with the imaginative power of the approach of the monster since Grendel himself will soon be characterized as the *scea-dugenga* ("walker in darkness," 703a, another unique formation). The emphatic *semninga* ("suddenly," 644b) of Hrothgar's need to seek his evening rest has suddenly got too much implied explanation, and it threatens his heroic standing.

It is hard for a leader to keep his dignity while he is watching with too much attention the movement of the sun and rapidly giving up the hall that he rules over in order to move out of harm's way into the women's quarters. Hrothgar nevertheless does what he can to re-establish verbal control, for all the awkward circumstance. This first comes in reported speech as he offers Beowulf a conventional greeting ("him hæl abead" 653b, "offered him good health") which is joined in a striking zeugma with a far less conventional offer ("abead, | winærnes geweald," 653b–54a, "offered him control of the hall"), something which he explains he has never done before (and the *hapax legomena* built on ðryþ continue as Hrothgar offers the "ðryþærn Dena" 657a, "the strong/brave/mighty hall of the Danes"). Hrothgar then makes his tactical exit with his troop of heroes to seek Wealhtheow, "cwen to gebeddan" ("the queen as a bed companion," 665a). This is clearly a retreat, even as the phrasing provides for the king a compensating suggestion of virility, with the hint of royal sexual activity, although not, presumably, for the troop of heroes (*hæleþa gedryht*, 662b) headed in the same direction.

The hint of a verbal joke lingers in Hrothgar's reported speech:

> Hæfde kyningwuldor
> Grendle togeanes, swa guman gefrungon,
> seleweard aseted; sundornytte beheold
> ymb aldor Dena, eotonweard' abead.
> (665b–68)

> The king of glory had set,
> as men have heard tell, a hall-guardian against Grendel;
> he observed a special office about the lord of the Danes,
> he offered a guardianship against giants.

This is a passage rich in unique formations (*kyningwuldor, seleweard, eotonweard*), suggesting a high degree of poetic attention, even if the sense of the passage is contested. The most likely meaning is that Hrothgar has set Beowulf up as hall-guardian, and we have watched him do precisely that. The unique designation of Hrothgar in the present recapitulation as *kyningwuldor* ("the most glorious of kings") continues the poet's irony at his expense, since he is not presently undertaking an action that looks particularly glorious, all the more so since the compound so clearly echoes the more common *wuldorcyning*, which usually renders the divine king.[36] In the ensuing line and a half, *eotenweard* may be the subject or may be the object of the second verb with a subject only implied.[37] In either event, the function described is clearly allotted to Beowulf, and it is a distinctive and unusual function: *eotenweard* (668b, "a watch against a giant"; Fulk et al., "protection against giants/monsters," DOE) and one not likely to have been commonly called for. Verbal patterning is established through the verb *abead* ("offered," 668b), echoing the same verb used of Hrothgar's salutation to Beowulf just a few lines earlier (653b). The present passage, then, hints at high verbal ingenuity, perhaps even the creation of a joke, with the striking coinage *eotenweard* so neatly chiming with *seleweard*. The crafter of this verbal artistry is implicitly the one who is hovering over this whole passage, namely Hrothgar. He may be retreating to the women's quarters and he may be handing off the control of his hall for the first time ever, but it looks like he exited with a verbal witticism, a joking coinage, and thereby reclaimed a degree of verbal if not martial control. There is power in being the one who crafts verbal witticisms, even as this is something of a forlorn hope for saving face when the narrator is gently but busily mocking Hrothgar. Beowulf, on the other hand, is working very hard not to.

These issues remain fraught after the detailed account of Beowulf's fight with Grendel. Hrothgar's return to the hall leads to a resumption of the same comic digs from the narrator. In the morning, after the account of the energetic retainers following the bloody tracks of the dismembered Grendel and returning with exuberant storytelling and

---

36 This is the understanding of Bruce Mitchell and Fred C. Robinson, eds., *Beowulf: An Edition with Relevant Shorter Texts* (Oxford: Blackwell, 1998), and of most editors. Fulk et al., however, consider the referent here to be God in their glossary entry for *kyningwuldor*.

37 The former is assumed by Mitchell and Robinson; the latter is suggested in Fulk et al.'s note to 667f.

horse racing (lines 837–917a), Hrothgar rises and enters the hall with his troop and his wife:

> swylce self cyning
> of brydbure,   beahhorda weard,
> tryddode tirfæst   getrume micle,
> cystum gecyþed,   ond his cwen mid him
> medostigge mæt   mægþa hose.
> (920b–24)

likewise the king himself, the guardian of the ring-hoard,
the one fast in glory, stepped from the female-chamber
with a great force, well known for excellence,
and his queen along with him
traversed the path to the mead hall with a company of women.

Beahhorda weard ("guardian of the treasure-hoard," 921b) certainly sounds like an entirely standard epithet for a king,[38] even if it is perhaps unfortunate that it so audibly alliterates with the *brydbure* ("the bridal chamber," 921a) from which this ineffectual guardian is emerging. The king is a married man, so it is suitable that he is stepping out from the chamber that he shares with his queen, who is also present here. But if a king is usually well served by having a *getrume micle* ("a great troop," 922b), the size of the retinue is not so clearly meritorious here as these are the hall-thanes who escaped by keeping themselves farther away and safer (cf. lines 168–73). This is an awkward moment to be *gecyþed* ("widely known," 923a). The ironies are amplified by the verb of motion given the group: *mæt* 924a matches the verb used so recently of the horse-riders coming back from the mere, who *mæton*, 917a, the lengthy streets, but it is hard to see the distance traversed as all that great on the *medostigge* ("path to the mead hall," 924a, another *hapax legomenon*). Hrothgar may have exited making a joke; he re-enters joked at by the narrator.

The attention of the poem moves to different aspects of court etiquette as Beowulf is rewarded for his deed and the Danes listen to a celebratory tale told by the *scop*, namely the Finnsburh Episode, which lacks in this retelling the insouciant humour of Hnæf seen in *The Finnsburh Fragment* and described above. The powerful potential of language is prominent in the story, though, with a treaty attempting to fend off ignominy by prohibiting speech (lines 1096b–106) as unsuccessful as one would expect.[39] The direct

---

38 The compound uniquely survives in its three uses in *Beowulf*.
39 The speech presents a dizzying sequence of conditions and qualifications; see, *inter alia*, perceptive studies of Shippey, *Beowulf*; J.R.R. Tolkien, *Finn and Hengest: The Fragment*

and indirect impact of what is said and not said by Wealhtheow, who re-establishes courtly custom (in lines 1162b–91) while manoeuvring to shore up the position of her children in relation to the threat of Hrothgar's too-quick adoption of Beowulf as a surrogate son and the likely threat from their uncle Hrothulf, has been analysed well by others.[40] The poet revels as ever in the complexities and subtleties of court culture, albeit in these cases not exploiting humour to do so.[41]

After such turns, retiring to bed on the night following the defeat of Grendel is finally not fraught with embarrassment, even as the narrator instead plays up the irony of the doom impending unawares for one of the retainers (lines 1239–55). This time Beowulf is one of those sleep-ing elsewhere, and the night attack by Grendel's mother briefly makes him vulnerable as the butt of the comedy of manners, but in this case any comic embarrassment is quickly allayed. Unaware of what has transpired overnight, Beowulf and his men enter into Hrothgar's presence in another entry-into-the-hall scene with an approach that is altogether too breezy for the mood of the moment, as Beowulf:

> frægn gif him wære
> æfter neodlaðum   niht getæse.
> (1319b–20)

> asked him if the night
> had been agreeable to him after the urgent summons.

---

and the Episode, ed. Alan Bliss (London: Allen, 1982); Michael Benskin, "The Narrative Structure of the Finnsburh Episode in *Beowulf*," *Amsterdamer Beiträge zur älteren Germanistik* 77 (2017): 37–64.

40 In addition to *Klaeber's Beowulf*, 192, note to 1169ff., see Jane Chance, *Woman as Hero in Old English Literature* (Syracuse: Syracuse University Press, 1986), chap. 1; Michael J. Enright, *Lady with a Mead Cup: Prophecy and Lordship in the European Warband from La Tène to the Viking Age* (Dublin: Four Courts, 1996); Shari Horner, *The Discourse of Enclosure: Representing Women in Old English Literature* (Albany: State University of New York Press, 2001), chap. 2; Stacy S. Klein, *Ruling Women: Queenship and Gender in Anglo-Saxon Literature* (Notre Dame, IN: University of Notre Dame Press, 2006), chap. 3; Helen Damico, *Beowulf and the Grendel-Kin: Politics and Poetry in Eleventh-Century England* (Morgantown: West Virginia University Press, 2015), chap. 4.

41 See also Eric G. Stanley, "Courtliness and Courtesy in *Beowulf* and Elsewhere in English Medieval Literature," in *Words and Works: Studies in Medieval English Language and Literature in Honour of Fred C. Robinson*, eds. Peter S. Baker and Nicholas Howe (Toronto: University of Toronto Press, 1998), 67–103. As Orchard, *Critical Companion*, 216, puts it: "The careful patterning of the first seventeen speeches in *Beowulf* seems clearly designed to point up Heorot as a courtly, cultured, mannered place."

Although not stated, Beowulf likely used some version of a standard Old English greeting, *wes þu sæl* (literally "be happy"), in view of the phrasing of Hrothgar's rejoinder:

'Ne frin þu æfter sælum!   Sorh is geniwod
Denigea leodum: dead is Æschere ...
(1322–3)

Don't ask about happiness! Sorrow is renewed
among the people of the Danes: Æchere is dead...

Beowulf has been wrong-footed: a polite, even banal, greeting now looks like a serious *faux pas*. Instead of accentuating the embarrassment and laughing at Beowulf, the narrator shows the hero recover with speed and poise. In his very next speech, at the end of Hrothgar's lengthy lament, Beowulf is in tune with the king's mood, shaping the king's response, and displaying the greatest verbal artistry:

'Ne sorga, snotor guma.   Selre bið æghwæm
þæt he his freond wrece   þonne he fela murne.
Ure æghwylc sceal   ende gebidan
worolde lifes;   wyrce se þe mote
domes ær deaþe;   þæt bið drihtguman
unlifgendum   æfter selest.
(1384–9)

Don't sorrow, wise man. It is better for everyone
that he avenge his friend than mourn much.
Each of us must experience an end
of life in the world; let him who may work
glory before death; that is afterwards best
for the warrior no longer living.

Beowulf is forcefully articulating the ideology of the heroic world in an affirmation of action presented with considerable rhetorical finesse as he draws upon the eternal verities of gnomic wisdom with what sound like aphorisms and clinches the case with the climactic and emphatic "domes ær deaþe" ("glory before death," 1388a). One who speaks like this is not a character to be laughed at.

The hero follows earnest words with earnest action in his encounter with Grendel's mother, while the king recovers the status of dispenser of wisdom as he reacts to the hilt of the giants' sword with his so-called sermon (lines 1700–84). One final narrative trick in the Heorot scene, though, probably involves the narrator playing a joke on an audience in tune with the patterns of the poem. After so much bed-time business, an audience is surely extra attentive when the helm of night once more descends dark over the warriors ("Nihthelm geswearc/deorc ofer dryhtgumum," 1789b–90a). It is no longer ignoble to sleep among the *buras*, and so nobody need be laughed at for their nightly routines, but something monstrous has happened following both the two previous going-to-bed scenes, so it does not require consciousness of the epic laws of folk narrative to suspect that the third iteration is likely to be significant, too.[42] The poet seems to play with that assumption, both with that martial characterization of night falling and by articulating the senior Scylding's desire for bed and the bold Geat's immeasurable desire for rest (lines 1790b–98) – all very reasonable after two days of action – but with such narrative attention to the business of going to bed as to prime an alert audience to be anxious about what will happen next. And what does happen next is ... one character rested (*Reste* 1799a), one slept (*swæf* 1800b) – and that's it!

> oþ þat hrefn blaca   heofones wynne
> bliðheort bodode.   Ða com beorht [leoma]
> [ofer sceadwa] scacan
> (1801–3a)

> until the black raven, happy in heart,
> announced the joy of the sky. Then the bright light came
> hastening over the shadows.

Nothing but rest and sleep happening in the nighttime is not in itself any cause for surprise, but for the listener well-attuned to the narrative flow who has got this far in the story it is a radical incongruity. No monsters, and no night attacks, and day comes over the shadows with none of the tension of lines 646b–51a![43] There may be a further joke in the choice for the harbinger of the dawn, which is a role not usually allotted to the raven, a bird which is not usually characterized as happy except as a beast of battle, when happiness comes from the prospect of upcoming slaughter.[44] But apparently a

---

42 On the ubiquity of patterning by threes, see Axel Olrik, "Epic Laws of Folk Narratives," in *The Study of Folklore*, ed. Alan Dundes (Englewood Cliffs, NJ: Prentice-Hall, 1965).

43 The shadows are speculative, if likely: there seems to be an omission in view of the want of sense at lines 1802–3, filled in with the emendation accepted in Fulk et al., presented in brackets.

44 Sylvia Huntley Horowitz, "The Ravens in *Beowulf*," *The Journal of English and Germanic Philology* 80, no. 4 (1981): 502–11; Mo Pareles, "What the Raven Told the Eagle: Animal Language and the Return of Loss in *Beowulf*," in *Dating*

raven is sometimes just a rooster, and the raven here appears to be a simple sign of a happy dawn. The whole rhythm of a night in and around Heorot in which there is no story to tell creates comic bathos in the denial of expectations.

With Beowulf's departure and return to Geatland, the poem transitions to the story of the dragon fight much later in his life. The tone of this last part is altogether more bleak and not punctuated by the kind of court humour described here. Cowardly retainers are roundly shamed as they fail to help Beowulf and Wiglaf in the final encounter, but there is little of the comedy of manners seen in maintaining face for an aging Hrothgar. Indeed, the contrast clarifies how the humour of the Denmark section, for all its potential satirical bite, works to establish a happy tone.

The reading of tone in the poem suggested here indicates the way *Beowulf* might have appealed to many different audiences. Events in Denmark give the narrator the opportunity to augment a story of martial prowess with one of court etiquette and manners – a kind of humour different from the sardonic deflection of fear seen more widely in heroic literature and analysed in the first half of this chapter. The combination of the different forms of humour suggests how *Beowulf*, despite its modern designation as an epic, is hardly monologic in its style. Comedy of manners in the context of court etiquette is more characteristic of romance than of epic, as can be seen, for example, in the Old English *Apollonius of Tyre* discussed in chapter 8, but adds a twist to the description of hall-centred heroism.

This chapter will end with consideration of the primal scene of heroic performance – in a hall peopled by warriors – even as the complexities of laughter at figures of power suggests a critique of just such an audience. Indeed, this pursuit of humour in *Beowulf* has uncovered a paradox of interpretation – both a celebration of martial heroic humour seen in the skilful deployment of insouciance, and a critique of the leaders who pursue such values, seen in laughing at the embarrassments of such leaders – that is matched by a paradox of possible audiences – both martial celebrants gathered in a mead hall and those who would laugh at those very people.

Beowulf: Studies in Intimacy, eds. Daniel C. Remein and Erica Weaver (Manchester: Manchester University Press, 2020), 164–86. Note also Durham Proverb 6 discussed in chap. 1 above.

The Community of Laughter in the Hall

The Rune Poem, considered in chapter 2 above, includes the following stanza:

> "Peorð" byþ symble   plega and hlehter
> wlancum …,   ðar wigan sittaþ
> on beorsele   bliþe ætsomne.
> (*Rune Poem*, lines 38–40)

> "Peorð" (a dice-game? a gaming piece?) is always play and laughter
> for the proud ones …, where warriors sit
> in the beer hall happy together.

A poem aimed at those learned in runic wisdom presents here an idealized portrait of community in the hall, one where laughing together cements that community. The poem clearly depicts the pleasure enjoyed by martial men, *wigan* ("warriors," 39b), gathered together at drinking, *on beorsele* ("in the beer hall," 40a), even if the sense of the runic name in this case is uncertain,[45] and the middle line of the stanza is missing a word or two. As they indulge in play and laughter (*plega and hlehter*, 38b), these men constitute a happy community (*bliþe ætsomne*). Such a bibulous secular hall community presents a portrait of joyful communitarianism that the learned and literate may aspire to. Laughter is associated with play in the happy hall, which could come as easily from listening to the literature examined in this study as from the enigmatic *peorð*.

That joyful communitarianism is seen in the performance scenes imagined in *Beowulf*, where the poet repeatedly portrays the recital of poetry or scenes of mirth as moments enjoyed by a masculine elite audience drinking in the hall. Early on, this takes the form of the "swutol sang scopes" ("clear song of the poet," 90a) as the *scop* tells the story of creation with such volume as to infuriate the *ellengæst* (86a), Grendel, who thereupon comes to attack. This first scene of merriment, while described from the

---

45 Page, *Introduction*, 79–80 says, "This word is a mystery…. Scholars have been ready enough to suggest meanings, more or less elegant, to fit this vague context, but none is convincing"; Niles, *Enigmatic Poems*, suggests the rune is an initialism and should be read as *pipe*, flute, pipe, or bagpipes creating a festive air in the mead hall. See Halsall for the suggestions in the translation.

perspective of the listening hostile spirit, still presents key elements of a happy recital. Grendel:

> dream gehyrde
> hludne in healle.   Þær wæs hearpan sweg,
> swutol sang scopes.
> (88b–90a)

> heard loud joy in the hall. There was the sound of the harp
> the clear song of the poet.

The emphasis here is on happy sounds: *dream*, "joy" (a noun that also conjures up happy sound)[46] as well as *sang*, "song," presented at high volume (*hludne*) and with clarity (*swutol*). It seems reasonable to assume that the happy sounds that so provoke the excluded spirit are sounds of mirth, which occur *in healle* ("in the hall," 89a) characterized by the social consumption of alcohol (*æfter beorþege*, 117a, "after partaking of beer") and of feasting (*æfter wiste*, 128a, "after feasting"). The recital immediately follows the construction of Heorot, so that the hall easily stands as a spatial metaphor for the happy sound of an imagined community of laughers within that constructed space.[47] Right at the start of the poem, then, the poet projects an imagined place and occasion for convivial performance and exchange, a place for the solving of riddles or for appreciating the sardonic humour of heroic insouciance, the mead or beer hall.

That hall as a place of comic performance is seen on other occasions in the poem, too. Laughter rings out in that hall at the end of the exchange between Unferth and Beowulf, when Hrothgar is cheered by the hero's resolute thought:

> Ðær wæs hæleþa hleahtor,   hlyn swynsode,
> word wæron wynsume.
> (611–12a)

> There was the laughter of heroes, the noise resounded,
> words were joyous.

---

46 See the range of senses listed by DOE s.v. *dream*, including "1 joy, bliss" and "3 sound, music, noise; that which produces sound or music."

47 On the hall as metaphor for martial society, see Kathryn Hume, "The Concept of the Hall in Old English Poetry," *Anglo-Saxon England* 3 (1974): 63–74; James W. Earl, *Thinking About Beowulf* (Stanford, CA: Stanford University Press, 1994); Hugh Magennis, *Images of Community in Old English Poetry* (Cambridge: Cambridge University Press, 1996).

As noted above, such laughter is ringed around with ironies as Hrothgar is here effectively undercutting his own *þyle*, Unferth, and perhaps being laughed at in his turn by the narrator. Nevertheless, the scene also suggests a straightforward venue for the performance of humour with a strong hint that the flyting has been seen as just such. Pleasure in such agonistic verbal exchange suggests an audience that would enjoy the goading included in the Old English riddles or the humour of the dialogue poems.

The poet later suggests that Beowulf himself was seen by his peers as one who appreciated humour and fun, when the anonymous messenger of the Geats comments on the parlous prospects of the Geatish people at the end of the poem:

> nu se herewisa   hleahtor alegde,
> gamen ond gleodream.
> (3020–1a)

> now the battle leader has laid aside laughter,
> amusement and entertainment-joy.

We may not have seen Beowulf doing a lot of *hleahtor* or *gamen ond gleodream*, but apparently, the messenger can imagine the lack of these as a token of the demise of the hero. Beowulf's put-down of Unferth is one of the few moments when we see an audience respond to his performance with laughter, establishing the flyting as a scene of *gamen ond gleodream* and cementing the idea of the hall community as one formed through communal laughter.

Scenes of mirthful performance are overwhelmingly associated with the hall in *Beowulf*, but there is one portrayal of poetry outdoors, as the leading men of Heorot follow the track of the maimed Grendel and tell poems and compete on horse-back on their return (853–917a). Otherwise, poetry performances occur in the hall with a strong association with happy sounds. This is seen most fully in the poetic recital of the Finnsburh Episode, when *sang ond sweg* ("song and sound") get joined with the *gid* ("story" or "poem" or "song") of Hrothgar's *scop* (poet) along the mead benches (1063–8a) at the feast following Beowulf's successful encounter with Grendel. That performance is received with an outpouring of happy sounds:

> Leoð wæs asungen,
> gleomannes gyd.   Gamen eft astah,
> beorhtode bencsweg;   byrelas sealdon
> win of wunderfatum.
> (1159b–62a)

The song had been sung,
the story of the entertainer. Merriment arose again,
the noise from those on the benches brightened; cup-bearers gave out
wine from wonderful vessels.

Striking here is the synesthesia of the happy sound which brightens as it
rises, along with the inevitable association of the hall (represented here by
the benches) with convivial drinking in merriment (*gamen*).

The picture of such a mirth-filled performance context gets repeated in
Beowulf's report back to Hygelac in Geatland, when he observes of the
morning after the encounter with Grendel:

Þær wæs gidd ond gleo;   gomela Scilding,
felafricgende   feorran rehte;
hwilum hildedeor   hearpan wynne,
gomenwudu grette.
(2105–10)

There was poetry and pleasure; the old Scilding
knowing much related from far back;
sometimes the battle-bold one touched the instrument of pleasure,
the harp, with joy.

Although we did not see it at the time, Beowulf here reports on Hrothgar
himself telling tales to the accompaniment of the harp, generating mirth as
well as stories (*gidd ond gleo*), even as the account here goes on to stress
the old king telling with heightened emotion the passing of his youth. This
shows that performers could include the most elite, and they are envisaged
as telling tales of mirth and humour as well as those of sorrow in the idealized performance context of the mead hall.

The group of revellers drinking in the hall constitute a paradigmatic
heroic audience who would surely appreciate stories of joking in the face
of death, defiance through understatement, and the performed insouciance
of heroes. They would be well placed for enjoying Old English riddles.
It is easy to imagine a boisterous and agonistic group of men entertained
by riddles revolving around a sword or a drinking horn. Group dynamic
was probably fuelled by communal drinking, making the hall-thanes a
particularly appropriate audience for riddles that describe the perils of
booze,[48] even as such lubrication probably made them all the more prone
to laughter. If one of the key components for finding things funny is an

---

48 See Riddles 11, 18, 27, 28, discussed below.

audience primed to expect humour, such was apparently the case for any gathering of hall-thanes faced with a poet or performer. They would surely have loved the sardonic heroic humour drawn out in the first half of this chapter.

Pleasure in the comedy of embarrassment drawn out in the second half of this chapter might resonate with quite different audiences, of course, since such humour implicitly undercuts the imagined glories of the martial elite and their sense of power. It is easy to imagine broad swathes of society who might be happy to quietly laugh at the privileges of the warrior elite. Given the social stratification and gender hierarchy of early medieval England, such a counter-audience might include women of any rank, who are excluded from most of the martial camaraderie and whose resentment at the work of the sword is made explicit in Riddle 20; the slaves and the servants who were serving the tables for all the drinking thanes, who might listen to poetic performances in the household but not be inclined to identify with the elite warriors contained in them; men and women of a religious calling, who might question the terms of earthly glory in such heroic literature, and whose competition with the imagined warrior elite was seen in the analysis of Riddle 51 above; the farmers and freemen whose lives could be upturned by a call for military action or by the disruption of military campaigns; artisans and city-dwellers, who might have a significant social distance from the imagined communities of warriors; and the peasants working in the fields, who would have laboured to create the food for the warriors that does not get described in Old English feast scenes. Any or all of these audiences might appreciate following what is not said and enjoy laughing quietly while watching King Hrothgar squirm.

The imagined community of the mead hall, then, excluded many in society. Nevertheless, that audience of elite secular martial men coming together as they enjoyed a convivial performance is a clear-cut community of laughter, and the cohesion seen in Heorot after the flyting with Unferth or the tale of the Fight at Finnsburh suggests the power of humour to create community in such a place. This is a paradigmatic imagined audience for all kinds of performance. It proves handy to conjure such an audience for enjoying much of the humour in this study, particularly bawdy riddles and playful challenges, even as it will be seen that this audience gets laughed at more often than it gets portrayed laughing. Humour can cut in many directions, and the two different forms of humour investigated in this chapter give a good sense of how an ideology of heroism can both get built up by moments of comedy (as in the insouciance of the hero) and taken down through laughter (as in the comedy of embarrassment in the portrayal of court etiquette). Humour serves competing social functions, even as it entertains broadly.

Chapter Five

Playing with Parody to Comic Effect

Mocking one of the heroes in a heroic narrative – seen in the undercutting of King Hrothgar described in the last chapter – suggests how humour can serve a satirical purpose. The present chapter will build on that insight with poems that work more forcefully against the expectations of their genre and to fuller comic effect. The clash between Christian stories and the trappings of heroic narrative set up moments of comedy in the poems *Judith* and *Andreas*. In such cases, the humour has both local and larger effects, potentially laughing at an ideology of heroism that is getting displaced by that of Christianity. In both instances, the humour arises from inverting the expectations that are generated by this form. To contextualize that process, it will be useful to first consider the extreme case of a riddle that inverts the expectations of what a riddle should do.

Monster Riddles: Riddling with the Riddle Form

Riddles imply a compact with their audience. The riddler provides clues, many of which will be blinds suggesting false possibilities, but some of which will provide useful details, albeit presented from a surprising point of view, and all of which will retrospectively fit in the description of a recognizable riddle subject.[1] Some riddles, though, cheat on that compact, and that very cheating can generate humour. Riddle 86 of the Exeter Book collection provides an extreme example:

Wiht cwom gongan   þær weras sæton
monige on mæðle,   mode snottre;

---

[1] Part of the definition of riddles proposed by W.J. Pepicello and Thomas A. Green, *The Language of Riddles: New Perspectives* (Columbus: Ohio State University Press, 1984), 88; see, further, chap. 1 above.

hæfde an eage   ond earan twa,
ond twegen fet,   twelf hund heafda,
hryc ond wombe   ond honda twa,   5
earmas ond eaxle,   anne sweoran
ond sidan twa.   Saga hwæt ic hatte.[2]
(Riddle 86)

A creature came walking where men sat,
many at a meeting, wise in mind;
it had one eye and two ears,
and two feet, twelve hundred heads,
a back and a belly and two hands,
arms and shoulders, one neck
and two sides. Say what I am called.

The clues here seem obvious enough. Itemizing body parts is a common
trope in the riddles, and it is not unusual for the parts not to fit together in
an obvious way, as in Riddle 31, where elements of human or animal anatomy fail to add up to a regular whole, creating at first a kind of monster
before a perceptive reader resolves the clues into a bagpipe.[3] The inventory
of body parts in Riddle 86 looks close to regular, presenting a creature
that can walk (*gongan*), and that is one eye shy of the regular count (line
3a), but is otherwise provided with a wholesome tally of body parts (two
ears, two feet, back and belly, two hands, arms, and shoulders, one neck,
and two sides), apart from one casual but rather significant exception: the
presence of twelve hundred heads (line 4b). With the addition of that profusion of heads, what otherwise would look like a slightly odd creature is
suddenly monstrous indeed.

The very process of enumerating in this riddle sounds like an arithmetical puzzle, another recognizable subset of riddles, and one that often
inverts conventional arithmetical logic, showing how two plus two does
not always equal four.[4] Riddle 46, discussed in chapter 8 below, provides

---

2 Text from Bernard J. Muir, *The Exeter Anthology of Old English Poetry*, 2 vols. (Exeter:
   University of Exeter Press, 1994; revised ed., 2000), who numbers this his Riddle 85, but
   rejecting his emendation of line 7b.
3 See Nigel Barley, "Structural Aspects of the Anglo-Saxon Riddle," *Semiotica* 10 (1974):
   143–75; and my "Incongruity in Riddle 31."
4 See Dieter Bitterli, *Say What I am Called: The Old English Riddles of the Exeter Book
   and the Anglo-Latin Riddle Tradition* (Toronto: University of Toronto Press, 2009),
   chap. 3, on riddles as arithmetical puzzles.

a good example, where five people constitute an unlikely plethora of relations that seem not to add up until a riddle solver thinks through the disruptive effects of incest and the personnel in a famous biblical story. In Riddle 86, the effect of the tricky numbers is amplified by an opening that builds up the riddler's agonistic baiting of the audience. This particular *wiht* came where men (*weras*, line 1b, a gendered word, suggesting those with relative power in early medieval England) were sitting at a meeting or assembly (*on mæðle*, line 2a), presumably an opportunity for these men to show their intellectual prowess that will be challenged by the entering creature. Indeed, this internal audience is characterized as *mode snottre* ("wise in mind," 2b), adding to the sense of their anticipated skills. Such a wise group of men at the meeting place had better be able to name a *wiht* that walks in! And the numbers in the itemization suggest that the internal and external audience ought to be able to solve the riddle through arithmetical prowess, with some paradoxical turn, as in Riddle 46.

And yet, as commentators concede, the creature would be nigh impossible to name were it not for a surviving Latin analogue in Symphosius's Enigma 94, which is provided with a solution: *Luscus alium uendens*, One-Eyed Seller of Garlic. This is a solution that is arbitrary and capricious. The super-abundance of heads might reasonably hint at a special sense, namely the carrying of some bulbous vegetable matter, and so a Seller of Garlic is a reasonable solution to the riddling paradox, but there is no reason within the Exeter Book riddle for such a person to have a single eye. The extra detail is motivated within the Symphosius riddle, which suggests how the plenitude of heads fails to compensate for the missing part of the seller's own anatomy, asking of the vegetable vendor, "From where can he, who sells what he has, procure what he has not?"[5] Without that nudge (and the provision of an explanatory title), the very notion of the vendor of this heady and healthy vegetable being one-eyed is an arbitrary trick which makes the solution of the riddle available only to the one posing the riddle. Setting an arbitrary rather than a knowable solution subverts the fundamental compact of the riddle, denying expectations in a comic incongruity. It thereby mocks both those wise men at the meeting and the audience of would-be riddle solvers.

Such riddling trickery is common enough to constitute a recognized subgenre, namely that of the neck-riddle, defined by Archer Taylor as "a description of a scene that can be interpreted only by the one who sets the

---

5 T.J. Leary, ed., *Symphosius, the Aenigmata: An Introduction, Text, and Commentary* (London: Bloomsbury, 2014), enigma 94; translation from the commentary (294).

puzzle."[6] Such riddles are almost always funny because of the way they frustrate the most basic rule of the riddle form, thereby establishing incongruity by upsetting expectations. They proceed through a kind of metalepsis that forces the audience to jump levels from engaging the puzzle inside the genre to noticing the expectations of the genre. Presumably such a shift could frustrate an audience enough for it to react with anger but, given the low-stakes play-world of most riddle contests, it is more likely to amuse. An audience might react with laughter on the release of pent-up problem-solving energy or in recognition of the meta-incongruity of the form.

In the case of Riddle 86, that meta-incongruity may go further still. The riddle begins with a third-person perspective, common in many of the Exeter Book riddles, but the final line is presented with a first-person perspective, also common in many riddles, as the creature concludes by asking, "Saga hwæt ic hatte," "say what I am called."[7] This seems to be a mistake after so much third-person description and is duly corrected in the editions of Williamson and of Muir, who emend the final half-line to "Saga hwæt hio hatte" ("say what it is called").[8] And yet the reading in the manuscript may be deliberate, bringing about a different version of the neck-riddle. If the manuscript reading is allowed to stand, the monstrous and impossibly difficult creature described does not need to be guessed after all. In this reading, the difficult clues of the riddle were merely a blind for distracting an audience from a straightforward response. A wise riddle solver could answer the question posed by saying that you are the riddler.[9] The switching of levels from an imagined world within the riddle text to a literal response to the one telling that text is another form of metalepsis that cheats on a different implied contract with the audience. As so often with metalepsis, the upsetting of expectation is funny, as the shock of shifting levels presents an appropriately inappropriate incongruity. Instead of

---

6 Archer Taylor, "The Varieties of Riddles," in *Philologica: The Malone Anniversary Studies*, eds. Thomas A. Kirby and Henry Bosley Woolf (Baltimore: Johns Hopkins University Press, 1949), 1–8, at 6.

7 Orton, "The Exeter Book *Riddles*," divides the riddles by whether they present their subject in the first or third person. The closing formula "say what I am called" is more common, occurring in Riddles 1 (in modified form), 3, 8, 10, 12, 23, 62, 66, 73, 80, 83, while "say what it is called" occurs only in Riddle 39, although numerous riddles use the third-person viewpoint.

8 Williamson, *Old English Riddles*, 115, where this is his Riddle 82; Muir ed., *Exeter Anthology*, 373. Most other editors and commentators assume such an error but do not correct the line.

9 See further my "Mock-Riddles in Old English: Exeter Riddles 86 and 19," *Studies in Philology* 93, no. 2 (Spring 1996): 180–7, and compare the most famous folk example, "As I was traveling to St. Ives, I met a man with seven wives."

doing the work of engaging the extended content of the riddle, the audience only needs to react to the framing.

In a scribal culture that includes frequent scribal substitutions, it is hard to tell if this is a deliberate trick of the riddler or a scribal error, but the same displacement is now apparent in one other Exeter Book riddle, the runically challenging Riddle 19, explored above in chapter 2, which may be another mock riddle in the same manner as Riddle 86.[10] In both cases, the joke of the ending is the more appealing because the clues of the main text are so very difficult to resolve. In both cases, too, the metalepsis of the solution means that the riddles play with the conventions of the riddling genre, presenting what might be seen as a parody of the form, and creating comic effect by messing with conventions.

Other Exeter Book riddles play with expectations in different ways. Riddle 47 appears to provide its answer in the first words of the riddle, as was seen in chapter 2 above, and Stewart argues that it, too, constitutes a parody of the riddle form.[11] The incorporation of runes as both letters and words defies aural expectations of poetry, as explored in chapter 2. In all such cases, an audience struggling to solve the clues is going to react to the realization that they are pursuing the wrong terms of reference – that the solver does not need to tackle the apparent clues proffered – with both a groan and laughter, partly from the release of psychic energy so far expended on the puzzle, partly from the instantaneous re-visioning from the high domain of pondering metaphor to the lower one of literal message, and partly from a sense of superiority on realizing the answer. Riddle 86 presents play that makes the form particularly obvious and mocks the audience through humour for not being sufficiently cautious about accepting the implicit contract of the genre.

Similar play, but with a different genre, is evident in the two religious poems to be considered in this chapter that take over the conventions of heroic poetry and use them for distinctive Christian purposes. *Andreas* presents a complicated case that is repeatedly funny as it exploits momentary incongruities to create humour in a poem that may directly parody the heroic conventions as a whole. Before considering that example, I will turn to another work that has long been recognized for moments of mock-heroic form, namely the Old English poem *Judith*. The humour here clearly serves the purpose of telling a Christian story with renewed power by exploiting and inverting some heroic conventions.

---

10 I pursue the claim in more detail in "Mock-Riddles."
11 Ann Harleman Stewart, "Old English Riddle 47 as Stylistic Parody," *Papers on Language and Literature* 11 (1975): 227–45.

Mock-Heroic *Judith*

In the biblical story of Judith, a woman, humble, pure, little, and weak (in Ælfric's summary assessment), overcomes a military leader of great might.[12] The female protagonist achieves this end by deploying sexual allure in order to behead the martial leader of the Assyrians. The underlying paradox of the weak overpowering the strong, here embodied as a woman defeating a man, demonstrates in its Old Testament context God's support for his chosen people. It is consonant with and can prefigure the Christian doctrine of the weak inheriting the earth (cf. Matthew 23:12, Luke 14:11), and that is one of the explicit morals drawn by Ælfric, who translates the story into Old English and provides a commentary. In another interpretation common in exegetical tradition, Ælfric also suggests that Judith represents the congregation of the faithful and the power of the church to cut off the head of the old devil, which is sin. Through such interpretations, Ælfric allays a certain anxiety manifest in dealing with a story that is premised upon sexual allure, an aspect which he strikingly downplays in his translation.[13] Ælfric's version is instructive in another way, too, since it shows how this story, for all its underlying incongruities, can be successfully conveyed without humour. The anonymous translation into Old English verse, by contrast, embraces and enhances the paradoxes of the story, re-telling it in a way that plays up the humour.

The Old English poem *Judith* survives in a fragmentary state in MS London, BL Cotton Vitellius A. xv, where it comes beside the poem *Beowulf*, with which it shares a scribe.[14] In its current state, the Old English *Judith* relates just part of the biblical story, Judith 12:10–16:1. Most modern

---

12 "Heo eadmod 7 clæne, 7 ofercom þone modigan, lytel 7 unstrang, 7 alede þone
    miclan" ("She was humble and pure, and overcame the proud one, little and weak, and
    cast down the great one"), Ælfric's *Homily on Judith*, ed. S.D. Lee, lines 344–5; also,
    Bruno Assmann, ed., *Angelsächsische Homilien und Heiligenleben*, Bibliothek der
    angelsächsischen Prosa 3 (Kassel, 1889; repr. with a suppl. intro. by Peter Clemoes,
    Darmstadt, 1964), 102–16, homily IX, lines 410–11. The Book of Judith is considered
    part of the apocrypha in the Protestant tradition but was a canonical book of the Bible
    in the Middle Ages. On Ælfric, see chap. 6 below.
13 For an outstanding reading of the homily and the underlying unease, see Mary Clayton,
    "Ælfric's *Judith*: Manipulative or Manipulated?" *Anglo-Saxon England* 23 (1994): 215–27.
14 Mark Griffith, ed., *Judith* (Exeter: University of Exeter Press, 1997), with a full
    introduction, including useful information on the biblical source. *Judith* is written by
    Scribe B of *Beowulf*, which it now follows, but most likely once preceded with some
    intervening texts; see Simon C. Thomson, *Communal Creativity in the Making of the
    'Beowulf' Manuscript: Towards a History of Reception for the Nowell Codex* (Leiden:
    Brill, 2018).

commentators assume that not much text is lost from the beginning and that the poem only dealt with the second half of the biblical book, as is suggested by the poet's omission of characters from the first half who appear in the surviving part of the story, including any mention of Holofernes's superior, Nebuchadnezzar, or of the prominent character Achior.[15] Within the surviving part, the poet makes some substantial changes in shaping the story, reducing the main thrust to a contrast between a virtuous Judith and villainous Holofernes. The poet shields Judith from the role of instigating Holofernes's drunkenness by not having her present at the (much-expanded) drinking scene, rearranges Judith's incitement of the Bethulians to play up both her role and her emotion, and adds a battle scene between the Assyrians and the Bethulians at the end.[16] In a story about a woman wielding a sword and galvanizing her people, much critical attention has appropriately focused on what the poem reveals about attitudes to gender.[17] The poet's version of the story reveals the influence of Christian exegesis even as it dwells on the literal narrative.[18] I will focus on the humour, first by looking closely at one particular scene that the poet chooses to convey with high comedy and then by looking more briefly at how humour runs across the poem as a whole.[19]

---

15 See, for example, Griffith, *Judith*; Thomson, *Communal Creativity*; David Chamberlain, "*Judith*: A Fragmentary and Political Poem," in *Anglo-Saxon Poetry: Essays in Appreciation*, eds. Lewis E. Nicholson and Dolores Warwick Frese (Notre Dame, IN: University of Notre Dame Press, 1975), 135–59, presents the opposite case.

16 In addition to Griffith, *Judith*, see, in particular, Hugh Magennis, "Contrasting Narrative Emphases in the Old English Poem 'Judith' and Ælfric's Paraphrase of the Book of Judith," *Neuphilologische Mitteilungen* 96 (1995): 61–6; Lori Ann Garner, "The Art of Translation in the Old English *Judith*," *Studia Neophilologica* 73 (2001): 171–83; Haruko Momma, "Epanalepsis: A Retelling of the Judith Story in the Anglo-Saxon Poetic Language," *Studies in the Literary Imagination* 36, no. 1 (Spring 2003): 59–73.

17 Karma Lochrie, "Gender, Sexual Violence, and the Politics of War in the Old English *Judith*," in *Class and Gender in Early English Literature*, eds. Britton J. Harwood and Gillian R. Overing (Bloomington: Indiana University Press, 1994), 1–20, points to the intersection of sexual and political violence; Stacy S. Klein, "Gender," in *A Handbook of Anglo-Saxon Studies*, eds. Jacqueline Stodnick and Renée Trilling (Oxford: Blackwell, 2012), 39–54, reads the poem optimistically as revealing the lability of gender identity and the possibility of overcoming toxic martial masculinity.

18 See, in particular, Ann W. Astell, "Holofernes's Head: *tacen* and Teaching in the Old English *Judith*," *Anglo-Saxon England* 18 (1989): 117–33; Griffith, *Judith*.

19 For a good brief account that highlights some of the humour, see Orchard, *Critical Companion*, 5–12. Ivan Herbison, "Heroism and Comic Subversion in the Old English *Judith*," *English Studies* 91 (2010): 1–25, attempts the fullest reading of comedy in the poem, although is often unconvincing because he does not explain why he sees passages as funny.

One of the funniest moments comes towards the end of the poem. The Assyrian soldiers are desperately in need of their battle leader since the Bethulian army is suddenly attacking them, but they believe that their lord is busy in *wifcyþþe* (intimacy with a woman)[20] inside his tent, so they are extremely loath to interrupt him. The scene is implicated in all kinds of serious issues – the gender violence of Holofernes's imagined sexual desire is obvious and scary, while the retainers' paralysis suggests a breakdown in lord–retainer relationships and the bonds of the loyalty system – and yet the moment is presented here as one of high comedy.[21] Pinpointing the techniques for creating humour is facilitated by comparison both with the source and with Ælfric's handling of the same scene in his Old English prose version.

The scene is presented with gentle hints of comedy in Jerome's Vulgate version of Judith 14:9–13, here presented in the Douai–Rheims translation. The Assyrian watchmen run to the tent of Holofernes:

> 9 And they that were in the tent came, and made a noise [perstrepentes] before the door of the chamber to awake him, endeavouring by art to break his rest, that Holofernes might awake, not by their calling him, but by their noise [a sonantibus].

> 10 For no man durst knock, or open and go into the chamber of the general of the Assyrians.

> ...

> 13 Then Vagao going into his chamber, stood before the curtain, and made a clapping with his hands [et plausum fecit manibus suis]: for he thought that he was sleeping with Judith.

The circumspection of the Assyrian inner circle pushes them into an action that is funny in its timidity and inappropriateness to the situation – making a noise in an attempt to get their leader's attention through directed indirection at a moment when more direct action seems called for – comically hinting at their discomfiture in a circumstance where the dramatic irony is obvious since we, the audience, know that Holofernes is

---

20 The word is used of King Cynewulf's visit to a mistress in the chronicle story of "Cynewulf and Cyneheard" (s.a. 755 for 757); conveniently ed. Baker, *Introduction*, 186, text 3, sentence 4.

21 An early reading of the humour of the scene, with particular attention to the structure, is provided by Fredrik J. Heinemann, "*Judith* 236–91a: A Mock-Heroic Approach-to-Battle Type-Scene," *Neuphilologische Mitteilungen* 71 (1970): 83–96; Thomson, *Communal Creativity*, 61 sees it as "one of the most comic scenes in Old English literature."

dead and beheaded, even as they do not yet know this, but surely soon will. Ælfric translates the scene with efficiency and compression without any hint of humour:

> 7 hi [þa Syriscan] þa woldon awreccan heora ealdorman. Ac nan man ne dorste þa duru unlucan, ac hi woldon elles mid gehlyde hine awreccan.
> (Ælfric's homily on Judith, ed. Lee, lines 301–3)

> and they [the Assyrians] then wanted to arouse their leader from sleep. But no-one dared to open the door, but they wanted rather to arouse him with noise.

With characteristic brevity and efficiency, Ælfric presents the action and its motivation, but without pausing on the event long enough to pull out the dramatic irony or to allow the audience to dwell on the discomfiture of the Assyrian retainers, whose motivation is simply and explicitly stated by the narrator (*nan man ne dorste*) rather than shown in narrative time. This is both efficient and not funny.

The poet, on the other hand, presents the scene in a far more leisurely manner that allows full play of the humour:

> Beornas stodon
> ymbe hyra þeodnes træf   þearle gebylde,
> sweorcendferhðe.   Hi ða somod ealle
> ongunnon cohhetan,   cirman hlude
> ond gristbitian   – gode orfeorme –
> mid toðon, torn þoligende ...
>   Hogedon þa eorlas aweccan
> hyra winedryhten: him wiht ne speow.
> (*Judith*, lines 267b–74)[22]

> Warriors stood
> about their lord's tent considerably roused [or greatly emboldened],[23]
> gloomy in mind. They then all together

---

22 The poem is cited from Griffith, ed., *Judith*.

23 DOE, following earlier editors, takes *gebylde* here in the special sense of "roused" s.v. *gebylded, gebyld*; Griffith *Judith* (note to line 268b) assumes the more customary sense of the verb *gebyldan*, "to make bold," arguing for its ironic use as the Assyrians become bold enough to make a noise.

began to clear their throats, to ahem loudly
and to gnash their teeth – estranged from good –
suffering grief....
The men intended to awaken
their liege lord: they did not succeed at all.

Many elements, from the micro to the macro, play up the humour here.
While it is true that the Vulgate gives the wake-up noises as a group
action, the choric nature of the activity is brought out more fully in the
Old English poem through the qualification of the plural pronoun in line
269b (*hi... somod ealle*, "they... all together"). The two adverbs provide
added emphasis to an idea of solidarity, an idea that is perhaps given yet
more emphasis by the pleonastic onset verb *ongunnon*, all of which is thoroughly deflated by the semantic weight of the verbs that follow. This group
solidarity is in order to collectively *cohhetan* (270a), a *hapax legomenon*
that is striking in its onomatopoeic power, the sense of which is summed
up in the DOE's definition which cautiously relates it to its later cognate: "to make a noise, perhaps specifically: to cough to gain attention."
Griffith picks up on Marckwardt's suggestion that the suffix "represents
an 'unsustained durative', indicating repeated or continuous action where
the repetition is not regular" and so arrives at a definition to "clear the
throat noisily and frequently." Whatever the detail – and the precise nature
of the activity is probably best hinted by the sound of the infinitive in Old
English, including its central guttural consonant – it is hard to imagine that
this is a particularly noble sound. The undignified choric throat-clearing is
amplified through the variation with two further verbs: *cirman*, "to make a
noise, (a) to utter sounds, cry out, wail (in poetry)," another sound which
is rarely happy and which probably carries extra onomatopoeic weight
here, and *gristbitian... mid toðon*, "to gnash/grind one's teeth," which is
recurringly used as a sound of despair.[24] Such indirect action would be
undignified in a single retainer. Here it is coming from the inner group of
retainers, which is the group close to the leader, the elite central corp. Such
activity is a massive deflation from what is expected of the *heorðwerod*
("hearth-retainers," "inner troop"), a comic incongruity, with the comedy
played up through the leisure of the narration, the emphatic redundancies,
and the ear-catching sound effects of the verbs.

The irony is also spelled out in a much more pointed manner than in the
source (or in Ælfric's rendering). The poet describes the action such that
we know why the retainers are doing what they are doing, but then adds

---

24 Definitions from DOE, s.v. *cirman* and *gristbitian*.

a narratorial explanation, emphatic in its redundancy, telling us outright what the retainers are intending, namely to awaken their lord. The reason for such emphatic redundancy is to provide a contrast with the following pithy summation through litotes: *him wiht ne speow* (274b, expressed in an impersonal structure, i.e. "it did not succeed at all for them"). As is apparent throughout this study, use of such litotes is often comic, especially if there is a substantial difference between the assertion and the action, as here, since it is so difficult to awaken the dead with the sound of throat clearing, however loudly a group tries. The poet knows that we the audience know what is going on, but the characters look extra foolish because they do not know. Dramatic irony joins comic incongruity in a humour of embarrassment at the discomfiture of the troop.

Such explicit incongruities are not the only sources of humour here. The vocabulary for the men and their lord contributes to the effect. *Beornas* (267b) in poetry are generally men of a certain martial calibre, captured by the DOE definition "1a with emphasis on martial vigour: noble, hero, warrior." That seems an unfortunate designation for a group of men facing defeat whose nearest approach to boldness comprises loudly clearing their throats. *Eorlas* (273b) probably follows a similar pattern, playing up the martial.[25] The inappropriateness is still clearer in the designation for the leader: *winedryhten* (274a) has a first element emphasizing amity and so gets defined by BT as "A friendly, gracious lord" and by Griffith as "lord and friend," even as it is specifically Holofernes's unfriendly nature that is causing the present predicament for his followers, who are so habituated to fear him that they cannot act straightforwardly. This kind of appropriate inappropriateness in the overtones of the vocabulary runs through the whole poem and adds a level of ironic humour throughout,[26] and is particularly concentrated here.

Diction, point of view, sound effects, and narrative pacing all point to humour that laughs at the heroic inadequacy of the Assyrian retainers, but this is not all. At a larger structural level, an audience is keyed at this point to expect the narrative to be setting up a coming battle in what can be characterized as an approach-to-battle type-scene.[27] Heinemann demonstrates that one of the characteristic elements building to such a scene is "The Narrator Relates the Troops' Intentions and Thoughts," and these intentions usually centre on the troops' plan to defeat the enemy. This is

---

25 DOE s.v. *eorl* "1b in poetry: warrior, man."
26 See below and Elizabeth M. Tyler, "Style and Meaning in *Judith*," *Notes Queries* 237 (1992): 16–19.
27 See Heinemann, "Mock Heroic."

a context for the logically redundant statement of intention at line 273, which is anticipated by the poet with an earlier redundant statement of intention,

> Hogedon aninga
> hyra hlaforde   hilde bodian
> (*Judith*, lines 250b–51)

> They intended at once
> to announce the battle to their lord.

This certainly sets up an expectation of the turn to battle, and the adverb of time (*aninga*) is particularly ironically inappropriate – the retainers may intend to announce the battle at once, but it takes up many lines of narrative as well as much imagined passing of time (*sið ond late*, 275a, "at last") to work through the non-announcement. Ironies continue – the retainers will not actually announce the battle since there will not actually be a battle but rather a running away, while there is not actually a lord to make the announcement to, since their ex-lord is currently headless, leaving the retainers headless and hence vulnerable.

The structural play also continues. As Heinemann observes, the actions of the one picked out to contact their leader play against the expectations of another conventional topos, here of the brave retainer who gets picked out for special treatment, such as the ones who make defiant speeches and push themselves forward to die in battle in *The Battle of Maldon*. Rather than such heroic action, the special retainer here, *niðheard* ("the battle-bold one," 277a) *nedde* ("ventured," 277a) to such an extent that he entered the tent. Already a travesty of the bold retainer who fights, this battle-bold one works through the feminized gestures of grief by falling down, tearing his hair and clothes, and articulating sorrow (280b–89a).[28] Where the expected motif sees a leader rising up and brandishing weapons while making an inspirational speech, this manifestation sees the individual dropping down and expressing despondency before abandoning weapons. The speech of despondency inverts the contents of Judith's earlier speech of inspiration to the Bethulians (lines 177–98), playing up the fundamental dichotomy between the side blessed by God and the mock-heroic status of

---

28 Lochrie, "Gender," suggests that these gestures of grief are marked as feminine, pointing to the mourner at the end of *Beowulf*; Heinemann, "Mock Heroic," shows how this is inverting the expected heroic scene.

the side that is not. The structural inversions here create such a huge gulf between expectation and action as to craft an incongruity that is marked by context and technique as thoroughly funny.

The comedy benefits from one further big-picture element of the poem, the reorganization of the biblical story into a more streamlined and dichotomous contrast of good opposed to evil. In this way, the poet has taken a story told through the conventions of heroic verse but adopted the conventions of a saint's life, a genre dominated by the contest between good and evil.[29] In hagiography evil has the upper hand in relation to conventional structures of secular power, but good has the benefit of divine authority and so is sure to win out in the end. That dichotomy creates a storyline where the outcome is ultimately happy, however horrifying the current tribulations, and where an audience in tune with the religious sympathy need never feel bad at laughing at the villains. The result is a genre that is surprisingly open to humour, as is explored in chapter 7 below. In *Judith*, those hagiographic sympathies invert the standard hierarchies of heroic narrative, where fighting men are habitually given the most sympathetic attention. Here a woman is presented as the hero and fighting men are mocked mercilessly. Manly physical superiority is shown to be ultimately valueless in a Christian ethic of supporting the meek.[30]

What is so effectively achieved in this one scene is also broadly present throughout the poem as a whole. The surviving fragment opens with a feast scene (lines 7–34), greatly amplified over the biblical source (Judith 12 and 13). This draws on the Germanic heroic tradition of the feast as an emblem of joy and community building, but here presented "as a travesty of such order and cohesion."[31] The audience is keyed to funny business by verse that pushes at an onomatopoeic effect, including the often-comic heightening of internal rhyme:

> Ða wearð Holofernus,
> goldwine gumena,   on gytesalum:
> hloh ond hlydde,   hlynede ond dynede,
> þæt mihten fira bearn   feorran gehyran
> hu se stiðmoda   styrmde ond gylede,
> modig ond medugal,   manode geneahhe
> bencsittende   þæt hi gebærdon wel.
> (21b–27)

---

29 Many commentators have pointed out how *Judith* appeals to the dichotomizing conventions of hagiography; see, especially, Magennis, "Contrasting"; Griffith, *Judith*.

30 Herbison, "Comic Subversion," suggests a very different valorization of the use of humour through the poem.

31 As shown by Magennis, "Adaptation," 332. See, more generally, Magennis, *Images of Community*.

         Then Holofernus,
the gold-friend of men, was in a festive mood:
he laughed and roared, bellowed and hail-fellowed,
so that the children of men might hear from afar
how the fierce-hearted one raged and yelled,
proud and flush with mead, he often exhorted
those sitting on the benches that they should have a great time.

The sequence of verbs at line 23, "hloh ond hlydde, hlynede ond dynede," stands out for multiple chiming effects, from the true rhyme of *hlynede* and *dynede* to the off-rhyme of *hlydde* to the striking alliterative consonant cluster of *hl-* to the echo from guttural *-h* to *-de*. Four verbs in a line is always striking in Old English and these four resound in an onomatopoeic manner, suggesting the frenetic noise that their semantic weight denotes. This is an instance of the ominous nature of laughter.[32] The problems of excess are evident in the following chiming verbs, as the leader *styrmde and gylede* and pushes his retainers into a moral and practical abyss (*manode... þæt hi gebærdon*). The sound effects encourage an attentive audience to be alert to the heightened passage and probably sounded comic in their overblown acoustical effect.

    Not just the sounds make this feast sound funny. The choice of vocabulary throughout the scene carries deeply ironic weight. *Medugal* ("flush with mead," 26a) has strongly negative overtones since the adjective *gal* means "wanton, lascivious, evil," and the comparable term *ealugal* "ale-gal" is used of the inhabitants of Sodom in *Genesis A*.[33] The word resonates here with retainers who are *medowerig* ("mead-weary," 229, 245) and *winsæd* ("wine-sated," 71), emphasizing the deleterious effects of alcohol as seen in Riddle 28 (if that is booze rather than book) described above. *Gytesalum* is a *hapax legomenon*, combining *sæl*, "happiness," with an outpouring (*gyte*), here of alcohol, a compound which is steeped in irony in this context. Holofernus is called *goldwine gumena* ("gold-friend of men," 22a) although it is notable that he is never portrayed as sharing treasure in the way of the positive *goldwine*, while his failure to be a friend to his men has already been remarked on, making both halves of that compound ironic. *Stiðmod* ("fierce-hearted," 25a) is overly appropriate for such a leader, whose strength of mind is in leading his followers to perdition. Even the term for the retainers as *bencsittende* ("those

---

32 As discussed in the introduction above, and Magennis, "Images of Laughter."
33 See DOE, s.v. *gal*, *ealu-gal*.

sitting on the bench," 27a) gets ironized, as Momma has nicely demonstrated. The term here is a variation on another common compound word for such retainers, used just before this passage, *fletsittende* (19a), "those sitting in the hall," where the root-word, *flett*, usually denotes "hall" through synecdoche from its primary sense of "floor."[34] When the same term is used just a little later for the retainers who have been subject to the heavy drinking (32b–34a), Momma suggests that the root form is now literally appropriate after the retainers have lost contact with the benches on which they had been sitting, slumped down to the literal floor level.[35] So the mighty feasting of warriors has fallen, creating such glaring incongruity between description and expectation as humour thrives on, particularly as the reality proves so much more degraded (both literally and metaphorically lower) than the ideal.

The deleterious effects of the alcoholic flow are played up through what comes next:

Swa se inwidda   ofer ealne dæg
dryhtguman sine   drencte mid wine,
swiðmod sinces brytta,   oðþæt hie on swiman lagon,
oferdrencte his duguðe ealle,   swylce hie wæron deaðe geslegene,
agotene goda gehwylces.
(*Judith*, lines 28–32a)

So the wicked one throughout the whole day
made his retainers drunk with wine,
the strong-minded distributor of treasure, until they lay in a swoon,
he inebriated all of his followers, as if they had been slain in death,
drained of all good.

The arresting central effect here depends again on the finite verbs, this time *drencte* and *oferdrencte*, in a way that is hard to convey in translation. *Drencan* is a weak class I causative verb created from the noun *drinc*.[36] It is defined by DOE with a useful range: "1. to cause to drink, give drink to; 1a. to intoxicate; 2. to drench, saturate; 3. to submerge, dip; 4. to drown (trans. and intrans.)." The verb borders on the wholesome possibility of giving drink in a positive upbeat Germanic feasting scene,

---

34 See DOE, s.v. *flett*.
35 Momma, "Epanalepsis," 62–3.
36 Richard M. Hogg and R.D. Fulk, *A Grammar of Old English; Volume 2: Morphology* (Chichester: Wiley-Blackwell, 2011), 258–9, §6.78.

but inclines more to the negative of forcing drink upon people, intoxicating them, drenching them, or, indeed, drowning them. Negative connotations are confirmed in the more explicit excess of *oferdrencte*, "excessively gave drink to in an intoxicating manner,"[37] which clearly conveys an over-suffusing with alcohol and an under-pouring of goodness (cf. line 32a). The effect is clarified by the simile at line 31b, "as if they had been slain in death," which, of course, they metaphorically have been and soon literally will be. Line 30b continues the play as the retainers lay "on swiman," with hints of both swimming (in the head) and swooning, activating the idea of not waving but drowning.[38] The poet is laughing at the retainers and explicitly condemning the leader, now *se inwidda* ("the wicked one," 28a). He is an ironic distributor of treasure, since he is dealing out the false treasure of intoxication rather than the material goods seen as more wholesome in heroic verse. His designation as *brytta* ("distributor," "giver"), both here at line 30a and again at line 90a, is the more ironic as the same term is used affirmatively by Judith of God at line 93a. Even the descriptive *swiðmod* ("strong-minded," 30a), carries heavy irony since this leader is certainly authoritarianly strong-willed, and yet his strong mind is about to completely desert him as he collapses in an alcohol-induced swoon that leaves him first mindless and then headless. Such hefty ironies emphasize the moral dichotomies of the story by disparaging the villainous, and do this with appropriate inappropriateness that would generate happy laughter of contempt in an attentive audience.

Ironies of heroic action and vocabulary run throughout the poem, as has been nicely explicated by Tyler. She shows how *wiggend* and *hæleð*, terms for "warrior" or "hero" which carry martial connotations in heroic verse, are used in appropriately inappropriate ways when applied to the Assyrians. The irony stretches even to the use of a verb of action. *Steppan*, "to march, advance," is used with its traditional valence of the Bethulians in their advance into battle at the end of the poem, but the Assyrians *stopon* (in lines 39 and 69) as selected soldiers lead Judith into Holofernes's tent and then march out – "hardly martial activity," as Tyler wryly observes.[39]

The comic play continues in the description of the interior of Holofernes's tent. In another modification of the source that has seen much critical

---

37 BT defines *oferdrencan*: "to overdrench, give a person too much to drink, to inebriate, intoxicate," and cf. the negative overtones of *ofer-* in *The Durham Proverbs*.

38 BT, s.v. *swima* offers two definitions: I. swimming in the head, dizziness, giddiness, vertigo; II. a state of unconsciousness, swoon.

39 Tyler, "Style and Meaning," 17.

attention, an "eallgylden | fleohnet fæger" ("an all golden beautiful fly-net," 46b–47a) is hung around the leader's bed, a screen which allows him to see out, but no-one to see in, unless he allows them to come up close. This mosquito net has significance as a prop for the plot since it explains why the Assyrian inner troops dare not approach Holofernes in his bed to tell him of the Bethulian attack, as described above. It also speaks to his character since it dramatizes the leader's uninterrupted and unknowable gaze upon his subjects even as they cannot gaze upon him, an asymmetry of sight that dramatizes the asymmetry of power in a leader who does not cultivate the usual bonds of trust. At a poetic level, the overtones of a net from the psalms is as a device of the trickster tricked, while the idea of a fly-net hints at a spider's web, where the spider will capture and consume those who enter it (with a sense of Judith's peril), even as, in ironic reversal, it is the spider at the centre who ends up dead and dismembered.[40] Again, the difference between expectation and reality, presented with appropriate sudden reversal, creates humour here.

The action proceeds as it must: Holofernes passes out from drink, Judith prays to God for strength and then beheads the mighty leader. The radical inversion of the wise woman wielding a sword to behead the battle-bold heathen hound is presented as something to be marvelled at with full poetic force. Judith grabs Holofernes "fæste be feaxum sinum" ("fast by his hair," 99a), which makes the more striking her characterization as *ða wundenlocc* ("the one with curly or braided hair," 103b) just four lines later as she chops off the leader's hair-covered head. The substantive probably plays up her gender, since she was characterized by the same substantive earlier (77b), although such a reading is complicated by the use of the same term for the Bethulians (325a).[41] Another crux here may also be relevant as Judith pulls the unconscious Holofernes towards her *bysmerlice* (100a), a term that would normally mean "shamefully" (perhaps as ironic reading of such an action in a more expected context?), although the latest editor deflects the risk of criticism by suggesting "ignominiously," even as the term keys us in to the shame of Holofernes in his powerlessness.[42] Judith and her maid take the severed head back to Bethulia where the motif of fortunes reversed continues as the once repressed turn to triumph

---

40 See Carl T. Berkhout and J.F. Doubleday, "The Net in *Judith* 46b–54a," *Neuphilologische Mitteilungen* 74 (1973): 630–4; Griffith, *Judith*.

41 See, for example, Heide Estes, "Feasting with Holofernes: Digesting Judith in Anglo-Saxon England," *Exemplaria* 15, no. 2 (2003): 325–50.

42 Griffith, *Judith*, 123, note to line 100a. DOE sense 1a seems to apply best, "of affliction visited on someone: shamefully, ignominiously, contemptuously."

after Judith's speech of inspiration and display of the bloody head. The poet then turns to a battle scene, complete with beasts of battle, which is the context for the comic scene of Assyrian timidity before the tent of their slain leader, discussed above. The poem ends with Assyrian rout and Bethulian triumph.

The poem as a whole, then, makes use of humour to present what appears to be a comedy in Christian terms as good triumphs over evil. The humour works particularly well to undercut the martial exploits of the belittled Assyrian force. The poet draws on the language and conventions that celebrate martial action and mocks them in a story where ultimate success has everything to do with divine support rather than traditional heroic strength and those that are meek can expect to triumph. The poem does not so much parody heroic poetry as deploy the conventions in unexpected ways and thereby create comic inversions. This is humour of inversion in the cause of Christian triumphalism rather than subversive humour. Such a technique will be seen again in the saints' lives discussed in chapter 7 below, but first I will consider one further poem, the account of the apostle Andrew among the Mermedonians in *Andreas*, that might work in similar ways or might just go one stage further into full-blown parody.

How Far Can You Go? A Rollicking Reading of *Andreas*

There is something funny, in the sense of disconcertingly odd, about the poem, *Andreas*. It provides an account of the misadventures and yet ultimate success of the apostle Andrew, who saves the apostle Matthew from the clutches of the Mermedonian cannibals at the edge of the world. The underlying story is a hagiographic romance – a form that combines the conventions of a saint's life with those of an adventure tale in a way that could make a good theologian feel uncomfortable, and Ælfric, for one, chooses to relate a completely different story about Andrew.[43] The Old English poem uses the style and language of traditional martial Old English poetics, most obviously echoing language seen in *Beowulf*, and by doing so creates a striking dissonance between expectations of such a storytelling style and the saintly action of an apostle. Indeed, the poem is so rife with incongruity

---

43 Ælfric, CH I.38 (ed. Clemoes, 507–19). For his source, see Malcolm Godden, *Ælfric's Catholic Homilies: Introduction, Commentary and Glossary*, EETS s.s. 18 (Oxford: Oxford University Press, 2000), 318–29; for Ælfric's treatment of the occasion in contrast with the hagiographic romance story, see Scott DeGregorio, "'Þegenlic' or 'Flæsclic': The Old English Prose Legends of St. Andrew," *The Journal of English and Germanic Philology* 102 (2003): 449–64.

that it is easy to see funny moments. How fully such humour extends and what that humour is doing are questions I will tackle here.[44]

Andreas tells the story of Andrew's mission to save Matthew from the Mermedonians, who capture foreign visitors as a food source, blind them, give them a mind-destroying potion that makes them like animals, and then hold them for thirty days before slaughtering them for food. On the twenty-seventh day of Matthew's captivity, the Lord comes to Andrew in the city of Achaia and sets him the mission of rescue. Andrew is reluctant at first, cavilling over the initial practical difficulty – how could he get to Mermedonia in time? – and suggesting that the Lord's angels could better be set to what he cannot do. After this initial hesitation of faith, Andrew takes on the task. He goes with his followers to the seashore, where he finds a boat and steersman fortuitously bound for Mermedonia. The steersman, who turns out to be Jesus disguised as a boatsman, encourages Andrew to recount his experience as an apostle to his followers within earshot of his unrecognized Lord. After a further exchange, Andrew and his companions sleep and are miraculously conveyed to the walls of Mermedonia. Awakening, he realizes the true nature of the steersman, while his companions recount confirmatory visions. In Mermedonia, Andrew soon sets Matthew and the other captives free, who then leave the story along with Andrew's companions. The Mermedonians, now discomfited by lack of food, draw lots to decide which of their own people to sacrifice for the good of the collective meat supply. Later, spurred on by the devil in disguise, they capture Andrew and torture him for three days. Andrew is tormented by being dragged around the town, but, after an expression of anguish, the trail of his blood becomes a primrose path and his body is miraculously restored. Andrew summons up a huge flood that kills many of the Mermedonians. Realizing the folly of their ways, the remainder decide to convert to his faith and appeal to his God. The flood stops and is reversed; most of the slain are brought back to life; and the Mermedonians convert en masse. Andrew wants to leave but is required by the Lord to stay for a further week. He becomes the spiritual leader of the Mermedonians, establishes a church and preaches to them before returning to the city of Achaia.[45]

---

44 I have discussed the use of humour in this narrative in "Eating People Is Wrong: Funny Style in *Andreas* and Its Analogues," in *Anglo-Saxon Styles*, eds. Catherine E. Karkov and George Hardin Brown (Albany: State University of New York Press, 2003), 201–22, and some elements of the present discussion borrow wording from my treatment there.

45 Richard North and Michael D.J. Bintley, eds., *Andreas: An Edition* (Liverpool: Liverpool University Press, 2016) provides text, translation, and commentary. Useful

Such is the story that the Old English poet chooses to recount, drawing on a now-lost Latin source that is best reflected in a surviving Greek text, the *Praxeis Andreou kai Matheian eis ten Polin ton Anthropophagon* (*Acts of Andrew and Matthias in the city of the cannibals*).[46] The Old English poem survives uniquely in the Vercelli Book, the late tenth-century compilation from Kent that probably reflects an ecclesiast's reading material. The same story is also told in an Old English prose version, which lacks the heightening effect of the poetic discourse, and so the poem will be the centre of discussion here.

Critical reception of *Andreas* has often reflected the interpretive trends of a scholarly age. Nineteenth-century critics uncovered with delight the overlaps in wording with *Beowulf*, and these have been prominently deployed ever since either to denigrate the artistry of the poem, or to elucidate the nature of poetic composition in an oral culture, or to demonstrate a patina of literate and textual allusion.[47] The oddity of the story has been much remarked, and one reaction has been to sublate the surface narrative by attending to the symbolic significance through typological readings, with particular emphasis on the poem's projection of the rite of baptism and the process of conversion.[48] While illuminating, such interpretations tend to overlook humour since they downplay attention to the surface of the narrative, which is of interest only as a vehicle for carrying more fundamental, and more serious, ideas. In reaction, a counter-flow of studies worked to recover the surface by offering close readings of the poem.[49] Recent interest has centred

---

earlier editions include Kenneth R. Brooks, ed., *Andreas and the Fates of the Apostles* (Oxford: Oxford University Press, 1961); Mary Clayton, ed. and trans., *Old English Poems of Christ and His Saints*, DOML (Cambridge, MA: Harvard University Press, 2013), 183–299.

46 The Greek text and a later Latin version, the Casanatensis, are made accessible in translation in Robert Boenig, trans., *The Acts of Andrew in the Country of the Cannibals: Translations from the Greek, Latin, and Old English* (New York: Garland, 1991).

47 For recent overviews, see F.J. Rozano-Garcia, "*Hwær Is Wuldor Þin?* Traditional Poetic Diction and the Alien Text in the Old English *Andreas*," *Peritia* 28 (2017): 177–94; Francis Leneghan, "The Departure of the Hero in a Ship: The Intertextuality of *Beowulf*, Cynewulf and *Andreas*," *SELIM* 24 (2019): 105–32.

48 Amity Reading, "Baptism, Conversion, and Selfhood in the Old English *Andreas*," *Studies in Philology* 112 (2015): 1–23 provides a recent example.

49 Most notably Edward B. Irving, Jr., "A Reading of *Andreas*: The Poem as Poem," *Anglo-Saxon England* 12 (1983): 215–37; see also Nathan A. Breen, "'What a Long, Strange Trip It's Been': Narration, Movement and Revelation in the Old English *Andreas*," *Essays in Medieval Studies* 25 (2008): 71–9.

more on the poem's portrayal of cannibalism and its intriguingly rich accounts of built structures and place.[50]

Humour in the poem has received some acknowledgment but is rarely a central focus of critical attention.[51] And yet, at times, the poem is clearly funny, with moments of irony, word play, and inversions of expectation. The incongruities at the root of that humour often depend on the mismatch between subject matter and the way in which it is described. "The familiar heroic language applied in such strange circumstances makes the monstrosity of the Mermedonians all the more evident," observes Bolintineanu, and the parading of that clash between style and subject matter, while often seen as a weakness by critics, makes an opening for comedy.[52] While the comedy often serves the pedagogical, catechetical, and poetic effect of the work, as has been seen in *Judith*, it may go yet further and parody and critique the underlying heroic tradition. I will explore here the mechanisms that mark certain scenes as clearly comic and then consider how far such interpretation can be taken in pondering what the humour is doing.

50 On cannibalism: Shannon N. Godlove, "Bodies as Borders: Cannibalism and Conversion in the Old English *Andreas*," *Studies in Philology* 106 (2009): 137–60; Fabienne L. Michelet, "Eating Bodies in the Old English *Andreas*," in *Fleshly Things and Spiritual Matters: Studies in the Medieval Body in Honour of Margaret Bridges*, eds. N. Nyffenegger and K. Rupp (Newcastle upon Tyne: Cambridge Scholars, 2011), 165–92; Aaron Hostetter, *Political Appetites: Food in Medieval English Romance* (Columbus: Ohio State University Press, 2017), chap. 1. On place, environment, and built structures: Lori Ann Garner, "The Old English *Andreas* and the Mermedonian Cityscape," *Essays in Medieval Studies* 24 (2008): 53–63; Michael D.J. Bintley, "Demythologising Urban Landscapes in *Andreas*," *Leeds Studies in English* 40 (2009): 105–18; Lindy Brady, "Echoes of Britons on a Fenland Frontier in the Old English *Andreas*," *Review of English Studies* 61 (2010): 669–89; Denis Ferhatović, "*Spolia*-Inflected Poetics of the Old English *Andreas*," *Studies in Philology* 110, no. 2 (2013): 199–219; Heide Estes, *Anglo-Saxon Literary Landscapes: Ecotheory and the Anglo-Saxon Environmental Imagination* (Amsterdam: Amsterdam University Press, 2017), chap. 2.
51 Roberta Frank, "North-Sea Soundings in *Andreas*," in *Early Medieval English Texts and Interpretations: Studies Presented to Donald G. Scragg*, eds. Elaine Treharne and Susan Rosser (Tempe, AZ: ACMRS, 2002), 1–11, in a brilliant reading of the kennings and imagery of the poem in light of the Old Norse tradition, points to some of the humour in showing how important it is not to be too doggedly literal.
52 Alexandra Bolintineanu, "The Land of Mermedonia in the Old English *Andreas*," *Neophilologus* 93 (2009): 149–64, at 156; see also Ivan Herbison, "Generic Adaptation in *Andreas*," in *Essays on Anglo-Saxon and Related Themes in Memory of Lynne Grundy*, eds. Jane Roberts and Janet Nelson (King's College London: Centre for Late Antique and Medieval Studies, 2000), 181–211.

Preaching to the Preacher in Chief:
Comic Ironies in *Andreas*

Ironies are rampant in the story and are often presented in such a way as to suggest they are deliberately funny. The presence of Christ himself in disguise as the pilot of the ship that takes Andrew and his followers to Mermedonia is a clear irony in the plot, playing on Christ's role as a pilot of all Christians, and the nautical grounding for some of the parables, and the comedy is played up as the apostle fails to recognize the ship's steersman.[53] The Old English poem deploys elements of traditional technique to heighten the effect. For example, the description of arranging and embarking on the sea journey is amplified through elements that critics sensitive to oral formulaic composition characterize as "the hero on the beach" type-scene so that the preparations are told with "high heroic decorum."[54] This adds to the incongruity because such poetic language anticipates a heroic and martial tale, expectations which are repeatedly conjured up to be denied. On the other hand, there are ways in which the inappropriate expectations are, nevertheless, appropriate since the saint's activities are, indeed, like the martial exploits of a hero as Andrew defeats the devils that come to torment him and the cannibals who have captured him. Such action is seen simultaneously from a Christian and a heroic perspective that embraces both the surface action of the story and its doctrinal implications.

The ironies pile on as Andrew adopts the assertive language of the verbally challenged battle leader – reminiscent of Beowulf rebutting Unferth – but in this case adapted to Christian sententiousness. Thus, in a discussion of payment for the sea journey, the Old English Andrew outdoes the analogues by turning on the ship captain to berate him for pride for asking about payment, rather than sharing his God-given gifts with those in need:

Ne gedafenað þe,   nu þe dryhten geaf
welan ond wiste   ond woruldspede,
ðæt ðu ondsware   mid oferhygdum
sece, sarcwide.
(*Andreas*, lines 317–20a)[55]

---

53 Dumitrescu, *Experience of Education*, chap. 4, demonstrates that such riddling elements also contribute to a serious critique of the failure of education in the poem.

54 As observed by Irving, "Reading," 220–1; cf. D.K. Crowne, "The Hero on the Beach: An Example of Composition by Theme in Anglo-Saxon Poetry," *Neuphilologische Mitteilungen* 61 (1960): 362–72.

55 The poem is cited from North and Bintley, eds., *Andreas*, but without showing vowel length-markers.

It is not fitting for you, now the Lord has given you
wealth and prosperity and success in the world,
that you seek an answer with pride,
searing words.

There is jaw-dropping incongruity in the dramatic irony as Andrew
is here preaching at the Preacher in Chief, asserting the good fortune
of the one who creates all fortune (the ship captain was earlier named by the
poet as "Drihten sylf, dugeða wealdend, ece ælmihtig," lines 248–9a, "the
Lord himself, the ruler of hosts, the eternal Almighty"). Andrew is accusing
Christ, the fount of all virtue, of the sin of pride. The humour of the incongruity is amplified by the frisson of possible heresy in such talking back at
Christ, even as the hagiographic frame relaxes any ultimate concerns.

In a context of such excruciating irony, even the speech tags that introduce Andrew's speech carry added resonance:

Đa him Andreas   ðurh ondsware,
wis on gewitte,   wordhord onleac
(315–16)

Then Andrew, wise in wit,
unlocked his word-hoard in answer to him.

Once again, irony runs rampant in characterizing as "wise in wit" the one
who uses his words to accuse God Almighty of the sin of pride, and the
point is reinforced by the style of the speech tag, since "wordhord onleac"
conjures up *Beowulf*ian sententiousness in speaking to the coastguard
(*Beowulf*, line 259). The mock-heroic presentation encourages laughter
through the doubleness of vision that the incongruity creates as well as
laughter of embarrassment at the apostle's *faux pas*, and also laughter of
Christian triumph at the lesson such incongruity encodes.

Indeed, Andrew continues with *Beowulf*ian sententiousness and breathtaking incongruity:

                    selre bið æghwam
þæt he eaðmedum   ellorfusne
oncnawe cuðlice,   swa þæt Crist bebead,
þeoden þrymfæst.
(320b–23a)

it is better for everyone
that he humbly may acknowledge
openly the one eager to depart, just as Christ,
the glorious Lord, commanded.

The language here echoes Beowulf's statement to Hrothgar in favour of revenge (*Beowulf*, lines 1384–9, discussed above in chapter 4). As Foley suggests, such language keys into the "inescapable and resonant web of traditional implication,"[56] and yet what is presented is Christian morality rather than the revenge ethic espoused by Beowulf with such similar phrasing, even as, ironically, that Christian wisdom is being misdirected at a non-fallible part of the Godhead. The humour here, then, comes both from piling irony upon irony and through a deployment of mock-heroic style that misdirects expectations to a world of heroic action.

Such comic misdirection is particularly apparent in the portrayal of the martial activity of the cannibal Mermedonians. Again and again, the poet presents their dining practices as incongruous in ways sure to resonate as appropriately inappropriate for humour. They treat their human captives like cattle, but with an unlikely emphasis on civilized practicalities for such an uncivil practice as eating people. Irving points to the incongruities as Mermedonians, who in the source are "tidy-minded bureaucrats who assign each captive a tablet with his number of days on it, check it daily, and duly eat him when his thirty days are up," and who in the poem get portrayed through language used of "ravening ogres of the Grendel type."[57] The clash is played up by the poet's language:

> wæs him neod micel
> þæt hie tobrugdon   blodigum ceaflum
> fira flæschoman   him to foddorþege.
> (158b–60)

> there was a great need
> that they tear to pieces the bodies of men
> with bloody jaws as a food source for themselves.

Tearing apart the bodies of men with bloody jaws contrasts strikingly with Mermedonian civilized husbandry and shared governance.

Not all ironies are funny, of course, and sometimes the poem presents irony with a serious face. A large part of the poem comprises Andrew's statement of doctrine as he recounts a version of early Christian history. This comes in a deeply ironic frame as the apostle preaches in dialogue

---

56 Foley John Miles, *The Singer of Tales in Performance* (Bloomington: Indiana University Press, 1995), 196.
57 Irving, "Reading," 218.

with an interlocutor who is Christ in disguise and distracts his followers from their fear during a storm at sea by telling the miracle of Christ's calming of a storm at sea, but it is presented here as a leisurely exposition of catechetical knowledge in a sermon style that it is not humorous. The passage lacks comic timing, and the narration lacks the markers of specially appropriate incongruity that are deployed in the mock-heroic depictions.

As the story relaunches in Mermedonia, the clash of frameworks becomes apparent once more:

Đa wæs gemyndig   modgeþyldig,
beorn beaduwe heard;   eode in burh hraðe,
anræd oretta,   elne gefyrðred,
maga mode rof,   meotude getreowe.
(981–4)

Then the mind-patient one, the man bold in battle,
was mindful; he went quickly into the city,
the resolute warrior, sustained by courage,
the man brave in spirit, faithful to the creator.

The passage drips with heroic vocabulary of thoughtful bravery as the protagonist is portrayed in five variations as *modgeþyldig, beorn beaduwe heard, anræd oretta, elne gefyrðred, maga mode rof* – marking Andrew as a hero with a plenitude of bravery. By such means, the poet uses a traditional register to establish the hero entering hostile territory, and yet the story here provides Andrew with a somewhat different role. Instead of heroic battle action, this poem is going to combine the magic of romance and the victory-in-defeat of hagiography. That special status is immediately apparent as the bold warrior quickly advanced (*Stop*, 985a, cf. the word in *Judith*), "swa hine nænig gumena ongitan ne mihte,| synfulra geseon" ("as none of the people, of those sinners, could perceive him, could see him," 986–7a) since the Lord has made him invisible to enable his mission. This is a useful practical plot device, but it is one that sets up a clash between the language of bravery and the developing story. Irving registers the incongruity as "a genuinely absurd and incongruous clash of style and content"[58] – just the kind of instantaneously registered gulf between expectation and exposition that creates the frisson of humour.

---

58 Irving, "Reading," 228.

The comic clash between the register of Old English heroic poetic language and the action of this story continues as the story advances. In a scene that has inevitably been compared with Grendel's approach to Heorot, Andrew approaches the prison, breaks open the door with a touch, and enters to a scene of carnage with the prison guards dead (lines 990–1003). The battle-bold resonances establish the expectation that the approaching warrior will do his warrior business and gloriously defeat those heathen prison guards, but the exposition firmly places their death in an impersonal construction:

> Ealle swylt fornam;
> druron domlease.   Deaðræs forfeng
> hæleð heorodreorige.
> (994b–96a)

> Death took them all away;
> the inglorious ones fell. The onrush of death seized
> the blood-stained men.

The audience is presented with language that sets up an expectation that the approaching hero should be doing the killing, and a clear statement that killing has happened but, in this story, the fight scene of heroic poetry is not necessary. Such a passage would encourage a double take from the audience. Comedy comes from the clash between the resonances of a traditional poetic style designed for describing martial exploits and action that belongs to the distinctive genre of hagiography.

Similar incongruities continue. Within this poem "þurh heard gelac" ("through hard battle," 1092a) is used of Mermedonian consumption of their own kind. The Mermedonians cast lots to decide which of their group to eat and the *ealdgesiða* ("old retainer," 1104b) who is selected is named as *collenferhð* ("bold-spirited," 1108a) even as he undertakes the unbold and unspirited move of saving his skin by offering his own son. Here the inappropriate liturgical overtones give added frisson to the inappropriate heroic vocabulary. The distance between language and act is so vast as to create comic incongruity, funny in its audacity.

A similar skewering occurs for the full group of cannibals as they take on the task of killing and consuming the son of this battle leader:

> Þa wæs rinc manig,
> guðfrec guma,   ymb þæs geongan feorh
> breostum onbryrded   to þam beadulace.
> (1116b–18)

> Then many a warrior,
> battle-bold man, was inspired in his breast
> concerning the battle-play about that young man's life.

The stress on the victim's youth (*geongan*) in contradistinction to the martial vocabulary for the group (*rinc, guðfrec guma*) makes all the more inappropriate the designation of his capture and killing as a *beadulac*, "battle-play."[59]

If Mermedonians get cast as comic villains through a mock-heroic presentation of cannibals, the devils are laughed at even more thoroughly. During the torture scenes, a devil characterized as *atol æglæca* ("a terrible monster," 1312a) commands his minions – "þegnum þryðfullum" ("strength-endowed thanes," 1329a; cf. the *þryð*- compounds in *Beowulf* discussed in chapter 4) – to humble the saint's *gylp* ("boast," 1333b) in the language of heroic battle poetry:

> Lætað gares ord,
> earh attre gemæl,   in gedufan
> in fæges ferð.
> (1330b–32a)

> Let the spear's point,
> the arrow stained with poison, pierce
> into the heart of the doomed one.

Things look bad for Andrew as the *reowe* ("cruel," 1334a) demons rush on him with avaricious grasps. But the audience need have no fear: the attack is repulsed as soon as the devils see the glorious sign of Christ's cross on his visage (lines 1335b–40). While this makes sense from a theological perspective, the contradiction between aggressive martial heroic language and instantaneous retreat without a fight creates comedy at the level of plot. The poet's use of heroic style makes the scene humorous, with devils the butt of the joke in a way that the Assyrians had been in *Judith*.

Incongruity of language and action continues as the demon troop report back to the lead devil that they cannot succeed, adding unheroically "Do it yourself!" ("Ga þe sylfa to," 1348b), a retort unthinkable at Maldon. Instead of an attack, the troop decide to insult Andrew, "to have words ready, all prepared, against that monster [*þam æglæcan*]" (lines 1358b–59). Such a rapid shift from deeds to words (rather than the other way round, as in the heroic struggle at Maldon or in *Beowulf*) is strikingly anticlimactic,

---

59 The compound survives elsewhere only in *Beowulf*, line 1559.

while the demons' term for the sleeping Andrew – *þam æglæcan* – is arrest-ingly inappropriate: the beast to go around aggressively sleeping like that! The devils lose the ensuing verbal exchange, of course; after a single speech by Andrew "that one who previously once grimly mounted a feud against God was put to flight" (lines 1386–7). Even in a war of words, the devil is physically routed and sent ignominiously *on fleame* with bathetic ease. While the action may come from the lost Latin source, the mock-heroic treatment of it is peculiar to the Old English, drawing on the conventions of Old English heroic poetry to play up comic effects.

Andrew's encounter with the Mermedonians backed by devils comes to a climax on the third day, when there is a turning of the tide in the plot. The Old English poet once again exploits the potential of Old English heroic verse to inject comedy. The *Praxeis* narrative climaxes in a melodramatic but serious incident in a romance storytelling tradition that serves as a vehicle for an allegory of conversion and baptism, death and resurrection, and hints of the ceremony of the eucharist. The Old English poet adds to this climax by again exploiting the traditional register of Old English verse. After a climax-signalling pause while the poet parades an inadequacy topos (lines 1478–89a), Andrew commands the stone pillars to pour forth:

> Stream ut aweoll,
> fleow ofer foldan;   famige walcan
> mid ærdæge   eorðan þehton,
> myclade mereflod.   Meoduscerwen wearð
> æfter symbeldæge;   slæpe tobrugdon
> searuhæbbende.   Sund grunde onfeng,
> deope gedrefed;   duguð wearð afyrhted
> þurh þæs flodes fær.   Fæge swulton,
> geonge on geofone   guðræs fornam
> þurh sealtes swelg;   þæt wæs sorgbyrþen,
> biter beorþegu.   Byrlas ne gældon,
> ombehtþegnas;   þær wæs ælcum genog
> fram dæges orde   drync sona gearu.
> (1523b–35)

The stream surged out,
flowed over the earth; the foamy billows
engulfed the earth with the break of day,
the sea-flood increased. There was a serving of mead [*or* a deprivation of mead]
after the day of feasting; the armed men
started from sleep. The water engulfed the ground,
deeply stirred up; the troop was all frightened
through the sudden attack of the flood. The doomed died,

the battle-rush took off the young ones in the ocean
through the swallowing of the salt water; that was a brewing of sorrow,
a bitter beer drinking. The cupbearers, the serving men,
did not delay; there was enough drink
immediately ready for each from the beginning of the day.

This scene provides a climax of comic incongruity with the flood conceived as a really heavy drinking session. The first sentence presents the flood as an excessive sea surge. Then, however, it gets figured as *meoduscerwen*, either "a serving of mead" in an excessive act of hospitality by the Mermedonians who have shown so little hospitality, or "a deprivation of mead" in a heavily ironic comment on the lack of sustenance-providing drink for the Mermedonians drowning in an excess of water.[60] Whatever the precise valence of *meoduscerwen*, *æfter symbeldæge* (line 1527a) is also ironic: the day before was a perverse holiday for the Mermedonians insofar as they festively watched the torture of Andrew, but was certainly no "feast-day," since they were torturing Andrew precisely because he had deprived them of their food supply. As so often in *Andreas*, the event is seen in terms of appropriately inappropriate battle imagery. In this case, the *guðræs* is an unconventional battle onslaught against which those possessing armour (*searuhæbbende*) are ill-equipped. If Brooks's emendation of line 1532a is accepted, the *sealtes swelg* is surely as much "the swallowing of the salt" as "the abyss of salt water."[61] The ironic feast inversion is then exploited most fully at lines 1532b–35: Brooks suggests a metathetic "brewing of sorrow" for *sorgbyrþen*, clearly in keeping with the *biter beorþegu*, "bitter beer-partaking," that ironically conveys the unfestive consumption of salt water, or consumption by salt water, that is substituting for hospitable beer-sharing. The excessive consumption is expressed in terms reminiscent of Holofernes's overdrinking in *Judith*. Variation stresses the imaginary presence of serving folk – *byrlas, ombehtþegnas* (lines 1523b, 1524a) – who provide their abundance with temporal alacrity – *fram dæges orde, sona* (line 1535). The fundamental litotes – "þær wæs ælcum genog ... drync ... gearu" ("there was enough drink ready for each") – is embedded in such an ironically fatal context that it surely constitutes a killer case of Old English understatement. On the one hand, this whole counterfeast emphasizes the hospitality not shown by the Mermedonians to their guests; on the other hand, the excess here plays into the whole thematics of good

---

60 See *Klaeber's Beowulf*, 161–2, note to line 769 and North and Bintley, ed., *Andreas*,
       77–9, for summary discussions of the possibilities with bibliography.
61 Brooks, ed., *Andreas*, 114.

and bad consumption. Eating people is wrong; eating the Eucharist, as the Mermedonians will do at the end of the poem, is right. Now the partying is happening to excess, as the drinking proves to be a consumption of the Mermedonians themselves, eaten by the salt water, but drinking the eucharistic wine will turn this into a wholesome party for the soul.[62]

This vision of the flood as an excess of serving by eager servants is an element unique to the Old English poem that most clearly pushes the climax into comedy. At one level, drowning is no laughing matter, and it is clearly incongruous at a literal level to describe a flood as an excessive party. The way that description resonates with the broader themes of the poem and with the details of the moment make it, however, a particularly appropriate incongruity. That a set of grave issues – cannibalism and torture, death and conversion – are here figured through something as ungravid and indecorous as a heavy drinking session provides the kind of gulf that humour thrives on.

The broad framework for the poem is a comedy of Christian triumphalism in which good wins over evil, as always ultimately happens in saints' lives. That is an outcome that is happy enough to prevent the blocking of a humour response on account of alarm or horror, even if the plot features elements that appear scary and alarming, such as torture and mass drownings. The romance element to this hagiographic story relieves those plot tensions since, in *Andreas*, even death can be reversed, as it is when the Mermedonians go to Andrew ready to convert and the saint intercedes to end the flood and bring the drowned back to life (lines 1620–4). This has doctrinally useful thematic overtones of baptism, even as it is incongruous in either real life or heroic story. The plot continues with the practicalities of building a church, establishing a bishop, and baptizing the people, and finally the apostle returns to Achaia, where Andrew will subsequently be martyred in what the poem characteristically describes as "beadu-cwealm" ("death in battle," "battle-slaughter," 1702a), even though there will be no actual battle. The poet amplifies: "Þæt þam banan ne wearð/hleahtre behworfen" ("that was not a matter of laughter for the slayer," 1702b–3a), who was consigned to hell. Killing a saint is not a laughing matter for the worldly tormenter, although it may be for the saint, as is seen in chapter 7. In this case, the saint's exploits are surely a matter for laughter for the audience.

---

62 See, further, Hugh Magennis, *Anglo-Saxon Appetites: Food and Drink and Their Consumption in Old English and Related Literature* (Dublin: Four Courts, 1999), 158–9; Hostetter, *Political Appetites*, chap. 1.

Placing the Parody

Andreas, then, uses the trappings of heroic martial poetry to tell a hagiographic story that is underpinned by a different ideology from that of a heroic narrative like *Beowulf*. The humour in the poem derives above all from the stylistic misalignment between the story told and the overtones and connotations of the traditional language in which it is told. Such a clash of generic expectations was seen also in *Judith*, where the poet makes occasional use of comic devices to stress the discomfiture of the Assyrians. The *Andreas*-poet makes yet fuller play with the clash of styles, turning initial practicalities into a kind of heroic sea journey, playing up ironies, making fun even in torture scenes, and playing the drowning scene as a comic inversion of a heroic climax. Underlying this deliberately mismatched style are many affinities with *Beowulf*, and these raise the possibility that the humorous turn in this poem works to laugh at the values of that poem in particular.

The overlap of language has long been noticed, with early discussions pointing to direct influence from one poem to the other, oral formulaists pointing to it as evidence of characteristic poetic discourse, and more recent scholars convinced of the direct verbal borrowing from *Beowulf* to *Andreas*. The overlap is certainly strikingly extensive.[63] Orchard is convinced that the sheer bulk of the overlap conclusively proves direct verbal borrowing, which would suggest in turn that *Andreas* could be a self-conscious parody of *Beowulf*.[64] This possibility is developed further in the recent edition of North and Bintley. They consider the author of *Andreas* to be a masterful poet, skilfully manipulating poetic traditions in a literate and self-conscious way, who appreciated the poetic style of Cynewulf, which he reproduces, and who deliberately alludes to and mocks the style of *Beowulf* in particular. They point to many moments where they see the *Andreas*-poet as self-consciously alluding to details of *Beowulf* and expecting an audience to pick up the allusion. "Some of his loans may be read as barbed references to the compassion with which the poet of *Beowulf* ennobles heathens," they suggest, asserting that "this poet mocks *Beowulf* for its nostalgia for heathen values."[65]

---

63 It is most fully listed by Alison M. Powell, "Verbal Parallels in *Andreas* and Its Relationship to *Beowulf* and Cynewulf" (unpublished PhD diss., University of Cambridge, 2002).

64 Andy Orchard, "The Originality of *Andreas*," in *Old English Philology*, eds. Rafael J. Pascual, Leonard Neidorf, and Tom Shippey (Cambridge: Brewer, 2016), 331–70.

65 North and Bintley, ed., *Andreas*, 64 and 66. The idea is worked out more fully in Richard North, "Meet the Pagans: On the Misuse of *Beowulf* in *Andreas*," in *Aspects of Knowledge: Preserving and Reinventing Traditions of Learning in the Middle Ages*, eds. M. Cesario and Hugh Magennis (Manchester: Manchester University Press, 2018), 185–209.

This is an appealing idea, and I think North and Bintley are convincing in uncovering humorous moments in *Andreas*, yet I find their underlying model unconvincing. A lot depends on assumptions about how much Old English poetry fails to survive. If the surviving corpus is a substantial proportion of the verse that was written in this style, then the overlap of language with *Beowulf* (and with the works of Cynewulf) would likely indicate direct borrowing. If, on the other hand, the vast majority of Old English poetry has been lost to us and there were once hundreds or thousands of other poems deploying similar language and relating plots that sometimes resembled surviving works, then the overlaps would simply point to frequently deployed language drawn from multiple and unknowable other poems. While it is unwise to be dogmatic about what has not survived, it seems likely to me that oral storytelling and oral poetry-reciting were rife throughout early medieval England and that the vast majority of such tales and poems do not survive in writing.[66] In such a case, the overlaps with *Beowulf* are less remarkable in their specificity, if still meaningful in effect. They indicate a poet generating humour by adapting and reshaping an existing tradition rather than alluding to a single poem within that tradition.

Such a view aligns well with the insights of oral formulaic scholars. Foley suggests that the verbal overlaps in this poem are not specific citation and allusion, but rather the work of a literate poet working from a Latin source and choosing to make use of traditional poetic style. Through overlaps in theme and motif and formula and wording, the poet draws on and alludes to "an inescapable and resonant web of traditional implication," keying in to what Foley more generally calls "the traditional register."[67] Rather than creating a specific parody of *Beowulf*, then, I see the *Andreas*-poet as deliberately exploiting the resonant web of traditional implication to do something different, namely to present a Christian tale, drawn from a Latin source, in the trappings of heroic poetry. Such an understanding by no means discounts the presence of humour – the surprising and appropriately inappropriate shifts of register repeatedly make scenes funny – but does affect the targeted nature of that humour, which no longer looks like it is designed to mock *Beowulf*.

Andreas is far from funny all the way through, but the poet does exploit humour where possible, by playing up the comedy of the ironies, by

---

66 For a classic attempt to assess what is missing, see R.M. Wilson, *The Lost Literature of Medieval England* (New York: Philosophical Library, 1952).

67 Foley, *Singer of Tales*, chap. 6 "Indexed Translation: The Poet's Self-Interruption in the Old English *Andreas*"; quotations from 196 and 203.

casting characters and their actions in a mock-heroic tone, and through the climactic anti-battle imagery of the drowning scene. In all of this, humour functions above all to capture attention for what is ultimately an edifying story, even as underlying it may be a form of Christian supersessionism that is suggesting the inadequacy of heroic values by adapting the style to new ends. Even if Ælfric would not have approved, *Andreas* matches *Judith* in a tradition of pious works that use humour to celebrate the edification of the ultimate Christian comedy. Christian faith is premised upon multiple incongruities, as will be explored in the next two chapters, including the incongruity between the travails of this world and the ultimate satisfaction of the next. This leads to a tradition of Christian comedy most fully seen in humorous hagiography, even as it derives from a theology with ambivalent attitudes to humour, as will be seen in the next chapter.

Community of Laughers: Appreciating the Trick

The ideal community of laughers for these poems is one well versed in traditional poetic techniques who would enjoy experiencing those techniques deployed for a Christian purpose. The secular but pious poetry connoisseurs described in chapter 3 – King Alfred or the non-literate farmhands at Whitby – would surely delight in this use of the poetic tradition. It is a turn that would also be enjoyed by the explicitly religious communities of laughter – the monastic and unreformed communities who listened to the Exeter Book of chapter 1 or the scholars in training in the classroom imagined in chapter 2.

In addition, there is something distinctly tricky about the humour explored in this chapter. The mock-heroic techniques of *Judith* and the inversions of traditional language in *Andreas* would particularly appeal to an audience that enjoyed the comic trickery of a riddle describing a One-Eyed Seller of Garlic. While any audience might enjoy such comic mischief, these portrayals seem particularly well suited for a comic trickster, and one such character appears in the same manuscript as *Judith* and *Beowulf*, namely, Alexander in *The Letter of Alexander the Great to Aristotle*, a work that portrays Alexander's exploits in India told from the first-person perspective of the practical joke–playing hero.[68]

Alexander is built up throughout this work for strength, bravery, and cunning. The latter is particularly apparent when he opposes the regional leader, King Porus. After besting threatening beasts in the desert by force,

---

68 R.D. Fulk, ed. and trans., *The Beowulf Manuscript*, DOML 3 (Cambridge, MA: Harvard University Press, 2010). Reference is by sentence number in this edition.

Alexander takes on Porus through trickery. He goes into Porus's court disguised as a beggar, where he gives Porus a false description of his supposed leader:

> Đa bysmrode ic hine mid minum ondswarum ond him sæde þæt he forealdod wære ond to þæs eald wære þæt he ne mihte elcor gewearmigan buton æt fyre ond æt gledum.
> (Fulk, 60, sentence 159)

> Then I mocked him with my answers and told him [Porus] that he [Alexander] was ancient and was so old that he could not stay warm except at a fire and at coals.

Alexander-in-disguise describes Alexander-the-leader to Porus as an old and feeble man. King Porus takes the bait and is duly delighted: "Þa wæs he sona swiðe glæd ond gefeonde þara minra ondswaro ond worda" (Fulk, 60, sentence 160, "Then he was immediately very pleased and rejoicing at my answers and my words"). Porus employs Alexander-disguised-as-beggar to give a letter to Alexander-the-leader. Alexander-in-disguise takes the letter, returns to his camp, and when he reads the letter cannot stop laughing: "ic wæs swiðe mid hleahtre onstyred" (Fulk, 62, sentence 164, "I was completely consumed by laughter"). Alexander as practical joker appreciates inversion with an aggressive turn as deeply comic.

Alexander shows an acute consciousness of the agonistic power of humour again later in the narrative. When two old men tell him about fortune-speaking trees of the sun and the moon, he worries that they are mocking him ("Đa ne gelyfde ic him ac wende þæt hi mec on hyscte ond on bismer sægdon," Fulk, 72, sentence 233; "Then I did not believe them but thought that they spoke to me in derision and in mockery"). He complains that, despite all his power, these two old foreigners "mec ... nu her bysmergeað" ("now here are mocking me"). Fear of such mockery is enough to make him go and check on the wonder, which turns out to be for real. Such explicit fear of derision by one who identifies as the most powerful man in the world suggests the remarkable strength of mockery and derision. Humour is imagined as a powerful tool. Placed alongside the comic readings of *Judith* and, to a lesser extent, of *Beowulf*, the joking of Alexander might indicate that the compiler of the *Beowulf* and *Judith* manuscript was not just a connoisseur of monsters, as has long been suggested, but also of jokesters.

The tyrant's vulnerability to humour is thematized in another surviving poem, too, namely *Widsith* in the Exeter Book. When the widely travelled imagined persona of this poem first mentions Eormanric, he gives the king of the Goths his usual character for villainy, describing his home as that of *wrapes wærlogan*, ("the cruel breaker of covenants," 9a), which reflects the way this character is thought of in *Beowulf* and elsewhere.[69] By the end of the poem, however, Widsith lists Eormanric's household among those containing *gesiþa þa selestan* ("the best of companions," 110). The fulcrum for this change of attitude lies in the revelation that this King of the Goths treated the visiting poet Widsith well, giving him a ring worth 600 pieces of gold (lines 88–92). A prodigious gift to a poet can apparently earn a prodigiously notable villain a good poetic presentation. This turns a rather cynical light on Widsith's gnomic-sounding conclusion that the one who works *lof*, i.e. deeds worthy of praise, will have *heahfæstne dom* ("everlasting glory," 142b–43), a statement made in the context of minstrels, *gleomen*, speaking words of thanks for those who are generous with gifts (line 135–42a). Widsith is laughing with the humour of superiority at how a poet can out-do even a tyrant with the power of poetry and of laughter, humorously conveying a message of humour's power.

The rapid and striking reversal in attitude to Eormanric hints at the power of satire to make or break the reputation of a leader, suggesting that Alexander the Great is right to worry about the possibility of mockery. The previous chapter showed how such satire could be directed at a high-status character within a heroic story in the case of King Hrothgar in *Beowulf*. The present chapter shows how similar satire can help to belittle the villains in the Christian cosmography of biblical or hagiographic verse narrative, and possibly mock the storytelling expectations of heroic literature. When a One-Eyed Seller of Garlic enters the scene, even the most powerful men drinking their wine in the mead hall had better pay attention.

---

69 The poem is ed. and trans. in Mitchell and Robinson, *Beowulf*, 196–203. *Klaeber's Beowulf*, 193, note to lines 1197–201, sums up how Eormenric "became in heroic poetry the type for the ferocious, covetous, and treacherous tyrant."

Chapter Six

Homiletic Humour:
Christian Laughter and Clerical Satire

For all the hints of comedy in *Judith* and *Andreas*, Christianity is in general strikingly hostile to humour in this world, as I will suggest by pointing to Christ's teaching on ultimate salvation. Accordingly, while a rich tradition of Christian preaching survives in Old English, it makes little use of humour, even as it often dwells on pious paradoxes. While a decorum of seriousness is widespread, it is particularly acute in one author, Ælfric of Eynsham, who has an out-size presence in the surviving preaching record, and who is strikingly disinclined to use humour in his works. Preachers from a later period sometimes deploy funny *exempla*, and I will suggest that there are hints of this in an Old English collection of pious stories. I will also analyse more fully two sermons by unknown preachers that buck the serious trend. I will round out this exploration of preaching humour by examining a fragment of clerical satire that uses humour to police those preachers.

This chapter, then, will lay out some of the foundational vernacular Christian literature from early medieval England and pursue the rather slim pickings for Christian comedy within it. I will then turn in the following chapter to religious narratives which prove most conducive to the deployment of humour, namely the lives of saints. As with the homilies, Ælfric once again dominates the surviving record, and that careful Old English exegete will allow only a significantly circumscribed version of humour within his works. Other examples of saints' lives translated and developed by anonymous writers attest to the potential for more robust use of pious humour. In general, though, the cautious attitude to Christian humour contributes to the dour impression made by the corpus of surviving Old English writings.

Almost Funny: Riddle 48

A riddle which dwells on paradox without being funny serves well to introduce the state of most surviving Old English Christian literature.

Ic gefrægn for hæleþum   hring gyddian,[1]
torhtne butan tungan,   tila þeah he hlude
stefne ne cirmde,   strongum wordum.
Sinc for secgum   swigende cwæð:
"Gehæle mec,   helpend gæsta."   5
Ryne ongietan   readan goldes
guman galdorcwide,   gleawe beþencan
hyra hælo to gode,   swa se hring gecwæð.
(Riddle 48)

I heard a round thing, a bright one without a tongue,
speak before men, speak well even though he
did not cry out loudly in strong words with a voice.
The treasure, being silent, said in front of men:
"Heal me, helper of souls."
May men understand the mystery,
the incantation of the red gold, may they wisely entrust
their well-being to God, as the round one said.

In the central paradox of this riddle, something circular speaks, even though it lacks a tongue, a treasure talks silently. This sounds like another monster riddle, a creature with body parts that cannot add up, like the One-Eyed Seller of Garlic discussed in the previous chapter. Speech sans tongue is emphasized here through the clashing verbal forms in line 4b, which juxtaposes a present participle of the verb *swigian*, "to be silent," with a finite verb of speaking, *cweðan*, "to say," usually thought of as the opposite to being silent. That juxtaposition sets up a jolt of incongruity in a mini-riddle that is not hard to solve in a literate society (silent speaking = writing), albeit one that revivifies wonder at the qualities of the written word. This matches the immediately preceding riddle, the book moth of Riddle 47, touched on in chapter 2 above, which, by consuming words without comprehending them, also brought to life the paradoxical power of writing.[2] The present riddle, then, uses the techniques of paradox that

---

1 MS *hringende an* is organized by Krapp and Dobbie as *hring endean* (but this defies sense) and emended by Williamson to *hring gyddian*, which is accepted by Bernard J. Muir, *The Exeter Anthology of Old English Poetry*, 2 vols. (Exeter: University of Exeter Press, 1994; revised ed., 2000).

2 The two riddles share codicological as well as conceptual links since the usual punctuation for ending a riddle is lacking from the end of Riddle 47; see Martin Foys, "The Undoing of Exeter Book Riddle 47: 'Bookmoth'," in *Transitional States: Change,*

can create comic incongruity, but the tone is strikingly different. Rather than a shift from high to low register with the appropriate inappropriateness to create a comic jolt, the present riddle emphasizes a sense of wonder in a context that tamps down any humour.

That different tone is partly created by the words the round creature speaks in line 5, which immediately key into a Christian register through the overtones of an imperative form of the verb *gehælan* ("to heal or save") and the semantic and associative range of *gæst* ("soul," "spirit," "ghost") particularly in relation to *helpend* ("helper"). The association is all the stronger if the collocated forms here punningly suggest the common word for the Christian God, *hælend*.[3] The utterance keys into a biblical text, Psalm 11:2, or part of the liturgy of the mass, even as it also (secondarily and ironically) conjures up a secular healing practice involving writing on religious implements to create a *galdor* ("charm") for health (cf. line 7a).[4] There is a double hint of doubleness in the revelation occurring *for hæleþum* (line 1a), where the term for the imagined audience falsely conjures the specialized sense of *hæleþ* ("heroes") and thereby suggests a mead-hall performance, rather than the broader sense of "men," which keys to a religious performance presided over by a masculine sacerdotal class, while the repeated prepositional phrase (*for* 1a and 4a) can mean both "before, in front of" and "on account of, on behalf of," with the first sense activated by a secular reading, the second by a religious one. The audience that is watching or being served is imagined as markedly male (*hæleþ* 1a, *secg* 4a, and *guma* 7a, all usually denote male people), perhaps augmenting the mead-hall feint, while also nodding to a liturgical context where an early medieval audience would take for granted the sexual segregation of an audience in church.[5]

Tradition, and Memory in Medieval Literature and Culture, eds. Graham D. Caie and Michael D.C. Drout (Tempe, AZ: ACMRS, 2018). The power of the image of silent speaking in these riddles is brilliantly explored in Mary Hayes, "The Talking Dead: Resounding Voices in Old English Riddles," *Exemplaria* 20 (2008): 123–42. For context, see Peter Ramey, "Writing Speaks: Oral Poetics and Writing Technology in the Exeter Book Riddles," *Philological Quarterly* 92, no. 3 (2013): 335–56.

3 A suggestion of Andy Orchard, "Performing Writing and Singing Silence in the Anglo-Saxon Riddle Tradition," in *Or Words to That Effect: Orality and the Writing of Literary History*, eds. Daniel F. Chamberlain and J. Edward Chamberlin (Amsterdam: Benjamins, 2016), 73–91 at 78–9.

4 See Megan Cavell, "Powerful Patens in the Anglo-Saxon Medical Tradition and Exeter Book *Riddle 48*," *Neophilologus* 101 (2017): 129–38.

5 See Margaret Aston, "Segregation in Church," in *Women in the Church*, eds. W.J. Sheils and Diana Wood (Oxford: Blackwell, 1990), 237–94.

The precious round object that speaks is probably a religious vessel featuring a religious inscription, most likely a paten (OE *husel-disc*) used for carrying the bread-turned-host during the liturgy, or possibly a chalice filled with wine-turned-blood. Incongruities abound. The subject of the riddle toggles between animate and inanimate, silent and speaking, earthly treasure and gateway to heaven, basic carrying device and provider of ultimate salvation, in paradoxes that match some of the fundamental paradoxes of the Christian faith, in which the last shall be first, consecrated bread and wine is flesh and blood, and salvation comes from digesting the Godhead. Rather than being comic, these are incongruities underlying the ultimate values of a faith system and so get treated as triggers for awe rather than laughter. Such a damping of humour proves to be usual throughout the Old English homiletic tradition.

The Old English Homiletic Tradition

Preaching in English would have been a feature of pastoral care from the time of Augustine's mission to Kent in 597 CE onwards, even though surviving preaching texts date overwhelmingly from the late tenth century or after. Preaching texts from the period are generally short tracts of religious explanation and moral edification, termed homilies or sermons interchangeably both by Old English scribes and by modern scholars. They often begin by explaining the gospel reading of the day (a form that some modern scholars consider as homilies strictly speaking), but sometimes they simply present moral exhortation (the form sometimes distinguished as sermons). Such tracts were delivered in English by a priest on Sundays and other major feast days as part of the mass.[6] Old English homilies are often catechetical, that is, they endeavour to convey the essential tenets of the faith, laying out the basic outline of the Christian story and essential Christian morality.[7] The priest as preacher exhorts his audience around familiar themes, such as love of God and neighbour or the requirement to do good and avoid sin.

---

6 For a good introduction to homilies, see Aaron J. Kleist, ed., *The Old English Homily: Precedent, Practice, and Appropriation* (Turnhout: Brepols, 2007). On pastoral care, see Francesca Tinti, ed., *Pastoral Care in Late Anglo-Saxon England* (Woodbridge: Boydell, 2005); Catherine Cubitt, "Pastoral Care and Religious Belief," in *A Companion to the Early Middle Ages: Britain and Ireland, c. 500–c. 1100*, ed. Pauline Stafford (Chichester: Blackwell, 2009), 394–413.

7 See Virginia Day, "The Influence of the Catechetical *Narratio* on Old English and Some Other Medieval Literature," *Anglo-Saxon England* 3 (1974): 51–61; Mary Clayton, "Homiliaries and Preaching in Anglo-Saxon England," *Peritia* 4 (1985): 207–42.

A remarkable quantity of such preaching texts in Old English survive, numbering into the hundreds. Two authors reveal their name in some of their works and write with such distinctive style that it is easy to establish a fuller body of their preaching. The leading such homilist is Ælfric of Eynsham, writing in the 990s and 1000s. The Dictionary of Old English counts some 136 surviving homilies written by him,[8] along with many surviving saints' lives (as will be seen in the next chapter). Wulfstan, Archbishop of York, is the other named writer with a substantial if smaller body of surviving homilies,[9] which, while stylistically impressive, rarely deploy humour as they incline to the sensational in making moral points. Other pieces surely once circulated as the work of recognizable and acknowledged preachers, but further authors are not now recoverable, so the remaining homilies are viewed as anonymous. A healthy number of such works survive, although not as many as the homilies by Ælfric.[10] Some of those which predate Ælfric are contained in a pair of manuscripts, the Vercelli Book and the Blickling Homilies, named after where those books later came to reside.[11] While most anonymous homilists are as reluctant as Ælfric and Wulfstan to use humour in their preaching, a few will prove more open to it.

---

8 Works listed by the Dictionary of Old English [DOE] under ÆCHom, ÆHom, ÆHomM. On this body of work, see Aaron J. Kleist, "Ælfric's Corpus: A Conspectus," *Florilegium* 18, no. 2 (2001): 113–64; Aaron J. Kleist, *The Chronology and Canon of Ælfric of Eynsham* (Cambridge: Brewer, 2019). For a maximal interpretation of their circulation, see my "Ælfric in Dorset."

9 The DOE list 27 homilies by Wulfstan under WHom, but omits examples not edited by Bethurum; see further my "The Dissemination of Wulfstan's Homilies: The Wulfstan Tradition in Eleventh-Century Vernacular Preaching," in *England in the Eleventh Century*, ed. Carola Hicks (Stamford: Watkins, 1992), 199–217; Joyce Tally Lionarons, *The Homiletic Writings of Archbishop Wulfstan* (Woodbridge: Brewer, 2010).

10 The DOE lists 142 texts with the designation HomM, HomS, or HomU, although this over-counts since it includes a number that are overlapping texts, fragmentary, or not really homilies, and a number more that are by Wulfstan (as explained in the preceding note); see D.G. Scragg, "The Corpus of Vernacular Homilies and Prose Saints' Lives before Ælfric," *Anglo-Saxon England* 8 (1979): 223–77, for fuller details on the anonymous homilies.

11 Vercelli Homilies edition: D.G. Scragg, ed., *The Vercelli Homilies and Related Texts*, EETS o.s. 300 (Oxford: Oxford University Press, 1992); translation: Lewis E. Nicholson, ed., *The Vercelli Book Homilies: Translations from the Anglo-Saxon* (Lanham, MD: University Press of America, 1991). Blickling Homilies: Richard Morris, ed. and trans., *The Blickling Homilies*, EETS o.s. 58, 63, 73 (1874, 1876, 1880, repr. as one volume, London: Oxford University Press, 1967); and, less reliably, in Richard J. Kelly, ed. and trans., *Blickling Homilies: Edition and Translation* (London: Continuum, 2003).

These preaching texts as a whole represent a substantial proportion of surviving writing in the vernacular from early medieval England. They have not, however, received proportional attention from modern scholars and that partly reflects a judgment on the unexciting nature of their content. Homilies are doctrinal or, more often, moral and, for the most part, thoroughly not funny. I will consider some reasons for this by engaging with Christian hostility to humour before considering the few exceptions that survive. First, I will introduce the most prolific writer of homilies, Ælfric, in view of his dominance in the surviving record, and consider what can be said about his idea of humour.

The Controlling Voice of Ælfric

Ælfric's overwhelming preponderance in the surviving homiletic record can be explained by both the effectiveness of his preaching and the pastoral needs of his historical moment. Monk and mass-priest of Cerne Abbas, Dorset, probably from 987, and then Abbot of Eynsham, Oxfordshire, from 1005, Ælfric crafted homilies that edify while controlling an audience's response. His work is carefully developed to avoid the risk of introducing heretical ideas or what he would call *gedwyld*, "error."[12] Working at Cerne Abbas in the 990s, he crafted two sequences of homilies that run through the church year (known by modern scholars as the *Catholic Homilies* for their broad range and universal applicability), sequences which he then revised and augmented.[13] These collections are an achievement by any standard, but their impact was magnified as they were picked up by Sigeric, Archbishop of Canterbury, who, along with his successors, circulated them on a massive scale. At this time, the model of pastoral care was changing with a proliferation of small churches, each presided over by a priest working independently, in place of larger minsters that gathered priests in a regulated community.[14] These local priests would benefit from reliable and standardized

---

12 For introductions to Ælfric and his works, see Jonathan Wilcox, ed., *Ælfric's Prefaces* (Durham: Durham Medieval Texts, 1994); Hugh Magennis and Mary Swan, eds., *A Companion to Ælfric* (Leiden: Brill, 2009).

13 Editions: Peter Clemoes, ed., *Ælfric's Catholic Homilies: The First Series; Text*, EETS s.s. 17 (Oxford: Oxford University Press, 1997); Malcolm Godden, ed., *Ælfric's Catholic Homilies: The Second Series; Text*, EETS, s.s. 5 (London: Oxford University Press, 1979); translations: Benjamin Thorpe, ed. and trans., *Sermones Catholici or Homilies of Ælfric*, 2 vols. (London, 1844–6).

14 See, especially, John Blair, *The Church in Anglo-Saxon Society* (Oxford: Oxford University Press, 2005).

preaching material, and Ælfric's works supplied that need. The evidence comes from some forty-two surviving manuscripts of Ælfric's *Catholic Homilies*, a strikingly large number for anything written in Old English, most of which can be traced back to copying at Canterbury.[15] Between the practicalities of wear and tear to everyday books, the shift in language which made Old English unintelligible by the late Middle Ages, and the dissolution of the monasteries in the early modern period, with the consequent break up and destruction of monastic libraries, the chances for the survival of Old English manuscripts were slight, so the attested record is likely to be a tiny proportion of the copies that once existed.[16] Ælfric's homilies probably circulated in hundreds, perhaps even thousands, of manuscripts in the late Old English period such that their contents could be heard on Sundays and feast days in just about every church under the influence of Canterbury and so potentially throughout early medieval England.[17] The success of Ælfric's homilies for the most part displaced earlier vernacular preaching texts, and this helps to explain the rather thin and sporadic evidence for earlier preaching. They may well constitute the most widely known works in Old English that we can now access.

The popularity of Ælfric's homilies derived in part from their sound doctrine and in part from their successful formula of historical and moral explanation of the day's assigned biblical text, with complex doctrine explained with clarity, while concluding with predictable edifying morality. In addition, Ælfric developed a particularly effective style for conveying his message. He does something remarkable with his language to keep an audience's attention, taking the fundamentals of Old English poetry (based on alliteration in a four-stress line) and replicating its catchy rhythmical and alliterative effect but leaching it of the distinctive poetic vocabulary. His discourse maintains enough difference from poetic conventions that his work does not read like poetry, which he probably rejected as too secular in tradition, and too open to ambiguity and interpretation,

---

15 In addition to the editions by Clemoes and Godden, see Kleist, *Chronology and Canon*. N.R. Ker, *Catalogue of Manuscripts Containing Anglo-Saxon* (Oxford: Oxford University Press, 1957), lists some 412 manuscripts which contain Old English, and so Ælfric's *Catholic Homilies* account for over 10 per cent of the surviving manuscripts containing Old English.

16 See my "The Use of Ælfric's Homilies: MSS Oxford, Bodleian Library, Junius 85 and 86 in the Field," in *A Companion to Ælfric*, eds. Hugh Magennis and Mary Swan (Leiden: Brill, 2009), 345–68.

17 I make this argument more fully in "Ælfric in Dorset."

and perhaps even to humour.[18] Instead, he develops an ear-catching style that serves well the tempered control of an audience's response that is the hallmark of his achievement.

Ælfric held his audience's attention on sound doctrine, then, in part through the force of his prose style, in part through the clarity of his doctrine, but rarely by being funny. This is most likely because of an unwillingness to risk losing control over the audience's response. Ælfric carefully avoids offering up the duality or ambiguity that the creation of comic incongruity entails. He does not entirely eschew all possibility of humour, as will be seen next and in the following chapter, but examples are rare and strikingly controlled.

Ælfric's Sense of Humour

Ælfric's idea of a comic story can be illustrated from the preface to another of his religious writings, his translation into Old English of part of the book of Genesis. He uses a short comic story here to reflect upon the significance of the Old Testament and ultimately to argue for the interpretive style of his homilies:

> Hwilon ic wiste þæt sum mæssepreost, se þe min magister wæs on þam timan, hæfde þa boc Genesis, and he cuðe be dæle Lyden understandan; þa cwæþ he be þam heahfædere Iacobe, þæt he hæfde feower wif, twa geswustra and heora twa þinena. Ful soð he sæde, ac he nyste, ne ic þa git, hu micel todal ys betweohx þære ealdan æ and þære niwan.[19]

> Once I knew a certain masspriest, who was my teacher at the time, who owned the book of Genesis, and he could understand Latin a little; then he said about the patriarch Jacob, that he had four wives, two sisters and their two handmaidens. What he said was completely true, but he did not know, as did not I at that time, how great a difference there is between the old law and the new.

---

18 Ælfric's rhythmical style is discussed by John C. Pope, ed., *Homilies of Ælfric: A Supplementary Collection*, 2 vols., EETS o.s. 259–60 (London: Oxford University Press, 1967–8); Thomas A. Bredehoft, "Ælfric and Late Old English Verse," *Anglo-Saxon England* 33 (2004): 77–107. See also Kathleen Davis, "Boredom, Brevity and Last Things: Ælfric's Style and the Politcs of Time," in *A Companion to Ælfric*, 321–44. His distinctive rhythmical style is a feature of his later writings, including most of the saints' lives considered in the next chapter.

19 Wilcox, ed., *Ælfric's Prefaces*, text 4, lines 11–14.

There are multiple markers that this is intended as a joke. It starts with an opening formula and builds in rhythm towards a climax. It deals with a particular but unspecified target (*sum mæssepreost*) in a self-contained little story, validated through first person authentication. It touches on the taboo topic of sex and is rounded out with a punchline. The butt of the joke is the foolish teacher, a priest who can fantasize about multiple sexual partners and, perhaps as alarmingly, does not understand Latin properly, despite owning a book. The incongruity comes from this figure of religious authority hinting that it is just fine to have multiple wives, and perhaps even for religious authority figures like himself to be married, which are both ideas anathema to Ælfric's sense of sound doctrine. The imagined priest is surely something of a strawman: rampant polygamy does not seem to be an abuse that Ælfric treats as a serious threat, even if he is obsessed with maintaining clerical celibacy.[20] The possibility of multiple wives in Ælfric's world is surely a piece of comic business introduced to lead to the serious point about the priest's failure of interpretation, namely his inability to comprehend the relationship of Old to New Testament that is so fundamental to Ælfric's idea of Christian ideology.

In some ways, this is aggressive humour, making the priest the satirical butt of the invective in a manner treated by superiority theory, but Ælfric blunts the potential aggression by deflecting the target to be his own earlier self as well as the foolish priest. The whole episode is crafted as an amusing anecdote, complete with a touch of the salacious, and a hint at the personal, but it is quickly contained by palpably serving such a serious purpose. Ælfric captures attention with a moment of levity, but it is characteristic that he then works hard to contain that moment and to unambiguously make his serious point about the different *mores* of the Old and New Testament. It is also characteristic that this moment of levity does not occur in a piece for broad circulation. The context for this anecdote is Ælfric explaining to his powerful secular patron, Ealdorman Æthelweard, why he will not continue translating the Old Testament, and the preface has a strictly limited circulation. A comic and personal anecdote may be particularly useful here as Ælfric, a mere monk and mass-priest by his own self-definition, is defying the request of his high-status patron. The comic story serves his purpose, showing how crucial it is for an intellectual authority to explain the significance of biblical

---

20 On clerical celibacy as the marker of reformed monasticism, see Catherine Cubitt, "Virginity and Misogyny in Tenth- and Eleventh-Century England," *Gender History* 12, no. 1 (2000): 1–32; and on Ælfric's preoccupation with the issue, see Peter Jackson, "Ælfric and the Purpose of Christian Marriage: A Reconsideration of the Life of Æthelthryth, Lines 120–30," *Anglo-Saxon England* 29 (2000): 235–60.

text rather than giving readers easy access to "þa nacedan gerecednisse" ("the naked narrative," Preface 4, lines 42–3). Ælfric serves as that authority in his homilies, clothing biblical text with careful explanation and moral interpretation such that there is little space for humour.

Since the corpus of surviving Old English homilies is so dominated by the works of Ælfric, his cautious attitude to homiletic humour prevails widely and may have influenced subsequent homilists. The little story in this preface, though, reminds how a comic exemplum can be valued as a hook for attracting an audience, even by this decorous moralist, and this provides an opening for homiletic humour which will be considered later in this chapter. First, though, it will be useful to explore further the general attitude to humour in the Christian tradition, with particular emphasis on what was available to Old English writers.

Present Mirth Hath Present Laughter: The Christian Case against Humour

Christian doctrine is hesitant about humour, if not downright hostile. When Christ addresses the multitude on coming down from the mountain in the Sermon on the Plain (Luke's shorter version of Matthew's Sermon on the Mount), he includes the following:

Eadige synd ge ðe hingriað nu. forþam ge beoð gefyllede;   Eadige synt ge ðe nu wepað. forþam ge hlihaþ. …
Wa eow þe gefyllede synt: forþam þe ge hingriað; Wa eow þe nu hlihað. forþam þe ge heofað and wepað.
(Luke 6:21 and 25 in the Old English Gospels)[21]

beati qui nunc esuritis quia saturabimini beati qui nunc fletis quia ridebitis…
vae vobis qui saturati estis quia esurietis vae vobis qui ridetis nunc quia lugebitis et flebitis.
(Luke 6:21 and 25 in the Vulgate)

Blessed are ye that hunger now: for you shall be filled. Blessed are ye that weep now: for you shall laugh. …
Woe to you that are filled: for you shall hunger. Woe to you that now laugh: for you shall mourn and weep.
(Luke 6:21 and 25, trans. Douay Rheims)

---

21 Ed. R.M. Liuzza, ed., *The Old English Version of the Gospels*, EETS o.s. 304 (Oxford: Oxford University Press, 1994).

In laying out the paradoxes of reversal, Christ suggests that happiness is not to be had within the present world but in the one to come. This is part of a Christian message of hope for those disadvantaged and dispossessed within this world. The passage does not condemn laughter as such, since laughing stands beside a full stomach as a token of the ultimate pleasure of heaven. It does, however, give laughing within this world a bad name, since it correlates such laughter with gluttony and a lack of charity to others. Those who laugh here are tied to those with full bellies here in contrast with the needy: fat cats who will suffer in the long run for failing to provide those things to the virtuous poor who lack them. The underlying imagery is clearest in the case of food: the sated in this world are failing to make resources of food available to those who are deprived of them. Laughter is either imagined as a commodity like food that is limited in supply and is being squandered by the haves without regard to the needs of the have-nots, or the laughter of this world is encoding the callous disregard of such uncharitable well-fed people, unlike the meaning of laughter in the next world. Laughter itself may not ultimately be a bad thing, but it is inappropriate in this world, where humour seems to be a mark of the self-satisfied or the simply selfish. With such an ideology, biblical material looks set to offer slim pickings for the present study.

Such a dim view of amusement in this world is explicitly reinforced by some Christian apologists. Benedict of Aniane picks up on the above beatitude and observes: "Since the Lord condemns those who laugh now, it is clear that there is never a time for laughter for the faithful soul." Medieval biblical commentators assumed Christ must have had the ability to laugh, since they accept Aristotle's definition that laughter is a defining feature of human beings, but they observe that, while it is recorded that Christ wept, it is never recorded that Christ laughed. John Chrysostom articulates the case against merriment in this world by pointedly asking, "Christ is crucified and does thou laugh?"[22]

Ælfric is definitely on the side of the stern moralists. He makes use of Christ's teaching in the Sermon on the Plain in his homily for the First Sunday in Lent (CH I.11), but with a telling twist. In the course of emphasizing the need to give alms to the poor, Ælfric cites Christ's aphorism, but his wording misquotes Luke:

---

22 For a stimulating discussion of these and other biblical and classical attitudes to laughter, see Barry Sanders, *Sudden Glory: Laughter as Subversive History* (Boston: Beacon, 1995), chaps. 1–5.

crist cwæð. wa eow þe nu hlihgað: Ge scolon heofian. 7 wepan; eft he cwæð;
 Eadige beoð þa ðe nu wepað: for ðon þe hi scolon beon gefrefrode.
(CH I.11, lines 215–17)

Christ said: Woe to you who laugh now, you shall sigh and weep. Again he said,
Blessed are those who now weep, because they shall be comforted.

Ælfric conflates the comment in Luke with the equivalent part of the
Sermon on the Mount from Matthew 5:5, which makes no reference
to laughter ("beati qui lugent quoniam ipsi consolabuntur," "Blessed
are they that mourn: for they shall be comforted"). As a result of this
small conflation, Ælfric still condemns present laughter and promises
ultimate comfort, but in phrasing that omits any mention of the possibility of positive future laughter. This formulation conveys the same
fundamental inversion as Christ's sermon but declines to associate
heavenly happiness with laughter. For Ælfric, heaven of course constitutes eternal happiness, but he is not explicit on whether anyone gets
to laugh there, even as he is explicit that laughter in this world will be
condemned. While this could be a simple lapse of memory in engaging
familiar passages, it seems telling of an attitude. Apparently Ælfric was
loath to give laughter as much positive valence as it has in the passage
in Luke.

Many other Old English homilists are as dour as Ælfric, and this very
formulation, condemning worldly laughter and not recuperating it in
heaven, is seen also in some anonymous homilies. Blickling 2, for Quin-
quagesima Sunday, or the Sunday before Lent, is about Christ's healing
of the blind man on the road to Jericho (Luke 18:31–44). In concluding
exhortations, the homilist warns against sin generally and exhorts the audience to turn to penitence, again aligning Luke 6:25 with Matthew 5:5 and
thereby taking the laughter out of heaven.

Present mirth gets roundly condemned in a number of other homiletic formulations. In the anonymous homily, Vercelli 4, an extra adjective
expands the essential contrast of the beatitudes: "Her bið unglædlic hleahter,
ac þær is se ungeendoda heaf þam þe her mid unrihte gytsiaþ" ("here there
is cheerless laughter, but there will be unending lamentation for those who
here are wrongfully avaricious," Vercelli 4, lines 26–7). This homilist thereby
makes explicit that the laughter of this world is not actually happy but rather
unglædlic ("cheerless," "unsatisfying," "not delightful"), even though it will
still earn you eternal lamentation. Vercelli 11, an anonymous Rogationtide
homily, also warns against earthly laughter, exhorting the audience to abandon "unnytne hleahter 7 blisse" ("vain laughter and joy," Vercelli 11, lines
73–4), citing the caution of Luke 6:25, and adding an interpretation that

those who enjoy the greatest joy in the world will receive the greatest sadness without end (Vercelli 11, lines 77–81).

The same cluster of texts inform a slightly different condemnation of present mirth in Blickling 5, for the Fifth Sunday in Lent, with a warning that comes as a rhetorical question. The homilist wonders what becomes of present feasting and present laughter, with the clear implication that the answer is not good for the feasters or laughers:

> Hwær beoþ þonne þa symbelnessa, & þa idelnessa, & þa ungemetlican hleahtras, & se leasa gylp, & ealle þa idlan word þe he ær unrihtlice ut forlet?
> (Blickling 5, Morris, 59)

> Where then will be the feasts and the vanities and the unrestrained laughter and the false boast and all the vain speech which he previously sinfully practiced?

This time laughter is qualified with a different adjective (it is *ungemetlican*, "unmeasured" or "uncontained") and is collocated with other markers of sin. The homilist views the pleasures of the present world from the perspective of their deprivation in the ultimate future. Laughter joins the list of feasting, vanities, false boasts, and vain speech, all building a picture of a foolish sinner who is heedless of ultimate values but will receive ultimate comeuppance.[23] The laughter is qualified as unmeasured or unrestrained, suggesting that an unfitting kind of laughter is getting condemned, but the context as a whole suggests how mirth of any kind in this world is not something these homilists look on in a kindly manner.

In yet another version, the process of judgment is dramatized as the soul of a sinner berates its body, contrasting the body's delight in the world with the soul's discomfiture, and explaining "þonne þu smercodest and hloge, þonne weop ic biterlice" ("when you smirked and laughed, then I wept bitterly," Napier 29, 140/28–9). Humour and its reflexes are viewed unfavourably as pleasures of the body that pertain to this world and its vanities, rather than appropriate concerns of the soul, and so they will be rewarded with eternal sorrow. Given such concerns, it is unsurprising that few homilists work to make an audience laugh.

The Sermon on the Plain is not the only biblical passage that takes a dim view of worldly merriment.[24] A famous passage in Ecclesiastes 3:4,

---

23 There is a similar collocation of laughter and vain boasts with the sins of this world in a homily for the Third Sunday in Lent, Blickling 4, line 253.
24 For a discussion of how laughter is treated in Genesis, see my "The First Laugh."

"A time to weep, and a time to laugh. A time to mourn, and a time to dance,"
appears to allow a positive valence for mirth, at least some of the time, but
a later chapter severely limits the possibility:

> 4 melior est ira risu quia per tristitiam vultus corrigitur animus delinquentis
> 5 cor sapientium ubi tristitia est et cor stultorum ubi laetitia
> 6 melius est a sapiente corripi quam stultorum adulatione decipi
> 7 quia sicut sonitus spinarum ardentium sub olla sic risus stulti sed et hoc vanitas

> 4 Anger is better than laughter: because by the sadness of the countenance the
>   mind of the offender is corrected.
> 5 The heart of the wise is where there is mourning, and the heart of fools where
>   there is mirth.
> 6 It is better to be rebuked by a wise man, than to be deceived by the flattery of
>   fools.
> 7 For as the crackling of thorns burning under a pot, so is the laughter of a
>   fool: now this also is vanity.
> (Ecclesiastes 7:4–7, Vulgate and Douai-Rheims)

The wonderful image of the crackling of thorns burning under a pot conveys the short-lived nature of laughter in this world, which is here aligned
with the fool.

The idea is picked up in Vercelli 11, where the homilist warns:

> Twa tida on hiera endebyrdnesse her on worulde a singalice fyliað: *Tempus flendi
> et tempus ridendi*, þæt is wopes tid 7 oðer hleahtres tid. Ne magon we ða
> hleahtras a singalice habban.
> (Vercelli 11, lines 27–9)

> Two times follow one another continually here in the world in their order: *a time
> for weeping and a time for laughing*, that is a time for weeping and another time
> for laughter. We can't be continuously forever laughing.

The homilist here alludes to Ecclesiastes and appears to allow the possibility
of happy laughter in the world, even though the second sentence warns that
mortal folk cannot have outpourings of laughter (*ða hleahtras*, "laughter" in
the plural) continuously (*singalice*) forever (*a*). The source, though, clarifies
that there is not really any time for laughing in this world,[25] and that is probably what the Old English is conveying with characteristic understatement.

---

25 The homilist is closely translating Sermo ccxv of Caesarius of Arles: "Nemo se
   circumueniat, fratres, non est in hoc mundo tempus ridendi" ("No-one can get round it,
   brothers, it is not in this world a time for laughing"). See Scragg, *Vercelli Homilies*.

The homilist goes on to clarify how joy is not possible in this world but in the next, building to a suggestion of a contrast like that in the beatitudes, but here drawn from the Psalms, "Ða ðe sawað on tearum, hie eft on gefean ripað" ("those who sow in tears, they afterwards reap in joy," Vercelli 11, lines 44–5, translating Psalm 125:5). Even if the deadpan understatement suggests a hint of humour to point to the recurring homiletic theme of the vanity of humour in this world, the prospects for homiletic humour look bleak.

Fortunately, though, humour need not be entirely incompatible with Christian virtue. St. Francis is famously considered the holy joker,[26] and even the proscriptive literature aimed at the most pious shows a certain ambivalence. The Benedictine Rule warns monks against the sin of vain words, which include those that move to laughter and so would seem to prohibit making jokes, but there are also hints that laughter can have its place. Chapter 4 of the Rule includes the following warning:

> Os suum a malo vel prabo aeloquio custodire, multum loqui non amare, verba vana aut risui apta non loqui, risum multum aut excussum non amare.
> (Benedictine Rule, chap. 4, clauses 51–4)[27]

> Keep your mouth from harmful or wicked speech, do not love to chatter, speak nothing foolish or laughable, do not love excessive or raucous laughter.

The laughable here is parallel with the foolish and both are instances of sins of the mouth, suggesting a strong rejection of verbal humour, but the last clause leaves an opening for some positive laughter, since the exhortation is against laughter that is inappropriate either in its excess (*multum*) or in its disruptive sound (*excussum*). The Old English translation is close but with some telling differences that are less sympathetic to humour. It presents these injunctions in a third-person account of the ideal monk:

> His muð he sceal from ælcum þweoran and yflum wordum gehealdan; ne sceal he fela sprecan, ne idele word ne leahtorbere; ne hleahter ne sceal he lufian.
> (Old English Benedictine Rule, chap. 4, 18/6–9)[28]

---

26 See, for example, Sanders, *Sudden Glory*.

27 Latin version Bruce L. Venarde, ed. and trans., *The Rule of Saint Benedict*, DOML (Cambridge, MA: Harvard University Press, 2011), 34–5.

28 Arnold Schröer, ed., *Die angelsächsischen Prosabearbeitungen der Benedictinerregel* (Kassel: Wigand, 1888). *Leahtorbere* is the spelling of Schroer's text, but MS O has *hleahtorbære* and MS T has *hleahtorfull*.

He must keep his mouth from all depraved and wicked speeches; he must
not speak much, neither vain words nor words causing laughter; he must not
love laughter.

The prohibition on speaking frivolous words that would cause laughter
is similar to the Latin – monks are not to be comedians or the bearers
of comic speech – but the last clause in the Old English gives more of a
blanket prohibition than the Latin, with the suggestion that monks are
simply not to love laughter of any kind, without further qualification
about the type of laughter that is prohibited. This sounds more like
the Old English homiletic condemnations of present laughter, and the
impact may be the stronger since the Old English word for laughter,
usually spelled *hleahtor*, puns on and is sometimes confused with the
word for sin, usually spelled *leahter*. In Old English, laughter is close
to sin.

The ambivalence is evident again in a later requirement in the
Benedictine Rule. In describing the steps of humility for a monk, the
Latin says:

Latin original: Decimus humilitatis gradus est si non sit facilis ac promtus in risu
quia scriptum est: *Stultus in risu exaltat vocem suam* [Sir 21:23]
(chap. 7, verse 59).

The tenth step of humility is not to be easy or ready in laughter, for it is written,
"The fool raises his voice in laughter."

The Old English translation slightly expands on this:

Se teoða eaðmodnesse stæpe is, gif se munuc ne bið galsmære and eaðe and hræd
on hlehtre, forþy hit is awriten: "Se stunta on lehtre his stefne geuferað."
(OE Benedictine Rule, chap. 7b.10, 30/8–10)

It is the tenth step of humility if the monk is not inclined to frivolity and easily
and quickly into laughter, because it is written: "The fool raises his voice in
laughter."

The humble monk should not be acting like a jester nor easily or quickly
producing laughter. The monk is not to be "eaðe and hræd on hlehtre,"
which closely translates "facilis ac promtus in risu," but the same phrase
gives the prompt for the additional term *galsmære*, uniquely surviving
here, defined by DOE as "inclined/disposed excessively to laughter/fri-
volity," deriving from the adjective *gal*, "1 wanton, lustful, lascivious; 2
wanton, frivolous, capricious; 3 evil, wicked" and the adverb *smere* (used

in ME with the verb to laugh "happily, heartily, contemptuously").[29] The prohibition in the Old English appears to first imagine a kind of lascivious and/or contemptuous mirth and then an easy or fast laughter. Those are not allowed, but other laughter might be, as the continuation of the biblical passage hints: "A fool lifteth up his voice in laughter: but a wise man will scarce laugh low to himself" (Ecclesiasticus 21:23). The point is reinforced in the next step of humility, which commands that when the monk speaks, he speak gently "butan hlehtre" ("without laughter," chap. VIIb/11, 30/13; cf. chap. 7, verse 60). Laughter is not viewed favourably for a monk's decorum and loud laughter and jesting are out, but the idea of mirth is not entirely foreclosed.

For those in secular life, laughter might be less taboo, even within a pious context. This is the opening that allows for the edifying humour of some hagiography, as will be explored in the next chapter. Within a preaching context, one promising possibility for the deployment of humour lies in the use of comic exempla within a sermon, although again the evidence is rather thin.

Comic Exempla and the Translation of Gregory's *Dialogues*

Within a sermon, anecdotes can be useful for hooking an audience, and the late medieval preaching tradition famously makes much use of them for this purpose, although their use was always controversial. Most late medieval preaching tracts claim a preference for naked morality but concede that exempla could help keep an audience's attention.[30] Anecdotes within sermons were generally drawn from uncontroversially edifying sources such as the Bible, saints' lives, or works of the church fathers, but other stories could also be called upon for their attention-grabbing effect, as in the Ælfrician anecdote explored above. One scholar of late medieval sermons comments on the risks involved for the edifying message: "in late-medieval preaching the desire to entertain with 'quaint' stories and jokes tended to overshadow the preacher's earnest commitment to teaching faith and morals."[31] Misuse of such stories leads to abundant comic

---

29 See DOE s.v. *galsmære* and *gal* and MED s.v. *smere*.
30 On late medieval preaching practice, see H. Leith Spencer, *English Preaching in the Late Middle Ages* (Oxford: Oxford University Press, 1993). For a summary of late medieval preaching handbooks, see Siegfried Wenzel, *Medieval Artes Praedicandi: A Synthesis of Scholastic Sermon Structure* (Toronto: University of Toronto Press for Medieval Academy, 2015).
31 Siegfried Wenzel, *The Art of Preaching: Five Medieval Texts and Translations* (Washington, DC: Catholic University of America Press, 2013), 245.

satire in the works of Chaucer (including his self-revealing Pardoner) and of Langland.[32]

This is not a tradition that has been noticed in discussion of Old English preaching, but there are a few hints for the use of exempla. First, I will draw out the theoretical evidence for their use and look at one collection that includes such comic material before turning to two homilies that make fuller use of humour.

While Old English lacks the tradition of *artes praedicandi* laying out the theory of crafting a sermon, occasional references to the hortatory value of *bysen* or *bispel* (the Old English words for short anecdotes or examples) do survive. This can be seen in the Old English Boethius, a translation of the *Consolation of Philosophy* made within King Alfred's circle, possibly by Alfred himself.[33] Before launching into the story of Orpheus and Eurydice, presented for its moral of not looking back to old sins, Wisdom explains the value of such a story. Here the Old English version expands on the Latin source:

> Ne fo we na on þa bisna and on bispell for þara leasne spella lufan, ac forþam þe we woldan mid gebeacnian þa soðfæstnesse, and woldon þæt hit wurde to nytte þam geherendon.
> (*Old English Boethius*, book III, chap. 35, lines 187–9)[34]

> We do not take up the analogies and examples for love of those false stories, but because we wanted to indicate the truth with them, and wanted it to become useful to the listeners.

---

32 Preaching exempla and their overlap with the Middle English literary tradition have been well examined in modern scholarship: see Larry Scanlon, *Narrative, Authority, and Power: The Medieval Exemplum and the Chaucerian Tradition* (Cambridge: Cambridge University Press, 1994); Elizabeth Allen, *False Fables and Exemplary Truth in Later Middle English Literature* (New York: Palgrave, 2005); Susan E. Phillips, *Transforming Talk: The Problem with Gossip in Late Medieval England* (University Park: Penn State University Press, 2007). On humour in exempla, see in addition, Aron Gurevich, *Medieval Popular Culture: Problems of Belief and Perception*, trans. János M. Bak and Paul M. Hollingsworth (Cambridge: Cambridge University Press, 1988), 176–210.

33 For the controversy on Alfredian authorship, see M.R. Godden, "Did King Alfred Write Anything?" *Medium Aevum* 76, no. 1 (2007): 1–23; Janet Bately, "Did King Alfred Actually Translate Anything? The Integrity of the Alfredian Canon Revisited," *Medium Aevum* 78, no. 2 (2009): 189–215.

34 Malcolm Godden and Susan Irvine, eds., *The Old English Boethius: An Edition of the Old English Versions of Boetheius's 'De Consolatione Philosophiae'*, 2 vols. (Oxford: Oxford University Press, 2009), here citing MS B; text at vol. 1, pp. 335–6; translation at vol. 2, p. 65.

The comment suggests a certain ambivalence about the use of such stories. On the one hand, the translator hints that such exampla can be *leasne spella* ("false stories" or "lying narratives"); on the other hand, he defends the value of appropriate *bisna* or *bispell* as useful for revealing truth (*þa soðfæstnesse*).[35] Ælfric himself uses similar vocabulary and reasoning to defend occasional elaborations in his own sermons, as when he adds to his sources to describe the mixed but undivided nature of Christ's divinity and humanity through a "lytle bysne" (CH I.2, line 182, "little analogy"), comparing the concept with the mixed but undivided white and yolk of an egg (CH I.2, lines 181–5). Explanatory exempla, then, are given some respect.

One collection of Christian stories is described using similar language and may well have provided comic exempla for preaching. In the metrical preface to Bishop Wærferth's Old English Translation of Gregory the Great's *Dialogues*, the author points out that the book contains "gastlices lifes godre biesene" ("good exempla of the spiritual life").[36] These are worth considering further since many are distinctly humorous Christian stories.

Gregory's *Dialogues* present in four books a series of miracle stories, mostly short, centring on the deeds of sixth-century Italian bishops, monks, and priests (along with a fuller life of Benedict, which constitutes the whole of book II), all framed as a dialogue between Gregory and his deacon, Peter.[37] The collection was translated into Old English by Bishop Wærferth at the end of the ninth century in the context of King Alfred's program of translation of those books "most necessary for all people to know." The attribution to Wærferth is made in Asser's *Life of King Alfred*, and one version circulates with a preface in the name of King Alfred.[38]

Some of the stories included here were drawn on in Old English preaching. The anonymous homily, Vercelli 14, draws from the ending of the *Dialogues* (although probably taken over from a translation other than

---

35 For a recent sensitive handling of this language as early theorizing of fiction, see Jennifer A. Lorden, "Tale and Parable: Theorizing Fictions in the Old English *Boethius*," *PMLA* 136, no. 3 (2021): 340–55.

36 The Metrical Preface to Gregory's Dialogues in MS BL Cotton Otho C. i, ed. Elliott van Kirk Dobbie, ed., *The Anglo-Saxon Minor Poems*, ASPR 6 (New York: Columbia, 1942), 112–13, line 3.

37 Hans Hecht, ed., *Bischofs Wærferth von Worcester Übersetzung der Dialoge Gregors von Grosen*, Bibliothek der angelsächsischen Prosa 5 (Leipzig: Wigand, 1900).

38 For details, see Malcolm Godden, "Wærferth and King Alfred: The Fate of the Old English *Dialogues*," in *Alfred the Wise: Studies in Honour of Janet Bately on the Occasion of Her Sixty-Fifth Birthday*, eds. Jane Roberts, Janet L. Nelson, and Malcolm Godden (Cambridge: Brewer, 1997), 35–51, who suggests Alfred came to think not highly of the translation.

the surviving one).[39] The opening of the last book supplies material for a different anonymous homily (subsequently revised by Wulfstan), Napier 1. Ælfric makes occasional use of some of the stories in the *Dialogues*, notably for scenes of death and miraculously displayed doom, which he draws on in three different homilies.[40] Ælfric explicitly comments on the work in discussing the efficacy of the mass:

> Eac se halga papa Gregorius awrát on ðære bec dialegorum. hú micclum seo halige mæsse manegum fremode. Seo boc is on englisc awend. on ðære mæg gehwá be ðison genihtsumlice gehyran. se ðe hí oferrædan wile;
> (CH II.21, lines 176–80)

> Also Gregory the holy Pope wrote in the book *Dialogues* how much the holy mass did for many. That book is translated into English; anyone who wants to read it over can hear abundantly about this in that.

This sounds like an open invitation to use the stories of the *Dialogues*, albeit imagining an unclear (and perhaps unrealistic) access to a book in English which anyone can hear (*gehyran*) who will read it over (*oferrǣdan*). Further evidence for selective use of the *Dialogues* may lie in the chapter headings of the translation which were added in one eleventh-century manuscript and allow easier access to the individual stories, perhaps for the sake of mining them for exempla.[41]

There are hints, then, of a nascent exempla tradition drawing from Gregory's *Dialogues*. Surviving instances all draw on serious rather than humorous stories, reflecting the serious nature of the surviving homiletic corpus, but there are comic examples which could serve for such a purpose. One example, "Be þære nunfæmnan, þe bat þone leahtric" ("Concerning the nun, who bit the lettuce"), can give a sense of the comic potential of these stories.

> Soðlice sume dæge hit gelamp, þæt an nunne of þam ylcan mynstre þara fæmnena eode in þone wyrttun. Þa geseah heo ænne leahtric. Þa lyste hi þæs 7 hine genam 7 forgeat, þæt heo hine mid Cristes rodetacne gebletsode, ac heo hine freclice bat. Þa wearð heo sona fram deofle gegripen 7 niðer on þa eorðan gefeoll 7 wæs swiþe

---

39 The second part of Vercelli IV draws from *Dialogues* IV, 59–62; see Paul Szarmach, "Another Old English Translation of Gregory the Great's *Dialogues*?" *English Studies* 62 (1981): 91–109.

40 Such scenes are drawn from different stories in *Dialogues*, book IV in CH I.16, CH I.35, and CH II.19; see Godden, *Commentary*.

41 See David F. Johnson, "Who Read Gregory's Dialogues in Old English?" *The Power of Words: Anglo-Saxon Studies Presented to Donald Scragg on His Seventieth Birthday*, eds. Hugh Magennis and Jonathan Wilcox (Morgantown: West Virginia University Press, 2006), 171–204, who posits a range of possible uses.

geswenced. 7 hi þa hrædlice to heora fæder Equitio ærendracan sændon 7 him þis
sædon 7 hine bædon, þæt he hraðe come 7 mid gebedum heora swuster gehælde.
7 þa se halga man gebiddende arn. 7 sona swa se halga fæder in þone wyrtun
ineode, þa ongan se deofol, þe þa nunnan swencte, of hire muþe clypian[42] swylce
he dædbote don wolde 7 þus cwæð: 'Hwæt dyde ic hire? Hwæt dyde ic hire? Ic
me sæt on anum leahtrice, þa com heo 7 bat me.' He þa se Godes wer mid mycelre
æbylignysse bebead, þæt he of hire gewite, 7 þæt he þa stowe on þæs ælmihtigan
Godes fæmnan læng ne hæfde ne on hire ne wunede. 7 he þa sona onweg gewat, 7
he na onufan þæt hire gehrinan ne moste ne ne dorste.[43]

Truly, it happened one day that a nun from that same female monastery went
into the garden. She then saw a lettuce. Then she desired it and seized it and
forgot that she should bless it with sign of the cross, but she bit into it greedily.
She was then immediately gripped by the devil and fell down onto the ground
and was sorely afflicted. And then they quickly sent a message to their
spiritual father, Equitius, and told him this and asked that he come quickly
and save their sister with prayers. And the holy man then ran praying. And as
soon as the holy father entered into the garden, then the devil, who afflicted
the nun, began to call out from her mouth as if he wanted to do penance and
said thus: "What did I do to her? What did I do to her? I sat myself down on
a lettuce, then she came and bit me." The man of God then commanded with
great indignation that he depart from her, and that he no longer occupy that
place in that woman of Almighty God, and that he not dwell in her. And he
then departed away at once, and he after that could not nor dared not touch
her at all.

There are plenty of markers that this is a funny story. The episode opens
with formulas that establish it as an independent piece: the adverb of verac-
ity, soðlice (truly), the precise but unspecific temporal marker, sume dæge
(one day), and the impersonal and all-purpose verb, hit gelamp (it happened). The narrative develops with a self-contained story leading towards
a climax in the manner of a punchline ("What did I do to her? What did I
do to her?"), and then ends in resolution. This constitutes an independent
bisen, which proceeds through humour.

Part of that humour derives from the disconnection between the slight
narrative surface of a nun being overly hasty in her consumption of natural produce in the garden and such potentially weighty issues as the devil's
rights and the importance of exorcism. The comedy is ramped up through
the characterization of the devil. While his ontological status here is not

---

42 Hecht, Dialoge, has clypian presumably in error.
43 Hecht Dialoge, 30/28–31/26, left-hand column, with capitalization added.

entirely clear – is this the Prince of Darkness himself or some minor minion? his repeated speech tags and self-justification seem incongruously modest for any member of the demon-kind. There is a marked difference in the register between the colloquial and casual speech of the demon and the polysyllabic seriousness in the injunctions of the confessor. Humour arises from the incongruity between the apparently casual nature of the demon and the audience's awareness of the serious status of such beings in Christian cosmography, as also between the quotidian and modest status of a lettuce (or other greens of the genus *lactuca*) and the eschatological issues of demonology. The story ends not with a verbal witticism, but with a happy outcome, and yet surely works as something like a pious joke.[44]

Even though this particular story does not circulate further in Old English, it is clear how useful it could be as a memorable exemplum to demonstrate the omnipresence of the forces of evil which might trip up the inattentive Christian. It could also circulate, with slightly more bite, as a satire at the inattentiveness of people in holy orders. The gender of the lettuce-eating subject could be part of an anti-feminist critique, especially as the nun is displaying appetite and impulsiveness, which might be classed as greed. All of this is contained in a story that is brief and made memorable by the humour. It may be significant that humour comes into play in presenting a demon. Even as the devil serves a serious role in Christian cosmography as the locus of evil, the potential for his (semi-)vanquished tribe to be the butt of humour is seen fully in late medieval cycle and morality plays. If modern humour obsesses with crossing boundaries of the taboos of sex and violence, Old English homiletic humour might well be particularly interested in exploring the edges of the ultimate evil. As with saints' lives, such exploration can occur in an unanxious context in view of the ultimate downfall of the devil within the broad Christian story.

The *Dialogues* is built up from many brief stories such as this, and a number of others are funny, too. For example, in describing the divine perspicacity of a holy man called Isaac, in Book III, chapter 14 (202/17–203/3), Gregory describes how he is approached by a group of beggars, "oferhangene mid toslitenum claðum, swa þæt hi wæron ful neah nacode gesewen"

---

44 On the humour of the account in Gregory's original, see Danuta Shanzer, "Laughter and Humour in the Early Medieval Latin West," in *Humour, History and Politics in Late Antiquity and the Early Middle Ages*, ed. Guy Halsall (Cambridge: Cambridge University Press, 2002), 25–47 at 46, who relates it to a primal scene in Genesis, including Eve's desire for the apple, Adam's self-exculpation, and the devil's parade of injured innocence.

("hung about with torn clothes, so that they very nearly appeared naked," 202/19–20), who ask him for clothing. The holy man reacts by summoning one of his servants or followers ("ænne of his þegnum," 202/21) and telling him to bring the clothing that he will find in a hollow in a tree in a certain place. The holy man then invites the beggars in to dress themselves in the garments he provides:

> þa hi þas hrægl gesawon, hi gecneowon, þæt hi hi ær gehyddon, 7 wurdon afærede mid mycelre scame, 7 scamiende hi onfengon heora agenu hrægl, þa þe hi mid facne fræmde sohton.
> (Gregory's *Dialogues*, 202/28–203/3)

> When they saw these clothes, they knew that they had hidden them before, and they were fearful with great shame, and they received their own clothes shamefully, when they sought to get another's by deceit.

This little story, then, describes a practical joke played by the holy man as a witty response that shames false beggars. The story is funny because of the reversal of expectation, with the purveyor of charity not convey-ing the charity expected, and the tricksters not playing the trick they expect, but instead the pious man out-tricking the tricksters. The story can serve serious doctrinal points, such as the need for discernment in charity, the imperative not to try to cheat the system, and the all-know-ing nature of the Godhead, but makes those points through a short nar-rative that is funny.

Micro-Exempla in Action: Laughing at the Sinner in Napier 46

While deployment of such comic anecdotes is not the norm in the surviv-ing preaching record, there are a few cases where a homilist uses humour to build up a message. Napier 46, of unknown authorship, origin, or date, is one such, deploying a few funny scenes in the course of a broad-ranging sermon.[45] One such scene builds on laughing at demons and anticipates what will become a full-fledged comic exemplum in the later tradition, while another proves even more timeless, anticipating a scene depicted by

---

45 Arthur Napier, ed., *Wulfstan: Sammlung der ihm zugeschriebenen Homilien nebst Untersuchungen über ihre Echtheit* (1883; repr. with a bibliog. suppl. by Klaus Ostheeren, Dublin: Weidmann, 1967), 232–42. It survives in two MSS: CCCC 419 of

Freud. The humour is brief, but usefully hints at a sermon style that does not eschew entertainment in the cause of edification.

Napier 46 begins with an exhortation to observe correct behaviour in church, which is a recurring concern of the homily. Each person has two teachers, the homilist explains, an angel and a devil, who report the individual's actions to God and compete over the soul. These two make suggestions as the person enters a church, with the angel suggesting quietness, moderate speech, and consideration of God's commands, whereas the devil teaches:

> unstilnesse and ungemetlice hleahtras and unnytte spræce and unnytte geþancas and tælnesse and treowleasnesse godes beboda.
> (Napier 46, 233/18–20)

> unquietness and immoderate laughter and vain speech and vain thoughts and slander and faithlessness to God's commands.

This description of bad behaviour in church notably includes immoderate laughter (*ungemetlice hleahtras*), which is frowned on in other preaching contexts, too, but might hint at the possibility of joking in church. A little later, the homilist goes further in describing the nature of the bad behaviour. The devil teaches the distracted parishioner:

> þæt he stande and gorette and locige underbæc ut; þæt bið gymeleas gebed, and he hit ne mæg gebetan, forðan þe se deofol hæfð his heortan on his handa.
> (Napier 46, 234/17–20)

> that he may stand and stare about and look backwards from behind outwards; that is heedless prayer and he may not atone for it because the devil has his heart in his hands.

The description becomes fuller as we get to see the sinner's bodily contortions with hints of insouciant disregard for good etiquette in the bodily twisting (*gorette and locige underbæc ut*, "stare about and look backwards from behind outwards"), recalling the comic twisting of looking *underbæc* in Durham Proverb 28. This little vignette of bad behaviour in

---

the first half of the eleventh century, place of origin unknown, subsequently moved to Exeter, and Oxford, Bodleian MS, Bodley 343 of the second half of the twelfth century, probably from the West Midlands.

church anticipates what will become a staple for later medieval preaching humour, most developed in the tradition of the demon Tutivillus, who
records gossip and vain speech in church, and who, in one set of stories,
bangs his head on the church wall as he pulls on his parchment with his teeth
to give himself more space to record tittle-tattle.[46] Napier 46 anticipates the
scene of the negligent sinner in church and the role of the devil, even though
it does not present the full story of Tutivillus. In the incipient satire here the
preacher uses humour to police the behaviour of those preached at. Humour
can be useful for the controlling aspect of the homiletic voice.

Rather than develop further the humour of the controlling devil, Napier
46 plays up a different comic discomfiture to hold the audience's attention.
The homilist describes the passing of the souls of an impious and a steadfast man, drawn from the popular apocryphal account of the afterlife, the
Visio Sancti Pauli, and ends with an exhortation to consider the transitory
nature of life and to think of the world to come. In doing so, the homilist
calls for everyone to repent in front of a confessor, suggesting that it is
better to confess and be ashamed of one's sins before one man here in the
world than to be shamed at Judgment Day before God, the angels, the
citizens of earth, and the devils:

> se ðe nele her his synna nu andettan his scrifte and betan, swa he him tæcð, hine
> sceal on domes dæg gesceamian beforan gode and eallum his halgum and eac
> eallum deoflum, swa þam men dyde, þe wurde færinga nacod beforan eallon folce,
> and he nyste þonne, mid hwam he þone sceamiendan lichaman bewruge.
> (Napier 46, 238/10–16)

> he who will not here confess his sins now to his confessor and atone as he
> teaches him, he must be ashamed on Judgment Day before God and all
> his saints and also all the devils, just like it occurred to that man who was
> suddenly naked before all the people, and he did not know then with what he
> might cover his private parts.[47]

The homilist here is concerned to convey the fundamental Christian
idea of the shame derived from sins unshriven, which he does through

---

46 See Margaret Jennings, "Tutivillus: The Literary Career of the Recording Demon,"
    Studies in Philology 74, no. 5 (December 1977): 1–95; Phillips, *Transforming Talk*.
47 The same passage occurs in one other place, an anonymous homilist's expansion of an
    Ælfric sermon, Pope 27, lines 114–21 (ed. Pope 1967–8, II: 770–81), and that version
    clarifies the translation of the final phrase, which there is *his sceamigendlican*, i.e. "his
    naughty bits." I discuss this passage more fully in "Naked in Old English."

a comic simile that exploits the attention-grabbing potential of unexpected nudity. The extended simile here appeals to a squirming sense of situational inappropriateness that comes from finding oneself naked in front of a crowd; in other words, to comic embarrassment. Underlying the simile is the idea that such public exposure is an obvious trigger for comic embarrassment, an assumption that can be made as readily for an early medieval audience as it can by Freud in his dream of an analogous scene.[48]

Throughout this sermon, then, a homilist is using touches of humour and here a hint of the comically salacious to make serious moral points about conduct. This distinctive comic preaching aesthetic is seen even more clearly in another anonymous homily, now known as Vercelli 9.

Vercelli 9 and the Comic Exaggeration of Heaven and Hell

While it is strikingly unusual for Old English homilists to use humour to capture their audience's attention, the composer of Vercelli 9, a sermon on heaven and hell, does just that.[49] This is a broad-ranging, rhetorically crafted homily. It survives in different versions in three full accounts and five excerpts.[50] The homilist presents a forceful warning of the judgment coming to all individuals at the end of this transitory life for which, he warns, people are all too unprepared. Most of the homily describes the woes of hell and the joys of heaven, with a final injunction to cease sins, give alms, do good works, and seek out church with purity and humble prayer.

In developing these themes, the homilist shows a love of lists, enumerating the capital sins and the seven virtues, the seven pains of hell, the three deaths, which include a closing down of the five senses, and

---

48 See Sigmund Freud, *The Interpretation of Dreams*, trans. James Strachey (New York: Basic Books, 1955), 242–8.

49 Ed. Scragg, *Vercelli Homilies*, 151–90. Scragg's analysis is fundamental to understanding all aspects of the homily. The homily is translated from different versions in Charles D. Wright, *The Irish Tradition in Old English Literature* (Cambridge: Cambridge University Press, 1993), 277–91, and by Patricia Quattrin in Nicholson, *Vercelli Homilies*, 65–71. It has been the subject of relatively rich critical engagement and two studies are of particular value: Wright, *The Irish Tradition*; Samantha Zacher, *Preaching the Converted: The Style and Rhetoric of the Vercelli Book Homilies* (Toronto: University of Toronto Press, 2009), esp. chap. 6.

50 All versions are presented in Scragg's edition. Citations will use his sigla to indicate versions.

the five likenesses of hell.[51] Such lists probably serve to keep the audience oriented and attentive, even though the plenitude of their use risks seeming comically excessive. This homily also features memorable extended similes. In the most extended of these, the homilist uses the voice of the devil talking to an anchorite to provide images for the littleness of earth, the extreme noisiness of hell, and the sense of well-being in heaven, with an exuberance that suggests these are comic exempla.

In a work that has already spent considerable energy describing heaven and hell, continued expansion on the theme uses exaggeration to an extent that suggests the deliberate deployment of humour. For example, in describing the fifth torment of hell, the homilist has the devil explain to the anchorite:

> 7 þeah .vii. men sien, 7 þara hæbbe æghylc twa 7 hundsiofontig gereorda, swa feala swa ealles þysses middangeardes gereorda syndon, and þonne sy þara seofon manna æghwylc to alife gesceapen, 7 hyra hæbbe æghwylc siofon heafdu, 7 þara heafdu ælc hæbbe siofon tungan, 7 þara tungena ælc hæbbe isene stemne, 7 þonne hwæðre ne magon þa ealle ariman helle witu. (Vercelli 9 [AE], lines 108–13)

> and even if there were seven people, and each of those had seventy-two languages, as many languages as there are in all of this world, and then each of those seven people were created to eternal life, and each of them had seven heads, and each of those heads had seven tongues, and each of those tongues had a voice of iron, and even then they could not enumerate all the torments of hell.

The concatenation of numbers is striking, exemplifying the homilist's love of enumeration. The idea of inexpressible torments which could not be recited even if the speaker had a hundred tongues, a hundred mouths, and a voice of iron, is drawn from Virgil's account of Hades in the sixth book of the *Aeneid*, modified by way of the *Visio Pauli*'s account of hell, but here given its own twist.[52] The extremity of the listing points to the serious paradox of disquieting uncanniness presented in a rhetorical *tour de force*.

---

51 Wright, *Irish Tradition*, chap. 2, characterizes this as the enumerative style.
52 Wright, *Irish Tradition*, 145–8; "Nay, had I a hundred tongues, a hundred mouths, and voice of iron, I could not sum up all the forms of crime, or rehearse all the tale of torments," *Aeneid* VI.625–7.

This is articulated, ironically and yet appropriately, by a devil.[53] Torments that cannot be described are, by definition, beyond the power of human language to conjure, but stumping the devil expands the scope of such inexpressibility and makes a serious and cautionary point. And yet, for all such serious effects, the idea of inexpressibility articulated by an unlikely speaker at such expressive length is an incongruity with such appropriate inappropriateness as to be funny.[54]

I think that the breaking point where exaggeration becomes comedy can be specifically pinpointed in this example. The choice of seven individuals as the putative mouth-piece for the reported wisdom is hyperbolic but not unduly excessive, and any unease at the choric effect is disrupted by the apparently didactic parenthesis as the homilist cannot resist digressing on the number of languages known in the world, a piece of encyclopedic knowledge lacking any hint of comic tone.[55] The image moves to a more extreme level as those seven speakers are imagined for a moment "created to eternal life." Now we are in a counter-factual world of a thought experiment, but this does not seem disproportionate in the context of the eternal verities of the Last Judgment and heaven and hell. The tonal shift to the exuberant comes with the next item in the reduplicating series, as each speaker is imagined with seven heads. While this could be a serious nod to the many-headed beast of Revelation/Apocalypse, it sounds more like the topsy-turvy world of the riddles, where unreasonable numbers of body parts get resolved into forms likely (such as a plough or a rake) or unlikely (such as a bagpipe or the One-Eyed Seller of Garlic).[56] That element of exuberance through excess is repeated when each head is imagined to have seven tongues. Exaggeration is one technique for creating the incongruity of humour, and that is a likely effect of the grotesque imagery here.

Raising a smile at this point might be a deliberate performative ploy by the homilist. The broad context, the fear of hell for our misdeeds, may be

---

53 See Fred C. Robinson, "The Devil's Account of the Next World," *Neuphilologische Mitteilungen* 73 (1972): 362–71, repr. in his *The Editing of Old English* (Oxford: Blackwell, 1994), 196–205; D.G. Scragg, "The Devil's Account of the Next World Revisted," *ANQ* 24 (1986): 107–10; Wright, *Irish Tradition*, 145–56; Zacher, *Preaching*, 217.

54 Comedy is always possible in the excess of the inexpressibility topos, as is illustrated in the most famous example in modern literature, where Stephen Daedalus attempts to capture the flavour of eternity in the sermon in *Portrait of the Artist as a Young Man*.

55 The number is based on the tribes of Israel, as most modern commentators cannot resist explicating: see Hans Sauer, "Die 72 Völker und Sprachen der Welt: ein mittelalterliche Topos in der englischen Literatur," *Anglia* 101 (1982): 29–48.

56 See Exeter Book riddles 21, 34, 31, and 86; cf. the seven heads of the red dragon of Revelation 12:1 or the beast of Revelation 13:1 and 17:3–9.

no laughing matter, but audience members are not going to absorb the message if they cease attending to the homilist's extensive exhortations from exhaustion. What better way to keep them on track than to hold their attention with the comically grotesque? Confirmation that there is something striking here that is contrary to the expectations of Old English preachers is provided in the evidence of circulation. Two of the surviving manuscripts skip the seven heads, suggesting redactors who balked at deploying such homiletic humour.[57]

The homilist continues describing the woes of hell in a balanced rhetorical list, then switches again to the voice of the devil speaking to the anchorite, first explaining the narrow space of the earthly *middangeard* surrounded by ocean as like a mere prick in a wax tablet (Vercelli 9 (AE), 144–50), and then amplifying on this with an extended simile establishing the soundscape of hell:

> And he, se deofol, þa gyt cwæð to þam ancran: "Gyf ænig mann wære ane niht on helle 7 he eft wære æfter þam ofalædd, 7 ðeah man þone garsecg mid isene utan ymbtynde, 7 þonne ealne gefylde mid fyres lige up oþ ðone heofonas hrof, 7 utan embsette hine þonne ealne mid byligeon 7 heora æghwylc oðres æthrinan mihte, 7 to æghwylcum þæra byligea wære man geset 7 se hæfde Samsones strengðe (se wæs ealra eorðwarena strengest þe ær oððe syððan æfre gewurde) 7 þeah man þonne gesette an brad isen þell ofer þæs fyres hrof, 7 þeah hit wære eall mid mannum afylled 7 ðæra æghwylc hæfde ænne hamor on handa, 7 þeah man bleowe mid eallum þam byligeon 7 mid þam hameron beote on þær isene þell and se lig brastlode, ne awacode he næfre for eallum þisum, to ðam werig he wære for þære anre nihthwile."
>
> (Vercelli 9, main text [here O as MS A is missing a leaf], lines 151–63)

And he, that devil, then said further to the anchorite: "If any person were a single night in hell and he was led away again after that, and even if a person surrounded the ocean around with iron, and then filled it all with flames of fire up to the roof of heaven, and set about it on the outside then completely with bellows and each of them might touch the next, and a person were set to each of those bellows and that one had the strength

---

57 The Vercelli Book and Bodleian MS, Bodley 340; for full details, see my "The Pains and Pleasures of Vercelli Homily IX and the Delights of Textual Transmission," in *The Anonymous Old English Homily: Sources, Composition, and Variation*, eds. Winfried Rudolf and Susan Irvine (Leiden: Brill, 2021), 287–311.

of Samson (he was the strongest of all inhabitants of earth who ever was before or since) and even if one then set a broad iron cover over the roof of that fire, and even if it was completely filled up with people and each of those had a hammer in his hand, and even if they blew with all those bellows and beat with those hammers on the iron cover and the flame roared, he would not wake up for all of this, being weary to that extent on account of that single period of a night."

While the excessive commotion of hell may be commonplace, this homilist goes about giving that concept new attention-grabbing life through amplification in this epic simile that is uneconomical to such an extent as to suggest incongruity and the resulting possibility of humour. This image takes the idea of the racket of the smithy,[58] and amplifies it beyond measure, first by imagining a space for the commotion that is the size of the whole ocean, next by defining that space with an almost limitless construction of iron, and then by providing not just the hammers but also the bellows of all those iron-workers, themselves described in leisurely detail. The bellows is a comic focus for two Old English riddles (Riddles 37 and 87) which play with the strength and masculine prowess of the one who mans them, an apparent master, who nevertheless serves his servant's purpose. In the homily, the men pumping the bellows are imagined as having the strength of the strongest of men, namely Samson (whose strength is made apparent in one of those needless scholarly parentheses, matching the explanation of the 72 languages in the earlier extended simile), and the plenitude of such pumpers is emphasized by the fact that they are contiguous to the point of touching one another. A reprise of the bellows and the hammers and the flames blowing and beating and crackling in the pre-penultimate clause maintains a kind of leisurely pacing in the wording that contributes to the expansiveness of the account. Indeed, the image overflows with such exuberant excess as to invite a smile.

One added touch seems to me to clinch the case for deliberate humour, namely the extreme anti-climax of the ending. After so much crowding and so much effort describing so much noise, it is a disproportionate falling-off for all these rhetorical tricks of loudness simply to fall on deaf ears, to leave the putative escapee from hell not just not overwhelmed, but, apparently, still asleep. The extremity of such bathos, I suggest, encourages a smile at the comic incongruity.

---

58 Compare, for example, the fifteenth-century lyric in BL Arundel 292, fol. 71v (ed. as "The Smiths," in Thomas J. Garbáty, ed., *Medieval English Literature* [Lexington, MA: Heath, 1984], 671).

Once again, the subject matter may not be obviously suitable for laughing, and yet such an extended imagining of the terrors of hell surely benefits from changing tone from continuous strict seriousness. Once again, the reception history suggests that such a technique was controversial. The manuscript which had omitted the seven heads (Bodley 340), simply omits the whole extended image here. Apparently some compiler appreciated the homily but did not approve of its extravagances and so had a version copied such that a preacher could deliver it without excessive heads speaking or the fancifulness of excessive clamour. Such a desire to re-establish norms of homiletic decorum demonstrates how the Vercelli 9 homilist is doing something special by joking about hell.

The anonymous homilist of Vercelli 9 uses other unconventional methods, too, to keep an audience's attention. The account of heaven includes a salacious detail that may have shocked and amused, and is accordingly edited out of most manuscripts. Once again, the homilist describes heaven through an extended image placed in the mouth of a devil speaking to an anchorite. This time the inexpressibility topos imagines, with considerable leisure, the most beautiful and most wise man in the world in the most beautiful place on earth, with the greatest skills and greatest wealth, and living forever without sorrow, and brought each night the most beautiful woman, a new bride every night – and suggests that even this would be as nothing compared with one night in heaven (Vercelli 9 (A), lines 185–200). There is something distinctly comic in the *Land of Cockayne*–like excesses of such a dilatory description. This time the incongruity includes revelling in the pleasures of the sexual act, an emphasis that is strikingly unusual in the surviving Old English record.[59] Once again, the unusual nature of this description is marked by its omission in different versions of the homily, such that it survives in full in just one of the manuscripts, namely the Vercelli Book.[60] Such humour and salacious imagining was not to the taste of most Old English preachers, at least on the evidence of the record that survives in writing. Vercelli 9 as preserved in the Vercelli Book shows that humour and sensationalism could be put into service of a homiletic message in Old English, but it very rarely is so.

---

59 The paucity is discussed by Williams, "What's So New," and Melanie Heyworth, "Perceptions of Marriage in *Exeter Book Riddles 20* and *61*," *Studia Neophilologica* 79 (2007): 171–84, both of whom find relief only in descriptions in the Exeter Book riddles. Hugh Magennis, "'No Sex Please, We're Anglo-Saxons'? Attitudes to Sexuality in Old English Prose and Poetry," *Leeds Studies in English* 26 (1995): 1–26, usefully shows such hesitation towards sexual topics to be a recurring feature of surviving Old English literature, but without considering this example.

60 See my "Pains and Pleasures," for full details.

It is hard to tell, of course, whether the paucity of homiletic humour is simply a reflection of the high seriousness of anything that got preserved on parchment or whether it reflects a preaching style that eschewed the frivolity of such entertainment. One can imagine priests in the field stepping away from a written text and deploying their knowledge of their audience to keep the attention of their congregation with amusing anecdotes or extemporized comic business. Such good preaching may well have involved more use of humour than survives in writing, with the consequent risk of immeasurable laughter in the church. Napier 46 and Vercelli 9 give a hint of the comic possibilities within crafted sermons.

Preachers inclined to use devices of entertainment presumably laid themselves open to a risk of censure. While this is implied by a circulation record where the funny bits get excised, it is even clearer where sacerdotal misconduct becomes the subject of comic clerical satire, as occurs in one fragmentary Old English poem.

Sacerdotal Satire: *Seasons for Fasting*

Clerical satire becomes a stimulus for great poetry in the fourteenth century, as reflected in such works as *Piers Plowman* and *The Canterbury Tales*. There are hints of such a tradition in Old English, but the only surviving example is a turn within a fragmentary poem cut off by textual loss. *Seasons for Fasting* exemplifies the minimal case for the survival of an Old English text. The surviving fragment is recorded in a transcript of a manuscript that burnt in the 1731 fire at Ashburnham House, but that manuscript was presumably already fragmentary since the transcribed text ends incompletely in mid-flow.

Most of the surviving poem is homiletic and serious, laying out the appropriate date for a series of Christian fasts (known as Ember Days), and exploring and explaining the importance of fasting generally, especially at Lent.[61] This is a theme that is also covered in many Old English homilies, and the poem matches them in message and tone, expressed in a homiletic voice in verse. As such, it is an example of the didactic Christian poetry that is fairly common in the surviving record and usually not

---

61 The poem is edited, translated, and discussed by Mary P. Richards, ed. and trans., *The Old English Poem Seasons for Fasting: A Critical Edition* (Morgantown: West Virginia University Press, 2014); Christopher A. Jones, ed. and trans., *Old English Shorter Poems, Volume 1: Religious and Didactic*, DOML 15 (Cambridge, MA: Harvard University Press, 2012), 156–73.

funny.[62] The form of this poem is unusual, shaped into eight-line stanzas, but the serious didactic purpose is more common. Towards the end, however, the homilist-poet makes an unusual and comic turn.

This section begins with the serious and unsurprising exhortation that priests need to sing masses daily during fasts and that all people need to confess their sins to those priests (lines 184–91). That leads the homilist-poet to reflect on the importance of priests themselves exemplifying good Christian conduct. This, too, is a recurring preoccupation in many Old English homilies, and the poet provides common homiletic advice in exhorting layfolk to attend to the message rather than heeding the sins of the messenger if any priest proves wayward (lines 200–7).[63] Less characteristic is the subsequent turn to explicit condemnation of priests who anger the Lord daily and "mid æleste" ("with irreligion" or "with neglect of religious law," 211a) lead layfolk astray.[64] Here the homilist-poet crafts a strikingly unusual portrait of such irreligion:

> sona hie on mergan   mæssan syngað
> and forþegide,   þurste gebæded,
> æfter tæppere   teoþ geond stræta.
> (lines 213–15)

They sing masses in the morning and consumed and impelled by thirst, they at once roam through the streets after the tavern keeper.

The poet provides here a surprisingly specific imagined portrait of the malconduct of these misbehaving priests. Particularly striking is the brief entry into their thought-world with the recognition that they are driven by thirst (line 214). This is particularly ironic since it reminds an audience that the mass celebration has already involved their consumption of wine, albeit wine turned through their consecrating power into blood. Did the priests consume the Eucharistic wine because they were impelled by

---

62 Emily V. Thornbury, *Becoming a Poet in Anglo-Saxon England* (Cambridge: Cambridge University Press, 2014), chap. 5, calls this the Southern mode. See the poems collected in Jones, *Shorter Poems*.

63 For examples in the works of Wulfstan, see my "The Wolf on Shepherds: Wulfstan, Bishops, and the Context of the *Sermo Lupi ad Anglos*," in *Old English Prose: Basic Readings*, ed. Paul E. Szarmach (New York: Garland, 2000), 395–418; for Ælfric, see Robert K. Upchurch, "A Big Dog Barks: Ælfric of Eynsham's Indictment of the English Pastorate and *Witan*," *Speculum* 85 (2010): 505–33.

64 The noun is uniquely surviving here, defined by DOE s.v. *ælyste* as "neglect of (religious) law."

thirst? [65] That would be a shocking concession to the urges of the body at a moment of the most heightened sacral ceremony. Or has their thirst been triggered because of going through the work of consecrating the host and wine in celebrating the mass? That suggests a grotesque emphasis on, and complaint about, the laboriousness of a process that is supposed to be celebratory and miraculous, a response that is both ungrateful and apparently missing the point of the ceremony they have enacted. The poet provides no explicit condemnation, merely lays out the strikingly inappropriate thought and action as an established fact in the manner of satire. The satire is there, too, in the imagination of this group – anonymous, collective, and yet sacerdotal – wandering the streets seeking the professional dispenser of food and drink, a *tæppere* (tapster) – a word that survives in Old English only in this poem and in glosses. This is a surprisingly detailed and, on the surface, surprisingly unjudgmental portrait of conduct so unbecoming to the priests involved.

The poet continues:

> Hwæt! Hi leaslice   leogan ongynnað
> and þone tæppere   tyhtaþ gelome,
> secgaþ þæt he synleas   syllan mote
> ostran to æte   and æþele wyn
> emb morgentyd,
> (lines 216–20a)

> Indeed! They begin to falsely lie
> and urge the tapster repeatedly,
> they say that he may sinless give
> oysters for eating and noble wine
> in the morning time.

At first the viewpoint is clearly the external one of the homilist-poet, finally stirred to moral assessment, expressed with all the more force through the tautologous and echoing pair *leaslice leogan* ("lyingly lie") and the reiterative nature of the sin (*gelome*). As the sentence continues, though, the poet provides a portrait of action (here in the form of speech) without explicit condemnation, even though the sentiment is so contrary to the wisdom

---

65 *Forþecgan* at line 214a is a *hapax legomenon*. Jones, *Shorter Poems*, 171, assumes it goes with the second half of the line and translates "and, consumed and driven by thirst"; Richards, 109, assumes an implied object which she provides in her translation, "and have consumed (the Eucharist), impelled by thirst." DOE, s.v. *for-þecgan* implies that Jones's reading is more likely.

about fasting running through the rest of the poem that the critique is obvious. Rather than abstaining until evening time, these priests are telling the tapster that it is sinless for him to serve them, even though it is explicitly *morgentyd*, morning time, soon after the working of the mass on a day of fasting. A recurring definition of fasting, both in this poem and widely throughout the corpus of Old English, is refraining from food until the ninth hour (mid-afternoon or approximately 3:00 p.m. in the modern division of the day). Morning eating on fast days is a sin.[66] Rather than explicit condemnation in the usual homiletic manner, the specious reasoning and shocking action of the sinning satirical butts is described in detail. This approaches the satirical method Langland deploys in his more developed portrait of the actions and speech of Gluttony in *Piers Plowman*.

The choice of comestibles that these priests are defending is probably also significant. Oysters are neither fish nor fowl (or, more precisely, not meat, nor clearly fish) and so might be the subject of sophistical special pleading by the self-indulgent priests. Indeed, oysters are explicitly included in Ælfric's warning that priests may not eat or drink before celebrating the mass, either anticipating such sophistical reasoning or imagining a foodstuff that might be consumed in such circumstances.[67] The adjective qualifying the wine (not just any old wine but *æþele wyn*, high-class wine) adds to the satire, too. These priests are doing wrong by breaking the fast, by not taking their sacerdotal job seriously enough, by leading a layperson (the tapster) astray, by showing gluttony and disobedience, and also, apparently, by gourmandizing when they should be modest and humble. It is unsurprising, then, that the poet-homilist returns to outraged judgment in the next lines, condemning their lack of moderation as following eating practices more appropriate for a dog or a wolf (lines 220b–23).[68] The moralizing is more expected, even though the poet has switched from the first-person plural of homiletic exhortation (e.g. "and we bebeodað," "and we command," 178a) to the first-person singular, first introduced at line 208 ("Ac ic secgan mæg...," "But I can tell...," 208a), perhaps hinting at a more satirical voice.

---

66 Relevant texts are assembled by Roberta Frank, "Old English *æræt* – 'too much' or 'too soon'?" in *Words, Texts, and Manuscripts:Studies in Anglo-Saxon Culture Presented to Helmut Gneuss*, ed. Michael Korhammer (Cambridge: Brewer, 1992), 293–303.

67 Ælfric's *Second Pastoral Letter for Wulfstan*; see Richards, *Seasons*, 52–4, who sees this as a potential source for the poet. The bivalve is the subject of Riddle 77.

68 There are multiple possibilities for understanding the details of the text here, although the outline is clear; see Jones, *Shorter Poems*, 171; Richards, *Seasons*, 110; Hugh Magennis, *Anglo-Saxon Appetites: Food and Drink and Their Consumption in Old English and Related Literature* (Dubline: Four Courts, 1999), 85–92.

The poet returns to the apparent objectivity of a satirical portrait in the next lines:

Hi þonne sittende   sadian aginnað,
win seniað,   syllað gelome,
cweðað Godd life   gumena gehwilcum,
þæt wines dreng   welhwa mote,
siþþan he mæssan hafað,   meþig þicgan,
etan ostran eac   and oþerne
fisc of flode ...
(lines 224–30a)

Then, sitting down, they begin to be sated,
to bless the wine, give it frequently,
say that God would allow to every man
that almost everyone, weary after he has done mass
may partake of a drink of wine,
also eat oysters and other
fish from the sea...

While some of the details are hard to be sure of (reflecting the somewhat confused state of the surviving text), this is clearly a reprise and amplification of the account of the sinful priests in action, and there are plenty of clues that this is shocking conduct, even as the poet does not here explicitly moralize. The priests are in the dubious position of sitting (is that a critique in itself?[69]) and becoming sated with wine. This suggests over-consumption and plays into recurring critiques of drunkenness in general and clerical drunkenness in particular.[70] As shocking as the over-consumption is, the priests' justification for their action is even more shocking. They appear to be suggesting that such over-consumption is endorsed by God himself, whose voice they should habitually invoke in moral exhortation, but whose voice they are here ventriloquizing as permission for their moral backsliding into gluttony, laziness, impiety, and laxity. Line 228 replicates the alarming logic of lines 213–15 in suggesting that the weary (*meþig*) state

---

69 Hugh Magennis, "'Monig oft gesæt': Some Images of Sitting in Old English Poetry," *Neophilologus* 70 (1986): 442–52, shows how sitting in Old English is generally a dubious or denigrated position.

70 Wulfstan condemns excessive drinking in the morning time and boasting of such excess in his homily, Bethurum XI, lines 141–3. For clerical condemnations of drunkenness, see Hugh Magennis, "The Cup as Symbol and Metaphor in Old English Literature," *Speculum* 60 (1985): 517–36; "The Exegesis of Inebriation: Treading Carefully in Old English," *English Language Notes* 23 (1986): 3–6.

of the consumer of wine results from the labour of undertaking the mass ("siþþan he mæssan hafað"). This time there is an ambiguity as to whether that weary state has been induced in the priests, who have performed the mass, or in the parishioners, who have received it, but either sense is shockingly ungrateful in relation to the climactic redemptive miracle of the Christian faith. Such a brazen incongruity is also startlingly funny.

Juxtaposing eucharistic wine with the tapster's fine wine is a shocking shift of register which risks getting into theological hot water by reminding an audience of the central miracle of the mass that the priests are not doing. That association is loudly activated if the reading of line 225a is correctly that the priests bless (senian) the wine.[71] Presumably this is a potential blessing of the produce at a meal,[72] but it inevitably here conjures up the blessing of the eucharistic wine that the priests practised earlier in the morning (and now feel exhausted after), and turns the repast into a parody of the mass. Oysters make a return as the foodstuff of choice, apparently joined with fish from the sea as the explicit object of the sacerdotal sophistry in the claim that this consumption is just fine and would be approved by God (line 226).

It is unfortunate that the text breaks off at this point. Richards estimates that about fifty verse lines have been lost from the end of the poem, and these would presumably have pushed the satire further. Enough survives, though, to see that the homilist-poet has taken a turn very unlike other surviving devotional literature in Old English, with a satire of imagined misconduct presented with such incongruity of content that the poet can cease from editorial framing and present a description that the audience can revel in recognizing as all too wrong, the topsy-turvy world of sin unchecked. Given injunctions against Sunday work and Sunday frivolities and the constraints described in the rest of the poem, it is clear that such activity would be highly illicit on a fast day.[73] The incongruity of the passage resides in the objects of the critique acting out with particular brazenness practices that ought to be shamefully concealed. This is another form of homiletic humour, the humour of satire, which might appeal to

---

71 An emendation on which Jones and Richards agree, but with other suggestions in earlier editions. The whole passage is not altogether clear, probably through copying difficulties in making the transcript.

72 Excessive drunken blessings are condemned, alongside condemning the drunkenness, in an anonymous homily, Assmann 12I, lines 69–73.

73 For a handy survey of the expectations for fasting in early medieval England, see Christina Lee, "Reluctant Appetites: Anglo-Saxon Attitudes Towards Fasting," in Saints and Scholars: New Perspectives on Anglo-Saxon Literature and Culture in Honour of Hugh Magennis, ed. Stuart McWilliams (Cambridge: Brewer, 2012), 164–86.

parishioners who get to laugh at fallible priests, and the upstanding clerics who get to deploy laughter of superiority at their fallacious peers. This is humour with a purpose.

Christian Communities of Laughter:
The Church and the Ale House

Preaching was designed to shape an ideal Christian subject out of every individual and to thereby forge a community, as Riddle 26 explains of those who enjoy the religious book presented there:

> hy beoð þy gesundran ond þy sigefæstran,
> heortum þy hwætran ond þy hygebliþran,
> ferþe þy frodran, habbaþ freonda þy ma,
> swæsra ond gesibbra, soþra ond godra,
> tilra ond getreowra.
> (19–23a)

> they [the audience for the Bible] will be the healthier and the more victorious,
> the bolder in heart and the happier in mind,
> the wiser in spirit, they will have the more friends,
> companions and kin, true and good
> the better and the truer.

The material considered in this chapter is intended to help craft that broadest imaginable audience, turning a collection of individuals into a single Christian community. To that end, preaching texts would be heard in church on a Sunday or feast day by an audience of high born and low, free and enslaved, men and women, religious and secular. Most works that reached out to that mass audience, however, are not particularly funny. Ælfric's homilies in particular may have successfully shaped an idealized community of Christians precisely because the homiletic voice he projects is so careful to keep control that there is little opportunity for comic incongruity. That is not true of a few preachers, as seen here in the case of Napier 46 and Vercelli 9. These preachers, too, surely imagined themselves shaping the ideal Christian subject, but they did it with humour, allowing the risk of surprising or shocking the audience to better serve their ultimate goals. In these cases, the capaciously imagined fellowship of Christians would be a community defined by laughter. The humour by no means undermines the fundamental message, but rather serves the broad-ranging purpose of exhortation even better. For these homilists, laughter in church need not be a threat to a Christian order but might be a means of cohesion.

The locus for such community-building through laughter would be the church building itself. As has been seen, this was a period of rapid expansion of such venues, since local churches that would define English parishes were coming into being, even as larger corporate minster churches still supplied pastoral needs in some areas.[74] Comic exempla would help cement the community of the faithful in urban and rural places, both great and small, as a whole range of society heard hortatory literature in a church of some kind during a weekly service.

While the church building presents the most likely site for what humour was deployed by clerics, the work of this chapter foregrounds another venue for comic performances which nicely complements the church, namely the ale house. This is an institution for which there is strikingly little record, but in what evidence does survive the ale house has surprisingly strong associations with clowning priests. *The Seasons for Fasting* presents its satire of the bibulous imbibing priests in the ale house served by the tapster, with food and drink consumed at illicit times. Clerical legislation crafted by Wulfstan adds to the picture:

> And we lærað þæt ænig preost ne beo ealascop, ne on ænige wisan gliwige mid him silfum oðrum mannum, ac beo swa his hade gebirað, wis and weorðfull. (*Canons of Edgar*, para. 59).[75]

> And we teach that no priest may be an ale poet, nor in any way make other people merry, but should be appropriate to his order, wise and honourable.

The word *ealusceop*, "ale poet," defined by DOE as "one who recites poetry in the presence of those drinking" but carrying a strong suggestion that the poet himself may also be partaking, only survives as a practice condemned in clerical legislation.[76] The idea is clarified by the context here, with the suggestion that a bad priest might make people merry in the context of ale drinking in some way that is not "wise and honourable." Presumably, this would not be through the edification of homiletic discourse, even of a comic kind. Instead, priests are being warned off merry-making

---

74 See Blair, *Church*.

75 Roger Fowler, ed., *Wulfstan's Canons of Edgar*, EETS o.s. 266 (Oxford: Oxford University Press, 1972), 14–15.

76 In addition to the usage here, priests who practise such are commanded to atone in *The Northumbrian Priests' Law*, para. 41.

through scurrilous poetry. The sexual riddles of the Exeter Book seem the most likely surviving works to fit the bill, suggesting a surprising illicit mouthpiece for those works.

Nor is this the only hint of priests as comic performers. Other clerical legislation fleshes out the picture. Wulfstan comments about bishops in *The Institutes of Polity*: "Bisceopum gebyreþ, þæt hi ne beon to gliggeorne, ne hunda ne hafeca hedan to swyðe" ("it is fitting for bishops that they may not be too eager for entertainment, nor too much concerned with dogs and hawks," Jost, *Polity*, 213). Wulfstan is here prohibiting bishops from the pleasures of the elite secular life, which include dogs and hawks as well as being *gliwgeorne* (DOE defines as "eager for entertainment, fond of minstrelsy," and there may be a hint that the eagerness includes enacting the entertainment). This prohibition imagines the elite in society as a ready audience for poetry that brings pleasure, as has been seen in the fictional mead-hall audiences described in chapter 4, with elite ecclesiasts here warned not to be too involved in such entertainment. Legislation aimed at priests rather than bishops addresses similar issues while presupposing a less elite lifestyle. Ælfric commands priests in his *Second Old English Letter for Wulfstan*: "Ne ge gliwmenn ne beon" ("do not be entertainers," Fehr, *Hirtenbriefe*, 188), while also, in surrounding clauses, discouraging drunkenness. Priests play a role in Christian performance broadly comparable to the role of poets and entertainers in secular performance, even as the clerical reformers are keen to insist on the distinction. That very insistence shows how easy it is to imagine priests using their skills for comic and unedifying effect in a bibulous context.

The ale house conjured in *Seasons for Fasting* and implied by the clerical prohibitions joins the church, the mead hall, the monastery, and the classroom as imaginable sites for comic performance. While here satirized or condemned, it would presumably be an appropriate space for licit non-clerical performance, complete with the deployment of humour. With or without priestly comedians, a setting of secular, non-elite, bibulous entertainment is a likely venue for the reception of literature of all kinds, especially the trading of riddles, including obscene ones. In a later satirical portrait, Gluttony is imagined playing pub games that incite laughter in Book V of *Piers Plowman*. Many of the texts in this study may have been received favourably in just such a setting where an audience would be quick to laughter and encouraged to compete and shout out. The ale house complements the mead hall by imagining a venue for community and entertainment potentially lower on the social scale and more raucous than the gathering of agricultural workers at Whitby. The audience gathered in the ale house might particularly appreciate satire aimed at the more elite in society, including both the clerical class mocked in *Seasons for Fasting* and the secular martial elite mocked in the portrayal of King Hrothgar. The ale house of the ale poet comes into focus for early medieval England thanks to clerical legislation and clerical satire and suggests a sympathetic home for comic performance of all kinds.

Chapter Seven

Hagiographic Humour:
Decorous Delight and
Full-Throated Funniness

While Christian homiletic literature provides but slim pickings for the deployment of humour, hagiographic narrative offers more ample possibilities. The Christian community resulting from such literature is shown in the second half of Riddle 26, discussed at the end of the last chapter, describing the pleasure of community for those who benefit from the Bible or Gospel-book of the riddle. The opening, though, is strikingly different in tone:

> Mec feonda sum   feore besnyþede,
> woruldstrenga binom,   wætte siþþan,
> dyfde on wætre,   dyde eft þonan,
> sette on sunnan,   þær ic swiþe beleas
> herum þam þe ic hæfde.   Heard mec siþþan
> snað seaxses ecg,   sindrum begrunden;
> (Riddle 26, lines 1–6)

> One of my enemies deprived me of life,
> took away my worldly strength, afterwards wetted me,
> dipped me in water, took me out again from there,
> set me in the sun, where I was strenuously stripped
> of the hairs which I had. Afterwards, the hard edge of a knife
> honed with cinders, snipped me

In light of the rest of the riddle, this is distinctively the process of creation of parchment, with the skin taken from the creature, which has been killed, doused in liquid (the liming process), stretched in the sun, and then vigorously dehaired before cutting into bifolio pieces. The presentation stresses the pain of manufacture, an effect amplified by the sympathies created by the first-person point of view.[1] That point of view is emphasized in the first half-line, where the "feonda sum" ("one of the enemies" or "a certain one of the fiends") must be a human artisan, one of us humans listening to the riddle, establishing humans as enemies of the speaking once-living creature, even as we will become part of a happy and edified community by the end of the riddle. On a first hearing, the violent activity of the whole opening sounds less like book making and more like the torture of the human body, a defining characteristic of martyrdom, where death and flaying are frequent perils en route to the edifying saintly state.[2] Further details forestall this reading, but for a moment there is a particularly large incongruity between the false suggestion of possible martyrdom and the edifying book that transpires to be the *wiht* that is manufactured.

Or is there? The happy ending of the riddle mirrors the happy ending of martyrdom stories from a Christian perspective, since dying saints are born into eternal life. For all their gory subject matter, stories of saints are Christian comedies. The genre is premised upon an extreme incongruity between human and divine perspective, as will be seen in this chapter. With such incongruity in such an ultimately happy context, saints' lives prove to be strikingly open to deploying humour, even in a context of grotesque bodily suffering. While Christian decorum described in the last chapter is inimical to humour in this world, the inversions of the saintly narrative license some funny business.

Judith and *Andreas* give a sense of how relating a Christian story using traditional Old English poetic form opens an opportunity for humour in the gap between the expectations generated by form and story. Stories of Christian triumph are more often retold in Old English as prose saints' lives. The norms of the genre incline towards high moral seriousness, as with the sermon literature, but the form encourages the inclusion of entertaining anecdotes, while the basic plot is so predictable that there is a significant appeal in variations, sometimes comic, in order to make a particular saint's life memorable. As a consequence, saints' lives in Old English prove to be rich sites for humour, sometimes deployed quite decorously, sometimes in a more full-throated manner. I will first introduce the genre, and then consider those two different styles of hagiographic humour.

---

1 See Bruce Holsinger, "Of Pigs and Parchment: Medieval Studies and the Coming of the Animal," *PMLA* 124, no. 2 (2009): 616–23; Corinne Dale, *The Natural World in the Exeter Book Riddles* (Cambridge: Brewer, 2017), chap. 3.

2 The suggestion is made by Ruth Wehlau, *"The Riddle of Creation": Metaphor Structures in Old English Poetry* (New York: Peter Lang, 1997), 105–7.

The Lives of Saints, Told in Old English

Saints' lives work in predictable ways. They tell the story of men and women considered exemplary in the Christian faith who were culted for working miracles after their death.[3] There are two basic patterns. One tells of martyrs, early Christians who suffered for their faith and yet remained unbowed by the tortures of secular authorities. Their lives and deaths are retold as passions (Latin *passiones*, Old English *þrowunga*). These often dwell on the tortures, which the martyr transcends, thereby converting many who look on. After scenes of torture and defiance, such martyrs are generally finally despatched through beheading, whereupon their body or gravesite becomes a source of miraculous healing. A subset of the genre tells the story of virgin martyrs, usually women who die protecting their sexual purity as well as their faith, often fending off an arranged marriage to a pagan, who is sometimes converted in the process. The other standard form tells the lives of exemplary individuals, often institutional members of the church (Latin *vitae*, or *vitas* in medieval Latin, Old English *lif*). These tend to emphasize a good death, often anticipated by the saint, followed by posthumous miracles. The vast majority of saints' lives from the Middle Ages were written in the learned and international language of the church, namely Latin, and many thousand survive in both prose and verse.[4] A substantial number of these were translated into Old English, with over a hundred surviving examples.[5]

Saints' lives bear certain similarities to homilies and could serve a similar liturgical function since the life of the saint would substitute for a homily

---

3 The scholarly literature on saints' lives is predictably vast. For useful introductions, see Peter Brown, *The Cult of the Saints: Its Rise and Function in Latin Christianity* (Chicago: University of Chicago Press, 1981; enlarged second edition, 2015); Thomas J. Heffernan, *Sacred Biography: Saints and Their Biographers in the Middle Ages* (New York: Oxford University Press, 1988).

4 The *Acta Sanctorum* of the Bollandists attempts an exhaustive collection; David Hugh Farmer, *The Oxford Dictionary of Saints*, 3rd ed. (Oxford: Oxford University Press, 1992), provides a handy reference work.

5 Precise numbers depend upon definitions of what constitutes a saint's life and how to count fragments and appended items. Alex Nicholls, "The Corpus of Prose Saints' Lives and Hagiographic Pieces in Old English and Its Manuscript Distribution," *Reading Mediaeval Studies* 19 (1993): 73–96, and 20 (1994): 51–87, provides a useful introduction to the corpus and counts 103 distinct surviving hagiographic Old English prose texts, sixty-six of which were written by Ælfric. E. Gordon Whatley, "An Introduction to the Study of Old English Prose Hagiography: Sources and Resources," in *Holy Men and Holy Women: Old English Prose Saints' Lives and Their Contexts*, ed. Paul E. Szarmach (Albany: State University of New York Press, 1996), 3–32, makes slightly different assumptions and provides a list of some 106 lives in Old English prose.

in a church service held on a saint's festival day.[6] For example, celebrating the mass on 10 August would feature the reading of an account of the life and death of St. Laurence in place of a homily because this is the day of commemoration of St. Laurence's martyrdom. In view of that liturgical function, it is not surprising that Ælfric dominates the authorship of surviving Old English saints' lives, just as he does with homilies. Within the two series of his *Catholic Homilies*, he produced some thirty saints' lives, and these provide for the major saints who were celebrated in the annual round of church services. Ælfric duly provides the "Passio Beati Laurentii Martyris" ("Passion of the Blessed Martyr Laurence") for 10 August in his First Series of *Catholic Homilies*.[7] While thus related in purpose, Old English saints' lives differ from homilies in several interesting ways in the norms of their content. Even as a homily often includes some narrative, it is primarily concerned with catechetical instruction and moral exhortation, as seen in the previous chapter. A saint's life, on the other hand, usually provides far more narrative, even as it generally concludes with brief moral lessons or Christian instruction. The genre thus provides particularly extensive examples of storytelling.

In addition to a liturgical use, saints' lives in Old English could also serve as pious reading or listening material. Ælfric composed such extraliturgical lives, too, providing a further series, known as *Lives of Saints*, for saints celebrated in monasteries but not in services for the laity.[8] The best manuscript of that series, British Library MS Cotton Julius E. vii, preserves a further twenty-seven lives by Ælfric as well as four by other writers. Ælfric is thus the writer of some two thirds of the surviving Old English lives.[9] The audiences for the non-liturgical vernacular lives were probably quite various. Ælfric states in the preface to *Lives of Saints* that the impetus for translating them came from his powerful secular patrons,

---

6 Good introductions to the Old English lives are Michael Lapidge, "The Saintly Life in Anglo-Saxon England," in *The Cambridge Companion*, 251–72; David Rollason, *Saints and Relics in Anglo-Saxon England* (Oxford: Oxford University Press, 1989); and, with a pedagogical slant, Hugh Magennis, "Approaches to Saints' Lives," in *The Christian Tradition in Anglo-Saxon England: Approaches to Current Scholarship and Teaching*, ed. Paul Cavill (Cambridge: Brewer, 2004), 163–83.

7 CH I: 29, ed. Clemoes, 418–28.

8 Ed. and trans. Skeat, *Lives of Saints*, and now Mary Clayton and Juliet Mullins, eds. and trans., *Old English Lives of Saints: Ælfric*, 3 vols., DOML 58–60 (Cambridge, MA: Harvard University Press, 2019), who provide slightly different numbers for the lives. Quotations will be from Clayton and Mullins, with additional reference to Skeat to facilitate comparison. Both editions lay out Ælfric's rhythmical prose in verse-like lines, and so line references are usually identical for the two editions.

9 See note 5 above on the numbers.

and he envisages them as works both for reading and listening to. Elsewhere he comments how his pieces for specific occasions can also serve
a general audience and it is reasonable to assume that his saint's lives did,
too.[10] Lives in verse, such as *Andreas*, demonstrate how such narratives
could appeal to an audience with a taste for Old English poetry, while
those in prose probably reached an even larger audience, some in church
services, some beyond the church building.

The story that saints' lives unfold is broadly predictable because of the
constraints of the genre and perhaps for this very reason, there is a productive tension between the specific and the universal.[11] A saint is efficacious
because he or she led a life that is holy and will incline onlookers to God.
A martyr will inevitably be tortured and die for the cause of Christianity, a confessor will lead an exemplary Christian life and work miracles in
death. In some ways, then, all saints are alike and elements from one life
can fill in for those in another, as is apparent in the repeated modelling on
two paradigmatic examples, namely that of St. Antony in the desert, for
an account of a life of withdrawal, or that of St. Martin of Tours, for a life
of institutional effectiveness. On the other hand, saints are also, by definition, extraordinary people, and a life can revel in the way one particular
saint is even more extraordinary than others. The remarkable and unique
features help make the individual story memorable and therefore effective.
This can include playing up incongruity, since most aspects of a saint's life
break with everyday expectations. Ironies abound in the doubled perspective, earthly and celestial. Added to that, the outcome of a saint's life is
ultimately a happy one, since the saint's death is a birth into everlasting
life, even as events often look decidedly dire from the perspective of this
world.[12] Such elements make this a genre rife for exploiting storytelling
techniques of all kinds and sometimes the incongruities and ironies are
presented with considerable humour.

---

10 I explore the various possibilities in "The Audience of Ælfric's *Lives of Saints* and the
Face of Cotton Caligula A. xiv, fols. 93–130," in *Beatus Vir: Studies in Early English and
Norse Manuscripts in Memory of Phillip Pulsiano*, eds. A.N. Doane and Kirsten Wolf
(Tempe: ACMRS, 2006), 228–63.

11 For excellent accounts of the style of Old English prose saints' lives, see James W. Earl,
"Typology and Iconographic Style in Early Medieval Hagiography," *Studies in the
Literary Imagination* 8 (1978): 15–46; Thomas D. Hill, "*Imago Dei*: Genre, Symbolism,
and Anglo-Saxon Hagiography," in *Holy Men and Holy Women: Old English Prose
Saints' Lives and Their Contexts*, ed. Paul E. Szarmach (Albany: State University of
New York Press, 1996), 35–50, who suggests the variety extends to art-vitae.

12 See Jean Leclerq, "La joie de mourir selon Saint Bernard de Clairvaux," in *Dies Illa:
Death in the Middle Ages*, ed. Jane H.M. Taylor (Liverpool: Francis Cairns, 1984),
195–207, for a theoretical statement of the joyousness of the occasion.

Nevertheless, there are other factors militating against the use of humour. For a start, there is the general hostility of the church to humour and to laughter, as described in the preceding chapter. There is a kind of decorum of holiness, which tends to tamp down the elements of doubt or confusion or muddle that are productive for humour, and this tendency is particularly apparent in the works of Ælfric, who chooses to present any holy person as fully formed in unquestionable and unquestioning sanctity from the start, unruffled through the events of the narrative. Such a presentation emphasizes the inevitable triumph of good over evil in a Christian context, which may be good for reassuring the faithful, but tends to downplay the comic potential by eliminating all vulnerability or uncertainty. So long as the holy person's sanctity is not open to doubt, however, even Ælfric will sometimes exploit a kind of controlled humour in the cause of defiant sanctity.[13] The windbag torturers are deflated with glee and an audience gets to hear a story of Christian triumph memorable for the ever-more-outlandish details of the saint's mockery of those in apparent power. In part of this chapter, I will illustrate Ælfric's decorous hagiographic humour.[14]

Other writers are more willing to include details of human interest, parading moments of fallibility or particular foibles in the character of the individual who will become a saint. This allows for a less-controlled kind of narrative humour. In a handful of anonymous Old English saints' lives, humour is given full play, expanding beyond what was present in the source.[15] I will also explore this fuller humour evident in the work of some anonymous translators. Throughout, I hope to suggest that Old English saints' lives include narratives that are worthy of more consideration by contemporary readers than they tend to receive.

---

13 On the development of Ælfric's hagiographic style, see M.R. Godden, "Experiments in Genre: The Saints' Lives in Ælfric's *Catholic Homilies*," in *Holy Men and Holy Women: Old English Prose Saints' Lives and Their Contexts*, ed. Paul E. Szarmach (Albany: State University of New York Press, 1996), 261–87.

14 The use of humour in Ælfric's saint's lives is adeptly theorized in Niamh Kehoe, "The Importance of Being Foolish: Reconstruction of the Pagan and Saint in Ælfric's Life of St Cecilia," *SELIM* 23 (2018): 1–26, with reference to the Life of St. Cecilia. Fuller engagement with the humour of vernacular saints' lives is promised in Niamh Bridget Kehoe Rouchy, "Humour in Vernacular Hagiography from the Tenth to the Thirteenth Century in England" (PhD diss., University College Cork, 2018), currently embargoed, but with abstract available on ProQuest.

15 Anonymous lives are collected in the recent edition and translation of Johanna Kramer, Hugh Magennis, and Robin Norris, eds. and trans., *Anonymous Old English Lives of Saints*, DOML 63 (Cambridge, MA: Harvard University Press, 2020).

Humour in Ælfric's Saints' Lives: Laurence and Cecilia

As suggested in the introduction of this study, a thread in the story of Ælfric's Life of St. Laurence (CH I. 29) illustrates the power of humour in saints' lives. In a battle of wills, the emperor Decius threatens and then tortures Laurence to get him to honour the pagan gods of the Romans. Laurence refuses to bend to the emperor's will and responds with verbal defiance and mockery. When required to hand over his treasures, rather than complying, Laurence says he has already given the treasure of Christian salvation to the poor; when shown the torture implements, rather than cowering, he says that he looks forward to such luxuries; when placed on burning coals, rather than excruciating heat, he claims to feel cooling; and when told to offer a sacrifice to the pagan gods, Laurence, by now on the grid-iron, offers up his own flesh to the Almighty God. Finally, as his end approaches, Laurence responds to the bed of burning coals with a paradigmatic retort: "efne ðu earming brædest ænne dæl mines lichaman: wend nu þone oþerne. 7 et" ("Lo, wretch, you have roasted one side of my body: now turn the other, and eat," CH I. 29, lines 218–19). Laurence concedes that his body is mere meat for the roasting and yet, incongruously, the meat comments on its own state of culinary preparation. With such a statement of witty defiance followed by his appreciation of Christ he gives up his spirit and travels to "the higher kingdom."

The exchanges here are grotesquely incongruous from the perspective of this world as the one who is tortured goads his torturer, even when suffering physical duress. They are, however, entirely appropriate from the perspective of the transcendent other world of death and judgment, where bodily suffering is an ephemeral blip on the way to eternal reward and no pagan torturer is going to be ultimately successful. Defiant humour points attention to the secular power structures turned upside down. The incongruity reminds the audience of the upbeat message despite the seemingly bleak story. Effective verbal humour memorably aestheticizes a process of defiance that is baked into the genre of a martyr's life, with the saint's insouciance matching that of the heroes described in chapter 4. This is the kind of humour of which Ælfric apparently approves and happily deploys.

As with all the lives under consideration in this chapter, the Life of St. Laurence is a translation of an identifiable Latin source, and Laurence's witty verbal defiance here is all drawn from the source.[16] Indeed, the humour of the Latin version of this scene has long been recognized since it was E.R. Curtius's primary exhibit for his claim of grotesque humour in

---

16 See Godden, *Commentary*, 238–47.

hagiographical torture scenes.[17] Ælfric's sensitivity to the humour is apparent not in a new creation but in the distinctive way in which he chooses to translate this particular life. His usual practice is to abbreviate, simplify, and clarify his source, and he generally does this by curtailing or omitting details extraneous to the main plot and by turning many of the moments of direct speech into indirect discourse.[18] In this case, though, his translation style is noticeably different, retaining more details within the exchange and far more direct speech than is usual for him. Verbal lip is at the centre of this story, and this gets thematized by the tormentors' repeated attention to Laurence's "hihendum muðe" ("laughing mouth," CH I.29, 203–4), which is an early locus for his torture. Ælfric retains the relevant details and the humorously defiant speeches and shapes a punchline, cited above, that works well in Old English in view of the overtones of *brædan* (to roast as opposed to boil, characteristic of food preparation)[19] and the attention-grabbing brevity of the imperatives *wend* and *et*, placed in emphatic position in the clause. Such verbal repartee in the face of death echoes the sardonic humour of defiance seen in heroic literature, except that the martyr plays for eternal glory in heaven rather than for earthly glory. For the Christian saint, the ideology of the Last Judgment explicitly favours a posthumous reckoning over any outcome in this world, and the wit of the dying saint emblematizes confidence in eternal glory regardless of earthly agony.

The motif of witty verbal defiance by the saint is more marked when the victim is a woman, as is the case in a sequence of Lives of Virgin Martyrs, since an early medieval perception of relative powerlessness and frailty suggest a softer target for the physical intimidation by the ruthless male tyrant, which makes the reversal all the more striking.[20] This is seen, for example, in Ælfric's Life of St. Cecilia (Clayton and Mullins 30/Skeat 34).

---

17 E.R. Curtius, *European Literature and the Latin Middle Ages*, trans. Willard R. Trask (Princeton, NJ: Princeton University Press, 1953), 425–8, "Jest in Hagiography," where he traces the evolution of this comment of St. Laurence's from its earliest roots in Ambrose.

18 See Ruth Waterhouse, "Ælfric's Use of Discourse in Some Saints' Lives," *Anglo-Saxon England* 5 (1976): 83–103.

19 DOE, *s.v. brædan 1*, sense 1: "to cook (food, *acc.*); specifically: to roast or grill as opposed to boil."

20 The sequence is translated in Leslie A. Donovan, trans., *Women Saints' Lives in Old English Prose* (Cambridge: Brewer, 1999); for a reading of their underlying hermeneutic, see Shari Horner, "The Violence of Exegesis: Reading the Bodies of Ælfric's Female Saints," in *Violence against Women in Medieval Texts*, ed. Anna Roberts (Gainesville: University Press of Florida, 1998), 22–43.

In this case, the exasperated torturer, Almachius, sets himself up by asking the question "Do you not know my might?" The tortured saint replies:

Ælces mannes miht þe on modignysse færð
is soðlice þam gelic swilce man siwige
ane bytte and blawe hi fulle windes,
and wyrce siððan an þyrl, þonne heo toþunden bið
on hire greatnysse; þonne togæð seo miht.
(315–19)

The might of each person who walks in pride
is truly as if someone should sew up
a bladder, and blow it full of wind,
and afterwards should make a hole, when it is puffed up
in its greatness; then the might goes out.

The puffed-up torturer is always a wind-bag and describing him as an over-inflated bladder does a lot to prick his pretensions. The appropriate inappropriateness of the image from one who is subject to the power of the torturer is surely a cause for mirth.[21]

Any subversion from such humour is significantly contained. At one level, this is humour in the service of the disempowered. Cecilia is very visibly lacking earthly power in the story – she will soon be boiled in water and then beheaded – and so her deployment of humour gives her control in a situation where she otherwise appears to have none. Laurence was at the mercy of the emperor and his toasting duly leads to his death, and his defiance allows him to cock a snook at the one with the power to destroy him. At a broader level, though, this is clearly hegemonic humour, working to reinforce the message encoded in the genre, demonstrating the superiority of the Christian saint over any secular force of a pagan ruler. Structures of worldly power are trumped by the Christian triumph guaranteed through the persecuted martyr's transition to sainthood. The humour appears to upset established hierarchies of rank and gender, and yet it demonstrates the superiority of Christian values over pagan ones. Rather than subversion, humour gives a memorable edge to a story type that might otherwise be just too predictable to keep the audience's attention and thereby blunt its effectiveness. This is the sort of humour that Ælfric is happy to embrace.

---

21 The case is made more fully by Shari Horner, "'Why Do You Speak So Much Foolishness?' Gender, Humor, and Discourse in Ælfric's *Lives of Saints*," in *Humour in Anglo-Saxon Literature*, 127–36; Kehoe, "Importance."

Limiting Humour: Ælfric's Swithun and Eugenia

Ælfric is a master of restraint, and sometimes it is possible to see specific opportunities for comedy that he has declined and smoothed over, where he omits some of the funny stories from his sources or shapes his narrative in such a way as to avoid moments of humour. This is consistent with his general translation style both of abbreviating his sources and of down-playing human foibles and moral complexity in pursuit of a particularly clear-cut opposition of good versus evil.[22] In an account of the Apostles Peter and Paul (CH I. 26), for example, he removes two moments that seem to suggest hesitation or doubt in the apostles, while in an account of Apollinaris, Bishop of Ravenna, he omits the bishop's repeated exiles, beatings, and escapes to give a sense of a far more dignified episcopal mar-tyr than appears in his source.[23] In a similar manner, he flattens a humorous moment in the Life of St. Basil (Clayton and Mullins 3/Skeat 3) where the source portrays a frustrated sinner berating the dead saint for setting her on a runaround in the desert. In this case, he retains the underlying miracle story of the saint erasing her sins, thus keeping the underlying drama, but omits the inversions which give it a comic twist.[24] Ælfric puts a high value on decorum for his exemplary figures.

This is seen, too, in a life that is particularly close to him, the Life of St. Swithun (Clayton and Mullins 20/Skeat 21). Swithun was a ninth-century bishop of Winchester who suddenly came to posthumous prominence at about the time in 971 of the translation of his relics in the Old Minster, Winchester, under Bishop Æthelwold. Ælfric was presumably present for these events as he was trained and formed in the monastic school of Win-chester and repeatedly defined himself as "alumnus Æthelwoldi." As the cult of St. Swithun developed, Æthelwold commissioned an account of the saint's translation and miracles in Latin by a visiting Frankish monk, Lantfred.[25] This account is written in verbose hermeneutic Latin and is

---

22 See especially H. Magennis, "Contrasting Features in the non-Ælfrician Lives in the Old English *Lives of Saints*," *Anglia* 104 (1986): 316–48.

23 See, respectively, E. Gordon Whatley, "*Pearls before Swine*: Ælfric, Vernacular Hagiography, and the Lay Reader," in *Via Crucis: Essays on Early Medieval Sources and Ideas in Memory of J. E. Cross*, ed. Thomas N. Hall (Morgantown: West Virginia University Press, 2002), 158–84; E. Gordon Whatley, "Lost in Translation: Omission of Episodes in Some Old English Prose Saints' Legends," *Anglo-Saxon England* 26 (1997): 187–208.

24 See Gabriella Corona, ed., *Ælfric's Life of Saint Basil the Great* (Cambridge: Brewer, 2006), notes to chaps. 14 and 16 and especially note to lines 649–55 on 221.

25 See Michael Lapidge, ed., *The Cult of St Swithun* (Oxford: Oxford University Press, 2003), who edits and translates Lantfred's *Translatio et miracula S. Swithuni*, 217–334.

sprawling in structure. It is full of fascinating details of the life of the blind and the infirm of the day, and of the punished and the enslaved, many of whom turned to the saint for a cure for their woes. In retelling the life, Ælfric abbreviates this account massively and leeches it of much of the human interest, first in a Latin epitome, and then in the Old English life he includes in *Lives of Saints*.[26]

Within his narrative, Lantfred includes a mildly humorous incident that reflects on the success of the saint's cult. The monks of the monastic community get so exhausted by the saint's frequent miracle working, "hwilon þrywa on niht, hwilon feower syðum" ("sometimes three times in the night, sometimes four," 232) and the consequent requirement "to singenne þone lof-sang, þonne hi slapan sceoldon" ("to sing the song of praise, when they should be asleep," 233) that they slack off from their duty. The saint appears in a vision to a powerful figure who tells Bishop Æthelwold of the monk's laxity, which Æthelwold promptly has them correct. In his Old English version, Ælfric reflects on the moment in the first person:

Hi hit heoldon þa syððan symle on gewunon,
swa swa we gesawon sylfe foroft,
and þone sang we sungon unseldon mid him.
(262–4)

They always maintained the custom afterwards,
just as we ourselves saw very often,
and we have sung the hymn not seldomly with them.

There is a hint of humour in the litotes of *unseldon* ("not seldomly," 264), as a gloss on *foroft* ("very often," 263) as Ælfric here associates himself with the reformed practice rather than the momentary transgression. It is almost as if the episode includes the ingredients for a joke, one that Ælfric might share with fellow monks (oh, it was such a pain to have to get up for all those miracles), but he is not prepared to include that in a work aimed at a secular audience. It is more important for Ælfric to establish the moral standing of the monastery than to be an entertaining storyteller.[27]

---

26 Lapidge *Cult of St Swithun* establishes Ælfric's authorship of the Epitome and edits and translates it as the *Epitome translationis et miraculorum S. Swithuni*, 553–74. The Old English Life of St. Swithun is also ed. and trans. Lapidge, *Cult of St Swithun*; see also Mechthild Gretsch, *Ælfric and the Cult of Saints in Late Anglo-Saxon England* (Cambridge: Cambridge University Press, 2005).

27 The incident is conveyed with less personal involvement in the Epitome, chap. 14.

Another incident added to the source presents a display of humour of which Ælfric explicitly disapproves. He tells the story of a vigil over a dead body:

> ... and ðær wæs sum dysig mann,
> plegol ungemetlice, and to þam mannum cwæð,
> swylce for plegan, þæt he Swyðun wære:
> "Ge magon to soðum witan þæt ic Swyðun eom,
> se ðe wundra wyrcð, and ic wille þæt ge beran
> eower leoht to me and licgan on cneowum
> and ic forgife þæt þæt ge gyrnende beoð."
> He woffode ða swa lange mid wordum dyslice...
> (291–8)

> and there was a certain foolish man there,
> playful beyond measure, and he said to the people,
> as if in play, that he was Swithun:
> "You can know that I am truly Swithun,
> he who works miracles, and I want you to bear
> your lights/candles to me and kneel down
> and I will give you what you are desiring."
> He blasphemed then foolishly in words so for a long time...

Ælfric never wants his audience to doubt the folly of what is described here, stressed in the *dysig ... dyslice* with which the anecdote is framed, even as he gives a brief portrait of *plegan* (play) from one who is immoderate in that facility ("plegol ungemetlice"). The consequences are predictably dire. The man falls down unconscious and is only revived to health when his relatives carry him to the holy Swithun to whom he confesses and asks forgiveness. Ælfric editorializes at some length (lines 307–17), commenting how people do unwisely who *dwollice plegað* ("foolishly play," 308) at the body of a dead person, "and ælce fulnysse þær forð teoð mid plegan" ("and draw forth every foulness in play," 309). For Ælfric, such *plega* ("play") is *fulnysse* ("foulness"), and he is emphatically against it. He warns against drinking and partying next to the corpse, warning that such carousers anger God with their *gegaf-spæce* ("frivolous speech, wanton conversation, idle talk, gossip, ribaldry" in the capacious definition of DOE, 315). This is a warning Ælfric repeats in various contexts. Such condemnation matches the Wulfstanian prohibitions on inappropriate play by priests as ale poets, seen in the previous chapter, but here expands the warning to include secular people in a reverential space.

The scene in the Life of St. Swithun gives an unusually full sense of just what such merriment might look like, fuelled by alcohol consumption and featuring excessive talk of the non-pious kind. This sounds like a rich performance site for humour. Indeed, the afflicted joker here parodies a performance of sanctity, creating an impiety that leads the saint to take umbrage through a humorous appropriation of saintly and sacerdotal performance. Other instances of such *plega* might involve the telling of humorous tales or trading of funny riddles. Ælfric, however, would not be amused.

Given Ælfric's sensibilities, the prospect of his describing the activities of a cross-dressing woman are intriguing, even if she is also a saint.[28] Such is the task he faces in retelling the Life of St. Eugenia (Clayton and Mullins 2/ Skeat 2). A learned noble woman who converts to Christianity at the time of the Roman persecutions, Eugenia decides to dress as a man, both to evade her father, Philip, the Prefect of Alexandria, and to get close to the Christian community, which she enters as a monk. Opportunities for irony and comic misunderstanding are legion in such a story of trickery and confusion of identity, but these are not elements that Ælfric prizes. He takes his account from the anonymous Life of Eugenia included in the Cotton-Corpus Legendary, which he characteristically abbreviates and clarifies, and in the process he forestalls much of the potential for high drama as well as the comedy.[29]

A change of clothes and hair make Eugenia a man. The life damps down rather than plays up the inversion of hierarchy of this change since the disguise is pre-approved by a male authority figure, the visiting bishop, Helenus, who miraculously knows of Eugenia's gender shift and explicitly allows it until she receives baptism. Cross-dressing for disguise might seem inherently deceptive, but Ælfric presents her shift in a way that determinedly forestalls audience confusion:

Eugenia þa wunode on þam mynstre
mid wærlicum mode, þeah þe heo mæden wære.
(92–3)

---

28 For good accounts of the subgenre, see Valerie R. Hotchkiss, *Clothes Make the Man: Female Cross Dressing in Medieval Europe* (New York: Garland, 1996); Jonathan Walker, "The Transtextuality of Transvestite Sainthood: Or, How to Make the Gendered Form Fit the Generic Function," *Exemplaria* 15 (2003): 73–110. For more up-to-date cautions about the language used to engage such stories of gender choice, see Roland Betancourt, *Byzantine Intersectionality: Sexuality, Gender, and Race in the Middle Ages* (Princeton, NJ: Princeton University Press, 2020), chap. 4, and Alicia Spencer-Hall and Blake Gutt, eds., *Trans and Genderqueer Subjects in Medieval Hagiography* (Amsterdam: Amsterdam University Press, 2021).

29 For Ælfric's source in this life, see Gopa Roy, "A Virgin Acts Manfully: Ælfric's *Life of St Eugenia* and the Latin Versions," *Leeds Studies in English* 23 (1992): 1–27; E. Gordon Whatley, "Eugenia Before Ælfric: A Preliminary Report on the Transmission of an Early Medieval Legend," in *Intertexts: Studies in Anglo-Saxon Culture Presented to Paul E. Szarmach*, eds. Virginia Blanton and Helene Scheck (Tempe, AZ: ACMRS, 2009), 349–68.

Eugenia then lived in the monastery
with a manly spirit, although she was a maiden.

Much has been made by modern critics of Eugenia's "wærlicum mode" ("manly spirit") and its theological and gendered overtones,[30] but it is also worth noticing how rapidly and emphatically Ælfric controls against a true change of identity through the following half-line, complete with gendered pronoun. *Mæden* could be used for either sex, although it is most commonly used of a young woman; *heo* is unambiguously feminine.

Unlike the audience, her fellow monks are convinced and after three years, upon the death of their abbot, they elect her to that role, but the potential comedy of confused roles is diminished by the compression of the story. High drama does arise from Eugenia's fulfilment of one of her roles as abbot, that of doctor to the community. In this capacity she heals the wealthy widow, Melantia, who breaks out in passion for the abbot/Eugenia. The resulting complications sound like a romance plot of mistaken identity, misdirected desire, threatened peril, and dramatic resolution (lines 128–263), but again Ælfric downplays the drama by abbreviating the story and clarifying the outcome. After a verbal approach, Melantia gets physical:

Æfter þissere tihtinge and oðrum larum,
beclypte seo myltestre þæt clæne mæden
and wolde hi gebygan to bismorlicum hæmede.
(169–71)

After these exhortations and in other precepts,
the harlot embraced the pure maiden,
and intended to turn her to shameful fornication.

Ælfric adapts his source here to play up the contrast between *seo myltestre* (a loaded term for a prostitute or woman of ill-repute) and *þæt clæne mæden* ("the pure maiden") encapsulated in line 170. It is a characterization that forestalls the potential transgressiveness of the gender crossing

---

30 See Roy, "A Virgin Acts Manfully," who shows Ælfric downplays the symbolic overtones that are built up in the source; also Allen J. Frantzen, *Before the Closet: Same-Sex Love from Beowulf to Angels in America* (Chicago: University of Chicago Press, 1998), chap. 2; Shari Horner, "The Violence of Exegesis: Reading the Bodies of Ælfric's Female Saints," in *Violence against Women in Medieval Texts*, ed. Anna Roberts (Gainesville: University Press of Florida, 1998), 22–43; Alison Gulley, "*Heo Man Ne Wæs*: Cross-Dressing, Sex-Change, and Womanhood in Ælfric's Life of Eugenia," *Mediaevalia* 22 (1998): 113–31.

and instead distils and clarifies this as an encounter between good and bad. There is a hint of what a more adventurous presentation would look like in the version of this passage contained in one manuscript of the life, British Library MS Cotton Otho B. x, which once contained the complete text but was mostly destroyed in the fire at the Cotton library but which retains some legible passages. Lines 170–1 read "beclypte seo myltestre þone abbod. and wolde hine gebygan to hire bismærlicum hæmede" ("the harlot embraced the abbot and intended to turn him to her shameful fornication").[31] This is a crucial shift, since it puts the narrator and audience in the position of accepting Eugenia's gender shift, with Eugenia described simply as "the abbot" and as a masculine "him," in strong contrast with the "pure maiden." Throughout the episode of disguise, the Cotton Otho B. x text refers to Eugenia as the abbot and uses masculine pronouns, where Julius E. vii uses female forms *fæmne* and *mæden* or feminine pronouns. As the most recent editors say, "We believe that W [i.e. MS Julius E. vii] here preserves what Ælfric wrote."[32] An adapter in Otho B. x, then, plays with the counter-factual world as presented by Eugenia and as perceived by Melantia, drawing an audience into this alternative set of possibilities. This is just the kind of play that Ælfric so carefully avoids but that will be seen in the anonymous life of the cross-dressing Euphrosyne, considered next.

There is little surprise that Eugenia rejects the approach and rebuffs Melantia. Melantia then attempts to forestall exposure by pursuing a false charge of attempted rape against the abbot. The action gets played out in a court scene in front of the Prefect, who happens to be Eugenia's father, Philip, and this finally turns into a dramatic recognition and reunion scene, with Ælfric's unfolding of the plot remaining relatively restrained all the way to the climactic revelation. Eugenia tears open her garment to reveal her breast to her father, which re-establishes gender and family and justice in one sartorial rip, with the body acting as guarantor of gender identity, even as the drama is underplayed by passing so quickly.[33] Eugenia proceeds into a second half with further adventures as a non-cross-dressed holy maiden in Rome, including the gender re-grounding of founding a

---

31 See Clayton and Mullins: "Notes to the Text," I. 344.

32 Clayton and Mullins: "Notes to the Text," I. 343.

33 See in particular Clare A. Lees, "Engendering Religious Desire: Sex, Knowledge, and Christian Identity in Anglo-Saxon England," *Journal of Medieval and Early Modern Studies* 27 (1997): 17–45; Clare A. Lees and Gillian R. Overing, "Before History, before Difference: Bodies, Metaphor, and the Church in Anglo-Saxon England," *Yale Journal of Criticism* 11 (1998): 315–34. On the handling of this scene, see Roy, "A Virgin Acts Manfully," 8–11 and 18–19.

monastery for women, before facing her eventual martyrdom. The edification derived from the triumph of virginity is more important for Ælfric
than the potential drama of the plot.[34]

A large part of the pleasure of this kind of a saint's life lies in a version of dramatic irony: the difference between what the audience knows,
namely that the saint's life will end happily as a victory for Christian
triumph, and what the characters know, believing that they are imper-
illed and unable to see the outcome.[35] While this is the case in the Life
of Eugenia, Ælfric risks spoiling the balance by stacking the odds too
heavily in favour of the audience. With characteristic control, Ælfric
tells and retells the audience what is going on beneath the disguise and
so never allows the fluidity of identity – in terms of gender, class, religion, or morality – to seem like a reality. That leaves even a plot so rich
in potential for fluidity of identity largely unrealized. Ælfric proves to
be masterful at suppressing humour at the human level of farce or discomfiture. That such a plot could be handled differently is apparent by
considering the contrasting case of the Life of St. Euphrosyne, a cross-
dressing saint whose story was translated into Old English by someone
other than Ælfric.

Dramatic Humour of Cross-Dressing:
The Anonymous Life of St. Euphrosyne

The Life of St. Euphrosyne provides the story of another cross-dressing
woman who becomes a saint.[36] Although included in the main manuscript
of Ælfric's *Lives of Saints*,[37] the anonymous translator presents a more
dramatic rendering, with more attention to the human interest, than is
characteristic of Ælfric, and is readier to occasionally allow the humour of

---

34 See Cubitt, "Virginity and Misogyny," on how Ælfric's Lives of Virgin Martyrs underpin
   his essential ideology of support for the monasticism of the Benedictine reform.
35 See Jonathan Walker, "The Transtextuality of Transvestite Sainthood: Or, How to Make
   the Gendered Form Fit the Generic Function," *Exemplaria* 15 (2003): 73–110.
36 Ed. and trans. Kramer et al., *Anonymous Old English Lives of Saints*, 28–53. This
   edition presents lives in alphabetical order attached to names, rather than assigning
   numbers, with internal reference through numbered paragraphs rather than line
   numbers. This life is also ed. and trans. by Skeat, *Lives of Saints*, as LS 33. I will provide
   both the paragraph numbers of Kramer et al. and the line numbers of Skeat.
37 Its anomalous status in MS Julius E. vii is evident in that it is out of liturgical order:
   Euphrosyne is celebrated on 11 February, but the life comes here between lives of
   Edmund (20 November) and Cecilia (22 November). It also differs in vocabulary,
   syntax, and style from the works of Ælfric, as demonstrated by Magennis, "Contrasting
   Features."

the narrative full play.[38] Even as the narrator plays up the role of the father figure, Paphnutius, we also get more insight into the thinking of the cross-dressing heroine than in the Life of Eugenia. The result is an exploration of gender roles that has been celebrated by many critics.[39] The freer portrait of gender confusion also opens up more possibilities for humour.

The Life of Euphrosyne tells the story of the daughter of the wealthy and pious Paphnutius in Alexandria. At first childless, Paphnutius and his unnamed wife seek help in conceiving through the blessing of a local abbot. Euphrosyne, the resulting daughter, is a paragon of wisdom and virtue as well as beauty. Her mother dies, and the abbot is like a second parent to her. At eighteen, she is to be married to an eligible suitor but, in view of her piety, she is resistant to this norm of secular life. She decides, instead, to flee society and join the abbot's monastery, evading detection by dressing as a man (she adopts the name Smaragdus) and claiming to be a eunuch from the king's court. Euphrosyne/Smaragdus lives an exemplary pious life but, in an ironic complication, his/her beauty is so great that it enflames desire in the other monks in the community. The abbot resolves the resulting tension by withdrawing him/her from the general monastic community into a life of pious isolation. In a predictable ironic turn, Paphnutius visits the monastery, seeking solace for his overwhelming sense of loss at the absence of his daughter and the abbot chooses Smaragdus/Euphrosyne to console him. Through his/her wisdom and prayer he/she assuages Paphnutius's grief, without revealing his/her identity, for thirty-eight years. At the point of death, Smaragdus/Euphrosyne reveals his/her identity in confidence to the father. Against her/his wishes, the father reveals everything to the monks. In preparing the body for burial, a half-blind monk is miraculously cured of his sight, thereby establishing

---

38 On the source, a Latin vita not included in the Cotton-Corpus legendary, see Hugh Magennis, "On the Sources of Non-Ælfrician Lives in the Old English Lives of Saints, with Reference to the Cotton-Corpus Legendary," *N&Q* 32 (1985): 292–9; Magennis, "Contrasting Features," shows that this translator abbreviates almost as much as Ælfric does.

39 Lees, "Engendering," who points to the underlying gender tensions; Anke Bernau, "The Translation of Purity in the Old English *Lives* of St Eugenia and St Euphrosyne," *Bulletin of the John Rylands University Library of Manchester* 86, no. 2 (Summer 2004): 11–37, who also plays up such instability (although I disagree with her suggestion of similar play in Eugenia); Robin Norris, "Genre Trouble: Reading the Old English *Vita* of Saint Euphrosyne," in *Writing Women Saints in Anglo-Saxon England*, ed. Paul E. Szarmach (Toronto: University of Toronto Press, 2013), 121–39. For a reading of the French analogue in terms of more recent genderqueer analysis, see Amy V. Ogden, "*St Eufrosine*'s Invitation to Gender Transgression," in *Trans and Genderqueer Subjects in Medieval Hagiography*, eds. Alicia Spencer-Hall and Blake Gutt (Amsterdam: Amsterdam University Press, 2021), 201–21.

Euphrosyne's sanctity. Paphnutius gives his possessions to the monastery, as Smaragdus/Euphrosyne had instructed, occupies his/her monastic cell and is himself culted as a saint after his death.

The lability of identity is more embraced in this life than in Ælfric's portrayal of Eugenia. Pronouns to refer to the principal character shift from feminine to masculine at the point when Euphrosyne adopts a male identity, and back to feminine when the saint reveals her/himself to her/his father. Such a shift places the audience in the same frame as the characters rather than Ælfric's insistence on ensuring audience omniscience. The narrator does not always play up the comic potential of the story's ironies. The incident of the monks feeling passion for the attractive new monk in the monastery, which has received much attention from critics, is played surprisingly straight.[40] The ironies of (missing) daughter educating (forlorn) father on the Christian need to give up father and mother to embrace true faith touch upon serious issues of Christian value rather than appearing humorously incongruous.[41] But the narrator does bring out humorous effects some of the time, particularly at the beginning, when Euphrosyne decides to evade the suitor approved by her father and run away to the monastery. Here the narrator plays up the underlying practicalities of entries and exits, space and time, that are so crucial to farce, showing, in the process, the limited scope for manoeuvre for a female character. Euphrosyne uses that scope to the full in what an early audience would presumably have seen as an incongruous degree of self-direction for a woman, an incongruity that will play into her subsequent role as saint. I will pause on this early scene to show what is possible for a narrator who does not have Ælfric's instincts for controlling unambiguous edification.

As her doubled fathers – Paphnutius and the abbot – try to persuade her into marriage, Euphrosyne gets taken to the abbot's monastery and so comes to see and admire the way of life of the monks, "And heo wearð behydig be þissum" ("and she was heedful of this," §9, Skeat, line 47), a viewpoint that she gets to build on. With the seed now planted, we get to see the constraints imposed on her life in her father's household. A young monk visits (and monks, we are told, are always welcome to the

---

40 See Frantzen, *Before the Closet*, chap. 2; Andrew P. Scheil, "Somatic Ambiguity and Masculine Desire in the Old English Life of Euphrosyne," *Exemplaria* 11 (1999): 345–61.

41 See Stephen Stallcup, "The Old English *Life of Saint Euphrosyne* and the Economics of Sanctity," in *Anonymous Interpolations in Ælfric's "Lives of Saints"*, ed. Robin Norris (Kalamazoo, MI: Medieval Institute Publications, 2011), 13–28, and, on the alarming implications of incest in the displacement by the father, Erin Irene Mann, "Relative Identities: Father-Daughter Incest in Medieval Religious Literature" (unpublished Ph.D. diss., University of Iowa, 2011), chap. 2.

Paphnutius household) to bring Paphnutius an invitation to an upcoming feast at the monastery celebrating the ordination day of the abbot. Since Paphnutius is not at home, Euphrosyne gets to summon the monk and asks questions about life in the monastery, including whether the abbot will receive anyone who turns up there (§§12–13, lines 62–73). She continues to control the dialogue as she reveals to the young monk that she would like to turn to such a way of life but that she fears being disobedient to her father who, "for his idlum welum" ("for his vain riches," §14, line 76), wants to join her to a husband. This is not neutral phrasing, of course, but rather a clever protagonist controlling the response of the young man she is talking to, rather in the manner of the romance heroine in *Apollonius of Tyre*, examined in the next chapter. The young monk reacts with predictable youthful enthusiasm for an act of Christian rebellion. Euphrosyne has used her intelligence to invert conventional structures of power and initiate the plot.

After such priming, it is the young monk who explicitly suggests that Euphrosyne should go secretly to a monastery, lay aside worldly dress and adopt the garb of the monastic order. In saying this, he is presumably imagining a shift from secular to religious status, rather than from female to male status, although the potential further implication is apparent to an audience who knows the story. While the monk appears to initiate the suggestion, he has surely been prompted by the "wise" Euphrosyne, as the narrator signals with an understated nod ("Þa gelicode hire þeos spræc," "then this speech was pleasing to her," §15, lines 82–3). The pleasure of the story at this point comes from watching Euphrosyne control the action as she is finally given company of her own age, and finally given a voice in defiance of patriarchal norms.

There is one further objection to be overcome. Who will cut her hair? The practical act is also symbolic (both of clericizing and of gender crossing) and is one that she insists must be done by a Christian (§15, lines 84–5), even though it needs to be done covertly if she is to escape her father. This concern allows the young monk to articulate a plan (perhaps with a suggestion that she has already formulated it and is manipulating him into articulating it for her): he will be departing to the monastery with her father soon, where her father will be out of the way for three or four days, during which she can send for some other brother. By this point, the indirect language between Euphrosyne and this young monk looks like flirting, with its attendant pleasures and scope for comedy. One advantage of the monastic community proves to be that eligible young monks are plentiful and interchangeable. Once her father is out of the way, her trusted servant fetches another one, whom she gets to sit beside her, and to whom she retells her story (§§18–19 lines 101–11, again playing up that the marriage is on account of her father's "idlum welum"), and to whom she sets out her dilemma (without mentioning the previous monk's suggestion), and from whom she gets the predictable idealized Christian response (again). This gets her back to the point when she can ask for the monk's blessing and afterwards for him to cut her hair (§21, line 123). He then dresses her "mid munucreafe" ("with a monastic garment," §21, line 124). Was he carrying a spare? More likely, he is disrobing and giving her his outer dress, with a further frisson of flirtation in a cause of virtuous rebellion as she gets to adopt his apparel. The narrative drops mention of her hair, but the garment itself presumably bestows upon her an epicene status of monasticism. This young monk also gives her his blessing and departs. At this point, the narrator provides the internal thoughts of Euphrosyne, now acting alone, as she proceeds to dress herself in male garb to proceed to a monastery of men, namely the community of faith that sparked her desire for the monastic life, having engineered the many steps necessary to get herself admitted to it.

The piling up of circumstantial detail throughout this passage differs markedly from Ælfric's handling of narrative and reads more like the love scene in *Apollonius of Tyre*. It provides a different kind of pleasure to an audience, immersing us in the action as it happens, encouraging us to ponder the implications of what is described and not allowing us certainty as to the outcome while we are experiencing the details. With the bustle of these arrangements, which are ingenious and rebellious, even as they are pious and idealistic, the text positively oozes the pleasure of the youngsters, particularly Euphrosyne who, in a reversal of the expectations of age and gender, is now an acting subject, articulating her own desires, and stage-managing the scene to achieve what she wants. Rather than prior reassurance that this is the right thing to do (as in Ælfric's account of Eugenia), the audience may feel some anxiety about either the ethics or the practicality of what Euphrosyne is doing. Accepting the lability of identity as it gets worked out almost in real time forces the audience to go along for the ride to discover the outcome rather than making moral or practical judgments too quickly. All that stage managing of the activity is a building block for comedy.

After this opening set-up, the narrative gives less attention to the feelings of Euphrosyne as she becomes more of an icon for piety. The story proceeds with less circumstantial detail and less of a comic tone for the incidents of the monks' sexual desires and the lengthy ironic encounter of her consoling her father's grief. By the end, the life re-establishes normative roles by revealing Euphrosyne's identity and switching the focus to her father. As a whole, then, the life is rather restrained, yet it has more of the play of comedy than Ælfric's translation of the Life of Eugenia: human motivations and doubts are more apparent, and ironies pile up, even if the best humour here seems to get used up in the opening scene.

Delight in the moment of farce as Euphrosyne engineers her flight demonstrates the use of localized moments of humour in Old English prose hagiography. A few other lives deploy a sensationalist plot of adventure and misadventure that is still more open to uses of humour. Ælfric might not approve, but anonymous translations provide a glimpse of alternative traditions, and three lives in particular make considerable use of such sensational plots, namely the anonymous Old English translation of Jerome's Life of Malchus, the Life of Mary of Egypt, and the Legend of the Seven Sleepers of Ephesus. I will consider each of these narratives in turn.

Humour in the Desert: The Life of Malchus

The Life of Malchus (Assmann 18) survives in a manuscript compilation of pious reading, the whole of which represents a strikingly different sensibility from Ælfric's habitual caution.[42] BL Cotton Otho C. i (part two) is a collection written at Worcester by four hands in the early and mid-eleventh century (and now suffering some damage).[43] It opens with a copy of the Old English translation of Gregory's *Dialogues*, the pious collection of stories including some significant use of humour discussed above in chapter 6. Then come three items from the *Vitae Patrum* (Lives of the Desert Fathers), the third of which is the Life of Malchus, and the collection is rounded out with an Old English translation of a letter by Boniface and four homilies.[44]

---

42 Ed. Assmann, *Angelsächsische Homilien*, 195–207, item 18; trans. Peter J. Dendle, "The Old English 'Life of Malchus' and Two Vernacular Tales from the *Vitas Patrum* in MS Cotton Otho C.i: A Translation (Part 1)," *English Studies* 90 (2009): 505–17; "The Old English 'Life of Malchus' and Two Vernacular Tales from the *Vitas Patrum* in MS Cotton Otho C.i: A Translation (Part 2)," *English Studies* 90 (2009): 631–52, who also includes a useful introduction. It is not included in Kramer et al. The work has received little critical attention, but Katharine Scarf Beckett, "Worcester Sauce: Malchus in Anglo-Saxon England," in *Latin Learning and English Lore: Studies in Anglo-Saxon Literature for Michael Lapidge*, eds. Katherine O'Brien O'Keeffe and Andy Orchard (Toronto: University of Toronto Press, 2005), two volumes, II, 212–31, relates the Old English to its source and points out the very human character of Malchus.

43 See N.R. Ker, *Catalogue of Manuscripts Containing Anglo-Saxon* (Oxford: Oxford University Press, 1957), 236–8; Kenneth Sisam, "An Old English Translation of a Letter from Wynfrith to Eadburga (A.D. 716–17) in Cotton MS Otho C i," in *Studies in the History of Old English Literature* (Oxford: Oxford University Press, 1953), 199–224.

44 See Sisam, "Translation."

The two brief pieces preceding the Life of Malchus illustrate a taste for sensationalism in working through questions of faith. The first (named as a *sententia* in its *explicit*) revels in attention-grabbing and lurid detail, telling the story of a prostitute who determines to lead a monk sexually astray, egged on by his associates.[45] The monk holds off the devil's snares of temptation by burning each of his fingers in the flame of his lamp in order to override the burning flame of lust. Next morning, when the associates enter, the temptress is found dead within the monk's cell. After the associates chide the monk for a lack of charity, he intercedes to bring her back to life and she goes on to live a life of chastity. The explicit moral is laid out in the Old English translator's introduction: "to bysne and to lare þam ðe anrædlice deofles costnungum and his lotwræncum wiðstandan willað" ("to serve for example and instruction for those who want to withstand resolutely the temptations of the devil and his artifices").[46] The misogyny is obvious since the only female character proves to be the agent of the devil, with little other motivation.[47] While this story is not funny, the sensationalism created by the rapid reversals, along with such attention to sexual desire, serves a similar function of grasping an audience's attention, destabilizing expectations, and making the story memorable.

The following anecdote also revolves around the sexual desire of a monk, here desiring marriage to the daughter of a pagan priest, although he is ultimately returned to the faith.[48] The temptations of sex for the unwary monk prove to be the common thread running through all three stories, which gives them a sensational hook, even as they each work to reinforce the idea of clerical celibacy.[49] For all his concern with that issue, Ælfric would not approve such narratives, and he makes his disapproval explicit in the preface to his *Lives of Saints*, commenting "we remain silent concerning the book *Vitas Patrum* in which many subtleties are found which are not suitable to be shown to the laity."[50] Presumably he rejects these stories because they tend to show the fallibility of monks, who are here

---

45 Ed. Assmann 18, lines 15–65.
46 Text: Assmann 18, lines 3–5; translation: Dendle, "Malchus," 631.
47 See, further, Stacy S. Klein, "Ælfric's Sources and His Gendered Audiences," *Essays in Medieval Studies* 13 (1996): 111–19.
48 Ed. Assmann 18, line 66–123.
49 See Peter Jackson, "The *Vitas Patrum* in Eleventh-Century Worcester, in *England in the Eleventh Century: Proceedings of the 1990 Harlaxton Symposium*, ed. Carola Hicks (Stamford, CT: Paul Watkins, 1992), 119–34, who relates this theme to a possible user of the surviving manuscript, Bishop Wulfstan II of Worcester.
50 "Ideoque reticemus de libro *Vita Patrum*, in quo multa subtilia habentur, quæ non conveniunt aperiri laicis," Preface 5a, lines 11–13 (ed. Wilcox, 119).

often subject to temptation, particularly sexual temptation, as they attempt to pursue an eremetical life, which is antithetical to Ælfric's sense both of responsible pious narrative and of decent monastic practice.[51] Fortunately, not all Old English writers shared Ælfric's sensibilities.

Third in the sequence comes Jerome's Life of Malchus from the *Vitae Patrum*, probably translated in Mercia in the second half of the tenth century.[52] This life centres on a monk who is gently mocked throughout in an adventure story that includes further explicit engagement with sexual desire.[53] The story is framed by the figure of the narrator, Jerome, who is curious about the living arrangements of a particularly pious old couple, Malchus and an old woman "in his gesiðscipe" ("in his company").[54] In the Latin, this pious couple end up established in separate single-sex monasteries, a detail omitted in the Old English version, which thereby leaves the impression that they share a household as a chaste couple.[55] The whole work presents an exemplary Christian life of pious monastic practice in defiance of anticipated sexual temptation, narrated with a storytelling technique not scared of provoking laughter.

The story Malchus tells is rich with adventure. As a young man, he flees from his parents' wealth and status in order to become a monk (with hints of a male version of the plot seen in the Life of Euphrosyne). Less idealistically, he then vacillates in his monastic discipline after the death of his father and decides to return to settle his estate and tend to his mother.

---

51 On his rejection, see Peter Jackson, "Ælfric and the 'Uita Patrum' in Catholic Homily I.36," in *Essays on Anglo-Saxon and Related Themes in Memory of Lynne Grundy*, eds. Jane Roberts and Janet Nelson (London: Centre for Late Antique and Medieval Studies, King's College, University of London, 2000), 259–72. On Ælfric's sense of appropriate monasticism, see Mary Clayton, "Hermits and the Contemplative Life in Anglo-Saxon England," in *Holy Men and Holy Women: Old English Prose Saints' Lives and Their Contexts*, ed. Paul E. Szarmach (Albany: State University of New York Press, 1996), 147–75.

52 See Sisam, "Translation."

53 The Latin source is available in Charles Christopher Mierow, ed. and trans., *"Sancti Eusebii Hieronymi Vita Malchi Monachi Captivi,"* in *Classical Essays Presented to James A. Kleist, S.J.*, ed. Richard E. Arnold (St. Louis: Saint Louis University, 1946), 31–60. A more accessible translation, with a good introduction to the genre, is Carolinne White, trans., *Early Christian Lives* (London: Penguin, 1998), 119–28.

54 Assmann 18, line 155, Dendle, "Malchus," 639. The Old English translation is maladapted in handling the voice of the nested narrative, placing much of the framing material in the voice of Malchus rather than Jerome, creating a confusing opening; see Dendle, "Malchus," 638, n. 6.

55 The Old English has numerous small omissions from damage to the manuscript where it is occasionally hard to know what is missing, but it is unlikely that any major story element is lost in the lacuna at Assmann 18, line 418.

At this point, the full-fledged adventure story breaks out. Malchus is taken captive by Muslim traders when crossing the desert and is made a slave. This leads to motifs that would surely seem exotic in early medieval England as he is forced to ride a camel, eat half-cooked meat, and drink camel milk. He is also made to honour his master and mistress and go about nearly naked in the heat. Once at their estate, he is established as a shepherd and does this job responsibly, increasing the size of his master's flock. This has unforeseen negative consequences when his master, wanting to keep him tied to the establishment and discourage him from trying to escape, forces him to marry a fellow slave, a fate that Malchus considers worse than death, fearing the loss of his chastity and concerned at marrying somebody else's wife to boot, since the fellow slave was separated from her husband during the capture. Only after much lament does he (finally) discover that she is as little keen on their sexual union as he is. The two Christian slaves discover they can outsmart their master by collaboratively feigning marriage.

High drama continues as the two slaves finally decide to flee once Malchus is reminded of the virtues of the communal monastic life through watching a colony of ants. In more exotic adventures, they cross a river on goat skins, lose their food cache, travel over the desert by night, and get chased down by their master and an accomplice. In a providential turn, they hide in a cave where a she-lion proves to be lurking, and the lion saves them from their pursuers by killing the master and his accomplice before their eyes. Their terror increases when they spot the lion is with cubs, but it then proceeds to cede the cave to them. They continue to cower in terror but eventually run away on their pursuers' camels, get to Rome, and finally back to the starting monastery beyond Antioch.

Thus ends an exciting narrative of adventure and sudden reversal, of chance and sexual misadventure, more reminiscent of *Apollonius of Tyre* or of later romance than of Old English homilies, with a closing moral that true virtue can never be defiled. While the providential element hints at the underlying hagiographical motivation, this is a plot chock-full of incongruities in an exotic setting that would surely do its work by being both fun and, indeed, funny for an English audience. Considerable fear of the lion notwithstanding, it is fear of sex that is most powerful in the story, and this is where the greatest humour resides, already present in the Latin but amplified in the Old English translation.

Humour comes from incongruity established by the repeated reversals of expectations. This is clearly evident in the scene where Malchus balks at his master's command to marry his fellow slave. Dendle sees a pun when the master *ætfæste ... me* to the fellow slave (line 255) since the verb "can mean both 'to entrust, to pledge in marriage' and 'to inflict with,' a pointed double sense involving an implicit critique of marriage that is not present in Jerome's *tradidit mihi illam conservam mecum.*"⁵⁶ Malchus appears bold as he tells his lord that he will not marry her because he is a Christian and so is not permitted to take another man's wife, but the apparent bravery does not last long. The master gets angry and draws his sword, intending to kill him:

> Þær ic him ne æt onette, þæt ic þæt wif gegripe be hire earme and me toforan abræd, and þær þis nære, þonne wære min blod instæpe agoten.
> (chap. 6, Assmann 18, lines 263–5)

> If I had not anticipated him – in that I grabbed the woman by her arm and pulled her in front of me – if this had not been, then my blood would have been shed immediately.⁵⁷

Here Malchus is apparently taking the woman to interpose her body between him and the master's sword. Malchus is a monk rather than a warrior, so his failure to fight and nobly die standing his ground may be reasonable, but there is something strikingly unselfless as well as ungallant about grabbing the woman and turning her into a human shield to deflect the stroke coming his way. The gesture involves a rapid reversal from his previous defiance. It alludes to but parodies the more delicate touch that might have been expected if he had accepted the marriage proposal. The move is all the more charged as it is the first moment of touch since the pair were enduring the travails of being forced to ride on a single camel (chapter 4, lines 226–31). It also misrepresents Jerome's account. In the Latin, Malchus escapes his predicament by quickly embracing the woman ("Had I not at once anticipated him by taking the woman in my arms, he would have shed my blood on the spot"⁵⁸), presumably as a gesture of clear acquiescence in the proposed marriage. In the Old English, the different gesture suggests the strength of his resolve against sexual lust but appears incongruously lacking in either the expectations of a heroic narrative or the basics of Christian charity, a reversal of expectation that invites laughter at Malchus, especially in a context that anticipates some kind of happy outcome.

---

56 Dendle, "Malchus," 644, n. 21.
57 Translations are based on Dendle, "Malchus," with some modifications.
58 In White's translation of the Latin text, 124.

The comedy continues. In a descriptive detail analogous to the rapid passing of the day in Hygelac's Denmark, the narrator spells out with temporal emphasis the coming moment of challenge:

> And þa com þær swiðe hraðe þære nihte þysternys, þæt wit scoldan bion tosamne geþydde.
> (chap. 6, Assmann 18, lines 265–6)

> And then the darkness of night came very quickly there so that we two had to be joined together/brought together/united.

The double adverb (*swiðe hraðe*) shows Malchus's sense of the rapid approach of night, while *geþydde* presents a further ambiguity, punning on possible senses of "to join, connect, unite; to join together; to join, attach one person to another."[59] The term will chime throughout this passage, reflecting Malchus's foreboding:

> and wit þa wæron butu swiðe unrote geworden for þy hæmede, þe wit wendon, þæt wit hæman sceoldan, and uncer laþette ægþer oþer, þeah þe he hit oþrum ne sæde.
> (chap. 6, Assmann 18, lines 267–70)

> and we two both became very unhappy on account of the intercourse, which we two both expected that we would have to have, and each of us loathed the other, although neither said it to the other.

This observation comes after Malchus has led the woman into his private quarters, at which point his passivity sounds like comic discomfiture around the frisson of a taboo topic. The repeated dual pronoun is anything but romantic. The humour at the expense of Malchus amplifies as he laments at considerable length (given the brevity of most of the action here) in conversation with his own soul (but not with the other person in the room) as he ponders killing himself rather than giving up his chastity. He concludes he should be his own persecutor and make himself a martyr and prepares his sword for the deed, finally addressing his "wife" with further word play: "Hafa þu me ma to martire, þonne to were" ("have me more as a martyr than as a husband," 290), with the sounds of *martire* displaced into *ma ... to were*.

---

59 Citing some of the senses in BT and BTS for *geþeodan*.

The logical fallacy of the binary opposition in Malchus's mind only becomes apparent to him when the woman finally gets to have a voice in his narrative. She implores him not to die in what, in the Old English, sounds like a selfless statement of Christian love (whereas Jerome's Latin includes the more self-concerned rationalization that she will be blamed if he does so). Alternatively, she suggests that he should kill them both, since she wants to keep her chastity, too:

> Ic þe þonne andette, þæt ic swelte, ær ic wille beon to þe geþeodad, ac hafa þu me to þan geþungennestan wife, and wit syn ma þurh þa sawle tosamne geþiodad, þonne wit syn þurh þone lichman.
> (chap. 6, Assmann 18, lines 296–9)

> I vow to you, that I will die before I am joined/coupled/united to you, but have me as a most virtuous wife/woman, and we two will be joined/coupled/ united rather through the soul, than we will be through the body.

Their secular lord will believe that they are married, while Christ will know of their purity, she explains. The woman here gets both to embody the Christian virtue of chastity that Malchus is concerned with (in her case, rejecting both the coupling with him and her prior marriage in favour of chastity) and she also gets to articulate the smart plan, all the smarter in the Old English as she puns on *geþeodan*, to join together, which chimes four times through her short speech between lines 294 and 299, variously signalling them as united in one death, coupled in sex, or joined together in Christian love, echoing without precisely settling on a sense as "marriage."

Malchus is once more afraid, this time at the woman's speech, but has the wisdom to acquiesce, commenting, in another reversal of expectation: "I loved her then better than any lawful wife" ("ic hig þa lufode swiðor þonne ænig rihtwif," Assmann 18, line 303). The phrasing conjures up the idea of marriage by naming *rihtwif*, even as that is not what is here present. In a further version of the same trope, the implications of *rihtwif*-ness in bodily intimacy are brought into sharp focus by describing what it is that does not happen (but might be expected of such a couple):

> And ic næfre ne geseah hire nacode lichama, ne ic næfre ne æthran hire nacodum leomum. Ic þa ondræd, þæt ic in þære sibbe forlure, þæt ic ær in þæm gefiohte gehiold.
> (Assmann 18, lines 303–6)

> And I never saw her naked body, nor did I ever touch her naked limbs. I feared that I would lose in that peace what I had preserved in the battle.

The battle for Malchus is maintaining his chastity in the challenging plot offered him by this story. That battle against the temptations of sexual sin presumably continues even when the woman takes control and gets him out of the external threats through the couple's unconventional unsexual union. Multiple medieval expectations are getting reversed, as the woman leads the man away from sexual concupiscence, as nudity gets paraded to be not looked at, and as a monk establishes his exemplary chastity in an unconventional household that is here led by a woman.

Comedy here comes from the source and yet is amplified in the translation. Jerome uses humour and adventure in telling the story of miraculous celibacy within a horizon of expectation that differed from that of an early medieval English audience. A translation into Old English of such a story reverberates in ways that would seem both more exotic and more comic. When viewed from Rome, action in the Syrian desert, Muslim slave-trading, even the nature and expectations of monasticism and of celibacy, were all different from those ideas viewed from early medieval England. Where the translator specifically heightens comic effects, it is to play up the sexual discomfort of the would-be male celibate coming to terms with the miracle that communion with a woman may be possible without sex.

Ælfric's rejection of this kind of narrative has been remarked upon above, including his explicit refusal to include the *Vitae Patrum* in his *Lives of Saints*. Rather surprisingly, then, he did provide his own heavily abbreviated Life of Malchus at the end of one version of his homily on Judith, apparently in order to demonstrate the virtue of chastity. Unfortunately, that version is now almost all lost, damaged by the fire of the Cotton library, with just the beginning and ending surviving, but the limited space in the manuscript within which the account unfolded confirms that Ælfric radically abbreviated the translation as well as surely sanitizing it.[60] Nothing survives of the sexual encounter, alas, but most likely this was abbreviated into a mere antiseptic summary, if it was included at all. The extant ending includes a compressed version of the plot that sees Malchus and his companion flee the cave and return to Syria, with one small clue about Ælfric's technique. In what does survive, the pair escape the cave on horseback rather than on camel, suggesting Ælfric's characteristic domesticating translation style that downplayed the exotic in the story. The anonymous translation, on the other hand, shows how an Old English translator could revel in a plot of comic sexual embarrassment, even in the course of a pious story. This is a distinctive form of pious humour, very different from Ælfric's aesthetic, but akin to what is seen in two more anonymously translated lives.

---

60 See Lee, ed., *Ælfric's Homilies*, note to *Judith*, lines 372–81.

More Humour in the Desert: The Life of Mary of Egypt

With its interest in sexuality in the desert, with a fallible monk as point of entry, and even with a walk-on part for a she-lion, the Life of Mary of Egypt has numerous echoes of the Life of Malchus, and that goes for the deployment of humour, too. Once again, a story that revels in adventures and grand reversals told with a touch of hyperbole has been translated quite closely from the Latin source into Old English. This time sensational comedy comes in part from the extremity of the underlying swing from out-and-out sexual abandon to almost unimaginable ascetic renunciation by the character of Mary the Egyptian. The account of Mary's sexual past would likely have been shockingly sensational in the earlier Mediterranean milieu of the Greek original, from the sixth or seventh century, as it would have been in the ninth-century Latin version that is the immediate source for the Old English. It was certainly so in tenth-century England.

The Old English Life of Mary of Egypt is an anonymous prose translation of a widely circulating legend.[61] It is based on a Latin version written by Paul of Naples in the ninth century, which itself translates a Greek original, possibly written by Sophronius in the late sixth or early seventh century.[62] Like the Life of Euphrosyne, this is another life included among the sequence of Ælfric's *Lives of Saints* in MS Julius E. vii, even as it is very clearly not by him.[63] The Old English text came down to modern times in three manuscripts, but even so some gaps remain, since Julius E. vii has some omissions in the copying, one of which is substantial, and the two other manuscripts are fragmentary and can now provide only occasional added readings.[64]

At the centre of the story is a woman, Mary, who once embodied female sexuality run amok but who has come to an ascetic life of denial, isolation,

---

61 The Old English Mary of Egypt is ed. and trans. Skeat, *Lives of Saints*, as LS 23B, and by Kramer et al., *Anonymous Old English Lives of Saints*, 380–439. There is also a useful free-standing edition and translation with full apparatus by Magennis, *Life of Saint Mary of Egypt*, which is the edition cited here.

62 The Latin source text is ed. and trans. Magennis, *Mary of Egypt*, 139–209. The story's tradition is usefully discussed in the essays in Erich Poppe and Bianca Ross, eds., *The Legend of Mary of Egypt in Medieval Insular Hagiography* (Dublin: Four Courts Press, 1996).

63 See Magennis, *Mary of Egypt*, 24–35. Magennis describes the inappropriateness of the fit in "Contrasting Features," and "*Mary of Egypt* and Ælfric."

64 BL Cotton Otho B. x, and Gloucester, Cathedral Library, MS 35; details in Magennis, *Mary of Egypt*, 14–25; for the best recovered reading of the former, see Linda Cantara, "*Saint Mary of Egypt* in British Library, MS Cotton Otho B. x," in *Anonymous Interpolations in Ælfric's "Lives of Saints"*, ed. Robin Norris (Kalamazoo, MI: Medieval Institute, 2011), 29–69.

and piety in the desert. The audience encounters Mary through Zosimus, a monk who is questing for perfection. He finds Mary in the remote uninhabited desert, where she has lived for forty-seven years on two and a half loaves of bread, enacting an extreme version of pious eremeticism. She educates him by telling him of her earlier life of sexual abandon in Alexandria, which she pursued for seventeen years after leaving her home in her twelfth year. She then had a conversionary moment inspired by an image of the Virgin Mary when approaching the Church of the Resurrection in Jerusalem to celebrate the Feast of the Exaltation of the Holy Cross and turned to the desert. Zosimus meets with her a second time a year later at the River Jordan, where she receives the Eucharist from him. She encourages him to find her a year after that back in the desert, where he finds her dead body, which he buries with appropriate rites after receiving a miraculous message giving her name and time of death so that he can spread her story.

The whole narrative plays with role reversals as the authority figure of an elderly male monk and priest goes seeking a male figure of wisdom but finds himself edified instead by a non-literate and naked woman. Much of the situational humour gently mocks the male authority figure, appropriately enough, since Zosimus sets off on his quest into the desert because he believes he may have achieved spiritual perfection, with a strong hint of pride that merits comic deflation.[65] The plot plays up such humour when the celibate senior male gets characterized with tropes more applicable to a young lover. The most obvious source of humour in the story is the very extremity of the two roles that Mary gets to act out, as a woman with the most explicit sexual voracity imaginable, and as a hermit with such austere practice that she can subsist for forty-seven years on two and a half loaves of bread (and later three lentils) and with such piety that she levitates while praying.[66] The extreme contrast of these diametrically opposed imaginations of female embodiment is deeply incongruous. While the chasm between the two is designed to encourage faith through wonder, it is, at the same time, humorous, particularly since the super-pious present within the narrative makes an uncomfortable context

65 Robin Norris, "*Vitas Matrum*: Mary of Egypt as Female Confessor," in *The Old English Life of Mary of Egypt*, ed. Donald Scragg, OEN Subsidia (Kalamazoo, MI: Medieval Institute, 2005), 79–109; Paul E. Szarmach, "More Genre Trouble: The Life of Mary of Egypt," in *Writing Women Saints in Anglo-Saxon England*, ed. Paul E. Szarmach (Toronto: University of Toronto Press, 2013), 140–64, play up the educating of the male monastic figure.

66 This is the sole Old English example of a cluster of such lives described by Ruth Mazo Karras, "Holy Harlots: Prostitute Saints in Medieval Legend," *Journal of the History of Sexuality* 1 (1990): 3–32; Virginia Burrus, *The Sex Lives of Saints: An Erotics of Ancient Hagiography* (Philadelphia: University of Pennsylvania Press, 2004).

for viewing the salacious past. There is scope for localized comic incongruity, seen, for example, in excessive attention to a holy woman's nakedness. This is heavily exploited in the scene where Zosimus first meets her. Probably the funniest scene of all is the initial encounter between the two characters, which is worth exploring in more detail.

At the surface level, embarrassment is an ever-present risk in this scene because Mary's extreme ascetic lifestyle means she has no clothes to cover a body which she once chose to parade for sexual allure but which she now wants to conceal in the height of piety, and embarrassment is often good grist for humour.[67] As a result, on first encounter, Mary runs from Zosimus, who, full of enthusiasm, runs in pursuit of her. The scene is set up with comic incongruities from the start. Zosimus praying in the desert wilderness sees what he thinks may be "sumes gastes scinhyw" ("a phantom/illusion of some spirit," 209–10), which proves to be a human being, subsequently identified as a woman. She gets described:

> Swiðe sweartes lichaman heo wæs for þære sunnan hæto, and þa loccas hire heafdes wæron swa hwite swa wull and þa na siddran þonne oþ þone swuran. (215–18)

> She was of a very dark body on account of the heat of the sun, and the hair of her head was as white as wool and no longer than to her neck.

This is presumably what would be seen as an abject body, which makes Zosimus's response incongruous at the literal level, since he, eagerly gazing ("georne behealdende," 219), feels happiness "for þære gewilnedan swetnysse þære wuldorfæstan gesihðe" ("on account of the longed-for sweetness of that glorious sight," 220–1). Zosimus's high estimation of the sight of an abject body is a paradox that plays up the theological import of what is to come, with the humblest of ascetics able to teach the proudest of monks, the basest of sinners manifesting the greatest of salvations, all playing into the Christian paradox that the meek shall inherit the earth. At a theological or metaphorical level, Zosimus is certainly right to see Mary as *swetnysse*, to desire her, and run in pursuit of her.[68] At a literal level, though, it is incongruous and embarrassing for a pious and aged male

---

67 For the collision of humour, embarrassment, and nakedness in Old English texts, see my "Naked in Old English," which includes preliminary analysis of the present scene.

68 Although naked women are more often diabolical spirit of temptation from which to run away in lives of desert fathers, as Andrew P. Scheil, "Bodies and Boundaries in the Old English *Life of St. Mary of Egypt*," *Neophilologus* 84 (2000): 137–56 points out.

monk to be staring at, desiring, and running in pursuit of a naked woman. There is, then, a comic incongruity between the surface level of the physical action and the decorously pious possibilities of the allegorical action.

Even if his perception of *swetnysse* is entirely right at the metaphorical or theological level, Zosimus is not comprehending what he is seeing at the literal level and hence staring where he should not. His initial theological perceptiveness is undercut by his second response, as he wonders "hwæt þæt wildeora wære" ("what kind of a wild animal that was," 226), which shows that he has not understood what he has seen. The subsequent account of his pursuit of this wild creature is rich in description, which keeps an audience grounded at the literal level, where events are more obviously comic than edifying. Zosimus sets off in pursuit, "his ealdan ylde ofergetiligende" ("overcoming his old age," 227–8), "mid hrædestan ryne" ("with quickest running," 229), because he wanted "hine geðeodan" ("to unite himself," 230; "se coniungere" in the Latin source at line 235) with the one who fled, an ironic verb in view of all the awkward overtones that have been seen in the sexually charged scene in the Life of Malchus, namely "to join, connect, unite; to join together; to join, attach one person to another, etc." The text of Mary of Egypt gives extensive narrative time to the chase, in which the narrator spells out that Zosimus is pursuing her, and Mary is fleeing him (231), during which he gets closer *sticmælum* ("little by little," 232). While there is presumably no set upper age limit for running in early medieval England, the age of this pair establishes incongruity here, since Zosimus is repeatedly characterized as aged (and the plot sets him up as fifty-three years old or a little older) and the upcoming account will establish that Mary is seventy-six years old. At the surface level, an old monastic man running after a naked old woman out of desire is not congruous with either the characters' age or their status. Since the action seems to be undertaken without malice, each of those inappropriatenesses generates humour.[69] The distance between the cerebral high status of monastic perfection and the low (and taboo) status of bodily somatic and sexual concerns makes the incongruity funnier still.

Once Zosimus gets close enough to be heard, he (with continued emphasis on his advanced age: "forealdodne syngigan," "a very old sinner," 236)

---

69 Although Dumitrescu, *Experience of Education*, chap. 5, in the course of describing the dangers as well as pleasures of pedagogic desire, points to the norms of sexual violence in female hagiography and thus reads this as a parodic staging of a potential rape scene, which "renders the generic sexual aggression of hagiographies comical by replacing the virile pagan governor with a grasping senile ascetic, and the nubile virgin with a repentant, elderly harlot" (146).

calls out, asking her why she flees. She crosses a dried up streambed before giving an answer that explicitly negotiates issues of bodily decorum, while incidentally revealing her visionary powers. The proportions between those two elements suggest how happy the narrative is to play up the surface level and the comedy of embarrassment over the fundamentally miraculous here. Mary inspires awe with the first three words of her speech: "Ðu abbod Zosimus" ("Oh, Abbot Zosimus," 251; or, in the Latin source, two words: "Abba Zosima," 258). The next seventy-eight words, i.e. the vast majority of the speech, centre on the practicalities of decorum in this world as Mary explains her need for clothing to cover her naked body. The phrasing is striking, not only for the length, but also for the covert play with both Zosimus's and the audience's gaze. Mary asks Zosimus to have mercy on her, saying that she cannot show herself and turn towards him,

> forþon ic eom wifhades mann and eallunga lichamlicum wæfelsum bereafod, swa swa þu sylf gesihst, and þa sceame mines lichaman hæbbende unoferwrigene. (253–6)

> because I am a person of the female kind and completely lacking in bodily clothing, as you yourself see, and having the shame of my body uncovered.

Mary asks for Zosimus's cloak, "þe þu mid bewæfed eart" ("which you are covered with," 258–9), so that she can conceal "þa wiflican tyddernysse" ("that womanly frailty," 259) and turn to him and receive his prayers. This is a verbal account paradoxically rich in the descriptive display of that which is not to be gazed upon, as the two old people negotiate the concealment of what, the narrator says "mæst neod wæs to beheligenne" ("it was most necessary to conceal," 270). The language here is strikingly revealing for describing in such detail something that is being concealed. Mary both mentions her complete lack of bodily covering and then adds a logically redundant focus on the sexually charged specific part of her body that is uncovered, namely "þa sceame mines lichaman" ("the shameful part of my body," 255–6; in Latin "corporis turpitudinem," 260–1), itself a strikingly value-ladened term for the anatomy, since *sceamu* means the emotion of shame, or something which causes shame, including the sexual part of the body.[70] The revealing-concealing language continues in describing the

---

70 BT provides three definitions of *sceamu* s.v.: I "the emotion caused by consciousness of unworthiness or of disgrace, in a good sense, modesty, bashfulness; in a bad sense, shame, confusion"; II "what causes a feeling of shame, disgrace, shame"; III "the private part."

intimate parts of the body that establish *wifhad* to such an extent that it is impossible, in narrative terms, for an audience, no matter how pious in intention, not to be gazing on those very parts of the body that are not to be looked at. That trap of description is emphasized in diegetic time by that additional clause about Zosimus seeing, "swa swa þu sylf gesyhst" ("just as you yourself see," 255), which confirms the thing that is to be avoided, namely that such seeing of sexual signs *is* currently going on. Zosimus is looking where he should not, even if he is unaware that he is doing so. Gazing on the sexually specific parts of a female body mocks the pretensions of a monk, particularly one who thought that he might be perfect in his devotional practice.

It also mocks the audience. The exposition of the narrative forces the listener or reader to be attending to the sexual parts of the pious woman's body, "swa swa þu sylf gesyhst" ("just as you yourself see"). An audience needs to be attentive to this surface level of the unfolding narrative to arrive at the moral and theological point of a saint's life that emphasizes the transcendent pleasure of repentance and ascetic withdrawal over the pleasures of life in the world and the sexual urges of the body. Being laughed at for gazing at a holy woman's naughty bits encourages a humorous double-take in a self-aware audience, if we are capable of spotting that we have been drawn into just the sort of bodily attention that Mary will first describe and then transcend. That very doubleness of perspective, seeing the surface narrative, and then seeing the implications of that narrative, creates the double vision of incongruity, with the further delight here of spotting ourselves as butts of the joke.

Not that these are the only levels in operation in understanding the story. The body and its exposure have considerable metaphorical power.[71] In the monastery that Zosimus moves to, the monks aspire to be dead in the body but living in the spirit (lines 110–12). In the language of Zosimus in one of the lacunae in the Old English, Mary's nakedness is the human form which her divine power has chosen to put on to bring divinity to humanity (Latin source, lines 347–54). Mary herself equates Zosimus seeing her naked body to her laying bare her sinful past acts to him (Latin source, lines 368–72). As she puts it later, summarizing both garb and comestibles, in the desert she has been clothed in the garment of the word of God (lines 682–3), since man does not live by bread alone (lines 683–5). Such allusions point to a

---

71 With a very different emphasis, Clare A. Lees and Gillian R. Overing, *Double Agents: Women and Clerical Culture in Anglo-Saxon England* (Philadelphia: University of Pennsylvania Press, 2001), chap. 4, bring out well the theological and allegorical implications of Mary's naked body and the act of gazing.

clear allegorical sense for Mary's nakedness for an audience trained in techniques of allegorical reading. At a figural level, Mary represents, *inter alia*, Ecclesia, the church, ultimately redeemed by Christ. The first stage in the disciplining of Zosimus's spiritual understanding is "the clothing of Mary," a stage necessary to convert Mary's sexual knowledge "through penitential speech into spiritual knowledge," while the subsequent exchange of clothing "equalizes the distance between them," showing Zosimus's acquisition of the spiritual message.[72] Nevertheless, all that metaphorical and spiritual work is built on a surface narrative of palpable embarrassment and glaring incongruity, and hence one that is funny.

An unusually frank parading of senior nudity is thematically appropriate approaching a story that will in large part be about the taming of female sexuality. It is also something of a comic hook in its break from standard Old English decorum. A story of conversion depends upon reversals and this scene conjures up Mary's reversal from a body desiring to be gazed upon to one that has chosen isolation, from youthful sexuality of the body beautiful to aged bodies attempting to shake off sexual attention. Mary's observation of Zosimus's observing her nakedness ("swa þu sylf gesihst") presumably serves to tactfully educate him not to look (he turns his back as he throws his cloak), and thereby encapsulates another reversal as the woman of the story educates the man, and the repentant sinner educates the priest. The story here is rife with appealing gender reversals and is inverting expected conventions, social, religious, and literary.

Not that Zosimus seems to be paying much attention. Rather, he immediately reacts, at significant narrative length, to the first three words, wondering in great fear and awe how she, whom he has never seen before, could call on him by name (lines 261–5). He has the perspicacity to realize that she is equipped with divine foresight and to do what she has commanded *fæstlice* ("with firm purpose," 266). And so, Zosimus takes off the cloak "þe he mid bewæfed wæs" ("which he had been clothed with," 267), and throws it to her with his back turned (*on bæclincg gewend*, 267–8). The exchange of monastic garb recalls the intimacy of the analogous scene in the Life of Euphrosyne and, for an audience attentive to surface details, suggests a further piece of possible comic play. Twice now the cloak (*scyccels*) has been characterized as that with which Zosimus was clothed or covered ("mid bewæfed eart/wæs" lines 258–9, 267). If this had been the narrative of Euphrosyne's transformation from secular young woman to

---

72 Clare A. Lees, "Vision and Place in the Old English Life of Mary of Egypt," in *The Old English Life of Mary of Egypt*, ed. Donald Scragg (Kalamazoo: Medieval Institute, 2005), 57–78, quotations from 71, 72, 77.

masculine monk, we might think that handing over a monk's cloak was a flirtatious gesture, as apparel, intimate from recent wear, goes from a young man to the young woman who is revelling in the agency she can grasp by breaking from her father's control and acting out with people her own age. Just as there is no specific age limit for running games, so there is presumably no age limit for flirtation and thoughts of sexual desire, even if such thoughts seem comically incongruous to this older and more pious couple. Zosimus's fear and awe and *fæstlice* compliance suggest that he is not thinking sexual thoughts at all, even if his gaze is trained on the wrong place, but his lack of self-awareness might have us wonder if there is a different cause to laugh at him. How much clothing does a monk wandering in the desert for a month wear? Illustrations of cowled monks tend not to be revealing of undergarments, but the desert is a hot place, and we have twice been told that the cloak is Zosimus's covering. Once removed, is there a risk that he is presenting himself with undignified exposure? Does he play the rest of the scene in the desert in just an undergarment? Or less? The potential for sexual embarrassment simmers in this text, even when the characters manage explicitly to avoid it.

With Zosimus's cloak in hand, there is a reprise of the trick of bodily concealing-revealing as the narrator comments that Mary covered as much of her body as she could and which it was most necessary to conceal (lines 269–70). There is also a reprise of the emphasis on gazing, as her first question is to ask why it was necessary for Zosimus to work so hard *to geseonne* ("to see," 272–3) her, a sinful woman. An emphasis on such gazing runs throughout the life. Again and again, Zosimus pines for the *gesyhðe* "sight" or "vision" of this spiritual guide, even as he and we risk being laughed at for gazing at the surface of the body. As Lees points out, for all the Old English female saint's narratives, "The act of looking, always problematic in Anglo-Saxon culture, is indeed a potent moment in these lives, with the acquisition of correct knowledge its correlative: even when naturalized by the ideology of spiritual love, the dangers of the unspiritual gaze, the pleasures of eroticized scopophilia, sadism, and masochism lurk everywhere."[73] As we have seen, gazing in veneration is hard to tell apart from gazing in bodily desire. Looking at Mary's body is a crucial and yet fraught part of the meaning of this life, in which, even as the story calls for looking to get to interpretation, getting caught gazing at the wrong places encourages a corrective humour.

The age of the two participants is a significant part of the pleasure – and humour – of the encounter, and so it is worth noticing the unusually

---

73 Lees, "Engendering Religious Desire," 35.

abundant evidence on this matter provided by the narrator. We are told that Zosimus is in his fifty-third year when he leaves his original monastery to take on the challenge of the stricter monastery near the River Jordan (line 57), whence he sets out at Lent on his quest to seek spiritual guidance beyond that river. Since such private exploration is an annual Lenten practice for this monastic community, he presumably encounters Mary in his first year there, when he would be aged fifty-three or fifty-four. Throughout the narrative, he is repeatedly characterized as old or the aged one, perhaps to emphasize that he should bear the wisdom of age. For Mary, we are given specific periods of time as if we are supposed to be keeping track to establish her age. She lived twelve years at home (line 363), seventeen years as a libertine sexual sinner in Alexandria (line 372), and then forty-seven years in the wilderness of the desert (lines 594–5), which add up to make her about seventy-six years old at the first encounter. Unlike Zosimus, though, she is never characterized as aged. It is striking that the narrative of her life seems to move in seventeen-year chunks. She is a sinner for seventeen years, and then, in her own account of her time in the desert, she explains that she struggled against thoughts of sin for seventeen years (lines 616–17), a period that she twice more mentions (lines 665, 672), on one occasion as if it reaches to the present ("for seventeen years … until this present day" 665–8), on another as if there were then a few years after such struggles (line 672). Even though forty-seven years in the wilderness is in both Old English and Latin (Latin source, lines 581–2), it is tempting to assume this is an error for seventeen, perhaps with a further few years in the wilderness after achieving enlightenment. Instead of seventy-six, this would make her a few years older than forty-six when Zosimus first encounters her. While that would probably suggest a no-longer sexualized body in the Early Middle Ages, she need not be as old as Zosimus, who then more understandably gets characterized as the old man.[74] Credible chronology, though, is not a particularly high desideratum for this narrative, as seen at the end of the story, when Zosimus returns to the monastery for a stay there of one hundred years (lines 957–8; the Latin source has him live there until he was one hundred years old, line 898).

Whatever their specific ages, there is a comic distance between narrative motifs of these two characters as young lovers and the aging figures of pious wisdom they represent in the present. The possibility that the aging

---

74 See Diane Watt and Clare A. Lees, "Age and Desire in the Old English *Life of St Mary of Egypt:* A Queerer Time and Place?" in *Middle Aged Women in the Middle Ages*, ed. Sue Niebrzysdowski (Cambridge: Brewer, 2011), 53–67, for an alternative explanation of the numbers which sees Mary as "not only beyond gender, she is *beyond* age" (62).

questing monk will be seen as a desiring young lover is played with a few times later in the life. As Zosimus realizes Mary's prophetic powers, in addition to fear and awe and trembling, he sighs ("Ða ongan he sworettan," "then he began to sigh," 287). Before their second meeting, Zosimus worries whether Mary is going to show up in language that might well resonate as an anxious lover awaiting his beloved (lines 787–8). As she leaves him, he expresses his desire to have the vision of her precious countenance ("deorwurðan andwlitan," 841–2). On his way to their third encounter, he heads towards their desert rendezvous described in an image of the hunter seeking to seize the sweetest wild animal (873–5), which again might sound like the metaphorical language of a lover in pursuit.[75] With such language, the narrator laughs at the ideal celibate who has to become vulnerable to such potential mockery to pursue this spiritual quest.

At a bodily level, Zosimus even gets mocked for his piety. After Mary has put on the cloak, the two holy figures bow down in respect of each other's holiness, prostrate themselves on the ground, and ask the other to bless them (276–8). As a consequence, they lie prostrate on the ground before each other in a deadlock of politeness "manega tida fæce" ("for a period of many hours," 279; "Post multarum ... horarum spatium" in the Latin source, 283). While this is a motif probably drawing on Jerome's account of Antony and Paul meeting in the desert, the Old English narrator highlights the incongruity by introducing the prostration with rapidity ("sona," "immediately," 276) for all its long duration. When the dialogue finally resumes, Mary points out Zosimus's special status as a priest, something which she will need to remind him of repeatedly, while Zosimus points to her divine foreknowledge as he realizes her special status.

Mary fully establishes that special status by revealing the story of her miraculous transformation from sexual sybarite to saintly sage. She describes the details of her conversion to Zosimus (lines 452–590) and, to make clear its full miraculous power, she precedes this with an unusually extensive account of her life of sexual sin (lines 360–451). She explains that she lived in Alexandria not as a prostitute but pursuing sex for her own desire. Most of that activity is described with a degree of tactful displacement through such images as "on þam bryne forligeres licgende" ("lying in the fire of fornication," 373) or the non-specificity of satisfying "þa scyldfullan gewilnunga mines forligeres" ("the disgraceful desires of my sexual activity," 379). Occasionally, though, there are more circumstantial details, and some provide hints of a different context for the performance of humour that are worth drawing out.

---

75 As Schiel, "Bodies," 150 suggests.

As Mary moves from Alexandria, she joins a group of pilgrims going to Jerusalem. Determined to enjoy sexually the company of men that she sees flocking, she picks out one group and provides unusual detail of her interaction with them. She notes ten young men standing by the shore:

> genoh þæslice on lichaman and on gebærum, and ful licwurðe me þuhte to mines lichaman luste. Ic me þa unsceandlice swa swa ic gewuna wæs tomiddes heora gemengde and him to cwæð, "Nimað me on eower færeld mid eow. Ne beo ic na eow unlicwyrðe." And ic hi þa ealle sona to þam manfullum leahtrum and ceahhetungum bysmerlicum astyrede mid manegum oþrum fullicum and fracodlicum gespræcum.
> (417–25)

> comely enough in body and in bearing, and it seemed to me very agreeable for the desire of my body. I then mingled shamelessly in the midst of them, as was my custom, and said to them "Take me on your journey with you. I will not be at all unagreeable to you." And I immediately stirred them all up then to wicked sins and to shameful snickering with many other foul and wicked speeches.

The passage is fascinating for the projection of a female gaze and female desire, albeit within a familiar misogynist tradition that condemns women as excessively lustful.[76] While the emphasis is on voraciousness in sexual sin, this brief vignette also gives a hint of other ways in which Mary created a community. She uses humour both in her present description and in her actions in the scene she is presenting. She chooses her men here on the basis of physique and bearing ("on lichaman and on gebærum"), which she characterizes with a little joke of understatement, saying they are "genoh þæslice" ("suitable, seemly, becoming, fit, meet, congruous; comely, fair, elegant" enough for her purposes[77]). Like so much of the sinning scene, what is getting built up here is uncontained sexual activity, but what Mary actually describes are words rather than deeds (*fullicum and fracodlicum gespræcum*). With another small litotes, she describes how she mingled *unsceandlice* ("not-shamefully," i.e. brazenly) in the middle of the group. Once there she speaks in a way that stirs her audience up, with appealing zeugma, both to evil sin (*þam manfullum leahtrum*) *and* to laughter (*ceahhetungum bysmerlicum*). This is

---

76 See Jane Stevenson, "The Holy Sinner: The Life of Mary of Egypt," in *The Legend of Mary of Egypt in Medieval Insular Hagiography*, eds. Erich Poppe and Bianca Ross (Dublin: Four Courts Press, 1996), 19–50, for the tradition in the sources.

a process that she characterizes as her regular modus operandi (*swa swa ic gewuna wæs*).

Her speech presumably provoked laughter because it broke taboo through brazen *double entendre*, with comic distance between a veneer of potential respectability and a clear underlying suggestion of sexual advances. The brief example she cites uses a rhetorical form that has been seen throughout this study to be characteristic for the creation of dead-pan humour: the litotes which provides understatement through a denied opposite in saying, "I will not be unpleasing to you" ("Ne beo ic na eow unlicwyrðe"). The central term used twice here may embody a pun and certainly displays further linguistic artistry: *lic-wyrðe*, "fit to please, pleasant, well-pleasing, acceptable, agreeable, estimable..." (according to BT) is probably built from the adjective *līc* "like" and the adjective *weorð* "worth, of value, etc." but also conjures up the neuter noun *līc* "body"-worthy. In its two uses here, the bodily sense is triggered through the echo with the two uses of *lichaman* in close proximity, first conjuring the bodies of the men she fancies, then describing the desire in her own body, while the other sense is also activated by chiming with the adverbial or adjectival ending *-lice/licum*, which recurs five times in just this short passage. The loudly lilting ullulation of the *l*-alliteration running throughout this passage with its climax in *leahtrum* ("sins") lulls an audience into a sense that it is serving for moral uprightness, even as the true power of the lilting *l*s is to link the body (*lic, lichama*, "body") with desire (*lic* in the sense of "like," *-lice*, and *lust*, "desire"). This is seduction through a rhetorically powerful linguistic performance, namely sex talk with style and wit, which was rewarded at the time by generating laughter. From her present perspective, Mary portrays that response as unwholesome laughter, *ceahhetungum bysmerlicum*, "shameful cackling" or "disgraceful repeated laughter."[78] The effect may be heightened yet further in the version in MS Otho B. x, fol. 28 (17)r, lines 20–3, where this clause reads "to þam manfullum leahtrum . 7 bysmer ceahhettungum astyrode wurdon" as recovered by Cantara, who sees therein an otherwise unattested compound noun, *bysmerceahhetungum*, "shameful cackling,"[79] a poeticism that stresses the unwholesomeness of the response, but also the spell that Mary's artistry casts over her male audience.

---

77 BT s.v. *þæslice*, definitions I and II.
78 DOE s.v. *ceahhetung*, "repeated laughter, cackling"; s.v. *bysmor-full*, sense 1 "shameful, disgraceful."
79 Cantara, "St. Mary of Egypt," fig. 7; she points to the compound noun in her commentary at 39.

Mary presents her story with a hint of humour throughout her narration to Zosimus and hence to the audience of the life, but this incident shows how her past revolved around performing humour, now seen as sinful, but once seen as carefree desire. Her address to these young men presumably inverted expectations in part because such openness in sexual discourse was not normal, in part because this was a woman doing the propositioning (contrary to medieval gender expectations), and in part for the disproportion in numbers (this was one single woman proposing sexual play with ten men). Inappropriateness and excess create a comic persona for Mary in ways somewhat analogous to her later fictive cousin, Alisoun, the Wife of Bath, in *The Canterbury Tales*. Sex talk is funny in the broader context of a group going on a religious pilgrimage, who (for all the Wife of Bath's subsequent wandering by the way) are not supposed to be thinking about sexual dalliance. By her own account, Mary seduced many, and this was clearly not just with her body, but also with words that could make men laugh.[80] Mary presents us here, then, with the unusual portrait of a female sexual comedian.

Indeed, later, when she looks back on what temptations she felt during her first seventeen years in the desert, she reflects how she missed the indulgences of her previous life, listing meat and fish, wine, and also verbal artistry:

Me wæs swilce swiðlic lust þæra sceandlicra sceopleoða me gedrefdon, þonne hi me on mode gebrohton þa deoflican leoþ to singanne þe ic ær on worulde geleornode.
(626–8)

It was as if an intense desire for those shameful songs afflicted me, when they brought it into my mind to sing those diabolical songs which I had previously learned in the world.

Just as she once ate fine fish and indulged to excess in the pleasures of wine, the joy of *sceandlicra sceopleoða* ("shameful poetic songs"), which she now characterizes as *þa deoflican leoþ* ("the devil-inspired songs"), were likewise a part of her pleasure routines in Alexandria. She now characterizes these performances in ways that distance herself from them, but they join fine food and drink as part of the secular good life of the past. Perhaps accompanying the fine food and wine and/or the sexual activity, she had apparently memorized (*geleornode*) songs or poems to perform in singing which she can now characterize as inspired by the devil (*deoflic*) and as *sceandlic* "disgraceful, foul, shameful, obscene."[81] What *leoð* would an early

---

80 Szarmach, "More Genre Trouble," sees the sex acts themselves within the life as comic.
81 BT s.v. *sceandlic*, definition II.

medieval English audience think of with such a description? Would sexual riddles qualify? Or the other humorous poems of this study? Mary is
describing a world of secular entertainment, including salacious but witty
performances that could make people laugh. Unlikely as it may seem, this
life gives us a picture of the performance of humour by a licentious female
entertainer, like the performer imagined in the riddle portrait of the Jay in
Riddle 24 (discussed in chapter 2 above). Imagined as a female-led, sexually charged, salacious and witty world of entertainment, there are hints
here of the deployment and enjoyment of a whole side of early medieval
humour that otherwise would go unrecorded.

    This is a world of which the pious Zosimus appears to have no knowledge
and there is an ever-present danger of him coming across as a fool. At their
first meeting, he beheld a miraculous sign when he saw that Mary levitated
in prayer (lines 327–35). This stands alongside her foreknowledge of him to
key him in that she has a very special status and is worthy of his venerating
attention. At their second meeting, he worries how she is going to cross the
River Jordan to join him, only to see her walk on water (in both directions,
lines 807–8, 859–61). From his perspective, then, her miraculous power and
providential protection should be pretty evident and, by the time of their
third encounter, he should be ready for the workings of providence. In practice, when he spots her dead body he runs to the spot (line 886), recalling his
earlier running scene, and does not dare to touch her body (887–8), recalling
the bodiliness of the first meeting. Being a prophetic saint, she has arranged
her body in death in an appropriate manner, facing east, with a message written on the ground (a miracle itself, since Zosimus had established that she
could not write). From this, in addition to learning her name and death day,
Zosimus knows it is appropriate to pray for her and bury her (lines 893–8).[82]
As he faces the practical dilemma of digging a grave, a lion appears. The
audience is likely to spot a motif drawn from Jerome's account of Antony
burying Paul with the help of two miraculously tame lions, and Zosimus,
too, should realize the lion's providential value, which makes his initial reaction of fear suggest that he is a slow learner, although he passes through
fear to enlightenment when he evokes the lion's aid. Laughing at Zosimus's
human foibles may save him from the danger of pride, as well as providing
the audience a fallibly human point of entry into a story of sanctity.

    The burial scene returns also to the nudity of the opening encounter as Zosi-
mus covers the body in earth "swa nacode swa he ærest gemette" ("as naked as
he had first met her," 943–4) except for the protection of the torn cloak which

---

82 Zweck, *Epistolary Acts*, 131–45 reads the missive written in the earth in relation to
    Mary's desire to have her body return to earth, not to be fetishized as a relic.

he had thrown to her before, "of þam Maria sumne hire lichaman bewæfdc" ("by means of which Mary had clothed some part of her body," 945–6). The reprise of so many of the details of that first encounter suggests that the narrator wants to give weight to the human-level comedy of the opening scene, even as it is transcended by the edifying nature of the saint. A pious and edifying story achieves its effect here through extensive use of narrative humour. For all its description of salacious entertainment, and for all the revelling in sexual awkwardness, the humour in this life serves the pious purpose of the story, keeping an audience engaged, and making this saint particularly memorable.

Humour in Time Travel: The Legend of the Seven Sleepers of Ephesus

One more anonymously translated saints' life plays with comic possibilities in a narrative rife with human interest and will serve as a final case study in this chapter. The Old English Legend of the Seven Sleepers of Ephesus once again survives in the main manuscript of Ælfric's *Lives of Saints*, Julius E. vii, along with a fragmentary copy in the burned Cotton Otho B. x, but is once again clearly not by him.[83] Here, the narrative plays up the circumstantial elements of the story, and these are brought out particularly well in the Old English translation which, unusually, is longer than the Latin source.[84] The story is striking for providing rich details of daily life, including about the circulation of coinage and other aspects of city life.[85] It is also striking for the human interest in the narrative. While, at moments, this leads to a life

---

83 Ed. and trans. Skeat, *Lives of Saints*, as LS 23 (488–541), and by Kramer et al., *Anonymous Old English Lives of Saints*, 587–651. It is also edited with a full apparatus in Hugh Magennis, ed., *The Anonymous Old English Legend of the Seven Sleepers* (Durham: Durham Medieval Texts 7, 1994), which is the text cited here. For the definitive case against Ælfric's authorship, see Magennis, "Contrasting Features."

84 The Latin source is published with a translation in Magennis, *Legend*, 74–91, as an appendix to his edition. On the source and its handling, see Hugh Magennis, "The Anonymous Old English *Legend of the Seven Sleepers* and Its Latin Source," *Leeds Studies in English* 22 (1991): 43–56.

85 See Dorothy Whitelock, "The Numismatic Interest of the Old English Version of the Legend of the Seven Sleepers," in *Anglo-Saxon Coins: Studies Presented to F. M. Stenton*, ed. R.H.M. Dolley (London: Methuen, 1961), 188–94; Catherine Cubitt, "'As the Law-Book Teaches': Reeves, Lawbooks and Urban Life in the Anonymous Old English Legend of the Seven Sleepers," *English Historical Review* 124 (2009): 1021–49; Hugh Magennis, "Crowd Control? Depictions of the Many in Anglo-Saxon Literature, with Particular Reference to the Old English *Legend of the Seven Sleepers*," *English Studies* 93 (2012): 119–37.

that is unusually poignant, at other moments it is also unusually funny, particularly in exploiting the comedy-of-errors confusion of one of the protagonists, the fallible and fearful saint Malchus.[86] Once again, Ælfric would not have approved – demonstrably so, since a different version of this life survives in a translation by him, where he manages to minimize the human interest and effectively eliminate the potential for comedy. I will first consider the anonymous life for its capacious deployment of humour, and then, more briefly, contrast Ælfric's handling with its implied rejection of humour.

The Legend of the Seven Sleepers tells the story of seven leaders from Ephesus at the time of the Christian persecution under Emperor Decius. The emperor requires the seven to honour pagan idols, which they refuse to do. Because they are friends and advisors of the emperor, he gives them time to reconsider. They retreat to a cave outside of Ephesus. When the emperor learns of their continued intransigence, he has the mouth of the cave walled up. Two covert Christian sympathizers record the story on lead tablets placed in the entranceway. The seven martyrs go to sleep as if in the regular manner, even as God has their slumber last 372 years, until the reign of Emperor Theodosius, who is Christian but facing a widespread heresy denying the bodiliness of the resurrection of all people at the Last Judgment. The seven sleepers awake, thinking a single night has passed, and send one of their number (their steward, Malchus) to the city to buy bread secretly for them. As audience, we follow his misadventures as he approaches the town, confused by changes, especially the appearance of Christian symbols. He is finally tripped up by the coins he uses to buy the bread. A crowd at the marketplace assumes he has found a treasure-hoard of ancient coins and is keeping it for himself; the town reeve gets involved and is distinctly threatening as he tries to apply the law to the case; and resolution comes only when the case moves to the more sympathetic bishop of the town, who listens to Malchus and allows him to take the authorities and accumulated crowd back to the cave. Here they find the community of sleepers and the lead tablets corroborating their story. Emperor Theodosius comes to visit and, while the end is missing from the Old English, the source shows how the story ends with the death of the seven, who are duly honoured as saints.

---

86 This is a different Malchus from Malchus in the desert of the Life of Malchus. The humour in this case has been explored before by Hugh Magennis, "A Funny Thing Happened on the Way to Heaven: Humorous Incongruity in Old English Saints' Lives," in *Humour in Anglo-Saxon Literature*, 137–57.

The story is strikingly uncanny throughout.[87] It keys into the genre of the *passio*, with its entirely predictable pattern of persecution, defiance, miraculous unconcern, and death, seen in the examples of Laurence and Agatha described above, but disrupts the expectations both in terms of plot (the persecuted ones here enter an extended sleep until the time of their reanimation rather than dying) and in terms of affect, with real concern for describing the emotion of the characters. The striking degree of human interest has been noticed by past critics. Peter Clemoes suggests in passing that this is the sole surviving religious example of a type of storytelling "marked by a much more circumstantial, psychological, strain" than the symbolic stories of the religious poetry, as it narrates "from episode to episode set in the intimate experience of human beings on this side of the material/spiritual divide."[88] Unlike other martyrs, these seven show fear, running away to the cave and trying to avoid their persecutor. Much of the emotion portrayed is far from funny, and Eileen Joy shows how the narrative portrays "through a type of psychological realism unique for its time, the emotional suffering of highly socialized selves being wrenched out of a world which itself mourns that untimely separation."[89] Joy makes a convincing case by focusing in particular on the conflicted nature of Emperor Decius and the consoling but threatened community of the seven in the cave. Fear is also a dominant emotion as Malchus faces the cosmic trick of being out of time and the dangers of false accusation in the city. The incongruity of Malchus's experience also allows for humour, which the narrator revels in developing. To understand that fully it will be necessary to look closely at the multiple ironies and the storytelling technique presenting Malchus's trip to the marketplace.

---

87 On the uncanny and the affective quality of stories of time dislocation generally, and of this story in particular, see Carolyn Dinshaw, *How Soon Is Now? Medieval Texts, Amateur Readers, and the Queerness of Time* (Durham: Duke University Press, 2012), esp. 55–9.

88 Peter Clemoes, *Interactions of Thought and Language in Old English Poetry* (Cambridge: Cambridge University Press, 1995), 355. I would add the Life of Malchus and the Life of Mary of Egypt to the list. On the unusual playing up of emotion in the translation, see Hugh Magennis, "Style and Method in the Old English Version of the Legend of the Seven Sleepers," *English Studies* 66 (1985): 285–95.

89 Eileen A. Joy, "The Old English *Seven Sleepers*, Eros, and the Unincorporable Infinite of the Human Person," in *Anonymous Interpolations in Ælfric's "Lives of Saints"*, ed. Robin Norris (Kalamazoo, MI: Medieval Institute, 2011), 71–96, at 85, in the course of an exploration of the sense of self revealed by this story. See also R.M. Liuzza, "The Future Is a Foreign Country: The Legend of the Seven Sleepers and the Anglo-Saxon Sense of the Past," in *Medieval Science Fiction*, eds. Carl Kears and James Paz (King's College, London: Centre for Late Antique and Medieval Studies, 2016), 61–78, who stresses the affective quality of the temporal dislocation.

The narrator makes explicit the dramatic irony of the extended sleep: "Eall hit wæs him uncuð, ac hit wæs Gode ful cuð" ("It was completely unknown to them, but it was fully known to God," 236–7), and the humour begins as they wake up, asking, with a heavy dose of irony, what Malchus heard said about them yesterday evening in the town. Malchus replies, with much stress on the temporal markers: "Þæt ic eow *to æfen* ær sæde, þæt ilce ic eow *nu* secge, þæt mann us *toniht* ofer eall sohte…" ("What I said to you before *in the evening*, that I say to you again *now*, that people have sought for us everywhere *tonight*…," 409–10) The normal time sequence is thus emphatically called upon. Humour lies in this misalignment of perception, explored as Malchus pursues his task of buying bread and learning more news about how the group is being talked about. He is established as a fallible viewpoint as, with added irony, the group mildly berates him for his less-than-entirely-successful bread-buying of the day before:

> And bige us swa ðeah rumlicor todæg be hlafe þonne ðu gebohtest gyrstandæg, and bring us bet behlaf þonne ðu ær brohtest, for þon þe þa hlafas wæron swiðe eaðelice þe us gyrstanæfen comon.
> (425–8; Skeat LS 23, 467–70)

> And nevertheless buy us a more ample supply of bread today than you bought yesterday, and bring better bread than you have been bringing us, because the loaves were very scanty which came to us yesterday evening.

While this reinforces the perception that just one night has passed, it also characterizes Malchus, the companion and yet servant of the group, as a flawed and humble character.

With circumstantial detail rare in Old English, the narrative spells out Malchus's preparations and itemizes the coins he takes with him. His limitations are seen as he emerges from the cave and notices the worked stones that lie about all over:

> and he healfunga þæs wundrode, þeah na swiðe embe þæt ne smeade, ac he forht of þære dune mid micclan ege nyðereode.
> (448–9, Skeat LS 23, 491–2)

> and he half wondered about it, although he didn't think about it overmuch, but he, scared, went down from the hill with great fear.

The tautology (*forht … mid micclan ege*) plays up the emotion of fear that is controlling him and makes him not entirely rational in his not-very-inquisitive response to the oddly built and carved stones (*weor-cstanas*, 447) which lay about *ofer eall* ("all over," 447). The narrator is clearly playing with him (and with us the audience) as he wonderfully wonders *healfunga*, "halfingly." Malchus is far from perfect, so it is jarring when the narrator soon after, commenting on his ignorance about the fate of the emperor, describes him as "he ... se halga" ("he ... that saint," 451–2). This is a very fallible and human saint.

Wonder and audience bemusement continues to build as Malchus is amazed as he gazes upon the cross on the town gates and then as he hears the townsfolk invoking God. The narrator plays with repetition and balance in laying this out:

> and eac þa byrig he geseah eall on oþre wisan gewend on oþre heo ær wæs, and þa gebotla geond þa byrig eall getimbrode on oþre wisan on oþre hi ær wæron.
> (464–6, Skeat LS 23, 509–12)

> and he saw the town also all changed in other ways than the way it had been, and the buildings throughout the town all built up in other ways other than they had been.

The repetition creates an incantation that captures something of the hallucinatory air that is so appropriate here. The repeated *ær*, a word that means "before" or that moves the tense of the verb back, is a reminder to the audience of the temporal split, even as Malchus is thinking of a single night. The audience is in a position of superiority – we know built structures will have changed with the passage of 372 years – but we also see the world empathetically from the confused perspective of Malchus, with some squirming that he cannot comprehend the rupture in the continuum of time, even as our attention is captured by wondering when he will reach an impasse that forces him to see that rupture.

That does not come soon. Instead, he rationalizes:

> God ælmihtig, gebletsige me! Hwæþer hit furðon soð sy oððe hwæðer me on swæfne mæte eall þæt ic her geseo færlices wundres?
> (476–8; Skeat LS 23, 521–3)

> God Almighty bless me! Is it indeed true, or does all that I see here of such sudden wonder come to me in a dream?

In a tradition generally thin in direct speech, Malchus gives us direct speech even when alone as he reasons through his puzzlement with the not-unreasonable possibility that maybe he is dreaming.[90] After hearing the use of Christ's name, he puzzles further:

> And he stod þær stille ane lytle hwile and þohte on him sylfum hwæt his soðes wære.
> (496–7; Skeat LS 23, 543–5)

> And he stood still there for a little while and thought within himself what the truth of it might be.[91]

Malchus is thus caught in a moment of stasis and self-doubt uncharacteristic of a saint, if understandable in the face of the predicament this plot has placed him in.

Given that predicament, he makes a rational choice, namely to ask a passer-by for orientation, yet the form of the exchange again plays up his vulnerability, this time with an added touch of humour:

> Ða ofseah he ænne geongne man and eode him to þæm ylcan, and ongan hine axian, and cwæð, "La, wel gedo ðe, gode man. Ic wolde georne æt ðe gewitan þissere byrig rihtnaman, gif þu me woldest gewissigan."
> (498–500; Skeat LS 23, 545–8).

> Then he saw a young person and took himself to that same one, and began to ask him, and said, "Lo, fare you well, good person. I would like eagerly to know from you the correct name of this town, if you would inform me."

This has the ring of colloquial speech and is far wordier than the source:

> Et accurrit ad quendam iuuenem, et interrogauit eum dicens, "Quod est ciuitatis huius nomen?"
> (244–5)

> Then he went up to a certain young man and questioned him, saying, "What is the name of this city?"

---

90 The Old English expands the Latin (Magennis, *Legend*, lines 235–6): "Et cogitans in semetipso ... dicens, 'Ne somnium sit quod uideo'" ("He pondered in himself ... and said 'May this not be a dream which I see'").

91 The Latin has simply "Et cogitans in semetipso stetit" ("And he stood pondering in himself," Magennis, *Legend*, line 243).

While it is hard to read colloquial tone in a culture that preserves so little of it, there are clues here that all is not well. The wordiness suggests hesitation on Malchus's part as we get the verb of perception (*ofseah*, lacking equivalent in the source) as well as the reflexive verb of motion (*eode him*), the pleonistic repetition of the object (*þæm ylcan*), the verb of inquiry compounded through a temporal trick (*ongan … axian*) and another verb of speaking. What he says is polite, probably excessively so. "La, wel gedo ðe" ("Lo, fare you well"), is probably a polite phrase of initial engagement, with the second-person pronoun more in tune with number than politeness. Does the added opening interjection and closing vocative make it sound excessive? If that sentence isn't giving clues, the next one surely is. The Latin gives a straightforward form of question, *quod est…*, which could presumably be straightforwardly rendered, *hwæt bið…* but that would perhaps seem too abrupt to be polite in Old English. Malchus switches to a first-person statement, complete with periphrastic verb form (*ic wolde … gewitan*), but makes sure also to include the addressee (*æt ðe*). The additional unnecessary adverb of eagerness (*georne*) confirms a sense of verbal excess also apparent in the *riht-* of *rihtnaman*, part of a compound noun in Magennis's edition, alternatively apparent in the endingless adjective of Skeat's understanding (*riht naman*). A suspicion of excess is fully confirmed in the ending get-out clause ("gif þu me woldest gewissigan"), with its compound verb alliterating, grammatically rhyming, and thoroughly echoing the main verb (*gewitan*), allowing the interlocutor not to *gewissigan* him if he so chooses.

The sheer verbal excess here hints at excessive deference, and that is borne out by noticing the social status of the two actors involved. The interlocutor is marked only as a young person, characterized in his responding speech tag through the substantive *se geonga* ("the young one," 501). Malchus's own social standing is hard to pinpoint precisely. He has been established as the servant to the group of sleepers (*heora ðenigmann*, lines 217, 407), but he is also one of their companions (*se geþensuma* in the opening list, line 4, *heora geferena an*, line 407). Presumably he gets to do the provision- and information-gathering precisely because he is the most modest (and youngest?) of the group. That group, though, is of very high social standing as confidantes (*dyrlingas*, lines 70, 132, 247, 301) to the emperor (*hi him ær on hirede swiðe neahgangele wæron*, "they were before the very close attendants of him in the household," 116). The account on the lead tablets records the status of Maximianus ("wæs þæs burhgerefan sunu," "he was the son of the town reeve," 707–8; "filius prefecti," "son of the prefect in the Latin," 329), so even their servant must have significant social standing. It is hard to think that Malchus is not letting his social rank down in his deference to the young man, regardless of his social-status-to-be as a saint. His verbal obsequience here may be enough to make an attentive audience squirm – and laugh with embarrassment – as he breaks propriety by being too timid.

Such a characterization remains in play as things continue to go wrong. He decides to hurry back to his companions, conscious that he may be off the right path with his mind ("of þam rihtan wege mines ingeþances" lines 503–4),[92] but first he goes to the part of the market where people sell bread. Again we are at a level of circumstantial detail unusual in the Old English written record, even for this essential activity. Indeed, it is hard not to notice the symbolic overtones of acquiring the daily bread, an activity enjoined by the Lord's Prayer, but the activity also has practical utility, the more marked for a group hiding in a cave. Village life would presumably have involved households making their own bread, but bread purchase would have been commonplace in the towns coming into ever-better focus through the archaeological record of early medieval England.

The pleasure of this detailed account continues as the bread vendors have their suspicions aroused by the old coins.[93] The perceived antiquity of the coins creates further dramatic irony as the vendors suspect a trick which Malchus understands not at all. Malchus has assumed that his vulnerability is from the need to hide from Emperor Decius. The market vendors assume that his vulnerability arises from finding an old hoard of coins and being unwilling to share his good fortune. The scene of the clash of those two assumptions presents hints of the corruption and travails of everyday life in unusual detail, here played for laughs, before the responsible city officials, first the port-reeve and then the bishop, are introduced.[94] The Old English translation adds both psychological and practical realism to the scene. The narrative piles on the looking, gazing upon, and passing around from bench to bench of the suspect currency in an extended passage (lines 516–20) which has a significant effect of discomfiting Malchus even before the traders speak to express their suspicion that this young man has discovered an ancient gold hoard (lines 520–2, slightly expanding the Latin original, 252–4). The unheroic Malchus "cwacode and bifode" ("quaked and trembled," 524) and offers to let them keep the money if he can get away, a deal that is comic in its desperation and that gets more fully spelled out in the Old English than the source. Indeed, Malchus appears to be pursuing the verbal strategy of excessive deference again, referring to

---

92 I think this is grotesquely mistranslated by Skeat, *Lives of Saints*, who offers, "Now I was in the right way in my inward thought," lines 569–70 (521).

93 See Whitelock, "Numismatic Interest."

94 On the scene with special attention to the role of the port-reeve, see Cubitt, "Law-Book."

a group of marketeers who will soon manhandle him as "leof" (531) and (rather obsequiously) as "ealra manna betst" ("best of all people," 533), even as he suggests they "bruce ge ægþres ge penega ge hlafa" ("enjoy both the pennies and the bread," 533–4).[95]

It does not work, but the merchants make a further offer, which Malchus also fumbles. The merchants ask about him and the gold hoard, with the offer that if he tells the truth, as they are guessing it to be:

> we beoð þine geholan and ealne wæg þine midsprecan. Ne we nellað þe ameldian, ac hit eall stille lætan, þæt nan man ne þearf geaxian buton us sylfum. (540–2)
>
> we will be your protectors and your advocates in everything. We will not snitch on you, but let it all remain quiet, so that nobody need learn about it except for us ourselves.

This is clearly a nefarious offer, even if it is laid out with far more indirectness than the source's "Nuntia nobis, et erimus communes tecum et cooperiemus te" ("Tell us, and we will be in league with you and conceal you," 262–3). In Old English, apparently, it does not do to outright articulate a conspiracy of deception; instead, the would-be conspirators offer "protection" and "advocacy," and a promise of silence, without stating what they will be silent about. This is corruption through hints, which is potentially a realistic picture, even as such indirectness of language leads to the comedy of confusion. Malchus, obtuse to their offer, complains aloud about how bizarre the world is, whining with a strong degree of self-pity (544–50, in the source this is a briefer internal monologue, 264–5) and is finally silent in bafflement (555–6). These are cues to the market-sellers that he will not be a cooperative ally in ancient-treasure-sharing, whatever his reasons, and so they switch tack to making a spectacle of him.

As the crowd of spectators piles in, Malchus stays with his primary tactic, which finally gets explicitly articulated in an explanation lacking in his source: "and he þam folce æfre swa georne huru mid his eadmodnysse cweman wolde, þæt he þurh his fullan eadmodnysse hreowan sceolde" ("and he wanted to propitiate the people ever so eagerly indeed with his humility, so that he should arouse compassion through his great humility," 570–1). It continues not to work, and he is detained, bound, and a noose placed about his neck. At this stage, he (belatedly) bethinks of his kin, who are oddly

---

95 The Latin has the somewhat more confident sounding: "ecce habetis argenteos, et nolo panes" ("here, have the money, and I do not want the loaves," lines 259–60).

not to be seen in the crowd. He is led to the bishop and the town reeve, in front of whom the dramatic irony plays out as he is questioned about the coins, which he protests are legitimate. The town reeve grows angry as he interrogates him about his home and his parents, while the perplexed Malchus turns quiet, only to be saved by the more compassionate questioning of the bishop, under whose influence he finally provides enough detail to reveal the conundrum of the temporal shift. Bishop, town reeve, and people go with him to the cave, and the comedy of confusion is quickly cleared away as the explanatory lead tablets are found in sealed caskets and duly opened and read, thereby providing clarity and confirmation, resolving the confusions of the plot. Humour and circumstantial detail give way to wonder and celebration as Emperor Theodosius is contacted and duly arrives. The saints are acknowledging him when the text ends abruptly, presumably through a faulty exemplar, which fails to include any Old English equivalent to twenty-three lines of the Latin source.[96]

Engagement with the intimate experience of human beings within this world creates a storytelling style rife with possibilities for humour. Irony piles upon irony in the unfolding of the story, as real-world confusion from the clash of two time zones heightens until the turn back to piety with the radiance of the saints in the cave. Other ironies accumulate, too. Even as a translation of a Latin life first composed perhaps in the sixth century, drawing from a Greek original, describing events around the Mediterranean in the third and fifth centuries,[97] this work nevertheless provides the most detailed and realistic account of the quotidian activity of buying bread that survives in the Old English record. And if buying bread is not an inherently funny activity, the irony of the double-time perspective guarantees that this instance is, as the confusions pile up, centring on the fallible and at times feeble focalization of Malchus. The world of collaborative corruption deploys language realistically coded to mean one thing even as it says another, with the overtones of both audible to the audience. The real-world administration by the town reeve provides intriguing insight, if with increasing poignancy rather than humour, as the threats to Malchus start to feel potentially real, until the entry of the father-like bishop allows for a happy resolution. Within the surviving text, the energy of the story is

---

96 Lines 361–84. Wanley's transcript from the badly damaged MS Cotton Otho B. x preserves the closing doxology but still lacks most of this last part.

97 Once again, the numbers don't add up in a straightforward way. Decius ruled as emperor 249–51; Theodosius II, son of Archadius, ruled as Eastern Roman emperor 408–50, and the story is placed thirty-eight years into his reign (line, 323), i.e. 446 CE, a time frame that is not compatible with the reported passage of 372 years (lines 443–4 and 644–5).

heavily on the narrative elements, although the missing ending would pre-sumably have switched the terms of reference to a theological perspective.

The method of the narrative here is somewhat akin to the leisurely unfold-ing of the Life of Mary of Egypt or the heightened incidents of adventure in the Life of (the other) Malchus but presents layers of circumstantial detail and psychological acuity that make it feel closer to the form of romance which was to flourish in later medieval literature. In this way, it is closer to the Old English translation of *Apollonius of Tyre*, another narrative that allows the formation of episodes of humour in its psychological detail. The unusual style here creates a humane hagiographic romance, where the audience gets to laugh at Malchus's puzzlement and yet feel sympathy for his experience. Indeed, the humour in this case does the opposite of most Old English saints' lives, humanizing the saint and making him more of an endearing and fallible point of entry into the story, with whom the audience can empathize.

That such need not be the case can be seen in Ælfric's handling of the very same story. As Magennis says of Ælfric's hagiographic style in gen-eral, his approach is "one of studied unsensationalism, playing down the human feelings and sentiments of the characters as seen in the original, and sacrificing some of the dramatic heightening to which the story might lend itself."[98] That makes for a very different rendition of this story. Ælfric makes use of the Legend of the Seven Sleepers twice, retelling the story in an appendix to his homily on the Nativity of St James the Apostle, CH II.27, lines 182–231, and again in a late revision to his first series homily for the First Sunday after Easter (CH I.16, app. B2, lines 34–43). In Ælfric's handling, instead of bumbling vulnerability, the seven are "geleaffullan godes cempan" ("faithful champions of God," CH II.27, 187–8), whose story is told in overview without a narrative of confusions, without any reference to Malchus in the marketplace, without, indeed, direct speech or detailed narrative incident of any kind until the end, when the Emperor Theodosius speaks in joy to the saints and Maximianus (only the leader of the saints gets a speaking part) explains to Theodosius the theological point of their story, namely that Theodosius may believe in the resurrec-tion of the flesh (220–5). The theological point is unambiguously clear in a story that lacks any humour and is completely devoid of the human inter-est that is so present in the source and its anonymous translation.[99] The

---

98 Magennis, "Contrasting Features," 324.
99 See further Hugh Magennis, "St Mary of Egypt and Ælfric: Unlikely Bedfellows in Cotton Julius E.vii?" in *The Legend of Mary of Egypt in Medieval Insular Hagiography*, eds. Erich Poppe and Bianca Ross (Dublin: Four Courts Press, 1996), 99–112; Godden, *Commentary*, 575–82.

survival of the anonymous Seven Sleepers demonstrates a different model for pious storytelling, one which proceeds with humour.

Community of Laughers: A Broad Christian Audience

Monks in reformed monasteries probably enjoyed reading or listening to their saints' lives in Latin, but there are plenty of pious secular individuals who would have appreciated saints' lives in English. One example is named by Ælfric in his preface to *Lives of Saints*: Ealdorman Æthelweard and his son Æthelmær, for whose use he created this series.[100] Æthelweard was a powerful secular leader who ranked just below the king, serving as Ealdorman of the Western Provinces (975–c. 998), a position in which his son would later succeed him. Their patronage of Ælfric included commissioning the translation of Genesis and their own version of the sequence of *Catholic Homilies*, and they were instrumental in Ælfric's monastic appointments.[101] The translations they commissioned suggest that they were modelling their secular household on the pious reading practices of reformed monks, but in English rather than in Latin. If that is right, then Ælfric's *Lives of Saints* would have been recited in front of the broad audience that made up a high-ranking secular household, not just the ealdorman, but also his wife, their children and relatives, other household members associated with the martial and administrative business of running a region, all attended by servants, male and female, free and enslaved.[102] Such a broad audience would be brought together as a community of Christian faithful by listening to saints' lives as well as homilies and biblical translations and laughing together at the comic elements. That same broad household could have enjoyed other works included in this study, where humour is rarely incompatible with Christian learning, including the Old English riddles of the Exeter Book, proverbial wisdom, and poems like *Judith* and *Andreas*.[103]

Such a household provides one good setting for considering these works, but by no means the only possibility. In the Preface to the *Lives of*

100 Wilcox, *Ælfric's Prefaces*, Preface 5a, lines 28–31, Preface 5b, lines 3–6, and Preface 5d. See, further, my "Audience of Ælfric's *Lives of Saints*."

101 See Catherine Cubitt, "Ælfric's Lay Patrons," in *A Companion to Ælfric*, eds. Hugh Magennis and Mary Swan (Leiden: Brill, 2009), 165–92.

102 Ælfric himself comments how worldly kings must have many followers and serving-people, and the same would have been true for an ealdorman, Preface 5b, lines 21–4.

103 Robin Flower, in *The Exeter Book of Old English Poetry*, with introductory chapters by R.W. Chambers, Max Förster, and Robin Flower (London: Lund, Humphries, 1933), 87–90, speculates on Ealdorman Æthelweard as a potential commissioner of the Exeter Book.

Saints, Ælfric explicitly targets his collection at a broad-ranging group of the faithful, who can benefit from reading or listening to them, commenting how the lives will help those flagging in faith.[104] Ælfric anticipated multiple users for all of his works. In another occasional piece (the Letter to Sigeweard), he comments how the work was composed for one person but may serve to benefit many.[105] Ælfric's homily on Judith, briefly considered in chapter 6 above, is explicitly addressed to a female monastic audience enjoining chastity, even as the Letter to Sigeweard calls it an example to encourage men to defend their land against an invading army with weapons.[106] Ælfric, then, envisages his works reaching multiple audiences made up of different groups, secular as well as religious, women as well as men.

A pious female-led household would also provide a suitable audience for any of the lives considered in this chapter, and such a household might particularly appreciate the displays of female agency and the challenges to masculine privilege examined in this chapter. It is possible to reconstruct such high-status female-dominated audiences around the eleventh century. *Beowulf* hints at the significance of a queen through presenting Wealtheow's role in Hrothgar's court, and this role is codified in such gnomic poetry as *Maxims I* (lines 81–92).[107] Stafford puts flesh on the historical role of a queen as the overseer of an independent household by focusing on the queens who were literary patrons in the eleventh century, namely Queen Emma and Queen Edith.[108] The latter was a member of the powerful Anglo-Norman family of Earl Godwine, wife of King Edward (reigned 1042–66), and sister of the later King Harold (reigned 1066). In a passage about the queen's formation in the *Vita Ædwardi regis qui apud Westmonasterium requiescit* (*Life of King Edward who rests at Westminster*), there is commentary on Edith's education in the female monastery at Wilton: "She diligently read religious and secular books, and she herself excelled in the writing of prose and verse. She could speak the general language used in Gaul, as well as Danish and Irish, as though they were her mother-tongues; and in all these she attained not merely an average standard but perfection."[109] Queen Edith's elite female household that would have been

---

104 Preface 5a, lines 1–5, and 13–15.
105 Preface 8c, lines 1–2; cf. also the various uses made of the Letter to Wulfgeat, ed. Assmann 1.
106 See Clayton, "Ælfric's *Judith*."
107 See, further, Klein, *Ruling Women*.
108 Stafford, *Queen Emma and Queen Edith*, esp. chap. 5.
109 *Vita Ædwardi Regis*, I.2, trans. Barlow, 23. This passage is regrettably missing from the surviving manuscript but can be recreated by the evidence of a fourteenth-century account by Richard of Cirencester, which the work's editor thinks well reflects the missing original.

fully in tune with all the conventions of literature in Old English (as well as other languages) and so well suited for all the literary humour investigated in this study.[110]

Such a learned woman-centred household might have enjoyed the challenges of the Exeter Book riddles and easily commanded the level of linguistic acumen to enjoy the runic puzzles, as well as appreciating the philosophical conundrums of the wisdom literature. Stress on Edith's piety suggests that she and her household would have enjoyed listening to the saints' lives, and laughter at the comic moments would have brought together the multiple members of that household. Edith's skills at composing verse in addition to prose suggests a pleasure in engaging with the formal aspects of heightened language, making her receptive to laughing at the incongruous excess of the rhymes or the examples of parody that overplay existing conventions investigated in chapters 2 and 5.

Edith's household also provides grounding for a mixed-sex elite audience, since Stafford shows how her household and that of the king's court often merged. That combined group is an appealing audience for a poem like *Beowulf* and the martial riddles. Women in such a courtly audience might have enjoyed attending to the politesse revealed in the poem even as male warriors in training within the royal court may have dwelt on the action of the story line. That mixed household would provide a powerful setting for the weapon-centred riddles, with their ambivalent celebration of martial values alongside laughter at masculine braggadocio. The competing perspectives in such a household might best come together in shared appreciation of religious-secular poems like *Judith* and *Andreas* and of secular-religious prose like the extended saints' lives of this chapter. Entertaining narratives such as the Life of Mary of Egypt, the Life of Malchus, or the Legend of the Seven Sleepers would have broad appeal, holding the attention of many audiences, while also serving a readily licensed doctrinal purpose.

---

110 The implications of such learning in such a powerful woman for creating a multilingual literary community is brilliantly drawn out in Elizabeth M. Tyler, *England in Europe: English Royal Women and Literary Patronage, c. 1000–c. 1150* (Toronto: University of Toronto Press, 2017).

Chapter Eight

Relishing Romance: Horror and Happiness in *Apollonius of Tyre*

One recurring use made of humour throughout this study is to empower the disempowered. In addition to satire aimed at the privileged, a kind of gentle humour can serve to valorize the perspective and actions of the less privileged, as when the befuddlement of Malchus in The Legend of the Seven Sleepers makes him an object both of laughter and of sympathy. Controlling the creation of the humour can also empower the disempowered, as with the initial actions of Euphrosyne or the late-life actions of Mary of Egypt. One last example will illustrate more fully such empowerment through humour: the control exercised by a woman in the courtship scenes of *Apollonius of Tyre*.

As a species of romance, this is a narrative form that encourages attentive reading for social cues, a style of reading that has been pursued already here in relation to *Beowulf* and the saints' lives. *Apollonius of Tyre* presents a narrative both of trauma and of comedy, rich in riddling throughout. It shows that some riddles are far from funny, even as others are distinctly so, as can be seen in a contrasting pair of riddles about incest, a humorous one from the Exeter Book and one of deadly seriousness from *Apollonius of Tyre*.

Riddles of Incest

A riddle about incest can be a short exercise in the humour of paradox, as it is in Riddle 46 of the Exeter Book riddles, or a totally unfunny engagement with the horror of coercion and rape, as it is in the Old English *Apollonius of Tyre*. I will begin this chapter with the comic version:

Wer sæt æt wine   mid his wifum twam
ond his twegen suno   ond his twa dohtor,
swase gesweostor,   ond hyra suno twegen,

freolico frumbearn;   fæder wæs þær inne
þara æþelinga   æghwæðres mid,
eam ond nefa.   Ealra wæron fife
eorla ond idesa   insittendra.
(Riddle 46)

A man sat at wine-drinking with his two wives
and his two sons and his two daughters,
beloved sisters, and their two sons,
noble first-born children; the father of each
of those princes was in there alongside,
uncle and nephew. In all there were five
men and women sitting within.

This is a riddle rich in paradoxes, both arithmetical and social. How can this profusion of relations come about with just five people? This is a numbers game in the riddling world where 2 + 2 does not necessarily = 4.[1] In any family following conventional rules of exogamy there would need to be considerably more individuals to incorporate so many different relationships. There is a clear breach either of the rules of counting or of the norms of permissible marriage and kinship relationships to arrive at such a condensed number. The riddle quickly cues that this is not a family following regular rules of Christian marriage since the first line sets the man up with one more than the licit number of living wives. That encourages an audience to jettison conventional laws of marriage in working on a solution, with a necessary breaking of taboo that could either shock or amuse. Even then, the relationship web seems hard to pare down to just five individuals, so the riddle presents a puzzle that can only be solved by working out the most economical familial grouping possible. The difficulty of the puzzle probably helps override any response of shock. Presented as an abstract gaming challenge, and with no suggestions of trauma, humour is likely to win over horror as a response to the imagined set-up.

In addition, an audience knowledgeable about Christian stories will quickly spot a specific tableau that fits the description. The answer depends on a widely known biblical story: that of Lot and his two daughters, who procreate with their father in his cups (hinted at by the setting *æt wine*) as an act of charity to repopulate the world when they believe themselves to be

---

1 See Dieter Bitterli, *Say What I am Called: The Old English Riddles of the Exeter Book and the Anglo-Latin Riddle Tradition* (Toronto: University of Toronto Press, 2009), chap. 3, on numerical riddles, and the discussion of Riddle 86 in chap. 5 above.

the only people left living (Genesis 19: 30–8). The riddler pushes the idea to its limit by pondering all of the relationships in the household that results. The two mothers are sisters to each other and both daughters of their sexual partner, while the child of each is a first-born son and each of those children are also sons of the patriarch and each is both uncle and nephew to the other. The answer is conceptually satisfying as it imagines the minimum number of people for such a maximal pile up of relationships. It is also emotionally unthreatening because the incest that is necessary to make the numbers work is licit since it is contained in an Old Testament narrative (the "old law," where different rules apply from those of the present age, as Ælfric emphasized) and because of the high-minded and charitable intentions of this patriarch and his daughters, who initiate the encounter. The underlying paradox is therefore funny, as it is both highly incongruous and yet also benign.

A similar riddle at the start of *Apollonius of Tyre* is distinctly not funny. "I seek, and cannot find, my father, my mother's husband, my wife's daughter" is the riddle (*þone rædels*) posed by Antiochus at the start of *Apollonius of Tyre*, a riddle posed by a tyrant to hide and yet reveal the unspeakable practice of father–daughter incest, and perhaps designed to warn off any potential suitor smart enough to solve the riddle and see the implications of brute power. The Old English *Apollonius of Tyre* gives the text in both Latin and Old English:

"Quaero patrem meum, meae matris virum, uxoris meae filiam nec invenio." Þæt is on englisc: "Ic sece minne fæder, mynre modor wer, mines wifes dohtor and ic ne finde."
(*Apollonius of Tyre*, chap. 4, 6/12–15)[2]

It is not a very good riddle in either language, since the first two clauses give the perspective of the daughter, whereas the third clause switches to the perspective of the father, though perhaps that merging is part of the point.[3] Even if the situation presents incongruity through doubled roles,

---

2 Peter Goolden, ed., *The Old English "Apollonius of Tyre"* (Oxford: Oxford University Press, 1958), who also includes a reconstructed Latin source; citation by page/line number. There is a convenient translation in Elaine Treharne, ed., *Old and Middle English: An Anthology* (Oxford: Blackwell, 2000), 234–53.

3 It is preceded by another part that is even worse as a riddle, although here the Latin does have word play that the Old English misses: "I suffer guilt/guiltily, I use/enjoy the flesh of the mother" (6/10–12) is introduced in the text as *þone rædels* ("the riddle," 6/10), even though it is more a thinly coded statement of the practice of incest than a true riddle. Apollonius solves the riddle but does not take what might be a hint in the badness of the riddle not to say the answer.

it fails to be humorous because the violation of structures is not benign. Instead, the narrator builds up an audience response of shock and repulsion by stressing the emotion of the raped daughter, given in the first person in a dialogue with her foster-mother-nurse. This is an example of incongruity that alienates an audience enough to block any possibility of a humour response.

It is thematically and tonally appropriate that the reward for solving this riddle is death, as Apollonius discovers when he does just that. And yet Apollonius is not killed, and this exceedingly unfunny riddle introduces a tale full of riddles, many of which are funny. The opening riddle lays bare the breaking of a taboo, and after that characters and audience are primed to be hyper-vigilant in a story where the rules of normality are never entirely clear. The result is a comic romance where every act or speech is a riddle requiring interpretation in a way that makes an audience particularly alive to seeing irony, doubleness, and the potential for humour, as the story pushes to a happy ending in a world where relationships may or may not be what they seem.

Even as *Andreas* hints at a poetic genre of hagiographic romance which has occasional scope for humour (as discussed in chapter 5) and the longer and more fleshed-out saints' lives like the anonymous translations of Mary of Egypt, the Life of Malchus, and the Legend of the Seven Sleepers show the potential for humour in the human interest of hagiographic romance (as seen in chapter 7), *Apollonius of Tyre* is one work in Old English where the human interest of the story and the tone of wondrous exploration provide more clear-cut scope for humour. To give a sense of this, I will focus on one comic incident where the humour empowers the otherwise disempowered: the indirection whereby the king's daughter wins for herself the male lead.

Apollonius of Tyre

There is biblical precedent for romance-like stories of adventure, misadventure, reversal, trickery, and occasional incongruity seen not just in *Judith* (analysed in chapter 5 above), but also in *The Story of Joseph* within the Book of Genesis, which tells of Joseph's near murder by his brothers, his abduction, rise to power, imprisonment on false sexual charges, release and rise to greater power, governorship of a new nation, and final reconciliation with brothers and father (Genesis, chapters 37–50). An Old English translation of that story survives in MS Cambridge, Corpus Christi College 201, added in close proximity to the Old English *Apollonius of*

Tyre, a work that it partly matches.[4] There is, though, a striking contrast of tone. The predominant gesture in *The Story of Joseph* is weeping, which reflects the psychological pain and trauma of a narrative of favouritism, attempted fratricide, and revenge.[5] *Apollonius of Tyre*, on the other hand, works through traumatic plot elements to arrive at a surprising happy conclusion, which makes the story more open to reading for humour, despite the traumatic opening.

An Old English translation of a probably sixth-century Latin text that is presumably a translation of a now-lost Greek original, the Old English *Apollonius of Tyre* is a romance (the genre) featuring a romance (the squishy feeling of amour between young people and the manoeuvres it leads to) before either are established in the English literary tradition.[6] It tells the adventures of the eponymous hero, here described as an *ealdorman* (the Old English term for a regional leader second only to the king), who first turns up in Antioch to attempt to win the daughter of the king, Antiochus. By the rules of the challenge, anyone who can solve the riddle posed by the king will win the king's daughter, but failure to answer will earn death for the questing suitor. Adventures follow as Apollonius escapes Antiochus's assassin, is shipwrecked on the shore of Pentapolis, where he loses all he has but then earns favour from King Arcestrates and that king's daughter, Arcestrate, who wins him first as her tutor, then as her husband. The Old English text is lacking a substantial section due to the loss of a quire from the manuscript which would continue with the story of Arcestrate's apparent death in childbirth on a ship and her body cast off to sea in a chest; a depressed Apollonius wandering for fourteen

4 See Daniel Anlezark, "Reading 'The Story of Joseph' in MS Cambridge, Corpus Christi College 201," in *The Power of Words*, eds. Hugh Magennis and Mary Swan (Leiden: Brill, 2009), 61–94; Benjamin C. Withers, *The Illustrated Old English Hexateuch, Cotton Claudius B. iv: The Frontier of Seeing and Reading in Anglo-Saxon England* (Toronto: University of Toronto Press, 2007), chap. 7; Mark Atherton, "Cambridge, Corpus Christi College 201 as a Mirror for a Prince: *Apollonius of Tyre*, Archbishop Wulfstan and King Cnut," *English Studies* 97 (2016): 451–72.

5 As I work through in "A Place to Weep: Joseph in the Beer-Room and Anglo-Saxon Gestures of Emotion," in *Saints and Scholars: New Perspectives on Anglo-Saxon Literature and Culture in Honour of Hugh Magennis*, ed. Stuart McWilliams (Cambridge: Brewer, 2012), 14–32.

6 See Elizabeth Archibald, *Apollonius of Tyre: Medieval and Renaissance Themes and Variations* (Cambridge: Boydell, 1991) on all aspects of the tradition. On the Old English as romance, see Mercedes Salvador-Bello, "The Old English *Apollonius of Tyre* in the Light of Early Romance Tradition: An Assessmnent of Its Plot and Characterization in Relation to Marie de France's *Eliduc*," *English Studies* 93 (2012): 749–74.

years in Egypt; the daughter consigned to the care of a couple in Thar-sus who, after bringing her up, attempt to kill her but are foiled as she is snatched away by pirates and sold to a brothel, where she nevertheless remains chaste; a final meeting of daughter with father in a surprise recon-ciliation scene featuring much riddle telling; and the movement of father and daughter to the temple of Diana at Ephesus, where the chief priest-ess proves to be Arcestrate, who was alive after all. At this point the Old English version resumes, as Apollonius reveals his story unknowingly to Arcestrate, the family is reunited, and Apollonius metes out justice to the second-tier characters.

The clash between a spirit of humour surrounding Apollonius and the trauma of Antiochus's court is established early. The whole plot is initiated by King Antiochus's riddle about incest, examined above, which is contextualized through the daughter's feelings of eliminated identity, described in chilling detail (chaps. 1–3), where she continues in a fractured state of dissociation, as does the household, among whom Antiochus's act is famed even as it is officially suppressed. In such a world, where every utterance is a riddle and all interpretation is fraught, the bleak tone gets relieved as well as emphasized through a certain dark humour as Apollonius enters for the challenge. Antiochus speaks some-what pompously, asking if he knows the terms of seeking his daugh-ter ("canst ðu þone dom mynra dohtor gifta," "do you know the *dom* for the gift of my daughter?", 6/8). *Dom*, here translating *condicionem* "condition," is a weighty word in Old English, conjuring up law and law process, but also glory (to be achieved with a happy outcome?), and also judgment, namely the decapitation promised by Antiochus for a wrong guess. The weight of the word makes Apollonius's pithy response both witty and defiant: "Ic can þone dom and ic hine at þam geate seah" ("I know the *dom* and I saw him/it at the gate," 6/8–9) where, we have been told, the heads of past would-be suitors are on display. Such an economical response alludes to the grizzly fate of a failed riddle solver without spelling it out and establishes Apollonius's insouciance in the face of the threat in a manner similar to the heroic humour considered above in chapter 4. The clean-living hero occupies a world presented with a markedly different tone from the trauma of the tyrannical rapist father figure.

And so, later in the story, it is the comic tone of Apollonius that pre-vails as the narrator displays a much healthier father–daughter relation-ship, even though Apollonius himself proves to be somewhat obtuse as the daughter takes comic control of the courtship. After his shipwreck, Apol-lonius proceeds into the city of Pentapolis, where he, like the audience, is forced to interpret the norms and the potential of the bath-house and

Greek-style gaming practices at the bath.[7] Free of the constraints to dress a part, Apollonius can reveal his unvarnished worth to King Arcestrates, both in the ball game and in a further activity that flummoxes the Old English translator: anointing and massaging the king's person in the Latin but, apparently, spinning the top in the Old English.[8] The shipwrecked man is cultivated by the king, who brings him to the court and the company of his daughter.

From this point on, the narrative revels in a courtship initiated by that daughter, Arcestrate. Arcestrate's stature is slightly diminished in the Old English, as Riedinger has argued,[9] but even so the daughter's control is striking. Arcestrate matches the plotting of Euphrosyne in the key scene from her life, achieving her ends without appearing to do so and flirting with the object of her desire. Flirting involves advancing the action through indirection with endless opportunities for embarrassment, which turns out to be a scenario rich in potential for sympathetic humour. Arcestrate manipulates the men around her with consummate skill in a reversal of the daughter's powerlessness at Antioch.

Nothing is straightforward, and doubled senses are legion. When the king sees that his daughter's questioning has renewed Apollonius's sorrows and led the guest to weep, he enjoins her "þæt þu gife him swa hwæt swa ðu wille" ("that you give him whatsoever you want," 24/18–19). Her response is double-coded: "Apolloni, soðlice þu eart ure" ("Apollonius, truly you are ours," 24/21). On the surface, this is presumably a statement that while Apollonius may be the shipwrecked man, he is being absorbed

---

7 See, in particular, David Townsend, "The Naked Truth of the King's Affection in the Old English *Apollonius of Tyre*," *Journal of Medieval and Early Modern Studies* 34, no. 1 (2004): 173–95, for a brilliant reading of the interpretive challenges here.

8 "He swang þone top mid swa micelre swiftnesse þæt se cyngc wæs geþuht swilce he of ylde to iuguðe gewænd wære" ("he swung the top with such great swiftness that the king considered he was turned from age to youth," 20/16–18); see Joseph McGowan, "The Old English *Apollonius of Tyre* 19," *The Explicator* 49 (1991): 74–5. In a revisionist reading, William Sayers, "*Þoðer* and *Top* in the Old English *Apollonius of Tyre*," *N&Q* 56 (2009): 12–14, sees the activity as striking the top of the ball from the ball game, which may be rationally more probable but is still a spectacular mistranslation of the Latin.

9 Anita Riedinger, "The Englishing of Arcestrate: Woman in *Apollonius of Tyre*," in *New Readings on Women in Old English Literature*, eds. Helen Damico and Alexandra Hennessey Olsen (Bloomington: Indiana University Press, 1990), 292–306, at 297 shows, for example, that Apollonius is named fifty-one times in the love scene in the Old English translation, eleven times more than in the source, whereas Arcestrate is not named once in this part, which is the same as in the source. Riedinger shows that, with the exception of her power in the Temple of Diana towards the end, Arcestrate is made "slightly less able and important"; but contrast Salvador-Bello, "Early Romance Tradition."

into the Pentapolis royal household, becoming one of the group, as she proceeds to give him riches and servants that imply status. Less decorously, this is also a brazen statement of desire and of intention, which will be borne out by the subsequent scenes.

The explicit falling in love, so uncharacteristic of Old English literature, occurs after Apollonius has made a surprise performance in the guise of Apollo singing and playing the harp and revealing other unnamed performance skills (chap. 16):

> Soðlice mid þy þe þæs cynges dohtor geseah þæt Apollonius on eallum godum cræftum swa wel wæs getogen, þa gefeol hyre mod on his lufe.
> (chap. 17, 26/20–2)

> Truly, when the king's daughter saw that Apollonius was so well accomplished in all good skills, then her mind/spirit fell in love with him.

The statement has been pointed to by many critics as the first falling in love in English.[10] Arcestrate rewards Apollonius's performance handsomely, designating him, ahead of the plot, as "minum lareowe" ("my teacher," 28/1). She deflects responsibility, describing the gifts as "be mines fæder leafe" ("by my father's leave," 26/27–8), even as she controls the details. There is emphasis that the gifts are given in public, "beforan minum freondum" ("in front of my friends," 28/2), and they earn great praise from all who see them. As Apollonius prepares to move "secan ure gesthus" ("to seek out our guest-house," 28/10), Arcestrate is loath to see him go:

> Ða adred þæt mæden þæt heo næfre eft Apollonium ne gesawe swa raðe swa heo wolde.
> (28/11–13)

> Then the maiden feared that she would never again see Apollonius as quickly as she wanted.

The very phrasing here plays at presenting the impatience of the young lover with sympathetic comedy since the opening clause establishes a fearful prospect – that the maiden would never again (*næfre eft*) see Apollonius – that is significantly less fearful in light of the delayed qualifying clause – as quickly as she wanted. How quickly is that? Apparently her passion will

---

10 See, for example, Carla Morini, "The First English Love Romance Without 'Love'! The Old English *Apollonius of Tyre*," *SELIM* 12 (2003–4): 109–25.

not brook Apollonius's departure to a guest quarter somewhere within the town. Instead, she exerts her power while maintaining decorum by influencing her father without expressing the impatience of her passion:

Ðu goda cyningc, licað ðe wel þæt Apollonius þe þurh us todæg gegodod is þus heonon fare, and cuman yfele men and bereafian hine?
(28/13–15)

Good king, is it pleasing to you that Apollonius, who today is so enriched by us may travel away from here, and evil men may come and rob him?

Her attribution of causality for the gift giving, *þurh us*, "through us," maintains decorum with its nod to her father's authority even as it also claims her own part. Her fear of robbery may or may not be justified, but we know that this is not her motivation and that language does not straightforwardly say what it means. An audience is likely to smile at the dualities, while feeling sympathy for the ingenuity of the controlling daughter.

Chapter 18 continues showing Arcestrate's deployment of indirect power in ways unparalleled in Old English, as she persuades her father to make Apollonius her teacher. The king duly commissions Apollonius, commenting with chiastic irony that if Apollonius complies: "swa hwæt swa ðu on sæ forlure ic ðe þæt on lande gestaðelige" ("whatsoever you have lost at sea, I will restore that for you on land," 30/3–4). That Arcestrates is playing a part is apparent in his reaction to the three noble and learned men who are long-time suitors of his daughter, whom he meets while in company with Apollonius (chap. 19). He immediately *smercode* ("smiled," but also possibly "smirked," 30/12) as the three greet him with one voice and teases them with a question of why they speak in unison. When they request clarification about which one he will adopt as son-in-law, he defers to his daughter's wishes while suggesting, with a further joke, that they have not chosen a good time since his daughter is very busy "ymbe hyre leornunga" ("about her studies," 30/20–1). The practicalities of time are a little puzzling since we have been told that mere hours have passed since Arcestrates asked Apollonius to teach his daughter, and since that time we have seen the father step out hand in hand with the would-be tutor, but presumably mere clock time is not really relevant within the chronotope of romance and instead we the audience are expected to revel in the irony. The king has each suitor write his name and proposed *morgengifu*, the traditional gift that gets to be in the control of the bride, in a letter, which the king seals and entrusts to Apollonius to give to Arcestrate so that she can make her choice.

Tone becomes yet harder to decipher in the next chapter (chap. 20). Apollonius takes the letters to Arcestrate in the royal hall (*ðare cynelican healle*, 30/28–9), whereas in the Latin he takes them to her bed chamber (*cubiculum*, 31/29). It looks like the Old English translator is preserving decorum and lowering the emotional temperature of the scene in the choice of setting, but not in the content. The bedroom context would make more sense for the following exchange in which in the Latin Arcestrate teasingly asks *amores suos* ("her lover," 31/28, also omitted in the Old English) why he is entering her bed chamber alone, to which he responds by addressing her (teasingly or seriously?) *Domina, nondum mulier mala* ("oh, lady, not yet a bad [i.e. sexualized] woman," 31/29–30), an apostrophe that presumably justifies his presumption in entering such a space. In the Old English, her question of "Teacher, why do you walk alone?" (30/30) is harder to understand, if still potentially teasing (presumably the range of options are: why aren't you with the servants I gave you? Or, why aren't you with my father like you were when you left? Or, why don't you have a mate to go by your side [by the way, I'm available]?). Apollonius's response closely translates the Latin but comes off differently in this different context: "Hlæfdige, næs git yfel wif" ("Lady, not at all yet evil [as in sexualized] woman," 30/30–1). That response has puzzled critics in readings of the narrative but, assuming that *yfel wif* signals a sexualized sense of *wif* makes sense of the scene, but significantly escalates the banter, since it suggests that Apollonius understood Arcestrate's question in the third and most flirtatious sense. His strait-laced continuation, giving her the letters and commanding her to read, suggests that Apollonius is not entering into the spirit of flirtation that she has created. At this point a sensitive audience might be laughing in a cringing manner at the overly decorous Apollonius in a scene that is starting to sound like the courting in Chaucer's *Troilus and Criseyde*.

On reading the letters and not finding the name she wants, Arcestrate continues her more or less direct flirtation with an explicit question: "Lareow, ne ofþingð hit ðe gif ic þus wer geceose? ("Teacher, would it not cause you regret if I thus chose a husband?", 32/2–3). The clueless Apollonius remains a target of a perceptive audience's mirth as he interprets this as a question about process rather than outcome, expressing no regret but rather a modicum of pride in her literacy in hoping that she chooses to respond in writing. This is the humour of embarrassment so readily available in a courtship scene in which one of the players is missing the cues. Arcestrate's response is clearly poignant: "Eala lareow, gif ðu me lufodest, þu hit besorgodest" ("Oh, teacher, if you had loved me, you would have regretted it/you would have sorrowed over it," 32/7). Nevertheless, she continues to her purpose by writing her response in a further letter which

Apollonius carries to Arcestrates. Even though we watch her seal the letter, its content is not hidden from us, the audience, witnessing the daughter establishing that the choice is hers and then choosing "þone forlidenan man" ("the shipwrecked man," 32/12–13), and explaining away her forwardness as enabled by the medium, but there is tension from the dramatic irony that that content is not witnessed by Apollonius, who remains cringingly unaware.

Within the riddling context of this romance, the daughter's phrasing is pretty clear – "the shipwrecked man" has, after all, become definitional of Apollonius – but it still manages to cause comic confusion among the men who receive it. Arcestrates is clueless (or teasing) enough to ask of the three suitors "which of you is a shipwrecked man" (chap. 21, 32/20), and one of them is quick-witted and opportunistic enough to volunteer for the role ("Ic eom forliden," "I am shipwrecked," 32/21), until slapped down by one of his rivals in the language of comic insult ("Swiga ðu; adl þe fornime þæt þu ne beo hal ne gesund. Mid me þu boccræft leornodest and ðu næfre buton þare ceastre geate fram me ne cume. Hwar gefore ðu forlidennesse?" "Shut up, you; old age has addled you so that you are not right in your mind [or may old age take you so that you are not well or healthy]. You have studied learning with me and you have never come outside the gates of the city without me. Where have you suffered shipwreck?", 32/22–4). Arcestrates (obtuse or knowing?) then gives the letter to Apollonius with the idea that one who was present when it was written may better be able to understand it.

And so, and at last, Apollonius gets the message. The wording of the letter presents no puzzle to him; instead it is his response which re-establishes the riddle of reading the body even as, once again, it is not a difficult code. As he comes to understand that he is loved by the maiden, Apollonius does what lovers caught unawares habitually do, giving off an unwilled sign of his dawning understanding: "his andwlita eal areodode" ("his face went all red," 32/30, which is more intensive than the source's *erubuit*, 33/22, in its increased word count, intensifying *eal*, and gaze-directing statement of the seat of the blush on *his andwlita*).[11] Arcestrates remains harder to read. On seeing the blush, he takes Apollonius's hand, turns him a little away from the suitors, and asks if he knows the shipwrecked man – all of which could be the action of somebody who understands the significance of the

---

11 See my "An Embarrassment of Clues: Interpreting Anglo-Saxon Blushes," in *Anglo-Saxon Emotions: Reading the Heart in Old English Literature, Language and Culture*, eds. Alice Jorgensen, Frances McCormack, and Jonathan Wilcox (Farnham: Ashgate, 2015), 91–107, on blushing in Old English.

moment, or not. Apollonius responds with words which inarticulately do
the work of the next stage of a medieval courtship scene, namely securing
the father's consent: "Ðu goda cyning, gif þin willa bið, ic hine wat" ("Oh,
you good king, if it is your will, I know him," 34/1). His dissociation from
self in referencing himself in the third person is belied by the more articulate response of his countenance, which is now given in full force:

> Ða geseah se cyngc þæt Apollonius mid rosan rude wæs eal oferbræded, þa
> ongeat he þone cwyde.
> (34/2–3)

> When the king saw that Apollonius was completely overspread with a rosy red,
> then he understood the utterance.

Further speech from Apollonius is unnecessary, as his blush establishes his
identity as the object of romantic desire, and Arcestrates puts him at his
ease by clarifying that his daughter's desire is his desire and returning to
the official suitors to clarify to them that this is, indeed, not a suitable time
to ask for his daughter as she is so engaged in her studies. The whole scene
has progressed displaying heightened sensitivities and a certain playfulness
basked in an awkward but happy glow of emotion.

In the following chapter (chap. 22), Arcestrates in person seeks confirmation from his daughter, who first repeats the riddling formulation
("Ic lufige þone forlidenan man," "I love the shipwrecked man," 34/18)
but then becomes straightforwardly explicit ("Apollonium ic wille, minne
lareow," "I desire Apollonius, my teacher," 34/19–20). Arcestrates is in the
process of playing on the earlier offer to make good on whatever Apollonius lost at sea (34/26–30) when the Old English text breaks off, with the
quire missing from the manuscript. When it resumes for a final three pages
of the story, Apollonius provides a retrospective account of the courtship
that is far more dully conventional than the Arcestrate-initiated wooing
we have seen in the story. In the action presented, control through indirection, coded language, and a comedy of embarrassment all make this an
appealingly, and sympathetically, funny courtship.

Humour within *Apollonius of Tyre*, then, derives from many of the
devices seen throughout this study – irony, indirection, deferral, and delay –
but in this case their usage is amped up by such a clear tone of comic courtship, where private affairs are advanced in public through coded language,
and where there is a constant risk of embarrassment for the characters
who fail to read the clues. Riddles abound, and even as the opening riddle
is marked off as distinctly not funny, operating in a domain where outrage and horror flood any possible humour response, subsequent riddles
contribute to the comic tone, encouraging laughter of sympathy with the

characters or humane laughter of superiority at their understandable fol
lies. The human interest matches the more leisurely and humane elements
of the anonymous saints' lives with enough verve to provide an appropriate climax and end point for this study in a work that, for all its early
sources, anticipates traditions of literature of the High Middle Ages.

Community of Laughers: Audiences All Over

For all its casual references to God and Christian values, *Apollonius of Tyre*
is a secular rather than a religious tale, set in the days of the old religion
of the Roman Empire. It survives added into MS CCCC 201, a collection
primarily comprising homiletic and legislative writings associated with the
reforming (and strikingly earnest) Archbishop Wulfstan. This is a context that has earned much commentary from modern critics, who have
ingeniously explained the apparent contradiction of a pagan romance in
such an edifying Christian collection by seeing the work as suitable for
educating rising monk-bishops, for illustrating the reformers' concerns
over marriage and sexual stability, or for narrativizing the responsibili-
ties of law and law-making.[12] The surviving manuscript suggests the work
was appreciated, then, in the intellectual foment of clerical training in the
power-house of late tenth- or early eleventh-century Winchester.

Other audiences would also be likely to appreciate this tale. The story
operates in a courtly world and would appeal to an audience that enjoyed
the courtly elements of *Beowulf*. The prominence given to the role of the
young female protagonist and her display of effective indirect power suggests appeal for an audience of women, such as the household of Queen
Edith investigated in the previous chapter. Anlezark has argued that the collection in CCCC 201 may have been assembled for an elite female monastic audience, such as that of Nunnaminster, Winchester, which represents
a crossover between royal and monastic households with its inclusion of
royal nuns.[13] Women were likely present in many of the performance contexts imagined throughout this study, participating in ecclesiastical life in
female monasteries, participating in the household of nobles, assembled
in church, or listening to tales as part of the workforce. Laughing with

---

12 See Patrick Wormald, *The Making of English Law: King Alfred to the Twelfth Century;
    Vol. 1: Legislation and Its Limits* (Oxford: Blackwell, 1999), 206–10, and 330–66;
    Morini, "Love"; Anlezark, "Reading"; Melanie Heyworth, "Apollonius of Tyre in Its
    Manuscript Context: An Issue of Marriage," *Philological Quarterly* 86 (2007): 1–26;
    Atherton, "Mirror."

13 Anlezark, "Reading," 93–4.

the female protagonist helps craft a community of all those who proceed through indirection, be they women or the non-elite male audiences, the servants and slaves in a household, the agricultural workers on a monastic estate or the group assembled at the ale house. Humour, like fiction, has the power to entertain broadly.

Conclusion

Humour is in evidence, then, throughout much Old English literature, even if it is unlikely that anyone reading the surviving corpus will suffer the fate imagined for those who consume the plant *clufþunge* ("celery-leaved crowfoot") in one manuscript of the Old English *Herbarium*:

> swa hwylc man swa þas wyrte fæstende þigð, hlihhende he ðæt lif forlæteð.
> (DeVriend 1984: 52)

> whatever person partakes of this herb fasting, that one will give up this life laughing.[1]

Few die laughing from partaking of Old English literature, but I hope this study has suggested that moments of humour are present throughout the corpus and worth attending to.

What difference does it make to bring such a focus to bear? First and foremost, it removes the expectation for high seriousness that too dolorous a sense of the corpus otherwise imposes. That matters for allowing works to be appreciated for their comic effects. It encourages engaging with some otherwise neglected texts as well as reading well-recognized works in a new way, and so has potential for revitalizing engagement with this corpus of literature. The doubleness that a moment of humour depends upon brings fresh attention to the frame that is surreptitiously and yet firmly

---

1 The reading of MS London, BL, Cotton Vitellius C. iii, where MS BL, Harley 2258B has the less striking "he byð sona unhal" ("that person will immediately be unwell"). Funnily, I have made a variant of this joke in print before; see my "Anglo-Saxon Literary Humor: Towards a Taxonomy," *Thalia: Studies in Literary Humor* 14, nos. 1–2 (1994): 9–20, at 18.

present until it is undercut by the flash of the moment of funniness. The frameworks so illuminated (and flouted) are both the language-based formal devices of literature and the social rules and expectations of life in the world, both of which become more apparent by attending to their violation through comic inversion.

Riddles provide the backbone for this study of humour in Old English literature, showing incongruity that is both conceptual and linguistic. A bagpipe as a large upside-down bird or a large bird as a cumbersome musical instrument (in Riddle 31) is an audacious duality, for example, with just enough common links between the two ideas for them to be held in the mind simultaneously and yet clashing enough – in an attention-grabbing but non-threatening way – to generate a comic jolt as one is reanalysed as the other. The humour of such incongruity is compounded by tricks of language. A rune that is deployed as both a letter and a word is funny for the frame-breaking duality that makes language itself both the medium of the message and the object of attention. Puns work in similar ways, encouraging dualities at a micro level. Through such effects, alternative possibilities are rapidly embraced and discarded with enough lingering incongruity to raise a smile.

Riddles entertain. Beyond the tiny window provided by the surviving manuscripts, early medieval reception of any text is necessarily speculative, but riddles wear their audience engagement in their form. The very call of the riddle subject-object to "say what I am called" dramatizes interaction with an audience and that audience surely reciprocated. The manuscript evidence for the Exeter Book riddles points to their use by a contemplative Christian community in a monastery or a cathedral, but the form of the riddle challenge suggests that they were enjoyed by just about every audience uncovered in this study, from the monastic or clerical collectivity implied by the Exeter Book to the ale house described in *Seasons for Fasting*, from the elite men gathered in the mead hall in *Beowulf* to the mischievous scholars in training of Ælfric Bata's classroom, from the large Christian household of Ealdorman Æthelweard's establishment to the modest animal-minder at Privett's Flood, from the elite women gathered around Queen Edith to the agricultural workers of Hild's monastery at Whitby. The riddles encourage speaking back by any of these audiences, who would be entertained by the ambiguities, engaged by the complexities, and who would resolve the incongruities in ways that led to laughter.

The riddles' ability to entertain is reflected in their modern reception, too, as these works continue to delight audiences of an almost comparable range – from the classroom, where all Old English readers include at least a few riddles, to the audience clicking on the Riddle Ages website; from the poet-translators assembled in *The Word Exchange* to the poets collected in *The New Exeter Book of Riddles*.[2] The basis of their appeal to modern audiences probably matches their appeal to medieval ones – entertained by the ambiguities, engaged by the complexities, and resolving the incongruities in ways that lead to laughter. The Exeter Book riddles have demonstrable and long-standing value as humorous entertainment.

Riddles have further appeal. Their inclusion in the Exeter Book indicates that they were valued for their theological and pious revelation. These are poems that give fresh insight into God's plenty, both in the range of objects described and in the loving attention that the oblique description involves. It is easy to imagine a pious audience laughing in awe at the wonder of the created world, just as it is easy to envisage a secular audience laughing at risqué suggestions and the playing with taboo. A classroom like that of Ælfric Bata would appreciate them for parading different codes of interpretation and different metrical forms, all made more engaging through the high degree of hilarity.

Their medieval reception is probably matched by modern readers, who notice the sense of wonder the riddles encourage. Their range allows the humour to contribute to a range of issues, all presented in topsy-turvy form. We appreciate their sensitivity to ecological concerns as nature and the environment get to speak back to human exploitation through their humour. The language tricks bolster the pedagogical potential of the sequence as they make conventions visible. In all their comic twists – both in the aspects of the world that get described and in the language that describes those aspects – the comic inversion makes manifest the norms that are inverted, allowing riddles to illuminate many facets of interest in the period. The humour of the riddles is thus both educational and entertaining, then and now.

The appeal of the humour in the Old English riddles, then, is easy to see and widely acknowledged, but that is not the case for most other works within this study. This is where modern assumptions about the sombre nature of the Old English corpus have become self-fulfilling, restricting what is seen as valuable and the way it is approached. Wisdom literature, for example, receives relatively little modern critical attention, and yet manifests many of the same techniques as the riddles and potentially has much of the same appeal. Conceptual puzzles in the proverbs are premised upon ambiguities that generate comic incongruity. Arriving at the

---

2 Cavell, *The Riddle Ages*; Greg Delanty and Michael Matto, eds., *The Word Exchange: Anglo-Saxon Poems in Translation* (New York: Norton, 2011); Kevin Crossley-Holland and Lawrence Sail, eds., *The New Exeter Book of Riddles* (London: Enitharmon, 1999).

underlying wisdom frequently involves holding contradictory ideas in mind to be resolved through incongruity-resolution techniques. Wisdom is imparted through tricks of language that create linguistic incongruities appropriately inappropriate enough to be funny. For such reasons, wisdom literature can be fruitfully engaged by thinking through humour, as is demonstrated here by the extended reading of *The Durham Proverbs* beside the Exeter Book riddles in chapter 1 and of *The Rune Poem* beside the runic riddles in chapter 2. Attending to humour encourages fresh attention to such rarely engaged works and helps manifest their appeal.

Humour from the play of language chimes throughout this study. The kennings of Old English poetic technique are akin to mini-riddles and often generate comic incongruity, as in the *hleahtorsmiðas* ("laughter-smiths") whose hands are locked shut in *Exodus*, where the process of humour creation is briefly analogous to the physical heft of the black-smith's hammer-wielding craft in a humorous image for the idea of humour.[3] Such incongruities often involve a momentary shifting of levels, and this is particularly apparent in the code-switching between roman and runic alphabets explored in chapter 2. The frame-breaking makes manifest the magic of language made physical by the freezing of speech on the page. That central paradox has been well studied by poststructuralist critics, but emphasizing the sheer funniness of the lettered code can breathe new life into the feature, as seen, for example, in the discussion of *Solomon and Saturn I*. Frame-breaking is a facet of humour that draws attention to the constriction of the frame as well as giving pleasure by overthrowing those constraints. Laughter at the self-conscious display of written language is a form of humour attuned to a literate and hence a learned audience, who may appreciate moments of release from the regular rules of language.

The very sound of words can also be funny, as seen in Riddle 24 in the verbs describing animal expressions that clue an audience into the jangling acoustic world of an avian mimic. Tricks of language manifested through sound break the frame in a way that makes language manifest. This is seen in chapter 3 by examining examples of extended rhyme. *The Rhyming Poem* makes many fascinating moves in working through the stages of an Old English elegy, all conditioned by the audible incongruity that insistently shapes the whole work as an *esprit de formes* that summons up a continuous smile. Revelling in the outré effects of the massively over-extended rhymes may bring greater appreciation to a poem that has received little critical favour until recently. Engaging with the humour encourages understanding the framework of Old English poetics along

---

3 *Exodus*, lines 42–3, analysed in the introduction.

with the pleasure of the violation of that framework through an over-the-top display of artistry.

In these ways, attending to humour encourages expanding the range of Old English texts worthy of consideration, but such attention can also encourage a distinctive way of reading, even for a very familiar poem like *Beowulf*. There are so many outstanding interpretations of *Beowulf* that it is daunting to consider adding a new one. It is possible, though, that the expectations of a dour corpus have unduly encouraged monologically martial and straightforwardly serious approaches. What if a critic took the kind of close reading style that is most obviously begged by a romance like *Apollonius of Tyre* – a close reading attentive to nuance and irony and the implication of how any statement is made, and of what is not said (as is practised in chapter 8) – and applied this reading style to the court scenes in Heorot? The result, as shown in chapter 4, plays up humour constructed around the role of Hrothgar, with the insistent and repeated undercutting of his attempts to establish his firm-handed leadership. Such a reading is only very mildly revisionist, but I think it is valuable for showing the kind of hook that might appeal to audiences who were (and are) hesitant to embrace the ethos of praise for masculine martial glory running through the poem. Humour can undercut the pretensions of the powerful and provide openings for those not favoured as the elite in society. Detecting the humour can make manifest social frameworks that otherwise may be taken for granted.

A related form of inversion is seen in *Judith* and *Andreas* and examined in chapter 5, where Christian narrative is unfolded deploying and tweaking some of the conventions of secular battle poetry. The clash between expectations derived from style and content of the story creates recurring flashes of humour. The account of a Jewish woman besting and beheading a male battle leader in *Judith* inverts in its plot many of the expectations that a battle poem creates. It turns around structures of power in a way that inverts heroic values, thereby serving a Christian ideology that is socially dominant in early medieval England (as explored more fully in chapter 6), but not the primary point of reference for this kind of poetry. *Andreas*, too, plays at moments with the mismatch between its hagiographical story line and the expectations of heroic poetry. The comic inversions make the frame manifest and allow these poems to have flashes of humour as they narrate their Christian story lines.

Saints' lives present a more straightforwardly Christian genre that is sometimes leavened with humour. I have dwelt most fully on a small cluster of extended hagiographical prose narratives that once again benefit from a style of reading that more generally fits romance. Within this group, I argue that humour is often a consequence of incongruities that arise as an individual defies social expectations. If, as I suggest in chapter 8, Arcestrate's machinations of indirect power generate humour but also considerable sympathy in the Old English *Apollonius of Tyre*, something similar goes on, I suggest in chapter 7, when the narrator dwells on the machinations of Euphrosyne in her desire to move into a male monastery, again creating sympathy for the one at the centre of the humour. A more broad-ranging sympathy comes from the humour that revolves around the two Malchuses and Mary of Egypt. In these cases, humour derives from stories of human interest, especially those that play up the anxieties of the individual against the conventions of society, as in the discomfiture of the monastic Malchus, forced to dissemble marriage in his desert adventure; or of a naked Mary of Egypt, whose past incorporates the unembarrassed embrace of female sexuality, but who is embarrassed in the present by a would-be pious interlocutor; or in the recurring and extended misunderstanding of the other Malchus who finds himself out of time in the *Legend of the Seven Sleepers*. Uncovering such humour of embarrassment calls for a careful reading of surface narrative and the clues that establish incongruities. The pleasure of such humour may enrich the Old English corpus if it serves to bring saints' lives such as these to greater attention.

An even bolder claim for rehabilitation lies in my turn to the homiletic literature in chapter 6. Here I show that two anonymous sermons, Napier 46 and Vercelli 9, deploy humour, even though it is far from the dominant mode for Old English sermon literature in general or even these two examples in particular. The multiple manuscript witnesses to Vercelli 9 demonstrate just how controversial the use of comic or sensational elements is, since these very passages get omitted in many of the copies. What else has got omitted from the written record is impossible to know, of course, but edifying reading like the *Dialogues* of Gregory the Great suggests some of the comic potential in works adjacent to the sermon tradition. The most dominating sermon voice from the period, Ælfric, exemplifies a preacher who would not approve of much of the humour uncovered in this study, but even Ælfric occasionally entertains through the deployment of controlled moments of humour. The quest for entertainment in preaching uncovers some new potential for engaging with Old English sermons and can point to one additional work that surely merits more attention than it is usually afforded in the wonderful if fragmentary satire in *Seasons for Fasting*.

In such ways, this study hints at the contours of an alternative tradition of Old English literature, pointing to works that stand out for their deployment of humour and that accordingly may be worth new consideration by modern readers. Attending to the incongruities encourages attention to the congruities, or the frames that get broken through the recalibration of the humour. This is true both at the linguistic level, which makes attending to the humour so valuable for revivifying formalist analysis, and also at the social level, which allows the uncovering of norms of society and discontent with those norms. It remains to consider some of the patterns that become apparent by attending to what the humour achieves.

The most consistent achievement of the humour is entertainment *tout court*. This is seen most clearly in the riddles, where the entertainment value of the puzzles is self-evident, but is also the case throughout this study. But humour often instructs as well as delights, and this is apparent, too, in most of the works considered here. It is particularly obvious in the hortatory literature since a sermon that makes use of humour is doing so to hook or retain the audience's attention for an explicitly stated moral message. In this way, the humour works in tandem with the ideology of the piece and reinforces its effectiveness. This is the case, too, in saints' lives. The humour of a martyr's comic insouciance cocks a snook at worldly power and makes for a memorable story and in the process reinforces the ideology of a narrative designed to steer an audience to thoughts of last things and Christian salvation. The saints' lives given fullest consideration in chapter 7 use a somewhat different technique to the same ultimate end, where the narrative incongruities get deployed for a kind of humour of human fallibility which works to bring sympathy to the saint. These differing styles of humour are all serving the hegemonic purpose of this Christian literature. While Ælfric may not have approved, such humour may bring an audience more effectively to the Christian message of the text than the more unambiguous pathway of the Ælfrician lives.

Something similar is happening in the poems *Judith* and *Andreas*. Humour from the incongruity between biblical story and heroic literary technique serves to entertain an audience that may thereby be the more readily drawn into the world of the poem, with all its moral and ethical implications. In these cases, though, the humour may also have more bite. When the *Judith*-poet deploys the conventions of a heroic approach to battle in a scene that displays instead the cowardice of the retainers and the demagogic thuggery of their leader, the poet not only entertains through a comic hook, but also dramatizes the underlying inversions, displaying an ideology where the first shall be last and the weak shall inherit the earth, and, in the process, perhaps suggests the inadequacy of heroic norms. The humour that comes from the mismatch of stylistic expectations potentially mocks the more usual use of those conventions which are here inverted. This is even more apparent in the case of *Andreas*, helped on by the abundant and still visible overlap of the language with a recognizable surviving heroic poem. The humour here adds to the entertainment of an ultimately edifying story and, at moments, also satirizes the heroic style and the values such a style encodes.

The bite of satire, then, is one of the additional effects of much comic incongruity. This is relatively straightforward in the critique of greedy and slothful priests in *Seasons for Fasting*. A similar process is seen in Ælfric's anecdote about the uxorious priest who was his teacher examined in chapter 6, although Ælfric's desire to control his message leads him to backtrack on the bite of the satire by providing explicit interpretation. In this way, the little anecdote is characteristic of Ælfric's writings more generally, where the controlling homiletic voice is loath to risk the uncontrol that humour can unleash.

More covertly, but also more commonly, the target of humorous satire in much of the material proves to be the high status martial heroic leaders and their elite masculine privilege. In this way, the biggest surprise about early medieval humour may be how much it pokes fun at just the kind of heroic martial manly world that is a commonplace modern understanding of what makes up that world. One appealing use of humour uncovered in this study, then, is its empowerment of the disempowered. The warriors of the mead hall may be the target audience for the humour of insouciance discussed in chapter 4, but they are as often instead the target of the satirical bite. Mocking defiance of the audience is common in the riddles and, whenever it gets specific, it is taunting an imagined gathering of males drinking in what looks like the paradigmatic mead-hall setting. In Riddle 42, the riddler is explicit about where and to whom he is uncovering the name of the runes: "Ic on flette mæg þurh runstafas rincum secgan, þam þe bec witan" ("I can tell to warriors in the hall, to those who know books," 5b–7a), which provides a striking conflation of warriors in the hall (*rincum ... on flette*) and those who know their runic letters. By the end of the poem, it is the former audience that is named, with clues for "werum æt wine" ("men at wine," 16a). If those bibulous masculine characters do not have knowledge of runic letter forms, though, they are going to be out of luck at trying to solve this riddle by spelling out letters that signify a cock and a hen. Instead, as I suggested in chapter 2, they are more likely being mocked for revelling in the display of sex in public with which this riddle began and for failing to crack the code. Such mockery of masculine mead-hall solvers proves common in many of the riddles. The monster of Riddle 86 comes "þær weras sæton monige on mæðle" ("where men sat, many at a meeting," 1b–2a). This male company is explicitly set up as wise ("mode snottre," "wise in mind," 2b), but a set-up it is, given the monstrous complexities of this particular riddle (as discussed at the opening of chapter 5) that they have no chance of solving. The nod to their perspicacity is really a baiting of their inadequacy.

Versions of this kind of humour at the expense of the warriors in the hall run through much of the material. It is seen in *The Rune Poem* when deflating men who boast of riding while sitting in the warm hall. It is particularly apparent in much of the sexual humour. As explored in chapters 1 and 4, the key of Riddle 44 or the sword of Riddle 20 both mock manly men who think they are so much in charge, even as the riddler indicates they are blindly following their body's lead. That is seen in other sexual riddles, too, such as Riddles 37 and 87, which play with the strength and masculine prowess of the one who mans the bellows, an apparent master, who nevertheless serves his servant's purpose. A similar undercutting of male strutting is seen in the laughter at the high-status male fantasy of Vercelli 9. Even the relatively modest Malchus of the Life of Malchus is most laughed at when he assumes masculine sexual dominance in his forced marriage before the narrative gives the woman an opportunity to speak. The undercutting of Holofernes fits into this context easily, and I have suggested adding Hrothgar as a target of a milder version of such laughter. Men who drink and boast of sexual prowess get laughed at. Real manly men get cut down to size through the humour, where a phallic boast is more often an undercutting of the folly of the boaster than the braggadocio it might at first appear to be. Real men in Old English literature aren't really real men after all.

One likely reason the surviving literature is so rich in this kind of humour lies in the process whereby these works got recorded. As the analysis of Riddle 51 in chapter 1 suggests, the group that turns out to out-perform men with swords in many of the riddles proves to be men with quills. In this way, some of the social humour is a kind of estates' satire in which the class who pray (intellectual, celibate, Christian) get to show their superiority to those who fight (physical, sexual, untheological), even as the latter are usually seen as the top of society. But humour can turn on any group. The clerical class, too, is the butt of the humour in some of this material, not just in the clerical satire, but more subtly in many of the comic saint's lives, which sometimes undercut clerical authority or skewer the complacencies of ecclesiastical power, as in the folly of a Zosimus or in the elders that constrain a cross-dressing Euphrosyne and Eugenia. Indeed, the broader sweep of the humour lies in empowering a range of underclasses, which in this society includes most women and workers and the non-elite all over.

It is for appreciating this aspect of the humour that focusing on known and knowable audiences is so appealing. The potential performance contexts described here are ones which chanced to leave a record, and collectively they hint at the multiplicity of ways of appreciating the humour of these works. Different audiences would laugh at different elements and at different targets of humorous satire. Appreciating the humour would cement a sense of belonging within any community that laughs together.

Attending to this multiplicity of performance contexts encourages a sense of the diversity of perspective within early medieval England which validates imagining a range and plurality of interpretation for any particular work.

Survival of vernacular literature from the Early Middle Ages is much more scant and fragmentary than from later periods, and the survival of funny literature is more scant and fragmentary still. Humour was to become much more visible in the literature that survives in Middle English as seen in the works of Chaucer and Langland and others. There is enough in Old English, however, to suggest that the earlier period is not exclusively dour, even in the record that does survive. It is my hope that this study opens up methods and material that may be amenable to further analysis. To put it in a way characteristic of the works under consideration, I hope to have suggested that Old English humour is not half bad.

Bibliography

Primary Texts

Anlezark, Daniel, ed. and trans. *The Old English Dialogues of Solomon and Saturn*. Cambridge: Brewer, 2009.

Arngart, Olof, ed. and trans. "The Durham Proverbs." *Speculum* 56, no. 2 (1981): 288–300.

Assmann, Bruno, ed. *Angelsächsische Homilien und Heiligenleben*, Bibliothek der angelsächsischen Prosa 3. Kassel: G.H. Wigand, 1889. Reprinted with a supplementary introduction by Peter Clemoes, Darmstadt, 1964.

Baldwin, Barry, trans. *The Philogelos, or Laughter-Lover*. Amsterdam: Gieben, 1983.

Barlow, Frank, ed. and trans. *The Life of King Edward Who Rests at Westminster*. 2nd ed. Oxford: Oxford University Press, 1992.

Benson, Larry D., ed. *The Riverside Chaucer*. 3rd ed. Boston: Houghton Mifflin, 1987.

Bjork, Robert E., ed. and trans. *The Old English Poems of Cynewulf*, DOML 23. Cambridge, MA: Harvard University Press, 2013.

– *Old English Shorter Poems; Volume II: Wisdom and Lyric*, DOML 32. Cambridge, MA: Harvard University Press, 2014.

Boenig, Robert, trans. *The Acts of Andrew in the Country of the Cannibals: Translations from the Greek, Latin, and Old English*. New York: Garland, 1991.

Brooks, Kenneth R., ed. *Andreas and the Fates of the Apostles*. Oxford: Oxford University Press, 1961.

Byock, Jesse, trans. *Grettir's Saga*. Oxford: Oxford University Press, 2009.

Cavell, Megan, ed. and trans. *The Riddle Ages: Early Medieval Riddles, Translations, and Commentaries*, 2013, redeveloped 2020. https://theriddleages.com/.

Clayton, Mary, ed. and trans. *Old English Poems of Christ and His Saints*, DOML 27. Cambridge, MA: Harvard University Press, 2013.

Clayton, Mary, and Juliet Mullins, eds. and trans., *Old English Lives of Saints: Ælfric*, 3 vols., DOML 58–60. Cambridge, MA: Harvard University Press, 2019.

Clemoes, Peter, ed. *Ælfric's Catholic Homilies: The First Series; Text*, EETS s.s. 17. Oxford: Oxford University Press, 1997.

Colgrave, Bertrand, and R.A.B. Mynors, eds. and trans. *Bede's Ecclesiastical History of the English People*. Oxford: Oxford University Press, 1993.

Corona, Gabriella, ed. *Ælfric's Life of Saint Basil the Great*. Cambridge: Brewer, 2006.

Crossley-Holland, Kevin, trans. *The Anglo-Saxon World: An Anthology*. Oxford: Oxford University Press, 2009.

Delanty, Greg, and Michael Matto, eds. *The Word Exchange: Anglo-Saxon Poems in Translation*. New York: Norton, 2011.

Dendle, Peter J. "The Old English 'Life of Malchus' and Two Vernacular Tales from the *Vitas Patrum* in MS Cotton Otho C.i: A Translation (Part 1)." *English Studies* 90 (2009): 505–17 and "The Old English 'Life of Malchus' and Two Vernacular Tales from the *Vitas Patrum* in MS Cotton Otho C.i: A Translation (Part 2)." *English Studies* 90 (2009): 631–52. https://doi.org/10.1080/00138380903181122.

DeVriend, Hubert Jan, ed. *The Old English Herbarium and Medicina De Quadrupedibus*, EETS o.s. 286. London: Oxford University Press, 1984.

Dobbie, Elliott van Kirk, ed. *The Anglo-Saxon Minor Poems*, ASPR 6. New York: Columbia, 1942.

Donovan, Leslie A., trans. *Women Saints' Lives in Old English Prose*. Cambridge: Brewer, 1999.

The Exeter Book of Old English Poetry. With introductory chapters by R.W. Chambers, Max Förster, and Robin Flower. London: Lund, Humphries, 1933.

Fehr, Bernhard, ed. *Die Hirtenbriefe Ælfrics*, BdaP 9. Hamburg, 1914; repr. with a suppl. intro. by Peter Clemoes, Darmstadt, 1966.

Fowler, Roger, ed. *Wulfstan's Canons of Edgar*, EETS o.s. 266. Oxford: Oxford University Press, 1972.

Fulk, R.D., ed. and trans. *The Beowulf Manuscript*, DOML 3. Cambridge, MA: Harvard University Press, 2010.

Fulk, R.D., Robert E. Bjork, and John D. Niles, eds. *Klaeber's Beowulf: Fourth Edition*. Toronto: University of Toronto Press, 2008.

Gameson, Richard, ed. *The Cambridge History of the Book in Britain; Volume 1, c. 400–1100*. Cambridge: Cambridge University Press, 2012.

Garbáty, Thomas J., ed. *Medieval English Literature*. Lexington, MA: Heath, 1984.

Godden, Malcolm, ed. *Ælfric's Catholic Homilies: The Second Series; Text*, EETS, s.s. 5. London: Oxford University Press, 1979.

Godden, Malcolm, and Susan Irvine, eds. *The Old English Boethius: An Edition of the Old English Versions of Boetheius's 'De Consolatione Philosophiae'*, 2 vols. Oxford: Oxford University Press, 2009.

Goolden, Peter, ed. *The Old English "Apollonius of Tyre."* Oxford: Oxford University Press, 1958.

Griffith, Mark, ed. *Judith.* Exeter: University of Exeter Press, 1997.

Gwara, Scott, ed. and David W. Porter, trans. and intro. *Anglo-Saxon Conversations: The Colloquies of Ælfric Bata.* Cambridge: Boydell, 1997.

Halsall, Maureen, ed. *The Old English "Rune Poem": A Critical Edition.* Toronto: University of Toronto Press, 1981.

Headley, Maria Dahvana, trans. *Beowulf: A New Translation.* New York: Farrar, Straus, and Giroux, 2020.

Hecht, Hans, ed. *Bischofs Wærferth von Worcester Übersetzung der Dialoge Gregors von Grosen*, Bibliothek der angelsächsischen Prosa 5. Leipzig: Wigand, 1900.

Jones, Christopher A., ed. and trans. *Old English Shorter Poems, Volume 1: Religious and Didactic*, DOML 15. Cambridge, MA: Harvard University Press, 2012.

Jónsson, Guðni, ed. *Grettis saga Ásmundarsonar.* Reykjavik: Íslenzka Fornrit, 1936.

Jost, Karl, ed. *Die "Institutes of Polity, Civil and Ecclesiastical": ein Werk Erzbischof Wulfstans von York.* Bern: Francke, 1959.

Kelly, Richard J., ed. and trans. *Blickling Homilies: Edition and Translation.* London: Continuum, 2003.

Keynes, Simon, and Michael Lapidge, trans. *Alfred the Great: Asser's Life of King Alfred and Other Contemporary Sources.* Harmondsworth: Penguin, 1983.

Klinck, Anne L., ed. *The Old English Elegies: A Critical Edition and Genre Study.* Montreal: McGill-Queen's University Press, 1992.

Kramer, Johanna, Hugh Magennis, and Robin Norris, eds. and trans. *Anonymous Old English Lives of Saints*, DOML 63. Cambridge, MA: Harvard University Press, 2020.

Krapp, George Philip, and Elliott Van Kirk Dobbie, eds. *The Exeter Book.* New York: Columbia University Press, 1936.

Lapidge, Michael, ed. *The Cult of St Swithun*, Winchester Studies 4. ii. Oxford: Oxford University Press, 2003.

Leary, T.J., ed. *Symphosius, The Aenigmata: An Introduction, Text, and Commentary.* London: Bloomsbury, 2014.

Lee, S.D., ed. "Ælfric's Homilies on Judith, Esther and Maccabees" (1999). http://users.ox.ac.uk/~stuart/kings/main.htm.

Liuzza, R.M., ed. *The Old English Version of the Gospels*, EETS o.s. 304. Oxford: Oxford University Press, 1994.

Lucas, Peter J., ed. *Exodus.* London: Methuen, 1977.

Macrae-Gibson, O.D., ed. and trans. *The Old English Riming Poem.* Cambridge: Brewer, 1983.

Mackie, W.S., ed. and trans. *The Exeter Book, Part II: Poems IX-XXXII*, EETS o.s. 194. London: Oxford University Press, 1934.

Magennis, Hugh, ed. *The Anonymous Old English Legend of the Seven Sleepers*. Durham: Durham Medieval Texts 7, 1994.

– ed. and trans. *The Old English Life of Saint Mary of Egypt*. Exeter: Exeter University Press, 2002.

Magnusson, Magnus, and Hermann Palsson, trans. *Njal's Saga*. London: Penguin, 1960.

Marsden, Richard, ed. *The Cambridge Old English Reader*. Cambridge: Cambridge University Press, 2004.

Mierow, Charles Christopher, ed. and trans. "Sancti Eusebii Hieronymi Vita Malchi Monachi Captivi." In *Classical Essays Presented to James A. Kleist, S.J.*, edited by Richard E. Arnold, 31–60. St. Louis: Saint Louis University, 1946.

Miller, Thomas, ed. and trans. *The Old English Version of Bede's Ecclesiastical History of the English People*, EETS o.s. 95, 96. London: Oxford University Press, 1890–91.

Mitchell, Bruce, and Fred C. Robinson, eds. *Beowulf: An Edition with Relevant Shorter Texts*. Oxford: Blackwell, 1998.

Morris, Richard, ed. and trans. *The Blickling Homilies*, EETS o.s. 58, 63, 73, 1874, 1876, 1880, repr. as one volume. London: Oxford University Press, 1967.

Muir, Bernard J., ed. *The Exeter Anthology of Old English Poetry*. Exeter: University of Exeter Press, 1994; revised edition 2000.

Napier, Arthur, ed. *Wulfstan: Sammlung der ihm zugeschriebenen Homilien nebst Untersuchungen über ihre Echtheit*, 1883; repr. with a bibliog. suppl. by Klaus Ostheeren. Dublin: Weidmann, 1967.

Nicholson, Lewis E., ed. *The Vercelli Book Homilies: Translations from the Anglo-Saxon*. Lanham, MD: University Press of America, 1991.

North, Richard, and Michael D.J. Bintley, eds. *Andreas: An Edition*. Liverpool: Liverpool University Press, 2016.

Orchard, Andy, ed. and trans. *The Old English and Anglo-Latin Riddle Tradition*, DOML 69. Cambridge, MA: Harvard University Press, 2021.

Pinsker, Hans, and Waltraud Ziegler, eds. and trans. *Die altenglischen Rätsel des Exeterbuchs*. Heidelberg: Winter, 1985.

Pope, John C., ed. *Homilies of Ælfric: A Supplementary Collection*, 2 vols., EETS o.s. 259–60. London: Oxford University Press, 1967–68.

Rambaran-Olm, M.R., ed. and trans. *John the Baptist's Prayer, or The Descent into Hell from the Exeter Book: Text, Translation, and Critical Study*. Cambridge: Brewer, 2014.

Rauer, Christine, ed. and trans. *The Old English Martyrology: Edition, Translation and Commentary*. Cambridge: Brewer, 2013.

Richards, Mary P., ed. and trans. *The Old English Poem Seasons for Fasting: A Critical Edition*. Morgantown: West Virginia University Press, 2014.

Schaff, Philip, trans. *A Select Library of the Nicene and Post-Nicene Fathers*, vol. 10. New York, 1888.

Schröer, Arnold, ed. *Die angelsächsischen Prosabearbeitungen der Benedictinerregel*. Kassel: Wigand, 1888.

Scragg, D.G., ed. *The Battle of Maldon*. Manchester: Manchester University Press, 1981.

– *The Vercelli Homilies and Related Texts*, EETS o.s. 300. Oxford: Oxford University Press, 1992.

Shippey, T.A., ed. and trans. *Poems of Wisdom and Learning in Old English*. Cambridge: Brewer, 1976.

Skeat, W.W., ed. and trans. *Ælfric's Lives of Saints*, EETS o.s. 76, 82, 94, 114. London: Oxford University Press, 1881–1900; repr. as 2 vols. 1966.

Smith, A.H., ed. *Three Northumbrian Poems: Cædmon's Hymn, Bede's Death Song, and the Leiden Riddle*. London: Methuen, 1933.

Stevenson, William Henry, ed. *Asser's Life of King Alfred*, with an intro. by Dorothy Whitelock. Oxford: Oxford University Press, 1959.

Symons, Thomas, ed. *Regularis Concordia: The Monastic Agreement*. London: Nelson, 1953.

Thorpe, Benjamin, ed. and trans. *Codex Exoniensis*. London, 1842.

– *Sermones Catholici or Homilies of Ælfric*, 2 vols. London, 1844–46.

Treharne, Elaine, ed. *Old and Middle English: An Anthology*. Oxford: Blackwell, 2000.

Tupper, Frederick, Jr., ed. *The Riddles of the Exeter Book*. Boston: Ginn, 1910; reprint Darmstadt, 1968.

Venarde, Bruce L., ed. and trans. *The Rule of Saint Benedict*, DOML. Cambridge, MA: Harvard University Press, 2011.

White, Carolinne, trans. *Early Christian Lives*. London: Penguin, 1998.

Wilcox, Jonathan, ed. *Ælfric's Prefaces*. Durham: Durham Medieval Texts, 1994.

Williamson, Craig, ed. *The Old English Riddles of the 'Exeter Book'*. Chapel Hill: University of North Carolina Press, 1977.

– trans. *A Feast of Creatures: Anglo-Saxon Riddle-Songs Translated with Introduction, Notes and Commentary*. Philadelphia: University of Pennsylvania Press, 1982.

– trans. *The Complete Old English Poems*. Philadelphia: University of Pennsylvania Press, 2017.

Ziolkowski, Jan M., ed. and trans. *The Cambridge Songs (Carmina Cantabrigiensia)*. New York: Garland, 1994.

Zupitza, Julius, ed. *Ælfrics Grammatik und Glossar*. Berlin: Wiedmann, 1880.

Secondary Studies

Abram, Christopher. "The Errors in *The Rhyming Poem*." *Review of English Studies*, no. 58 (2007): 1–9.

Allen, Elizabeth. *False Fables and Exemplary Truth in Later Middle English Literature*. New York: Palgrave, 2005.

Anderson, Earl R. *Cynewulf: Structure, Style, and Theme in His Poetry*. London: Associated University Presses, 1983.

Anlezark, Daniel. "Reading 'The Story of Joseph' in MS Cambridge, Corpus Christi College 201." In *The Power of Words: Anglo-Saxon Studies Presented to Donald G. Scragg on His Seventieth Birthday*, edited by Hugh Magennis and Jonathan Wilcox, 61–94. Morgantown: West Virginia University Press, 2006.

Archibald, Elizabeth. *Apollonius of Tyre: Medieval and Renaissance Themes and Variations*. Cambridge: Boydell, 1991.

Astell, Ann W. "Holofernes's Head: *Tacen* and Teaching in the Old English *Judith*." *Anglo-Saxon England* 18 (1989): 117–33.

Aston, Margaret. "Segregation in Church." In *Women in the Church*, edited by W.J. Sheils and Diana Wood, 237–94. Oxford: Blackwell, 1990.

Atherton, Mark. "Cambridge, Corpus Christi College 201 as a Mirror for a Prince: *Apollonius of Tyre*, Archbishop Wulfstan and King Cnut." *English Studies* 97 (2016): 451–72.

Attardo, Salvatore. *Humorous Texts*. Berlin: de Gruyter, 2001.

– "A Primer for the Linguistics of Humor." In *The Primer of Humor Research*, edited by Victor Raskin, 101–55. Berlin: Mouton de Gruyter, 2008.

Attardo, Salvatore, and Victor Raskin. "Script Theory Revis(it)ed: Joke Similarity and Joke Representation Model." *HUMOR* 4, no. 3–4 (1991): 293–347. https://doi.org/10.1515/humr.1991.4.3-4.293.

Baker, Peter S. "Beowulf as Orator." *Journal of English Linguistics* 21 (1988): 3–23. https://doi.org/10.1177/007542428802100101.

– *Introduction to Old English*. 3rd ed. Chichester: Wiley-Blackwell, 2012.

– *Honour, Exchange and Violence in Beowulf*. Cambridge: Brewer, 2013.

Bakhtin, Mikhail. *Rabelais and His World*. Translated by Hélène Iswolsky. Bloomington: Indiana University Press, 1984.

Barley, Nigel. "Structural Aspects of the Anglo-Saxon Riddle." *Semiotica* 10 (1974): 143–75. https://doi.org/10.1515/semi.1974.10.2.143.

Barrow, Julia. *The Clergy in the Medieval World: Secular Clerics, Their Families and Careers in North-Western Europe, c. 800–c. 1200*. Cambridge: Cambridge University Press, 2015.

Bately, Janet. "Did King Alfred Actually Translate Anything? The Integrity of the Alfredian Canon Revisited." *Medium Aevum* 78, no. 2 (2009): 189–215. https://doi.org/10.2307/43632837.

Bayless, Martha. *Parody in the Middle Ages: The Latin Tradition*. Ann Arbor: University of Michigan Press, 1996.

– "Merriment, Entertainment, and Community in Anglo-Saxon Culture." In *The Daily Lives of the Anglo-Saxons*, edited by Carole Biggam, Carole Hough, and Daria Izdebska, 239–56. Tempe, AZ: ACMRS, 2017.

Beckett, Katharine Scarf. "Worcester Sauce: Malchus in Anglo-Saxon England." In *Latin Learning and English Lore: Studies in Anglo-Saxon Literature for*

Michael Lapidge, edited by Katherine O'Brien O'Keeffe and Andy Orchard, 2 vols, II, 212–31. Toronto: University of Toronto Press, 2005.

Beechy, Tiffany. *The Poetics of Old English*. Ashgate, 2010; repr. New York, Routledge, 2016.

– "Wisdom and the Poetics of Laughter in the Old English Dialogues of Solomon and Saturn." *The Journal of English and Germanic Philology* 116 (2017): 131–55. https://doi.org/10.5406/jenglgermphil.116.2.0131.

Benskin, Michael. "The Narrative Structure of the Finnsburh Episode in *Beowulf*." *Amsterdamer Beiträge zur älteren Germanistik* 77 (2017): 37–64. https://doi.org/10.1163/18756719-12340066.

Bergson, Henri. *Laughter: An Essay on the Meaning of the Comic*. Translated by Cloudesely Brereton and Fred Rothwell. New York, 1911.

Berkhout, Carl T., and J.F. Doubleday. "The Net in *Judith* 46b-54a." *Neuphilologische Mitteilungen* 74 (1973): 630–4.

Bernau, Anke. "The Translation of Purity in the Old English *Lives* of St Eugenia and St Euphrosyne." *Bulletin of the John Rylands University Library of Manchester* 86, no. 2 (Summer 2004): 11–37. https://doi.org/10.7227 /BJRL.86.2.2.

Betancourt, Roland. *Byzantine Intersectionality: Sexuality, Gender, and Race in the Middle Ages*. Princeton: Princeton University Press, 2020.

Bintley, Michael D.J. "Demythologising Urban Landscapes in *Andreas*." *Leeds Studies in English*, no. 40 (2009): 105–18.

Birkett, Tom. "Runes and *Revelatio*: Cynewulf's Signatures Reconsidered." *Review of English Studies* 65 (2014): 771–89.

Bitterli, Dieter. *Say What I am Called: The Old English Riddles of the Exeter Book and the Anglo-Latin Riddle Tradition*. Toronto: University of Toronto Press, 2009.

Bjork, Robert. "Speech as Gift in *Beowulf*." *Speculum* 69 (1994): 993–1020. https://doi.org/10.1017/S0038713400030177.

Blair, John. *The Church in Anglo-Saxon Society*. Oxford: Oxford University Press, 2005.

Boenig, Robert. *Saint and Hero: Andreas and Medieval Doctrine*. Lewisburg: Mellen, 1991.

Bolintineanu, Alexandra. "The Land of Mermedonia in the Old English *Andreas*." *Neophilologus* 93 (2009): 149–64. https://doi.org/10.1007/s11061 -007-9097-1.

Borysławski, Rafał. *The Old English Riddles and the Riddlic Elements in Old English Poetry*. Frankfurt am Main: Peter Lang, 2004.

Bosworth, Joseph, and T. Northcote Toller. *An Anglo-Saxon Dictionary*. Oxford: Oxford University Press, 1898, and T. Northcote Toller, *An Anglo-Saxon Dictionary: Supplement*. Oxford: Oxford University Press, 1921. Reprinted as *An Anglo-Saxon Dictionary Online*, edited by Thomas Northcote Toller,

Christ Sean, and Ondrej Tichy. Prague: Faculty of Arts, Charles University, 2014. https://bosworthtoller.com.

Bracher, Frederick. "Understatement in Old English Poetry." *PMLA* 52 (1937): 915–34. https://doi.org/10.2307/458493.

Brady, Lindy. "Echoes of Britons on a Fenland Frontier in the Old English *Andreas.*" *Review of English Studies* 61 (2010): 669–89. https://doi.org /10.1093/res/hgq047.

Bredehoft, Thomas A. "Ælfric and Late Old English Verse." *Anglo-Saxon England* 33 (2004): 77–107.

Breen, Nathan A. "'What a Long, Strange Trip It's Been': Narration, Movement and Revelation in the Old English *Andreas.*" *Essays in Medieval Studies* 25 (2008): 71–79. https://doi.org/10.1353/ems.0.0013.

Brooks, Nicholas P. "Arms, Status and Warfare in Late-Saxon England." In *Ethelred the Unready*, edited by David Hill, 81–103. Oxford: BAR, 1978.

Brown, Peter. *The Cult of the Saints: Its Rise and Function in Latin Christianity.* Chicago: University of Chicago Press, 1981; Enlarged 2nd ed., 2015.

Bullough, D.A. "What Has Ingeld to Do with Lindisfarne." *Anglo-Saxon England* 22 (1993): 93–125.

Burrows, Hannah. "Riddles and Kennings." *European Journal of Scandinavian Studies* 51, no. 1 (2021): 46–68. https://doi.org/10.1515/ejss-2020-2017.

Burrus, Virginia. *The Sex Lives of Saints: An Erotics of Ancient Hagiography.* Philadelphia: University of Pennsylvania Press, 2004.

Calder, Daniel J. *Cynewulf.* Boston: Twayne, 1981.

Cantara, Linda. "*Saint Mary of Egypt* in British Library, MS Cotton Otho B. x." In *Anonymous Interpolations in Ælfric's "Lives of Saints,"* edited by Robin Norris, 29–69. Kalamazoo: Medieval Institute Publications, 2011.

Carroll, Noel. *Humour: A Very Short Introduction.* Oxford: Oxford University Press, 2014.

Cavell, Megan. *Weaving Words and Binding Bodies: The Poetics of Human Experience in Old English Literature.* Toronto: University of Toronto Press, 2016.

– "Powerful Patens in the Anglo-Saxon Medical Tradition and Exeter Book *Riddle 48.*" *Neophilologus* 101 (2017): 129–38. https://doi.org/10.1007/s11061 -016-9490-8.

Chamberlain, David. "*Judith*: A Fragmentary and Political Poem." In *Anglo-Saxon Poetry: Essays in Appreciation*, edited by Lewis E. Nicholson and Dolores Warwick Frese, 135–59. Notre Dame: University of Notre Dame Press, 1975.

Chance, Jane. *Woman as Hero in Old English Literature.* Syracuse: Syracuse University Press, 1986.

Christie, E.J. "By Means of a Secret Alphabet: Dangerous Letters and the Semantics of *Gebregdstafas* (*Solomon and Saturn I*, line 2b)." *Modern Philology* 109, no. 2 (2011): 145–70. https://doi.org/10.1086/663211.

Clark, George. "The Hero and the Theme." In *A Beowulf Handbook*, edited by Robert E. Bjork and John D. Niles, chapter 14, 271–90. Lincoln: University of Nebraska Press, 1997.

Clark, Stephanie. *Compelling God: Theories of Prayer in Anglo-Saxon England*. Toronto: University of Toronto Press, 2018.

Clark, Tom. *A Case for Irony in Beowulf, with Particular Reference to Its Epithets*. New York: Lang, 2003.

Clayton, Mary. "Homiliaries and Preaching in Anglo-Saxon England." *Peritia* 4 (1985): 207–42. https://doi.org/10.1484/J.Peri.3.106.

– "Ælfric's *Judith*: Manipulative or Manipulated?" *Anglo-Saxon England* 23 (1994): 215–27. https://doi.org/10.1017/S0263675100004543.

– "Hermits and the Contemplative Life in Anglo-Saxon England." In *Holy Men and Holy Women: Old English Prose Saints' Lives and Their Contexts*, edited by Paul E. Szarmach, 147–75. Albany: State University of New York Press, 1996.

Clements, Jill Hamilton. "Reading, Writing, and Resurrection: Cynewulf's Runes as a Figure of the Body." *Anglo-Saxon England* 43 (2014): 133–54.

Clemoes, Peter. *Interactions of Thought and Language in Old English Poetry*. Cambridge: Cambridge University Press, 1995.

Clover, Carol J. "The Germanic Context of the Unferþ Episode." *Speculum* 55 (1980): 444–68. https://doi.org/10.2307/2847235.

Coleman, Julie. "Old English Sexual Euphemism." *Neuphilologische Mitteilungen* 93, no. 1 (1992): 93–98.

– *Love, Sex, and Marriage: A Historical Thesaurus*. Amsterdam: Rodopi, 1999.

Conner, Patrick W. *Anglo-Saxon Exeter: A Tenth-Century Cultural History*. Woodbridge: Boydell, 1993.

Crossley-Holland, Kevin, and Lawrence Sail, eds. *The New Exeter Book of Riddles*. London: Enitharmon, 1999.

Crowne, D.K. "The Hero on the Beach: An Example of Composition by Theme in Anglo-Saxon Poetry." *Neuphilologische Mitteilungen* 61 (1960): 362–72.

Cubitt, Catherine. "Virginity and Misogyny in Tenth- and Eleventh-Century England." *Gender History* 12, no. 1 (2000): 1–32. https://doi.org/10.1111/1468-0424.00170.

– "'As the Law-Book Teaches': Reeves, Lawbooks and Urban Life in the Anonymous Old English Legend of the Seven Sleepers." *English Historical Review* 124 (2009): 1021–49.

– "Pastoral Care and Religious Belief." In *A Companion to the Early Middle Ages: Britain and Ireland, c. 500–c. 1100*, edited by Pauline Stafford, 394–413. Chichester: Blackwell, 2009.

– "Ælfric's Lay Patrons." In *A Companion to Ælfric*, edited by Hugh Magennis and Mary Swan, 165–92. Leiden: Brill, 2009.

Curtius, E.R. *European Literature and the Latin Middle Ages*. Translated by Willard R. Trask. Princeton: Princeton University Press, 1953.

Dailey, Patricia. "Riddles, Wonder, and Responsiveness in Anglo-Saxon Literature." In *The Cambridge History of Early Medieval English Literature*, edited by Clare A. Lees, 451–72. Cambridge: Cambridge University Press, 2013.

Dale, Corinne. *The Natural World in the Exeter Book Riddles*. Cambridge: Brewer, 2017.

Damico, Helen. *Beowulf and the Grendel-Kin: Politics and Poetry in Eleventh-Century England*. Morgantown: West Virginia University Press, 2015.

Davis, Kathleen. "Boredom, Brevity and Last Things: Ælfric's Style and the Politcs of Time." In *A Companion to Ælfric*, edited by Hugh Magennis and Mary Swan, 321–44. 2009.

– "Old English Lyrics: A Poetics of Experience." In *The Cambridge History of Early Medieval English Literature*, edited by Clare A. Lees, 332–56. Cambridge: Cambridge University Press, 2013.

Day, Virginia. "The Influence of the Catechetical *Narratio* on Old English and Some Other Medieval Literature." *Anglo-Saxon England* 3 (1974): 51–61.

DeGregorio, Scott. "'Þegenlic' or 'Flæsclic': The Old English Prose Legends of St. Andrew." *The Journal of English and Germanic Philology* 102 (2003): 449–64.

Dekker, Kees. "King Alfred's Translation of Gregory's *Dalogi*: Tales for the Unlearned?" In *Rome and the North: The Early Reception of Gregory the Great in Germanic Europe*, edited by Rolf H. Bremmer, Kees Dekker, and David F. Johnson, 27–50. Leuven: Peeters, 2001.

Dewa, Roberta J. "The Runic Riddles of the Exeter Book: Language Games and Anglo-Saxon Scholarship." *Nottingham Medieval Studies* 39 (1995): 26–36. https://doi.org/10.1484/J.NMS.3.239.

Dictionary of Old English: A-I Online. Edited by Angus Cameron, Ashley Crandell Amos, Antonette di Paolo Healey. Toronto: Dictionary of Old English Project, 2007. https://tapor.library.utoronto.ca/doe/.

Dictionary of Old English: Web Corpus. Edited by Antonette di Paolo Healey et al. Toronto: Dictionary of Old English Project, 2004.

DiNapoli, Robert. "In the Kingdom of the Blind, the One-Eyed Man Is a Seller of Garlic: Depth-Perception and the Poet's Perspective in the Exeter Book Riddles." *English Studies* 81 (2000): 422–55. https://doi.org/10.1076/0013 -838X(200009)81:5;1-8:FT422.

– "Odd Characters: Runes in Old English Poetry." In *Verbal Encounters: Anglo-Saxon and Old Norse Studies for Roberta Frank*, edited by A. Harbus and R. Poole, 145–62. Toronto: University of Toronto Press, 2005.

Dinshaw, Carolyn. *How Soon Is Now? Medieval Texts, Amateur Readers, and the Queerness of Time*. Durham: Duke University Press, 2012.

Doane, A.N. "Spacing, Placing, and Effacing: Scribal Textuality and Exeter Riddle 30 a/b." In *New Approaches to Editing Old English Verse*, edited by

Sarah Larratt Keefer and Katherine O'Brien O'Keeffe, 45–65. Cambridge: Cambridge University Press, 1998.

Donoghue, Daniel. *How the Anglo-Saxons Read Their Poems*. Philadelphia: University of Pennsylvania Press, 2018.

Douglas, Mary. *Implicit Meanings: Essays on Anthropology*. London: Routledge, 1977.

Dumitrescu, Irina. *The Experience of Education in Anglo-Saxon Literature*. Cambridge: Cambridge University Press, 2018.

Earl, James W. "Typology and Iconographic Style in Early Medieval Hagiography." *Studies in the Literary Imagination* 8 (1978): 15–46.

– "A Translation of 'The Rhyming Poem'." *Old English Newsletter* 19, no. 1 (Fall 1985): 31–33.

– "Hisperic Style in the Old English 'Rhyming Poem'." *PMLA* 102 (1987): 187–96. https://doi.org/10.2307/462547.

– *Thinking About Beowulf*. Stanford: Stanford University Press, 1994.

Eco, Umberto et al. *Carnival!* Berlin: de Gruyter, 1984.

Elliott, R.W.V. "Cynewulf's Runes in *Juliana* and *Fates of the Apostles*." *English Studies* 34 (1953): 193–204. https://doi.org/10.1080/00138385308596900.

– *Runes: An Introduction*. Manchester: Manchester University Press, 1959.

Enright, Michael J. *Lady with a Mead Cup: Prophecy and Lordship in the European Warband from La Tène to the Viking Age*. Dublin: Four Courts, 1996.

Estes, Heide. "Feasting with Holofernes: Digesting Judith in Anglo-Saxon England." *Exemplaria* 15, no. 2 (2003): 325–50. https://doi.org/10.1179/exm.2003.15.2.325.

– *Anglo-Saxon Literary Landscapes: Ecotheory and the Anglo-Saxon Environmental Imagination*. Amsterdam: Amsterdam University Press, 2017.

Farmer, David Hugh. *The Oxford Dictionary of Saints*. 3rd ed. Oxford: Oxford University Press, 1992.

Ferhatović, Denis. "*Spolia*-Inflected Poetics of the Old English *Andreas*." *Studies in Philology* 110, no. 2 (2013): 199–219. https://doi.org/10.1353/sip.2013.0009.

Fleming, Robin. *Britain after Rome: The Fall and Rise, 400–1070*. London: Penguin, 2010.

Foley, John Miles. *The Singer of Tales in Performance*. Bloomington: Indiana University Press, 1995.

Foucault, Michel. *Discpline and Punish: The Birth of the Prison*. Translated by Alan Sheridan. New York: Pantheon, 1977.

Foys, Martin. "The Undoing of Exeter Book Riddle 47: 'Bookmoth'." In *Transitional States: Change, Tradition, and Memory in Medieval Literature and Culture*, edited by Graham D. Caie and Michael D.C. Drout. Tempe, AZ: ACMRS, 2018.

Frank, Roberta. "Old English *æræt* – 'Too Much' or 'Too Soon'?" In *Words, Texts, and Manuscripts:Studies in Anglo-Saxon Culture Presented to Helmut Gneuss*, edited by Michael Korhammer, 293–303. Cambridge: Brewer, 1992.

– "North-Sea Soundings in *Andreas*." In *Early Medieval English Texts and Interpretations: Studies Presented to Donald G. Scragg*, edited by Elaine Treharne and Susan Rosser, 1–11. Tempe, AZ: ACMRS, 2002.

– "*Beowulf* and the Intimacy of Large Parties." In *Dating Beowulf: Studies in Intimacy*, edited by Daniel C. Remein and Erica Weaver, 54–72. Manchester: Manchester University Press, 2020.

Frantzen, Allen J. *Before the Closet: Same-Sex Love from Beowulf to Angels in America*. Chicago: University of Chicago Press, 1998.

Frese, Dolores Warwick. "The Art of Cynewulf's Runic Signatures." In *Anglo-Saxon Poetry: Essays in Appreciation*, edited by Lewis E. Nicholson and Dolores Warwick Frese, 312–34. Notre Dame: University of Notre Dame Press, 1975.

Freud, Sigmund. *The Interpretation of Dreams*. Translated by James Strachey. New York: Basic Books, 1955.

– *Jokes and Their Relation to the Unconscious*. Translated by James Strachey. London: Routledge, 1960.

Fry, Donald K. "Exeter Book Riddle Solutions." *Old English Newsletter* 15, no. 1 (1981): 22–33.

Fulk, R.D. "Cynewulf: Canon, Dialect, and Date." In *Cynewulf: Basic Readings*. New York, 1997; repr. as *The Cynewulf Reader*, 3–21. New York: Routledge, 2001.

Fulk, R.D., and Christopher M. Cain. *A History of Old English Literature*. 2nd ed. Oxford: Wiley-Blackwell, 2013.

Gameson, Richard. "The Origin of the Exeter Book of Old English Poetry." *Anglo-Saxon England* 25 (1996): 135–85.

– "The Colophon of the Eadwig Gospels." *Anglo-Saxon England* 31 (2002): 201–22.

Gardner, T.J. "*Þreaniedla* and *þreamedla*: Notes on Two Old English Abstracta in '-Lan'." *Neuphilologische Mitteilungen* 70 (1969): 255–61.

Garner, Lori Ann. "The Art of Translation in the Old English *Judith*." *Studia Neophilologica* 73 (2001): 171–83. https://doi.org/10.1080/00393270175340I474.

– "The Old English *Andreas* and the Mermedonian Cityscape." *Essays in Medieval Studies* 24 (2008): 53–63.

Göbel, Heidi, and Rüdiger Göbel. "The Solution of an Old English Riddle." *Studia Neophilologica* 50 (1978): 185–91. https://doi.org/10.1080/00393277808587714.

Godden, M.R. "Experiments in Genre: The Saints' Lives in Ælfric's *Catholic Homilies*." In *Holy Men and Holy Women: Old English Prose Saints' Lives and*

Their Contexts, edited by Paul E. Szarmach, 261–87. Albany: State University of New York Press, 1996.

– "Did King Alfred Write Anything?" *Medium Aevum* 76, no. 1 (2007): 1–23. https://doi.org/10.2307/43632294.

Godden, Malcolm. "Wærferth and King Alfred: The Fate of the Old English *Dialogues*." In *Alfred the Wise: Studies in Honour of Janet Bately on the Occasion of Her Sixty-Fifth Birthday*, edited by Jane Roberts, Janet L. Nelson, and Malcolm Godden, 35–51. Cambridge: Brewer, 1997.

– *Ælfric's Catholic Homilies: Introduction, Commentary and Glossary*, EETS s.s. 18. Oxford: Oxford University Press, 2000.

Godlove, Shannon N. "Bodies as Borders: Cannibalism and Conversion in the Old English *Andreas*." *Studies in Philology* 106 (2009): 137–60.

Gretsch, Mechthild. *Ælfric and the Cult of Saints in Late Anglo-Saxon England*. Cambridge: Cambridge University Press, 2005.

Griffith, Mark. "Riddle 19 of the Exeter Book: *snac*, an Old English Acronym." *Notes Queries* 237 (1992): 15–16. https://doi.org/10.1093/nq/39.1.15.

Gulley, Alison. "*Heo Man Ne Wæs*: Cross-Dressing, Sex-Change, and Womanhood in Ælfric's Life of Eugenia." *Mediaevalia* 22 (1998): 113–31.

Gurevich, Aron. *Medieval Popular Culture: Problems of Belief and Perception*. Translated by János M. Bak and Paul M. Hollingsworth. Cambridge: Cambridge University Press, 1988.

Hall, J.R. "Perspective and Wordplay in the Old English *Rune Poem*." *Neophilologus* 61 (1973): 453–61. https://doi.org/10.1007/BF01513855.

Hansen, Elaine Tuttle. *The Solomon Complex*. Toronto: University of Toronto Press, 1988.

Hayes, Mary. "The Talking Dead: Resounding Voices in Old English Riddles." *Exemplaria* 20 (2008): 123–42. https://doi.org/10.1179/175330708X311344.

Heffernan, Thomas J. *Sacred Biography: Saints and Their Biographers in the Middle Ages*. New York: Oxford University Press, 1988.

Heinemann, Fredrik J. "*Judith* 236–91a: A Mock-Heroic Approach-to-Battle Type-Scene." *Neuphilologische Mitteilungen* 71 (1970): 83–96.

Herbison, Ivan. "Generic Adaptation in *Andreas*." In *Essays on Anglo-Saxon and Related Themes in Memory of Lynne Grundy*, edited by Jane Roberts and Janet Nelson. King's College, 181–211. London: Centre for Late Antique and Medieval Studies, 2000.

– "Heroism and Comic Subversion in the Old English *Judith*." *English Studies* 91 (2010): 1–25. https://doi.org/10.1080/0013838090335 5122.

Hermann, John P. "The Pater Noster Battle Sequence in *Solomon and Saturn* and the *Pyschomachia* of Prudentius." *Neuphilologische Mitteilungen* 77, no. 2 (1976): 206–10.

Heyworth, Melanie. "Apollonius of Tyre in Its Manuscript Context: An Issue of Marriage." *Philological Quarterly* 86 (2007): 1–26.

– "Perceptions of Marriage in *Exeter Book Riddles 20* and *61*." *Studia Neophilologica* 79 (2007): 171–84. https://doi.org/10.1080/00393270701692794.

Hill, Joyce. "The Dissemination of Ælfric's Lives of Saints: A Preliminary Survey." In *Holy Men and Holy Women: Old English Prose Saints' Lives and Their Contexts*, edited by Paul E. Szarmach. Albany: State University of New York Press, 1996.

Hill, Thomas D. "Figural Narrative in *Andreas*: The Conversion of the Mermedonians." *Neuphilologische Mitteilungen* 70 (1969): 261–72.

– "Sapiential Structure and Figural Narrative in the Old English *Elene*." *Traditio* 27 (1971): 159–77. https://doi.org/10.1017/S0362152900005304.

– "Tormenting the Devil with Boiling Drops: An Apotropaic Motif in the Old English 'Solomon and Saturn I' and Old Norse-Icelandic Literature." *The Journal of English and Germanic Philology* 92, no. 2 (1993): 157–66.

– "*Imago Dei*: Genre, Symbolism, and Anglo-Saxon Hagiography." In *Holy Men and Holy Women: Old English Prose Saints' Lives and Their Contexts*, edited by Paul E. Szarmach, 35–50. Albany: State University of New York Press, 1996.

Hines, John. "Egill's *Hǫfuðlausn* in Time and Place." *Saga-Book* 24 (1995): 83–104.

Hogg, Richard M., and R.D. Fulk. *A Grammar of Old English; Volume 2: Morphology.* Chichester: Wiley-Blackwell, 2011.

Holsinger, Bruce. "Of Pigs and Parchment: Medieval Studies and the Coming of the Animal." *PMLA* 124, no. 2 (2009): 616–23. https://doi.org/10.1632/pmla.2009.124.2.616.

Horner, Shari. "The Violence of Exegesis: Reading the Bodies of Ælfric's Female Saints." In *Violence against Women in Medieval Texts*, edited by Anna Roberts, 22–43. Gainesville, FL: University Press of Florida, 1998.

– "'Why Do You Speak So Much Foolishness?' Gender, Humor, and Discourse in Ælfric's *Lives of Saints*." In *Humour in Anglo-Saxon Literature* edited by Jonathan Wilcox, 127–36. Cambridge: Brewer, 2000.

– *The Discourse of Enclosure: Representing Women in Old English Literature.* Albany: State University of New York Press, 2001.

Horowitz, Sylvia Huntley. "The Ravens in *Beowulf*." *The Journal of English and Germanic Philology* 80, no. 4 (1981): 502–11.

Hostetter, Aaron. *Political Appetites: Food in Medieval English Romance.* Columbus: The Ohio State University Press, 2017.

Hotchkiss, Valerie R. *Clothes Make the Man: Female Cross Dressing in Medieval Europe.* New York: Garland, 1996.

Howe, Nicholas. "The Cultural Construction of Reading in Anglo-Saxon England." In *Old English Literature: Critical Essays*, edited by R.M. Liuzza, 1–22. New Haven: Yale University Press, 2002.

Huizinga, Johan. *Homo Ludens: A Study of the Play Element in Culture.* London: Routledge, 1949.

Hume, Kathryn. "The Concept of the Hall in Old English Poetry." *Anglo-Saxon England* 3 (1974): 63–74.

Hurley, Matthew M., Daniel C. Dennett, and Reginald B. Adams, Jr. *Inside Jokes: Using Humor to Reverse-Engineer the Mind*. Cambridge, MA: MIT Press, 2011.

Irving, Edward B., Jr. "A Reading of *Andreas*: The Poem as Poem." *Anglo-Saxon England* 12 (1983): 215–37.

– "Heroic Experience in the Old English Riddles." In *Old English Shorter Poems: Basic Readings*, edited by Katherine O'Brien O'Keeffe, 199–212. New York: Garland, 1994.

Jackson, Peter. "The *Vitas Patrum* in Eleventh-Century Worcester." In *England in the Eleventh Century: Proceedings of the 1990 Harlaxton Symposium*, edited by Carola Hicks, 119–34. Stamford: Paul Watkins, 1992.

– "Ælfric and the Purpose of Christian Marriage: A Reconsideration of the Life of Æthelthryth, Lines 120–30." *Anglo-Saxon England* 29 (2000): 235–60. https://doi.org/10.1017/S0263675100002477.

– "Ælfric and the 'Uita Patrum' in Catholic Homily I.36." In *Essays on Anglo-Saxon and Related Themes in Memory of Lynne Grundy*, edited by Jane Roberts and Janet Nelson, 259–72. London: Centre for Late Antique and Medieval Studies, King's College, University of London, 2000.

Janko, Richard. *Aristotle on Comedy: Towards a Reconstruction of Poetics II*. London: Duckworth, 1984.

Jennings, Margaret. "Tutivillus: The Literary Career of the Recording Demon." *Studies in Philology* 74, no. 5 (December 1977): 1–95.

Johnson, David F. "Who Read Gregory's Dialogues in Old English?" In *The Power of Words: Anglo-Saxon Studies Presented to Donald Scragg on His Seventieth Birthday*, edited by Hugh Magennis and Jonathan Wilcox, 171–204. Morgantown: West Virginia University Press, 2006.

Jones, Christopher A. "The Irregular Life in Ælfric Bata's *Colloquies*." *Leeds Studies in English* 37 (2006): 241–60.

Jorgensen, Alice, Frances McCormack, and Jonathan Wilcox, eds. *Anglo-Saxon Emotions: Reading the Heart in Old English Literature, Language and Culture*. Farnham: Ashgate, 2015.

Joy, Eileen A. "The Old English *Seven Sleepers*, Eros, and the Unincorporable Infinite of the Human Person." In *Anonymous Interpolations in Ælfric's "Lives of Saints"*, edited by Robin Norris, 71–96. Kalamazoo: Medieval Institute, 2011.

Kaivola-Bregenhøj, Annikki. *Riddles: Perspectives on the Use, Function, and Change in a Folklore Genre*. Helsinki: Finnish Literature Society, 2001.

Karras, Ruth Mazo. "Holy Harlots: Prostitute Saints in Medieval Legend." *Journal of the History of Sexuality* 1 (1990): 3–32.

Kaske, R.E. "*Sapientia et Fortitudo* as the Controlling Theme of *Beowulf*." *Studies in Philology* 55 (1958): 423–56.

Kehoe, Niamh. "The Importance of Being Foolish: Reconstruction of the Pagan and Saint in Ælfric's Life of St Cecilia." *SELIM* 23 (2018): 1–26.

Kehoe Rouchy, Niamh Bridget. "Humour in Vernacular Hagiography from the Tenth to the Thirteenth Century in England." PhD dissertation, University College Cork, 2018. Dissertation under embargo, abstract available on ProQuest.

Kendrick, Laura. *Chaucerian Play: Comedy and Control in the Canterbury Tales.* Berkeley: University of California Press, 1988.

Ker, N.R. *Catalogue of Manuscripts Containing Anglo-Saxon.* Oxford: Oxford University Press, 1957.

Keynes, Simon. "The Historical Context of the Battle of Maldon." In *The Battle of Maldon, AD 991*, edited by Donald Scragg, 81–113. Oxford: Blackwell, 1991.

Kim, Dorothy, ed. "Critical Race and the Middle Ages: A Special Cluster." *Literature Compass* 16, no. 9–10 (2019). https://doi.org/10.1111/lic3.12549.

Kitson, Peter. "Old English Bird-Names (1)." *English Studies* 78 (1997): 481–505. https://doi.org/10.1080/00138389708599099.

Klein, Stacy S. "Ælfric's Sources and His Gendered Audiences." *Essays in Medieval Studies* 13 (1996): 111–19.

– *Ruling Women: Queenship and Gender in Anglo-Saxon Literature.* Notre Dame: University of Notre Dame Press, 2006.

– "Gender." In *A Handbook of Anglo-Saxon Studies*, edited by Jacqueline Stodnick and Renée Trilling, 39–54. Oxford: Blackwell, 2012.

Kleist, Aaron J. "Ælfric's Corpus: A Conspectus." *Florilegium* 18, no. 2 (2001): 113–64.

– ed. *The Old English Homily: Precedent, Practice, and Appropriation.* Turnhout: Brepols, 2007.

– *The Chronology and Canon of Ælfric of Eynsham.* Cambridge: Brewer, 2019.

Klinck, Anne. "*The Riming Poem*: Design and Interpretation." *Neuphilologische Mitteilungen* 89 (1988): 266–79.

Kries, Susanne. "Laughter and Social Stability in Anglo-Saxon and Old Norse Literature." In *A History of English Laughter: Laughter from Beowulf to Beckett and Beyond*, edited by Manfred Pfister, 1–15. Amsterdam: Rodopi, 2002.

Kuipers, Giselinde. "The Sociology of Humor." In *The Primer of Humor Research*, edited by Victor Raskin, 361–98. Berlin: de Gruyter, 2008.

– *Good Humor, Bad Taste: A Sociology of the Joke.* Berlin: de Gruyter, 2006; 2nd ed., 2015.

Lapidge, Michael. "The Hermeneutic Style in Tenth-Century Anglo-Latin Literature." *Anglo-Saxon England* 4 (1975): 67–111.

– "Surviving Booklists from Anglo-Saxon England." In *Learning and Literature in Anglo-Saxon England; Studies Presented to Peter Clemoes*, edited by

Michael Lapidge and Helmut Gneuss, 33–89. Cambridge: Cambridge University Press, 1985.

– "The Saintly Life in Anglo-Saxon England." In *The Cambridge Companion to Old English Literature*, edited by Malcolm Godden and Michael Lapidge, 2nd ed., 251–72. Cambridge: Cambridge University Press, 2013.

Larrington, Carolyne. *A Store of Common Sense: Gnomic Theme and Style in Old Icelandic and Old English Wisdom Poetry*. Oxford: Oxford University Press, 1993.

Leclerq, Jean. "La joie de mourir selon Saint Bernard de Clairvaux." In *Dies illa: Death in the Middle Ages*, edited by Jane H.M. Taylor, 195–207. Liverpool: Francis Cairns, 1984.

Lee, Christina. "Reluctant Appetites: Anglo-Saxon Attitudes towards Fasting." In *Saints and Scholars: New Perspectives on Anglo-Saxon Literature and Culture in Honour of Hugh Magennis*, edited by Stuart McWilliams, 164–86. Cambridge: Brewer, 2012.

Lees, Clare A. "Engendering Religious Desire: Sex, Knowledge, and Christian Identity in Anglo-Saxon England." *Journal of Medieval and Early Modern Studies* 27 (1997): 17–45.

– "Vision and Place in the Old English Life of Mary of Egypt." In *The Old English Life of Mary of Egypt*, edited by Donald Scragg, 57–78. Kalamazoo: Medieval Institute, 2005.

Lees, Clare A., and Gillian R. Overing. "Before History, before Difference: Bodies, Metaphor, and the Church in Anglo-Saxon England." *Yale Journal of Criticism* 11 (1998): 315–34.

– *Double Agents: Women and Clerical Culture in Anglo-Saxon England*. Philadelphia: University of Pennsylvania Press, 2001.

Leneghan, Francis. "The Departure of the Hero in a Ship: The Intertextuality of *Beowulf*, Cynewulf and *Andreas*." *SELIM* 24 (2019): 105–32. https://doi .org/10.17811/selim.24.2019.

Lerer, Seth. *Literacy and Power in Anglo-Saxon Literature*. Lincoln: University of Nebraska Press, 1991.

Lionarons, Joyce Tally. *The Homiletic Writings of Archbishop Wulfstan*. Woodbridge: Brewer, 2010.

Liuzza, R.M. "The Texts of the Old English *Riddle 30*." *The Journal of English and Germanic Philology* 87 (1988): 1–15.

– "The Future Is a Foreign Country: The Legend of the Seven Sleepers and the Anglo-Saxon Sense of the Past." In *Medieval Science Fiction*, edited by Carl Kears and James Paz, 61–78. King's College, London: Centre for Late Antique and Medieval Studies, 2016.

Lochrie, Karma. "Gender, Sexual Violence, and the Politics of War in the Old English *Judith*." In *Class and Gender in Early English Literature*, edited by Britton J. Harwood and Gillian R. Overing, 1–20. Bloomington: Indiana University Press, 1994.

Lockyer, Sharon, and Michael Pickering, eds. *Beyond the Joke: The Limits of Humour*. Basingstoke: Palgrave, 2005.

Lorden, Jennifer A. "Tale and Parable: Theorizing Fictions in the Old English *Boethius*." *PMLA* 136, no. 3 (2021): 340–55. https://doi.org/10.1632 /S0030812921000249.

Louviot, Elise. *Direct Speech in Beowulf and Other Old English Narrative Poems*. Cambridge: Bewer, 2016.

Love, Rosalind. "Insular Latin Literature to 900." In *The Cambridge History of Early Medieval English Literature*, edited by Clare A. Lees, 120–57. Cambridge: Cambridge University Press, 2013.

Mackie, W.S. "Notes on the Text of the 'Exeter Book'." *Modern Language Review* 28 (1933): 75–78. https://doi.org/10.2307/3715887.

Macrae-Gibson, O.D. "The Literary Structure of 'The Riming Poem'." *Neuphilologische Mitteilungen* 74 (1973): 62–84.

Magennis, Hugh. "Adaptation of Biblical Detail in the Old English 'Judith': The Feast Scene." *Neuphilologische Mitteilungen* 84 (1983): 331–7.

– "The Cup as Symbol and Metaphor in Old English Literature." *Speculum* 60 (1985): 517–36. https://doi.org/10.2307/2848173.

– "On the Sources of Non-Ælfrician Lives in the Old English Lives of Saints, with Reference to the Cotton-Corpus Legendary." *N Q* 32 (1985): 292–9. https://doi.org/10.1093/notesj/32.3.292.

– "Style and Method in the Old English Version of the Legend of the Seven Sleepers." *English Studies* 66 (1985): 285–95. https://doi.org/10.1080 /00138388508598392.

– "Contrasting Features in the non-Ælfrician Lives in the Old English *Lives of Saints*." *Anglia* 104 (1986): 316–48. https://doi.org/10.1515/angl.1986 .1986.104.316.

– "The Exegesis of Inebriation: Treading Carefully in Old English." *English Language Notes* 23 (1986): 3–6.

– "'Monig oft gesæt': Some Images of Sitting in Old English Poetry." *Neophilologus* 70 (1986): 442–52. https://doi.org/10.1007/BF00459825.

– "The Anonymous Old English *Legend of the Seven Sleepers* and Its Latin Source." *Leeds Studies in English* 22 (1991): 43–56.

– "Images of Laughter in Old English Poetry, with Particular Reference to the 'Hleahtor Wera' of *The Seafarer*." *English Studies* 73 (1992): 193–204. https://doi.org/10.1080/00138389208598805.

– "Contrasting Narrative Emphases in the Old English Poem 'Judith' and Ælfric's Paraphrase of the Book of Judith." *Neuphilologische Mitteilungen* 96 (1995): 61–66.

– "'No Sex Please, We're Anglo-Saxons'? Attitudes to Sexuality in Old English Prose and Poetry." *Leeds Studies in English* 26 (1995): 1–26.

- "Ælfric and the Legend of the Seven Sleepers." In *Holy Men and Holy Women: Old English Prose Saints' Lives and Their Contexts*, edited by Paul E. Szarmach, 317–31. Albany: State University of New York Press, 1996.
- *Images of Community in Old English Poetry*. Cambridge: Cambridge University Press, 1996.
- "St Mary of Egypt and Ælfric: Unlikely Bedfellows in Cotton Julius E.vii?" In *The Legend of Mary of Egypt in Medieval Insular Hagiography*, edited by Erich Poppe and Bianca Ross, 99–112. Dublin: Four Courts Press, 1996.
- *Anglo-Saxon Appetites: Food and Drink and Their Consumption in Old English and Related Literature*. Dublin: Four Courts, 1999.
- "A Funny Thing Happened on the Way to Heaven: Humorous Incongruity in Old English Saints' Lives." In *Humour in Anglo-Saxon Literature*, edited by Jonathan Wilcox, 137–57. Cambridge: Brewer, 2000.
- "Approaches to Saints' Lives." In *The Christian Tradition in Anglo-Saxon England: Approaches to Current Scholarship and Teaching*, edited by Paul Cavill, 163–83. Cambridge: Brewer, 2004.
- "Crowd Control? Depictions of the Many in Anglo-Saxon Literature, with Particular Reference to the Old English *Legend of the Seven Sleepers*." *English Studies* 93 (2012): 119–37. https://doi.org/10.1080/0013838X.2011.649063.
Magennis, Hugh, and Mary Swan, eds. *A Companion to Ælfric*. Leiden: Brill, 2009.
Mann, Erin Irene. "Relative Identities: Father-Daughter Incest in Medieval Religious Literature." unpublished Ph.D. dissertation, University of Iowa, 2011.
McGowan, Joseph. "The Old English *Apollonius of Tyre* 19." *The Explicator* 49 (1991): 74–5. https://doi.org/10.1080/00144940.1991.11484008.
McGowan, Todd. *Only a Joke Can Save Us: A Theory of Comedy*. Evanston: Northwestern University Press, 2017.
McGraw, Peter, and Joel Warner. *The Humor Code: A Global Search for What Makes Things Funny*. New York: Simon and Schuster, 2014.
McIntosh, Angus. "Wulfstan's Prose." *Proceedings of the British Academy* 35 (1949): 109–42.
McKie, Michael. "The Origins and Early Development of Rhyme in English Verse." *Modern Language Review* 92 (1997): 817–31. https://doi.org/10.2307/3734202.
Michelet, Fabienne L. "Eating Bodies in the Old English *Andreas*." In *Fleshly Things and Spiritual Matters: Studies in the Medieval Body in Honour of Margaret Bridges*, edited by N. Nyffenegger and K. Rupp, 165–92. Newcastle upon Tyne: Cambridge Scholars, 2011.
Miyashiro, Adam. "Homeland Insecurity: Biopolitics and Sovereign Violence in *Beowulf*." *postmedieval: a journal of medieval cultural studies* 11 (2020): 384–95. https://doi.org/10.1057/s41280-020-00188-3.

Moloney, Bernadette. "Another Look at Ælfric's Use of Discourse in Some Saints' Lives." *English Studies* 63 (1982): 13–19. https://doi.org/10.1080 /00138388208598152.

Momma, Haruko. "Epanalepsis: A Retelling of the Judith Story in the Anglo-Saxon Poetic Language." *Studies in the Literary Imagination* 36, no. 1 (Spring 2003): 59–73.

– "Old English Poetic Form: Genre, Style, Prosody." In *The Cambridge History of Early Medieval English Literature*, edited by Clare A. Lees, 278–308. Cambridge: Cambridge University Press, 2013.

Morini, Carla. "The First English Love Romance without 'Love'! The Old English *Apollonius of Tyre*." *SELIM* 12 (2003–04): 109–25.

– "The Old English Apollonius and Wulfstan of York." *Leeds Studies in English* 36 (2005): 63–104.

Morreall, John. "Applications of Humor: Health, the Workplace, and Education." In *The Primer of Humor Research*, edited by Victor Raskin, 449–78. Berlin: Mouton de Gruyter, 2008.

– *Comic Relief: A Comprehensive Philosophy of Humor*. Hoboken: Wiley, 2009.

Mulkay, Michael. *On Humour: Its Nature and Place in Modern Society*. Oxford: Polity, 1988.

Murphy, Patrick J. *Unriddling the Exeter Book Riddles*. University Park, PA: Penn State University Press, 2011.

Naismith, Rory. *Early Medieval Britain, c. 500–1000*. Cambridge: Cambidge University Press, 2021.

Neville, Jennifer. "The Unexpected Treasure of the 'Implement Trope': Hierarchical Relationships in the Old English Riddles." *Review of English Studies* 62 (2011): 505–19. https://doi.org/10.1093/res/hgq131.

– "A Modest Proposal: Titles for *The Exeter Book Riddles*." *Medum Ævum* 88, no. 1 (2019): 116–23. https://doi.org/10.2307/26889859.

Nicholls, Alex. "The Corpus of Prose Saints' Lives and Hagiographic Pieces in Old English and Its Manuscript Distribution." *Reading Mediaeval Studies* 19 (1993): 73–96, and 20 (1994): 51–87.

Niles, John D. "Exeter Book Riddle 74 and the Play of the Text." *Anglo-Saxon England* 27 (1998): 169–207.

– "Byrhtnoth's Laughter and the Poetics of Gesture." In *Humour in Anglo-Saxon Literature*, edited by Jonathan Wilcox, 11–32. Cambridge: Brewer, 2000.

– *Old English Enigmatic Poems and the Play of the Texts*. Turnhout: Brepols, 2006.

– *Old English Literature: A Guide to Criticism with Selected Readings*. Chichester: Wiley-Blackwell, 2016.

– *God's Exiles and English Verse: On the Exeter Anthology of Old English Poetry*. Exeter: University of Exeter Press, 2019.

Norris, Robin. "*Vitas Matrum*: Mary of Egypt as Female Confessor." In *The Old English Life of Mary of Egypt*, edited by Donald Scragg, OEN Subsidia, 79–109. Kalamazoo: Medieval Institute, 2005.

– "Genre Trouble: Reading the Old English *Vita* of Saint Euphrosyne." In *Writing Women Saints in Anglo-Saxon England*, edited by Paul E. Szarmach, 121–39. Toronto: University of Toronto Press, 2013.

North, Richard. "Meet the Pagans: On the Misuse of *Beowulf* in *Andreas*." In *Aspects of Knowledge: Preserving and Reinventing Traditions of Learning in the Middle Ages*, edited by M. Cesario and Hugh Magennis, 185–209. Manchester: Manchester University Press, 2018.

O'Brien O'Keeffe, Katherine. *Visible Song: Transitional Literacy in Old English Verse*. Cambridge: Cambridge University Press, 1990.

Ó Carragáin, Éamonn. "Cynewulf's Epilogue to *Elene* and the Tastes of the Vercelli Compiler: A Paradigm of Meditative Reading." In *Lexis and Texts in Early English: Studies Presented to Jane Roberts*, edited by Christian J. Kay and Louise M. Sylvester, 187–201. Amsterdam: Rodopi, 2001.

Ogden, Amy V. "*St Eufrosine*'s Invitation to Gender Transgression." In *Trans and Genderqueer Subjects in Medieval Hagiography*, edited by Alicia Spencer-Hall and Blake Gutt, 201–21. Amsterdam: Amsterdam University Press, 2021.

Olrik, Axel. "Epic Laws of Folk Narratives." In *The Study of Folklore*, edited by Alan Dundes. Englewood Cliffs: Prentice-Hall, 1965.

Ooi, S. Beth Newman. "Crossed Lines: Reading a Riddle between Exeter Book Riddle 60 and "The Husband's Message." *Philological Quarterly* 100 (2021): 1–22.

Orchard, Andy. *Pride and Prodigies: Studies in the Monsters of the Beowulf-Manuscript*. Cambridge: Brewer, 1995.

– *A Critical Companion to Beowulf*. Cambridge: Brewer, 2003.

– "Enigma Variations: The Anglo-Saxon Riddle-Tradition." In *Latin Learning and English Lore: Studies in Anglo-Saxon Literature for Michael Lapidge*, 2 vols., edited by Katherine O'Brien O'Keeffe and Andy Orchard, vol. I, 284–304. Toronto: University of Toronto Press, 2005.

– "The Originality of *Andreas*." In *Old English Philology*, edited by Rafael J. Pascual, Leonard Neidorf, and Tom Shippey, 331–70. Cambridge: Brewer, 2016.

– "Performing Writing and Singing Silence in the Anglo-Saxon Riddle Tradition." In *Or Words to That Effect: Orality and the Writing of Literary History*, edited by Daniel F. Chamberlain and J. Edward Chamberlin, 73–91. Amsterdam: Benjamins, 2016.

– *A Commentary on The Old English and Anglo-Latin Riddle Tradition*. Cambridge, MA: Harvard University Press, 2021.

Oring, Elliott. *Jokes and Their Relations*. Lexington: University of Kentucky Press, 1992.

– *Joking Asides: The Theory, Analysis, and Aesthetics of Humor*. Logan: Utah State University Press, 2016.

Orton, Peter. "The Exeter Book *Riddles*: Authorship and Transmission." *Anglo-Saxon England* 44 (2015): 131–62.

Owen-Crocker, Gale R. *The Four Funerals in Beowulf and the Structure of the Poem*. Manchester: Manchester University Press, 2000.

– *Dress in Anglo-Saxon England*, revised and enlarged ed. Cambridge: Boydell, 2004.

Page, R.I. *An Introduction to English Runes*. London: Methuen, 1973.

Pareles, Mo. "What the Raven Told the Eagle: Animal Language and the Return of Loss in *Beowulf*." In *Dating Beowulf: Studies in Intimacy*, edited by Daniel C. Remein and Erica Weaver. Manchester: Manchester University Press, 2020.

Parkes, M.B. "*Rædan, Areccan, Smeagan*: How the Anglo-Saxons Read." *Anglo-Saxon England* 26 (1997): 1–22.

Parks, Ward. *Verbal Dueling in Heroic Narrative: The Homeric and Old English Traditions*. Princeton: Princeton University Press, 1990.

Pàroli, Teresa. "The Tears of the Heroes in Germanic Epic Poetry." In *Helden und Heldensage: Otto Geschwantler zum 60. Geburtstag*, edited by Hermann Reichert and Günter Zimmermann, 233–66. Vienna: Fassbaender, 1990.

Paz, James. "Magic That Works: Performing *Scientia* in the Old English Metrical Charms and Poetic Dialogues of Solomon and Saturn." *Journal of Medieval and Early Modern Studies* 45, no. 2 (2015): 219–43. https://doi.org /10.1215/10829636-2880875.

Pepicello, W.J., and Thomas A. Green, *The Language of Riddles: New Perspectives*. Columbus: The Ohio State University Press, 1984.

Phillips, Susan E. *Transforming Talk: The Problem with Gossip in Late Medieval England*. University Park: Penn State University Press, 2007.

Pigg, Daniel F. "Laughter in *Beowulf*: Ambiguity, Ambivalence, and Group Identity Formation." In *Laughter in the Middle Ages and Early Modern Times: Epistemology of a Fundamental Human Behavior, Its Meaning, and Consequences*, edited by Albrecht Classen, 201–13. Berlin: De Gruyter, 2010.

Poppe, Erich, and Bianca Ross, eds. *The Legend of Mary of Egypt in Medieval Insular Hagiography*. Dublin: Four Courts Press, 1996.

Porck, Thijs. "Treasures in a Sooty Bag? A Note on Durham Proverb 7." *Notes Queries* 62, no. 2 (2015): 203–6. https://doi.org/10.1093/notesj/gjvo66.

Porter, David W. "Anglo-Saxon Colloquies: Ælfric, Ælfric Bata and *De raris fabuilis retractata*." *Neophilologus* 81 (1997): 467–80. https://doi.org/10.1093 /notesj/gjvo66.

Powell, Alison M. "Verbal Parallels in *Andreas* and Its Relationship to *Beowulf* and Cynewulf." unpublished PhD diss., University of Cambridge, 2002.

Provine, Robert R. *Laughter: A Scientific Investigation*. New York: Viking, 2000.

Puskar, Jason R. "Hwa þas fitte fegde? Questioning Cynewulf's Claim of Authorship." *English Studies* 92 (2011): 1–19. https://doi.org/10.1080 /0013838X.2010.536683.

Rabbie, Edwin. "Wit and Humor in Roman Rhetoric." In *A Companion to Roman Rhetoric*, edited by William Dominik and John Hall, 207–17. Malden, MA: Blackwell, 2007.

Ramey, Peter. "Writing Speaks: Oral Poetics and Writing Technology in the Exeter Book Riddles." *Philological Quarterly* 92, no. 3 (2013): 335–56.

– "The Riddle of Beauty: The Aesthetics of *Wrætlic* in Old English Verse." *Modern Philology* 114 (2017): 457–81. https://doi.org/10.1086/688057.

– "Crafting Strangeness: Wonder Terminology in the Exeter Book Riddles and the Anglo-Latin Enigmata." *Review of English Studies* 69 (2018): 201–15. https://doi.org/10.1093/res/hgx093.

Raskin, Victor, ed. *The Primer of Humor Research*. Berlin: Mouton de Gruyter, 2008.

Reading, Amity. "Baptism, Conversion, and Selfhood in the Old English *Andreas*." *Studies in Philology* 112 (2015): 1–23. https://doi.org/10.1353 /sip.2015.0003.

Riedinger, Anita. "The Englishing of Arcestrate: Woman in *Apollonius of Tyre*." In *New Readings on Women in Old English Literature*, edited by Helen Damico and Alexandra Hennessey Olsen, 292–306. Bloomington: Indiana University Press, 1990.

Risden, E.L. "Heroic Humor in *Beowulf*." In *Humour in Anglo-Saxon Literature*, edited by Jonathan Wilcox, 71–8. Cambridge: Brewer, 2000.

Robertson, Nicola. "The Benedictine Reform: Current and Future Scholarship." *Literature Compass* 3, no. 3 (2006): 282–99. https://doi.org/10.1111/j.1741 -4113.2006.00319.x.

Robinson, Fred C. "The Devil's Account of the Next World." *Neuphilologische Mitteilungen* 73 (1972): 362–71, repr. in his *The Editing of Old English*, 196–205. Oxford: Blackwell, 1994.

– "The Artful Ambiguities in the Old English 'Book-Moth' Riddle." In *Anglo-Saxon Poetry: Essays in Appreciation*, edited by Lewis E. Nicholson and Dolores W. Frese, 355–62. Notre Dame: University of Notre Dame Press, 1975.

– "Some Aspects of the *Maldon* Poet's Artistry." *The Journal of English and Germanic Philology* 75 (1976): 25–40.

Rollason, David. *Saints and Relics in Anglo-Saxon England*. Oxford: Oxford University Press, 1989.

Rosenwein, Barbara H. *Emotional Communities in the Early Middle Ages*. Ithaca: Cornell University Press, 2006.

Roy, Gopa. "A Virgin Acts Manfully: Ælfric's *Life of St Eugenia* and the Latin Versions." *Leeds Studies in English* 23 (1992): 1–27.

Rozano-Garcia, F.J. "*Hwær Is Wuldor Þin?* Traditional Poetic Diction and the Alien Text in the Old English *Andreas*." *Peritia* 28 (2017): 177–94. https://doi .org/10.1484/J.PERIT.5.114568.

Rudolf, Winfried. "Riddling and Reading – Iconicity and Logogriphs in Exeter Book Riddles 23 and 45." *Anglia* 130, no. 4 (2012): 499–525. https://doi .org/10.1515/ang-2012-0526.

Saltzman, Benjamin A. *Bonds of Secrecy: Law, Spirituality, and the Literature of Concealment in Early Medieval England*. Philadelphia: University of Pennsylvania Press, 2019.

Salvador-Bello, Mercedes. "The Key to the Body: Unlocking Riddles 42–46." In *Naked before God: Uncovering the Body in Anglo-Saxon England* edited by Benjamin C. Withers and Jonathan Wilcox, 60–96. Morgantown: West Virginia University Press, 2003.

– *Isidorean Perceptions of Order: The Exeter Book Riddles and Medieval Latin Enigmata*. Morgantown: West Virginia University Press, 2015.

– "The Old English *Apollonius of Tyre* in the Light of Early Romance Tradition: An Assessment of Its Plot and Characterization in Relation to Marie de France's *Eliduc*." *English Studies* 93 (2012): 749–74. https://doi.org/10.1080 /0013838X.2012.700566.

– "Exeter Book Riddle 90 Under a New Light: A School Drill in Hisperic Robes." *Neophilologus* 102 (2018): 107–23. https://doi.org/10.1007/s11061 -017-9540-x.

Sanders, Barry. *Sudden Glory: Laughter as Subversive History*. Boston: Beacon, 1995.

Sauer, Hans. "Die 72 Völker und Sprachen der Welt: ein mittelalterliche Topos in der englischen Literatur." *Anglia* 101 (1982): 29–48. https://doi.org/10.1515 /angl.1983.1983.101.29.

Sawyer, Peter. *The Wealth of Anglo-Saxon England*. Oxford: Oxford University Press, 2013.

Sayers, William. "*Þoðer* and *Top* in the Old English *Apollonius of Tyre*." *N Q* 56 (2009): 12–14.

Scanlon, Larry. *Narrative, Authority, and Power: The Medieval Exemplum and the Chaucerian Tradition*. Cambridge: Cambridge University Press, 1994.

Scheil, Andrew P. "Somatic Ambiguity and Masculine Desire in the Old English Life of Euphrosyne." *Exemplaria* 11 (1999): 345–61. https://doi.org/10.1179 /exm.1999.11.2.345.

– "Bodies and Boundaries in the Old English *Life of St. Mary of Egypt*." *Neophilologus* 84 (2000): 137–56. https://doi.org/10.1023/A:1004628602435.

– *The Footsteps of Israel: Understanding Jews in Anglo-Saxon England*. Ann Arbor: University of Michigan Press, 2004.

Schorn, Brittany Erin. *Speaker and Authority in Old Norse Wisdom Poetry*. Berlin: de Gruyter, 2017.

Scragg, D.G. "The Corpus of Vernacular Homilies and Prose Saints' Lives before Ælfric." *Anglo-Saxon England* 8 (1979): 223–77.

– "The Devil's Account of the Next World Revisted." *ANQ* 24 (1986): 107–10.

– "The Corpus of Anonymous Lives and their Manuscript Context." In *Holy Men and Holy Women*, edited by Paul E. Szarmach, 209–30. Albany: State University of New York Press, 1996.

Scragg, Donald, ed. *The Old English Life of Mary of Egypt*. Kalamazoo: Medieval Institute Publications, 2005.

– "The Nature of Old English Verse." In *The Cambridge Companion to Old English Literature*, 2nd ed., edited by Malcolm Godden and Michael Lapidge, 50–65. Cambridge: Cambridge University Press, 2013.

Shanzer, Danuta. "Laughter and Humour in the Early Medieval Latin West." In *Humour, History and Politics in Late Antiquity and the Early Middle Ages*, edited by Guy Halsall, 25–47. Cambridge: Cambridge University Press, 2002.

Shippey, T.A. *Beowulf*. London: Arnold, 1978.

– "Principles of Conversation in Beowulfian Speech." In *Techniques of Description: Spoken and Written Discourse; A Festschrift for Malcolm Coulthard*, edited by John M. Sinclair, Michael Hoey, and Gwyneth Fox, 109–26. London Routledge, 1993.

– "'Grim Wordplay': Folly and Wisdom in Anglo-Saxon Humor." In *Humour in Anglo-Saxon Literature*, edited by Jonathan Wilcox, 33–48. Cambridge: Brewer, 2000.

Shippey, Tom. *Laughing Shall I Die: Lives and Deaths of the Great Vikings*. London: Reaktion, 2018.

Shook, Laurence K. "Old-English Riddle 28 – *Testudo* (Tortoise-Lyre)." *Mediaeval Studies* 20 (1958): 93–97. https://doi.org/10.1484/J.MS.2.306630.

– "Riddles Relating to the Anglo-Saxon Scriptorium." In *Essays in Honour of Anton Charles Pegis*, edited by J.R. O'Donnell, 215–36. Toronto: PIMS, 1974.

Sims Williams, Patrick. "'Is It Fog or Smoke or Warriors Fighting?': Irish and Welsh Parallels to the *Finnsburg* Fragment." *Bulletin of the Board of Celtic Studies* 27 (1978): 505–14.

Sisam, Kenneth. "An Old English Translation of a Letter from Wynfrith to Eadburga (A.D. 716–17) in Cotton MS Otho C i." In *Studies in the History of Old English Literature*, 199–224. Oxford: Oxford University Press, 1953.

Sorrell, Paul. "Oaks, Ships, and the Old English *Rune Poem*." *Anglo-Saxon England* 19 (1990): 103–16.

Spencer, H. Leith. *English Preaching in the Late Middle Ages*. Oxford: Oxford University Press, 1993.

Spencer-Hall, Alicia, and Blake Gutt, eds. *Trans and Genderqueer Subjects in Medieval Hagiography*. Amsterdam: Amsterdam University Press, 2021.

Stafford, Pauline. *Queen Emma and Queen Edith: Queenship and Women's Power in Eleventh-Century England*. Oxford: Blackwell, 1997.

Stallcup, Stephen. "The Old English *Life of Saint Euphrosyne* and the Economics of Sanctity." In *Anonymous Interpolations in Ælfric's "Lives of Saints"*, edited by Robin Norris, 13–28. Kalamazoo: Medieval Institute Publications, 2011.

Stanley, E.G. "Rhymes in English Medieval Verse: From Old English to Middle English." In *Medieval English Studies Presented to George Kane*, edited by Edward Donald Kennedy, Ronald Waldron, and Joseph S. Wittig, 19–54. Woodbridge: Brewer, 1988.

– "Heroic Aspects of the Exeter Book Riddles." In *Prosody and Poetics in the Early Middle Ages: Essays in Honor of C.B. Hieatt*, edited by M.J. Toswell, 197–218. Toronto: University of Toronto Press, 1995.

– "Courtliness and Courtesy in *Beowulf* and Elsewhere in English Medieval Literature." In *Words and Works: Studies in Medieval English Language and Literature in Honour of Fred C. Robinson*, edited by Peter S. Baker and Nicholas Howe, 67–103. Toronto: University of Toronto Press, 1998.

– "Wonder-Smiths and Others: *smið* Compounds in Old English Poetry, with an Excursus on *Hleahtor*." *Neophilologus* 101 (2017): 277–304. https://doi.org/10.1007/s11061-016-9504-6.

Stevenson, Jane. "The Holy Sinner: The Life of Mary of Egypt." In *The Legend of Mary of Egypt in Medieval Insular Hagiography*, edited by Erich Poppe and Bianca Ross, 19–50. Dublin: Four Courts Press, 1996.

Stewart, Ann Harleman. "Old English Riddle 47 as Stylistic Parody." *Papers on Language and Literature* 11 (1975): 227–45.

– "Kenning and Riddle in Old English." *Papers on Language and Literature* 15 (1979): 115–36.

Stodnick, Jacqueline A. "Cynewulf as Author: Medieval Reality or Modern Myth?" *Bulletin of the John Rylands University Library of Manchester* 79 (1997): 25–39. https://doi.org/10.7227/BJRL.79.3.5.

Stodnick, Jacqueline A., and Renée Trilling, eds. *A Handbook of Anglo-Saxon Studies*. Oxford: Blackwell, 2012.

Symons, Victoria. *Runes and Roman Letters in Anglo-Saxon Manuscripts*. Berlin: de Gruyter, 2016.

Szarmach, Paul E. "Another Old English Translation of Gregory the Great's *Dialogues*?" *English Studies* 62 (1981): 91–109.

– "Ælfric's Women Saints: Eugenia." In *New Readings on Women in Old English Literature*, edited by Helen Damico and Alexandra Hennessey Olsen, 146–57. Bloomington and Indianapolis: Indiana University Press, 1990.

– "St. Euphrosyne: Holy Transvestite." In *Holy Men and Holy Women: Old English Prose Saints' Lives and Their Contexts*, edited by Paul E. Szarmach, 353–65. Albany: State University of New York Press, 1996.

– "More Genre Trouble: The Life of Mary of Egypt." In *Writing Women Saints in Anglo-Saxon England*, edited by Paul E. Szarmach, 140–64. Toronto: University of Toronto Press, 2013.

Taylor, Archer. "The Varieties of Riddles." In *Philologica: The Malone Anniversary Studies*, edited by Thomas A. Kirby and Henry Bosley Woolf, 1–8. Baltimore: Johns Hopkins University Press, 1949.

Thomson, Simon C. *Communal Creativity in the Making of the 'Beowulf' Manuscript: Towards a History of Reception for the Nowell Codex*. Leiden: Brill, 2018.

Thornbury, Emily V. *Becoming A Poet in Anglo-Saxon England*. Cambridge: Cambridge University Press, 2014.

– "Light Verse in Anglo-Saxon England." In *The Shapes of Early English Poetry: Style, Form, History*, edited by Irina Dumitrescu and Eric Weiskott, 85–106. Kalamazoo: Medieval Institute Publications, 2019.

Tinti, Francesca, ed. *Pastoral Care in Late Anglo-Saxon England*. Woodbridge: Boydell, 2005.

Tolkien, J.R.R. *Finn and Hengest: The Fragment and the Episode*. Edited by Alan Bliss. London: Allen, 1982.

Townend, Matthew. "Pre-Cnut Praise-Poetry in Viking Age England." *Review of English Studies* 51 (2000): 349–70. https://doi.org/10.1093/res/51.203.349.

Townsend, David. "The Naked Truth of the King's Affection in the Old English *Apollonius of Tyre*." *Journal of Medieval and Early Modern Studies* 34, no. 1 (2004): 173–95. https://doi.org/10.1215/10829636-34-1-173.

Trautmann, Moritz. "Die Auflösungen der altenglischen Rätsel." *Beiblatt zur Anglia* 5 (1894): 46–51.

Treharne, Elaine. *Living Through Conquest: The Politics of Early English, 1020–1220*. Oxford: Oxford University Press, 2012.

– *Perceptions of Medieval Manuscripts: The Phenomenal Book*. Oxford: Oxford University Press, 2021.

Tyler, Elizabeth M. "Style and Meaning in *Judith*." *Notes Queries* 237 (1992): 16–19. https://doi.org/10.1093/nq/39.1.16.

– *England in Europe: English Royal Women and Literary Patronage, c. 1000–c. 1150*. Toronto: University of Toronto Press, 2017.

Upchurch, Robert K. "A Big Dog Barks: Ælfric of Eynsham's Indictment of the English Pastorate and *Witan*." *Speculum* 85 (2010): 505–33. https://doi.org/10.1017/S0038713410001296.

Wade, Erik. "Language, Letters, and Augustinian Origins in the Old English Poetic *Solomon and Saturn I*." *The Journal of English and Germanic Philology* 117, no. 2 (2018): 160–84. https://doi.org/10.5406/jenglgermphil.117.2.0160.

Walker, Jonathan. "The Transtextuality of Transvestite Sainthood: Or, How to Make the Gendered Form Fit the Generic Function." *Exemplaria* 15 (2003): 73–110. https://doi.org/10.1179/exm.2003.15.1.73.

Wallace, David, ed. *The Cambridge History of Medieval English Literature*. Cambridge: Cambridge University Press, 1999.

Walsh, Efthalia Makris. "The Ascetic Mother Mary of Egypt." *Greek Orthodox Theological Review* 34 (1989): 59–69.

Waterhouse, Ruth. "Ælfric's Use of Discourse in Some Saints' Lives." *Anglo-Saxon England* 5 (1976): 83–103.

Watt, Diane, and Clare A. Lees. "Age and Desire in the Old English *Life of St Mary of Egypt:* A Queerer Time and Place?" In *Middle Aged Women in the Middle Ages,* edited by Sue Niebrzysdowski, 53–67. Cambridge: Brewer, 2011.

Wehlau, Ruth. *"The Riddle of Creation": Metaphor Structures in Old English Poetry.* New York: Peter Lang, 1997.

Wentersdorf, Karl P. "The Old English *Rhyming Poem*: A Ruler's Lament." *Studies in Philology* 82 (1985): 265–94.

Wenzel, Siegfried. *The Art of Preaching: Five Medieval Texts and Translations.* Washington, DC: Catholic University of America Press, 2013.

– *Medieval Artes Praedicandi: A Synthesis of Scholastic Sermon Structure.* Toronto: University of Toronto Press for Medieval Academy, 2015.

Whatley, E. Gordon. "An Introduction to the Study of Old English Prose Hagiography: Sources and Resources." In *Holy Men and Holy Women: Old English Prose Saints' Lives and Their Contexts,* edited by Paul E. Szarmach, 3–32. Albany: State University of New York Press, 1996.

– "Lost in Translation: Omission of Episodes in Some Old English Prose Saints' Legends." *Anglo-Saxon England* 26 (1997): 187–208.

– *"Pearls before Swine*: Ælfric, Vernacular Hagiography, and the Lay Reader." In *Via Crucis: Essays on Early Medieval Sources and Ideas in Memory of J.E. Cross,* edited by Thomas N. Hall, 158–84. Morgantown: West Virginia University Press, 2002.

– "Eugenia Before Ælfric: A Preliminary Report on the Transmission of an Early Medieval Legend." In *Intertexts: Studies in Anglo-Saxon Culture Presented to Paul E. Szarmach,* edited by Virginia Blanton and Helene Scheck, 349–68. Tempe, AZ: ACMRS, 2009.

Whitelock, Dorothy. "The Numismatic Interest of the Old English Version of the Legend of the Seven Sleepers." In *Anglo-Saxon Coins: Studies Presented to F.M. Stenton,* edited by R.H.M. Dolley, 188–94. London: Methuen, 1961.

Wilcox, Jonathan. "The Dissemination of Wulfstan's Homilies: The Wulfstan Tradition in Eleventh-Century Vernacular Preaching." In *England in the Eleventh Century,* edited by Carola Hicks, 199–217. Stamford: Watkins, 1992.

– "Famous Last Words: Ælfric's Saints Facing Death." *Essays in Medieval Studies* 10 (1993): 1–13.

– "Anglo-Saxon Literary Humor: Towards a Taxonomy." *Thalia: Studies in Literary Humor* 14, no. 1 2 (1994): 9–20.

– "Mock-Riddles in Old English: Exeter Riddles 86 and 19." *Studies in Philology* 93, no. 2 (Spring 1996): 180–7.

– "The First Laugh: Laughter in Genesis and the Old English Tradition." In *The Old English Hexateuch: Aspects and Approaches,* edited by Rebecca Barnhouse and Benjamin C. Withers, 239–69. Kalamazoo: Medieval Institute Publications, 2000.

– "The Wolf on Shepherds: Wulfstan, Bishops, and the Context of the *Sermo Lupi ad Anglos*." In *Old English Prose: Basic Readings*, edited by Paul E. Szarmach, 395–418. New York: Garland, 2000.

– "Transmission of Literature and Learning: Anglo-Saxon Scribal Culture." In *A Companion to Anglo-Saxon Literature*, edited by Phillip Pulsiano and Elaine M. Treharne, 50–70. Oxford: Blackwell, 2001.

– "Naked in Old English: The Embarrassed and the Shamed." In *Naked before God: Uncovering the Body in Anglo-Saxon England*, edited by Benjamin C. Withers and Jonathan Wilcox, 275–309. Morgantown: West Virginia University Press, 2003.

– "Eating People Is Wrong: Funny Style in *Andreas* and Its Analogues." In *Anglo-Saxon Styles*, edited by Catherine E. Karkov and George Hardin Brown, 201–22. Albany: State University of New York Press, 2003.

– "Ælfric in Dorset and the Landscape of Pastoral Care." In *Pastoral Care in Late Anglo-Saxon England*, edited by Francesca Tinti, 52–62. Cambridge: Boydell, 2005.

– "'Tell Me What I Am': The Old English Riddles." In *Readings in Medieval Texts: Interpreting Old and Middle English Literature*, edited by David F. Johnson and Elaine Treharne, 46–59. Oxford: Oxford University Press, 2005.

– "The Audience of Ælfric's *Lives of Saints* and the Face of Cotton Caligula A. xiv, fols. 93–130." In *Beatus Vir: Studies in Early English and Norse Manuscripts in Memory of Phillip Pulsiano*, edited by A.N. Doane and Kirsten Wolf, 228–63. Tempe: Arizona Center for Medieval and Renaissance Studies, 2006.

– "The Use of Ælfric's Homilies: MSS Oxford, Bodleian Library, Junius 85 and 86 in the Field." In *A Companion to Ælfric*, edited by Hugh Magennis and Mary Swan, 345–68. Leiden: Brill, 2009.

– "A Place to Weep: Joseph in the Beer-Room and Anglo-Saxon Gestures of Emotion." In *Saints and Scholars: New Perspectives on Anglo-Saxon Literature and Culture in Honour of Hugh Magennis*, edited by Stuart McWilliams, 14–32. Cambridge: Brewer, 2012.

– ed. *Scraped, Stroked, and Bound: Materially Engaged Readings of Medieval Manuscripts*. Turnhout: Brepols, 2013.

– "An Embarrassment of Clues: Interpreting Anglo-Saxon Blushes." In *Anglo-Saxon Emotions: Reading the Heart in Old English Literature, Language and Culture*, edited by Alice Jorgensen, Frances McCormack, and Jonathan Wilcox, 91–107. Farnham: Ashgate, 2015.

– "The Riddle of the Page: Material Enticement to the Old English Riddles of the Exeter Book." In *Manuscript Materiality in the Classroom and Beyond*, edited by Ellen K. Rentz and Michelle M. Sauer, a special issue of *SMART: Studies in Medieval and Renaissance Teaching* 25, no. 2 (Fall 2018): 75–87.

- "Understatement and Incongruity: Humour in the Literature of Anglo-Saxon England." In *Humour in the Arts: New Perspectives*, edited by Vivienne Westbrook and Shun-liang Chao, 59–77. New York: Routledge, 2019.
- "Humour and the Exeter Book Riddles: Incongruity in Riddle 31." In *Riddles at Work in the Anglo-Saxon Tradition: Words, Ideas, Interactions*, edited by Megan Cavell and Jennifer Neville, 128–45. Manchester: Manchester University Press, 2020.
- "The Pains and Pleasures of Vercelli Homily IX and the Delights of Textual Transmission." In *The Anonymous Old English Homily: Sources, Composition, and Variation*, edited by Winfried Rudolf and Susan Irvine, 287–311. Leiden: Brill, 2021.
- "Objects That Object, Subjects That Subvert: Agency in Exeter Book Riddle 5." *Humanities* 11, no. 2 (2022): 33. https://doi.org/10.3390/h11020033.
Williams, Edith Whitehurst. "What's So New about the Sexual Revolution? Some Comments on Anglo-Saxon Attitudes toward Sexuality in Women Based on Four Exeter Book Riddles." *Texas Quarterly* 18 (1975): 46–55.
Wilson, R.M. *The Lost Literature of Medieval England*. New York: Philosophical Library, 1952.
Withers, Benjamin C. *The Illustrated Old English Hexateuch, Cotton Claudius B. iv: The Frontier of Seeing and Reading in Anglo-Saxon England*. Toronto: University of Toronto Press, 2007.
Wormald, Patrick. *The Making of English Law: King Alfred to the Twelfth Century; vol. 1: Legislation and Its Limits*. Oxford: Blackwell, 1999.
Wright, Charles D. *The Irish Tradition in Old English Literature*. Cambridge: Cambridge University Press, 1993.
Zacher, Samantha. "Cynewulf at the Interface of Literacy and Orality: The Evidence of the Puns in *Elene*." *Oral Tradition* 17, no. 2 (2002): 346–88.
- *Preaching the Converted: The Style and Rhetoric of the Vercelli Book Homilies*. Toronto: University of Toronto Press, 2009.
Ziegler, Waltraud. "Ein neuer Lösungsversuch für das altenglische Rätsel Nr. 28." *Arbeiten aus Anglistik und Amerikanistik* 7 (1982): 185–90.
Zimmerman, Harold C. "Drinking Feasts and Insult Battles: Bringing Anglo-Saxon Pedagogy into the Contemporary Classroom." *Pedagogy* 13, no. 2 (Spring 2013): 229–44. https://doi.org/10.1215/15314200-1958431.
Zweck, Jordan. "Silence in the Exeter Book Riddles." *Exemplaria* 28, no. 4 (2016): 319–36. https://doi.org/10.1080/10412573.2016.1219477.
- *Epistolary Acts: Anglo-Saxon Letters and Early English Media*. Toronto: University of Toronto Press, 2018.

Index

Milton Keynes UK
Ingram Content Group UK Ltd.
UKHW040133070224
437371UK00010B/122/J

9 781487 545307